*The Tuft of Primroses*

# The Cornell Wordsworth

*General Editor:* Stephen Parrish
*Associate Editor:* Mark L. Reed
*Assistant Editor:* James A. Butler



---

*An Evening Walk,* edited by James Averill
*Descriptive Sketches,* edited by Eric Birdsall
The Salisbury Plain Poems, edited by Stephen Gill
*The Borderers,* edited by Robert Osborn
*The Ruined Cottage* and *The Pedlar,* edited by James Butler
*Peter Bell,* edited by John E. Jordan
*The Prelude,* 1798–1799, edited by Stephen Parrish
*Home at Grasmere,* edited by Beth Darlington
*Poems, in Two Volumes,* and Other Poems, 1800–1807, edited by Jared Curtis
*Benjamin the Waggoner,* edited by Paul F. Betz
*The Tuft of Primroses,* edited by Joseph F. Kishel
The Fourteen-Book *Prelude,* edited by W. J. B. Owen

CENTER FOR
SCHOLARLY EDITIONS
*AN APPROVED EDITION*
MODERN LANGUAGE
ASSOCIATION OF AMERICA

# *The Tuft of Primroses*
## with Other Late Poems for *The Recluse*
## by William Wordsworth

*Edited by*

JOSEPH F. KISHEL

CORNELL UNIVERSITY PRESS

ITHACA AND LONDON

ITHACA AND LONDON

THIS BOOK HAS BEEN PUBLISHED WITH THE AID OF A GRANT FROM THE HULL MEMORIAL PUBLICATION FUND OF CORNELL UNIVERSITY.

THE PREPARATION OF THIS VOLUME WAS MADE POSSIBLE IN PART BY GRANTS FROM THE PROGRAM FOR EDITIONS AND THE PUBLICATIONS PROGRAM OF THE NATIONAL ENDOWMENT FOR THE HUMANITIES, AN INDEPENDENT FEDERAL AGENCY.



First published 1986 by Cornell University Press.
Published in the United Kingdom by
Cornell University Press Ltd., London.

Printed in the United States of America.

**Library of Congress Cataloging in Publication Data**

Wordsworth, William 1770–1850.
The tuft of primroses, with other late poems for The recluse.

(The Cornell Wordsworth)
Bibliography: p.
I. Kishel, Joseph F., 1954– . II. Title. III. Series: Wordsworth, William, 1770–1850. Selections. 1981.
PR5852.K57 1986 821′.7 84-27403
ISBN 0-8014-1819-4 (alk. paper)

# The Cornell Wordsworth

The individual volumes of the Cornell Wordsworth series, some devoted to long poems, some to collections of shorter poems, have two common aims. The first is to bring the early Wordsworth into view. Wordsworth's practice of leaving his poems unpublished for years after their completion, and his lifelong habit of revision—Ernest de Selincourt called it "obsessive"—have obscured the original, often the best, versions of his work. These original versions are here presented in the form of clean, continuous "reading texts" from which all layers of later revision have been stripped away. The second aim of the series is to provide, for the first time, a complete and accurate record of variant readings, from Wordsworth's earliest drafts down to the final lifetime (or first posthumous) publication. The most important manuscripts are shown in full transcription; on pages facing the transcriptions of the most complex and interesting of these manuscripts, photographs of the manuscript pages are also provided. Besides the transcriptions and the photographs, on which draft revisions may be seen, and an *apparatus criticus* in which printed variants are collected, a third device for the study of revisions is adopted: when two versions of a work match sufficiently well, they are arrayed on facing pages so that the steps by which one was converted into the other become visible.

Volumes in the series are unnumbered, but upon publication their titles are inserted into the list of volumes in print in the order in which the works were written. A more detailed introduction to the series may be found in the first volume published, *The Salisbury Plain Poems,* edited by Stephen Gill.

S. M. Parrish

*Ithaca, New York*

# Contents

# Preface

In his preface to *The Excursion,* published in 1814, Wordsworth announced that virtually all of his poems would be found "by the attentive Reader" to be parts of a single grand project, *The Recluse.* Likening his design to a Gothic church, he explained that an autobiographical poem, "long finished" and "addressed to a dear Friend," would form an "Ante-chapel" to the whole, while his minor pieces "will be found . . . to have such connection with the main Work as may give them claim to be likened to the little Cells, Oratories, and sepulchral Recesses, ordinarily included in those Edifices." Wordsworth's indirect language—the reader must find a connection that may give the shorter works a claim to the simile—may betray a lack of confidence in the details of his scheme, but its broad outlines are clear. The body of the church, *The Recluse* proper, would be made of three parts, the first and third of which would "consist chiefly of meditations in the Author's own Person." By contrast, the intermediate part, *The Excursion,* referred "more to passing events, and to an existing state of things," and employed "Characters speaking" in "something of a dramatic form." The first and third parts, then, were to be the core of the great work in which, Coleridge hoped, Wordsworth would "assume the station of a man in mental repose, one whose principles were made up," and "deliver upon authority a system of philosophy." "But this," wrote Helen Darbishire, "was what Wordsworth could not do."[1]

Having completed the first book of the first part, *Home at Grasmere,* Wordsworth made only two more sustained attempts, in 1808 and 1826, to write "the FIRST GENUINE PHILOSOPHICAL POEM"—a design he prepared for, postponed, and worried over for most of his poetic career.[2] In the spring of 1808, he began three poems—*To the Clouds, The Tuft of Primroses,* and *St. Paul's*—apparently as a group, entering them together in two separate note-

[1]*Specimens of the Table Talk of the Late Samuel Taylor Coleridge* (2 vols.; London, 1835), II, 70; Helen Darbishire, *The Poet Wordsworth* (Oxford, 1950), p. 90.

[2]The phrase in capitals is Coleridge's, from *Biographia Literaria* (2 vols.; London, 1817), II, 178. The story of Wordsworth's almost lifelong preoccupation with plans for *The Recluse* is told by Beth Darlington in the introduction to her Cornell Wordsworth edition of *Home at Grasmere* (Ithaca, 1977), pp. 3–32.

books. The first was an affirmation of the poet's creative strength, the third a visionary spot of time; the second, abandoned in mid-sentence after nearly 600 lines, was an extended elegiac meditation on the poet's loss of his home at Grasmere—the center of joyous repose and poetic expectation that was to have made it possible to write *The Recluse*.[3] In 1826, once again threatened with the loss of a crucially important home, Wordsworth turned for the last time to his "long Poem," writing a meditative farewell to his favorite spring: *Composed when a probability existed of our being obliged to quit Rydal Mount as a Residence*. Except for *To the Clouds,* which appeared, heavily revised, in *Poems, Chiefly of Early and Late Years* (1842), none of the poems was published during Wordsworth's lifetime.

This edition provides a complete textual history of the late *Recluse* poems, presenting the 1808 poems as a group, the way they stood in manuscript before portions of *The Tuft of Primroses* were adapted for use in *The Excursion* and *The Prelude* and before *To the Clouds* was revised for publication. The early version of *To the Clouds,* here printed for the first time, emerges as a far more confident poem, vastly different from the one published in 1842; Wordsworth's final intentions in *The Tuft of Primroses* are established; and *St. Paul's* is put back into the context of the poems that surround it in manuscript. Full, annotated transcriptions of all of the surviving manuscripts allow the reader to trace the many stages by which each poem grew, clarifying, for the first time, the shape of *The Recluse* in 1808 and revealing the way in which portions of it were reworked and salvaged for later use.[4]

The manuscripts of the 1826 poem reveal what was a series of complete fair-copy versions, three of which (the two latest and one of the earliest) survive intact. The early version, here reconstructed for the first time, appears, surprisingly, as a 101-line "conversation poem," roughly modeled on Coleridge's *This Lime-Tree Bower My Prison.* In its final form, the poem has grown to a length of more than 200 lines, largely through the addition of a substantial passage on Joan of Arc—modeled on an episode in Robert Southey's *Joan of Arc,* written in collaboration with Coleridge nearly thirty

---

[3]James A. Butler relates *The Tuft of Primroses* to the failure of Wordsworth's plans to write *The Recluse* in "Wordsworth's *Tuft of Primroses:* 'An Unrelenting Doom,'" *Studies in Romanticism,* 14 (Summer 1975), 237–248.

[4]Ernest de Selincourt printed only the final text of *To the Clouds,* including some earlier variants in an *apparatus criticus* (*PW*, II, 316–320). His text of *The Tuft of Primroses,* included as an appendix to his edition of *The Excursion,* generally adopts the clearest, not necessarily the latest, of the copious revisions made for that poem (*PW*, V, 348–362). Each of the three *Recluse* poems of 1808 appears in a separate volume of *PW* (*St. Paul's* is in IV, 374), and the fact that they were written as a group is relegated to a brief note (*PW*, V, 482). Kenneth R. Johnston's essay "Wordsworth's Last Beginning: *The Recluse* in 1808," *ELH*, 43 (1976), 316–341, is a critical evaluation of *St. Paul's* and *The Tuft of Primroses,* based on de Selincourt's texts. The essay is incorporated in *Wordsworth and "The Recluse"* (New Haven and London, 1984).

years earlier.[5] Reading texts of the two complete versions of this curious last poem for *The Recluse* are arrayed here on facing pages.

Preparation of this volume, as of all volumes in this series, was made possible by the Trustees of Dove Cottage, who generously gave access to manuscripts at the Wordsworth Library at Grasmere and authorized their publication. My thanks are due to the Pierpont Morgan Library for permission to publish readings from the final fair copy of *Composed when a probability existed* . . . and to The Board of Trinity College, Dublin, for permission to publish the transcription of Trinity College MS. 5901. I am grateful for the wisdom and generosity of my fellow editors, especially Stephen Parrish, Mark L. Reed, James A. Butler, Karen Green, Michael C. Jaye, Carl Ketcham, and Beth Darlington, and I thank Virginia Brady, Jon Stallworthy, and M. H. Abrams for very helpful advice. My research in Grasmere has been supported by the National Endowment for the Humanities, the Hays Fund of the American Philosophical Society, and the Cornell University Department of English.

JOSEPH F. KISHEL

*New York, New York*

[5]What appears to be the final fair copy, now in the Pierpont Morgan Library, New York, was unavailable to de Selincourt, whose text of the poem is based on the penultimate fair copy in DC MS. 89, which he calls MS. A, all other Grasmere manuscripts falling in his category of MS. B (*PW*, IV, 381–387 and 477–478) except MS. C, identified in 1985.

# Abbreviations

| | |
|---|---|
| *Chronology: MY* | Mark L. Reed, *Wordsworth: The Chronology of the Middle Years, 1800–1815* (Cambridge, Mass., 1975). |
| DC MS. | Dove Cottage manuscript (revised numbering). |
| DW | Dorothy Wordsworth. |
| *EY* | *The Letters of William and Dorothy Wordsworth: The Early Years, 1787–1805,* ed. Ernest de Selincourt (2d ed.; rev. Chester L. Shaver; Oxford, 1967). |
| JC | John Carter. |
| *Journals* | *The Journals of Dorothy Wordsworth,* ed. Mary Moorman (Oxford, 1971). |
| *LY,* I–III | *The Letters of William and Dorothy Wordsworth: The Later Years, 1821–1850,* ed. Ernest de Selincourt (2d ed., rev., arranged, and ed. Alan G. Hill, Oxford, 1978, 1979, 1982). |
| *Memoirs* | Christopher Wordsworth, *Memoirs of William Wordsworth* (2 vols.; London, 1851). |
| Moorman | Mary Moorman, *William Wordsworth: A Biography* (2 vols.; Oxford, 1957, 1965). |
| MW | Mary Wordsworth. |
| *MY* | *The Letters of William and Dorothy Wordsworth: The Middle Years, 1806–1820,* ed. Ernest de Selincourt (2 vols.; 2d ed.; Part I, 1806–1811, rev. Mary Moorman, Oxford, 1969; Part II, 1812–1820, rev. Mary Moorman and Alan G. Hill, Oxford, 1970). |
| *PELY* | William Wordsworth, *Poems, Chiefly of Early and Late Years* (London, 1842). |
| *Prel.* | William Wordsworth, *The Prelude,* ed. Ernest de Selincourt (2d ed.; rev. Helen Darbishire; Oxford, 1959); unless otherwise noted, citations are from the 1805 text. |
| *Prose* | *The Prose Works of William Wordsworth,* ed. W. J. B. Owen and Jane Worthington Smyser (3 vols.; Oxford, 1974). |
| *PW* | *The Poetical Works of William Wordsworth,* ed. Ernest de Selincourt and Helen Darbishire (5 vols.; Oxford, 1940–1949; rev. 1952–1959). |
| *SPP* | *The Salisbury Plain Poems of William Wordsworth,* ed. Stephen Gill (Ithaca, 1975). |
| *STCL* | *Collected Letters of Samuel Taylor Coleridge,* ed. Earl Leslie Griggs (6 vols.; Oxford, 1956–1971). |

| | |
|---|---|
| *STCNB* | *The Notebooks of Samuel Taylor Coleridge,* ed. Kathleen Coburn (3 vols. to date; London, 1957–). |
| WL | Wordsworth Library, Grasmere. |
| WW | William Wordsworth. |

*The Tuft of Primroses*

# Introduction

## I

When the Wordsworths returned to Grasmere from their extended stay at Coleorton in the winter and spring of 1807, what they saw caused them great sadness:

On our arrival here our spirits sank and our first walk in the evening was very melancholy. Many persons are dead, old Mr. Sympson, his son the parson, young George Dawson, the finest young Man in the vale. . . . All the trees in Bainriggs are cut down, and even worse, the giant sycamore near the parsonage house, and all the finest firtrees that overtopped the steeple tower.[1]

Slightly more than a year later, Wordsworth's own lament for this heavy change, *The Tuft of Primroses,* lay abandoned in manuscript—a heavily revised, blank-verse fragment of close to 600 lines. Two shorter poems had been composed in almost the same breath: an invocation "To the Clouds" and an untitled "spot of time" on Wordsworth's vision of St. Paul's Cathedral.

Work on the poems began in early April 1808. Wordsworth had just spent a month in London, trying to arrange publication of *The White Doe of Rylstone* and passing most of his evenings with Coleridge. Early on the morning of April 3 he left Coleridge's lodgings above the *Courier* offices in the Strand to start his journey home. On April 8, back in Grasmere, Wordsworth wrote to Sir George Beaumont:

You will deem it strange, but really some of the imagery of London has since my return hither been more present to my mind, than that of this noble Vale. I will tell you how this happens to be.—I left Coleridge at 7 o'clock on Sunday morning; and walked towards the City in a very thoughtful and melancholy state of mind; I had passed through Temple Bar and by St Dunstan's, noticing nothing, and entirely occupied with my own thoughts, when looking up, I saw before me the avenue of Fleet street, silent, empty, and pure white, with a sprinkling of new-fallen snow, not a cart or Carriage to obstruct the view, no noise, only a few soundless and dusky foot-

[1]Dorothy Wordsworth to Catherine Clarkson, July 19, 1807, in *MY,* I, 158–159.

passengers, here and there; you remember the elegant curve of Ludgate Hill in which this avenue would terminate, and beyond and towering above it was the huge and majestic form of St Pauls, solemnised by a thin veil of falling snow. I cannot say how much I was affected at this unthought-of sight, in such a place and what a blessing I felt there is in habits of exalted Imagination. My sorrow was controlled, and my uneasiness of mind not quieted and relieved altogether, seemed at once to receive the gift of an anchor of security. [*MY*, I, 209]

Drafting of the lines on St. Paul's must have begun soon after this letter was written. Chronically short of paper, Wordsworth turned to the blank versos in what was left, by then, of the first manuscript of *Peter Bell* (DC MS. 18), entering early work toward *St. Paul's* near the front of the notebook, on 3$^v$. The poem moved rapidly toward completion; the earliest entries are separated by only one page of further work (2$^v$, now largely torn away) from the rapid fair copy on 1$^v$.

What emerged was a fuller, subtler version of the account sent to Beaumont perhaps no more than a few days earlier. Now, in the great autobiographical voice of *The Prelude,* the poet addresses himself directly to Coleridge, the "Friend" of line two, and transforms the prose poem of the letter into a visionary "spot of time." As in so many of those earlier "moving episodes," the poet is separated from others (quotations are from the reading text):

> Moving Form was none,
> Save here and there a shadowy Passenger, [ll. 20–21]

and closed within himself,

> pacing with an eye
> Down cast, ear sleeping, and feet masterless,
> That were sufficient guide unto themselves, [ll. 3–5]

when, "instantly," his focus on the foreground of his own activity broadens to include an arresting new perspective. Wordsworth looks upward—reminding us of the importance of the horizon in the spots of time on skating (*Prel.,* I, 452–489), the stolen rowboat (*Prel.,* I, 372–427), the dedication to poetry (*Prel.,* IV, 315–345), the discharged soldier (*Prel.,* IV, 400–504)—and if he does not tell us that he "Stopp'd short" (*Prel.,* I, 484) in Fleet Street on that snowy morning, it is because the syntax and structure of the poem have much the same effect. The scene is introduced with incantatory reluctance:

> It chanced
> That, while I thus was pacing, I raised up

My heavy eyes and instantly beheld,
Saw at a glance in that familiar spot
A visionary scene [ll. 11–15],

weighted with adjectives:

Deep, hollow, unobstructed, vacant, smooth [l. 17]
Slow, shadowy, silent, dusky [l. 22]
Pure, silent, solemn, beautiful [l. 25]

and carefully divided into two parts, so that the lines on Fleet Street covered with snow both introduce and delay the culminating vision of "The huge majestic Temple of St. Paul" (l. 26).

After finishing the St. Paul's lines, Wordsworth turned to $4^v$ of the same scrap of notebook to begin work on what was to become *To the Clouds.* After further drafting at the top of $5^v$, he entered twenty lines of the poem in rapid fair copy on $6^v$. In these twenty lines, Wordsworth addresses the flight of clouds with a series of rhetorical surmises meant to emphasize their magnificent, restless energy:

of the Wind,
Companions, fear ye to be left behind,
Or racing on your blue aetherial field
Contend ye with each other? of the Sea,
Children, bright Children of the distant sea,
Thus post Ye over dale and mountain height
To sink upon your Mother's joyous lap?
[Ll. 5–11, 1808 reading text]

Immediately, he identifies the power of this natural scene with the strength of his own imagination:

Your motion is my own; my very blood
Is quickened to your pace—a thousand thoughts
Ten thousand winged Fancies have ye raised
And not a thought which is not fleet as ye are.
[DC MS. 18, $6^v$]

The lines recall the glad preamble to *The Prelude,* in which the poet's inspiration becomes "A tempest, a redundant energy / Vexing its own creation" (*Prel.,* I, 46–47). But the clouds disappear, and, until the poem is expanded, we hear no more of the promise of the poet's "thousand thoughts." Instead, a space left at the bottom of the page shows that Wordsworth paused here before continuing composition, on $5^v$ and $7^v$, and beginning a second rapid fair copy at the top of 8$^{v}$. This second form of *To the Clouds* breaks off on 10$^{v}$ after 53 lines, and is in turn revised in two distinct stages. An expanded passage in fair copy on 11$^{v}$ adds five lines; further expansion, on 23$^{v}$ and 24$^{v}$, brings the total to 61 lines. What we have in DC MS. 18 amounts to four clearly discernible early stages of the poem's development.

Wordsworth went on to draft one more block of seven lines for *To the Clouds* at the foot of 12$^{v}$, but probably not before he had filled three pages (13$^{v}$, 14$^{v}$, 15$^{v}$) with 57 lines of a springtime poem on the reappearance of the primrose and the recovery of a female friend from severe illness. Like the St. Paul's lines, this first stage of *Tuft of Primroses* composition reflected topical concerns. The letter to Beaumont in which Wordsworth tells of his walk up Fleet Street on April 3 includes four separate references to Sara Hutchinson's alarming illness that spring, "bad accounts" of which had reached him in London, prompting him to cancel a detour to Oxford and return directly to Grasmere. The structure of the letter may suggest an even closer connection between the two poems. Throughout it, Wordsworth's concern for Sara Hutchinson's health is interwoven with fears for the state of Coleridge's "health and spirits"; at last, the two concerns become one: "if but poor Coleridge were in the right way we should be content, in the fulness of contentment, as I trust that, with care, we shall bring Miss Hutchinson about again" (*MY,* I, 209). The "conflicting thoughts of love and fear" that preoccupied the poet as he left Coleridge in London are virtually inseparable from those that awaited him in Grasmere. The poet who takes his way "Through the great City, pacing with an eye / Down cast, ear sleeping, and feet masterless" reappears in *The Tuft of Primroses* as one of the "Travellers that do hourly pace / This road . . . those who droop / Sick poor or weary or disconsolate" (DC MS. 65, 31$^{r}$). In London, the poet looks upward to a "sudden gift": the vision of St. Paul's in "its own sacred veil of falling snow" (l. 28). In Grasmere, weary Travellers raise their eyes to the primrose, on its "sunny and obtrusive seat" (l. 18), "Brightening at once the winter of their souls" (l. 35).

It is impossible to determine when, during the late spring and summer, Wordsworth turned to a fresh notebook, DC MS. 65, to enter careful fair copies of the three poems whose earliest drafts had been crowded together in DC MS. 18. But the two shorter poems and an expanded, 375-line version of *The Tuft of Primroses* had certainly been entered by September 29, when Wordsworth wrote to Samuel Rogers: "I have written since I saw you about 500 lines of my long Poem, which is all I have done" (*MY,* I, 269).

At the front of the new notebook (3$^{r}$–7$^{r}$) Wordsworth had entered a complete fair copy of *To the Clouds,* now titled and in 88 lines. The finished poem on St. Paul's was copied virtually unchanged at the back (118$^{v}$–120$^{r}$). On 30$^{r}$, Wordsworth began *The Tuft of Primroses* (now titled) in rapid fair copy, adding new composition beyond the first 57 lines taken over from DC MS. 18, and numbering his work at intervals of 20 lines. Further revision and expansion made it necessary to enter a second set of line numbers, carefully incorporating new material. But after a pause in composition on 53$^r$, Wordsworth drew a horizontal line, wrote the number 375, and left the rest of the page blank. He made a fresh start at the top of the following recto, and *Tuft of Primroses* work continues through 70$^r$, but there are no more line numbers.

Wordsworth's remark, in the letter to Rogers, that he had written "about 500 lines" has puzzled literary scholars.[2] The estimate hardly accounts for all 592 lines of *The Tuft of Primroses*—the only work of the spring and summer of 1808 that qualifies as a "long Poem." Besides, Wordsworth's careful numbering of the poem extends only to 375 lines; work beyond this point, complicated by layers of revision and a series of fresh starts, would have been significantly more difficult to count. The most likely explanation is that Wordsworth thought of the three poems in DC MS. 65 as a group and added together *To the Clouds* (88 lines), *St. Paul's* (28 lines), and the 375 numbered lines of *The Tuft of Primroses,* for a total of 491, or "about 500 lines." The consistent association of the three poems in manuscript may thus be explained as a reflection of Wordsworth's intention to make them parts of a single, larger design: his "long Poem," *The Recluse.*

Of course, if Wordsworth did intend to link together the three poems in DC MS. 65, it is difficult to imagine how he meant to do it. The poems seem too heterogeneous to fit together easily, and two of them are given separate titles. But it seems clear that Wordsworth wrote the poems for *The Recluse,* kept them together in two separate manuscripts, and referred to them collectively as a "long Poem." The poems may seem less oddly assorted when we remember Wordsworth's insistence on the factual background of so much of his work; the grouping is at least partly the result of an actual experience, described by Dorothy Wordsworth in her journal entry for April 24, 1802:

> We walked in the evening to Rydale. Coleridge and I lingered behind. C. stopped up the little runner by the Road side to make a lake. We all stood to look at Glowworm Rock—a primrose that grew there, and just looked out on the Road from its own sheltered bower. The clouds moved as William observed in one regular body like a multitude in motion a sky all clouds over, not one cloud. On our return it broke a little out and we saw here and there a star. One appeared but for a moment in a lake [of] pale blue sky. [*Journals,* pp. 115–116]

---

[2]Both Mark Reed and Mary Moorman mention WW's count of "about 500 lines," but neither is able to explain the figure (*Chronology: MY,* p. 382; Moorman, II, 131–132).

Primroses, clouds, and a sudden vision on the horizon had been linked together in Wordsworth's imagination some six years before the first entries in DC MS. 18. And we know that as late as 1826 Wordsworth still thought of *To the Clouds* as *Recluse* material. In a poignant attempt to take fresh credit for work then almost two decades old, he announced his intention to publish "a fragment of the Recluse, viz an address to the Clouds [?from] which you may judge if any Spirit be left in me" (*LY*, I, 473–474).

*To the Clouds* was finally published, in a heavily revised and expanded form, in 1842. But by that time, the first full-length version at the beginning of DC MS. 65 had been worked through no fewer than five fresh fair copies—each made necessary by heavy revision of the one it replaced. The first of these copies, in Mary Wordsworth's hand, fills $8^r$–$10^v$ of DC MS. 65. Wordsworth himself began the second on $113^v$; the rest of this version, probably entered on leaves 114–116, has been cut or torn from the notebook and is now lost. These first two copies could date from 1826, when Wordsworth may have reworked the poem as he considered publishing it, but it is clear that the third, entered by Mary Wordsworth in DC MS. 143, was part of Wordsworth's preparation of the poem for his 1842 volume, *Poems, Chiefly of Early and Late Years.* Mary Wordsworth prepared a text for the printer, DC MS. 151/3, but late revisions made yet another copy necessary, and DC MS. 151/6 was finally sent to Edward Moxon.

The St. Paul's poem and *The Tuft of Primroses* remained unpublished until the middle of this century, when they were included in the de Selincourt–Darbishire *Poetical Works* (*PW*, IV, 374–375; V, 358–362). Together with *Composed when a probability existed of our being obliged to quit Rydal Mount as a Residence*—200 lines of blank verse written in 1826 but unpublished until William Knight included a version in his *Life of William Wordsworth* (Edinburgh, 1889), III, 117–123—the three poems of 1808 represent Wordsworth's only sustained attempts, after *Home at Grasmere,* to return to the core of the "Philosophical poem" that was to have been the great work of his maturity.

## II

In his diary entry for October 6, 1826, Henry Crabb Robinson wrote:

> Mr. Wordsworth showed me the field he has purchased on which he means to build should he be compelled to leave the Mount. . . . He also pointed out to my notice the beautiful spring, a description of which is to be an introduction to a portion of his great poem—containing a poetical view of water as an *element* in the composition of our globe. The passages he read me appear to be of the very highest excellence. The

anxiety of the whole family about Miss Dorothy Wordsworth threw a shade over the enjoyment of the day.[3]

The "introduction to a portion of his great poem" is, of course, *Composed when a probability existed of our being obliged to quit Rydal Mount as a Residence*—the poem known to Christopher Wordsworth as *To the Nab Well* (*Memoirs,* I, 23n). What Crabb Robinson's diary entry makes especially clear is that events surrounding composition of the 1826 poem were strikingly similar to those that had prompted composition of *The Tuft of Primroses* almost two decades earlier. Once again the "Dearest resting places of the heart" (*The Tuft of Primroses,* l. 278) seemed threatened; once again one of the women closest to Wordsworth was seriously ill.

The owner of Rydal Mount, Lady le Fleming, had never been on very good terms with her tenants the Wordsworths. Finally, in 1825, it became clear that she wanted them to leave, so that her aunt, a Mrs. Hudleston, could use the house. Dorothy Wordsworth wrote to her friend Jane Marshall: "My Brother took his resolution immediately (he and all of us being so unwilling to leave Rydal) and purchased a piece of Land on which to build a house—and the next morning wrote to Lady le Fleming" (*LY,* I, 416). The land Wordsworth purchased, "at an extravagant fancy price" (*LY,* I, 448), was an adjoining field; plainly, his intention was to threaten Lady le Fleming with a new building uncomfortably close to Rydal Mount. As Dorothy went on to explain, "even if she has a particular dislike to us as tenants, it would not be less disagreeable to have us as neighbours, in a house of our own, so close to her Chapel and her Hall" (*LY,* I, 417).

Wordsworth's "desperate intent to build" (*LY,* I, 472) was almost carried out; in May, Sara Hutchinson wrote, "the Timber is bought—the plan & elevation all upon Paper."[4] But Lady le Fleming, apparently realizing that a new house so near to Rydal Mount would be "quite a nuisance to her" (see Moorman, II, 422n), agreed to allow the Wordsworths to stay. By late October, they were looking forward to "a quiet and industrious winter—without any harassing fears that we are to be turned [out] of our favoured Residence—a fear that haunted us, if I remember right, the last time I had the pleasure of writing to you."[5]

One additional circumstance deserves to be noticed. William, Dorothy, and Mary mention the threat of eviction from Rydal Mount in a number of letters, dating from December 1825 to October 1826 (*LY,* I, 416–417, 437–

[3]*Henry Crabb Robinson on Books and Their Writers,* ed. Edith J. Morley (3 vols.; London, 1938), I, 339–340.

[4]*The Letters of Sara Hutchinson,* ed. Kathleen Coburn (London, 1954), p. 318.

[5]Mary Wordsworth to John Kenyon, October 27, 1826, *LY,* I, 490.

438, 448, 472, 490). In the midst of these references, in a letter to John Kenyon dated July 25, 1826, Mary Wordsworth writes: "If W. chooses to recur to the subject, and speak of the field he has purchased with a desperate intent to build, I leave the other page for him to do so" (*LY*, I, 472). By this time, Wordsworth had probably begun work on *Composed when a probability existed . . .* , but instead of filling his page of the letter with further details about "the disagreeable prospect" of being driven from Rydal Mount (p. 472), Wordsworth discusses the weather and then a plan for a new edition of his poems, finally excusing himself in a postscript: "I have not spoken about my House, for I hate care" (p. 474). Consciously avoiding the topic of Rydal Mount, or at least aware that he is expected to write about it, Wordsworth chooses instead to make his boast about publishing "a fragment of the Recluse, viz an address to the Clouds [?from] which you may judge if any Spirit be left in me" (pp. 473–474). Writing in the grip of what Mary Wordsworth later called "a fear that haunted us" (*LY*, I, 490), Wordsworth makes his only recorded reference—aside from the Fenwick note dictated in 1843—to a poem then almost twenty years old, a sweeping assertion of the restless strength and freedom of his own mind. That he did so may be some indication of what *To the Clouds* meant to Wordsworth and to his plans for *The Recluse,* both in 1808 and in 1826.

Work on *Composed when a probability existed . . .* cannot have begun much earlier than December 23, 1825, when Dorothy Wordsworth could still refer to the dismissal from Rydal Mount as "sad news" (*LY*, I, 416). And it was certainly well under way, if not completed, by October 6, 1826, when Wordsworth read passages "of the very highest excellence" to Crabb Robinson. The first version of the poem now recoverable is a 101-line fair copy, largely in the hand of Mary Wordsworth: MS. A in DC MS. 105. But at least two earlier, and presumably shorter, versions must have existed: Mary Wordsworth saved some of the labor of preparing MS. A by pasting on two sections of fair copy taken from earlier manuscripts, one in her own hand and one in Dora Wordsworth's (ll. 28–44 and 94–101 in the early reading text); the versos of these paste-overs, lifted away during recent restoration of the manuscript, preserve scraps of still earlier work, in Mary's hand.

The 101-line poem in MS. A falls into four verse paragraphs. In the first, the poet bids farewell to the "Pellucid Spring"—the Nab Well, at Rydal Mount—that has served him for fourteen years (ll. 1–21).[6] In the second, he

---

[6]The poet's grandson, Gordon Graham Wordsworth, prepared the following handwritten note (WL MS. 7/23a) in response to a letter from Middleton's, the Ambleside printers, who were preparing a book on local wells. The "Mrs Tyson" is Agnes Tyson, a servant at Rydal Mount:

*The Nab Wells.*

Mrs Tyson tells me that the two wells outside the gate of the far Terrace at Rydal Mount have remained unchanged during the 70 years or more in which she has known them—The

describes his own visions in the "crystal depths" of the well, wondering if any future visitors will appreciate the wonders of what is "a mere goblet to the careless eye":

> Who, hurrying on
> With a step quickened by November-cold,
> Shall pause, the skill admiring that can work
> Upon thy chance defilements—wither'd twigs
> That, lodg'd within thy crystal depths, grow bright
> As if they from a silver tree had fallen . . . ? [Ll. 27–32]

The visions in the fountain are fragile:

> should a luckless hand, from off the floor
> On which the gleaming relics lie, uplift them,
> However gently, into vulgar air,
> At once their tender brightness disappears [ll. 38–41]

and they lead the poet to reflect, elegiacally, on the vulnerability of his own thoughts:

> And O how much of all that Love creates
> Or beautifies like changes undergoes,
> Suffers like loss when drawn out of the Soul,
> Its silent laboratory. [Ll. 45–48]

But he is consoled by a second analogy between the visions in the fountain and the workings of his own mind. As the world reflected in the fountain can seem limitless and "of etherial texture" (l. 61),

> So, in moods
> Of thought pervaded by supernal grace,
> Is the firm base of ordinary sense
> Supplanted, and the residues of flesh

---

upper one would have been "over-arched" to protect it from contamination, or from any collapse of the steep bank above it; the lower one would be constructed when the overarching was found to interfere with the ease of cattle in drinking. Every day a jug of water for drinking purposes had to be brought in; Mrs Tyson has often fetched it herself, and remembers how particular the Poet was that it should be drawn from the upper well—

The beautiful poem of 200 lines addressed to the Spring about 1826, and first published by Knight in the Eversley Edition Vol. viii. p. 289 is not as well known as it should be.

GGW. Nov: 28. 1911

The "overarching" of the well appears in ll. 28–32 of the late reading text; Wordsworth's concern that cattle not share his drinking water appears in draft lines on $1^v$ and $2^v$ of MS. B in DC MS. 105.

> Are linked with spirit; shallow life is lost
> In being; to the idealizing soul,
> Time wears the colors of Eternity,
> And Nature deepens into Nature's God.— [Ll. 63–70.]

The third verse paragraph opens with a glance at the "Millions of kneeling Hindoos" who worship "the watery element" in "their vast stream" (ll. 71–73), but this rather hollow epic overture is dropped in favor of a benediction:

> —Peace to the Matron who shall bend to dip
> Her pitcher in the favourite lymph, by me
> No longer greeted . . . [Ll. 83–85]

Finally, the "evening uproar" of a "cloud of rooks" introduces the last section of the poem, a farewell that recapitulates the consoling analogy between the mind of the poet and the scene he observes. Once again Wordsworth emphasizes the seeming insignificance of the spring—"unknown beyond the verge / Of a small Hamlet" (ll. 1–2)—and the poem ends in a second affirmation of religious faith:

> —if thy composure be not ours,
> Yet, if thou still, when we are gone, will keep
> Thy living chaplet of moist fern and flowers
> Cherished in shade tho' peeped at by the Sun,
> So shall our bosoms feed a covert growth
> Of grateful recollections, tribute due,
> (Not less than to wide lake and foaming rill)
> To thy obscure and modest attributes,
> To thee, clear Spring! and all-sustaining Heaven. [Ll. 93–101]

Once completed, the fair copy in MS. A was extensively reworked. Revision and expansion spilled onto two additional paste-overs (again containing earlier work on their versos), and an entirely new section of the poem, some fifty lines on Joan of Arc, was copied onto two leaves torn from another notebook, *Peter Bell* MS. 7, now MS. A(1) of DC MS. 105. Thus cobbled together, the expanded poem had assumed a bewildering shape, and a new fair copy was clearly necessary.

In MS. B of DC MS. 105, again in Mary Wordsworth's hand, the poem has jumped to a length of 182 lines (19 of these lines, which would have been on the missing leaf 6, have to be supplied editorially from MS. A). Further revision throughout MS. B, and two additional scraps of fair copy in Wordsworth's hand—MSS. B(1) and B(2)—bring the poem to very nearly its final state. In the penultimate fair copy in DC MS. 89, and in the final fair copy, at the Pierpont Morgan Library, it is more than 200 lines long.

## III

The care that Wordsworth bestowed on the *Recluse* poems of 1808 and 1826 may show how important they were to him. The seven fair-copy versions of *Composed when a probability existed . . .* ,[7] the six fair copies of *To the Clouds,*[8] and the multiple layers of revision in the *Tuft of Primroses* manuscript point to a significant and sustained effort at composition. The direction of this effort, traced through the manuscripts, brings us to the heart of the "Philosophical poem" Wordsworth never completed.

The early stages of *To the Clouds* composition in DC MS. 18 might almost be considered four separate poems, except for the apparent rapidity with which each succeeded the one before it. In the first of these versions, on $6^v$, the poet addresses six questions to the clouds (ll. 1–11 of the early reading text) and identifies their motion with a corresponding quickening of his emotions and thoughts: "Your motion is my own; my very blood / Is quickned to your pace . . ." (these lines became ll. 34–37 of the early reading text). He implores the clouds to speak—"Speak, silent Creatures!"—but they disappear, and the poem, at this early stage of its development, breaks off. The flight of clouds, like the "Eolian visitations" of the glad preamble to *The Prelude,* is a "power / That does not come unrecogniz'd" (*Prel.,* I, 47–48), and Wordsworth is quick to assert his corresponding inner vitality.

In the second stage of the poem's growth ($8^v$–$10^v$), the initial list of six questions (ll. 1–11) grows, with the addition of lines 16–29, to an anthology of nine. The third stage ($11^v$–$12^v$) adds an additional speculation (ll. 29–34), and the fourth stage ($23^v$–$24^v$), in lines later dropped, elaborates and lengthens an earlier one. By the time Wordsworth entered the first complete fair copy of the poem in DC MS. 65 ($3^r$–$7^r$), he had added two more conjectures (ll. 12–15) to the burgeoning catalogue. If, as Geoffrey Hartman suggests, the Romantic lyric can be considered as a development of the rhetorical surmise, *To the Clouds* may represent the decadence of the form.[9] But a still more striking feature of the poem's growth in DC MS. 18 is Wordsworth's doubling of the central assertion of a unity between the mind of the poet and the natural scene he observes. The second stage of work

[7]The versions in DC MS. 89 and in the Pierpont Morgan MS. are complete; in DC MS. 105, MS. A is complete, MS. B is missing one leaf, and MS. B(2) contains the first half of the poem; MS C is a fragmentary draft. Scraps of the two earliest fair copies survive as paste-overs in MS. A.

[8]DC MS. 65 contains two complete fair copies and clear evidence of a third, now cut or torn away; the other fair copies are in DC MSS. 143, 151/3, and 151/6.

[9]*Wordsworth's Poetry, 1787–1814* (New Haven, 1964), pp. 9–12.

begins as a fresh copy of the first, expanding the catalogue of questions, as we have seen. But now the poem continues with the appearance of a second flight of clouds that leads to another, more emphatic assertion of the poet's own imaginative strength:

> welcome to mine eye
> That sees them, to my Soul, which owns in them
> An image a reflection visible
> Of her capacious self, of what she is
> With all her restless offspring what she is
> And what she doth possess. [DC MS. 18, $10^{v}$]

This second stage—like the first, it might almost be considered a complete poem in itself—breaks off here. Stages three and four are limited to minor refinements and the expansion of the introductory catalogue of questions.

Wordsworth drafted a single additional block of lines for *To the Clouds* in DC MS. 18, but the lines are in a noticeably different hand and hence probably later than the other 1808 entries in the manuscript. Squeezed onto the foot of $12^{v}$, the passage is certainly later than the first four stages of *To the Clouds* work and would appear to be later than the beginning of *Tuft of Primroses* fair copy at the top of the following leaf ($13^{v}$). It continues *To the Clouds* with lines that became 64–71 of the early reading text—a transitional passage of autobiographical reflection that juxtaposes the "humble walk" the poet is "doomed to tread" to the consolation offered by the "perfect freedom" of his thoughts: "I pace it unrepining" (l. 69). Not only their position and appearance in manuscript but their content and phrasing suggest the possibility that the seven and one-half lines at the foot of $12^{v}$ were meant to connect the assertions of poetic strength in the early stages of *To the Clouds* work to the first 57 lines of *Tuft of Primroses* fair copy that follow, untitled, on $13^{v}$, $14^{v}$, and $15^{v}$. *The Tuft of Primroses* begins, of course, as another "humble walk," and in it the poet, like the other "Travellers that do hourly climb / This steep," finds consolation in the paradoxical beauty and power of the fragile and defenseless flowers.

The "humble walk" passage, whether or not it was first meant as the beginning of a link between *To the Clouds* and *Tuft of Primroses* work in DC MS. 18, remains a transitional passage in the first complete *To the Clouds* fair copy in DC MS. 65 ($3^{r}$–$7^{r}$). There it introduces a new conclusion to the poem (ll. 72–88 of the early reading text), in which the poet speaks for the first time of a song that will soar beyond the conventionally epic music of "Orphean Lyre or Druid Harp":

> the mountain Wind
> Shall be our hand of music! it shall sweep

> The rocks & quivering trees & billowy lake,
> And search the fibres of the inner caves & they
> Shall answer. . . . [$6^{r}$–$7^{r}$]

Of course it is somewhat odd that these assertions in the future tense should occupy the concluding lines of the poet's address; indeed, any assertion so sweeping and energetically confident might make more sense at the beginning of a long poem than at the end of a relatively short one. Given Wordsworth's apparently deliberate spacing of the 1808 entries in DC MS. 65—*To the Clouds* at the front ($3^{r}$–$7^{r}$), *The Tuft of Primroses* at the middle ($29^{v}$–$70^{r}$), *St. Paul's* at the end ($118^{v}$–$120^{r}$)—we can at least wonder whether a poem that sounds so much like the invocation to an epic was, at some point, intended to serve as one. The fair copy ends triumphantly with a third identification between the mind of man and the flight of clouds he beholds, but now it is not only the individual poet but the Sun himself, "Type of Man's far darting reason" and god of verse, who "Loves his own glory in their looks" (ll. 82, 86). Wordsworth calls on no lesser muse than Apollo, who follows the poet's lead in finding an image or type of his own mind in the natural scene.[10]

Wordsworth's fair copy at the front of DC MS. 65 is the last that might fittingly have prefaced an ambitious poem; the later fair copies, beginning with Mary Wordsworth's on $8^{r}$–$10^{v}$, reflect the gradual process of modification that led, finally, to publication of the poem as a single work in the volume of 1842. The most striking changes embodied in Mary Wordsworth's fair copy can be summarized briefly. The poet's first identification with the clouds—"Ye clouds, the very blood within my veins / Is quickened to your pace" (ll. 34–35, early reading text)—is simply dropped, perhaps as too immediate or too emotional an utterance. And the poem is expanded in two ways. First, Wordsworth indulges in some rather empty mythological embroidery. The clouds that were "apparell'd in the virgin garb / Of radiance yet unknown, transcendent hues" (ll. 27–28, early reading text) now stand

> Thronging like Cherubim what time they cower
> Before the insufferable Throne of light
> With wings advanced to veil their timid eyes [DC MS. 65, $9^{v}$]

and three new lines spell out the function of the "gentle gales" (l. 78, early reading text),

---

[10]The words "Image" (l. 61) and "type" (l. 82) are used in the first complete fair copy; "type" is used in both lines in the second fair copy (DC MS. 65, $10^{r}$–$10^{v}$).

Whose office is to clothe the naked lawn
With annual verdure & revive the woods
And moisten the parched lips of thirsty flowers. [DC MS. 65, 10v]

Other new passages lend the poem an elegiac tone. The clouds no longer simply disappear (ll. 38–44, early reading text); now they

vanish fleet as days & months & years
Life glory empire as the world itself
The lingering world when Time hath ceased to be. [DC MS. 65, 9v]

And for the first time in what had been an emphatically energetic, daylight poem, Wordsworth introduces a description of the clouds at rest, at night:

Moon & Stars
Keep their most solemn vigils when the clouds
Watch also changing peaceably their place
Like bands of ministering Spirits or when they lie
Blank forms and listless through the azure deep
Dispers'd in island quiet.
[DC MS. 65, 10v; I quote the lines as revised]

These passages, with their emphasis on time (in the deleted first version of the lines just quoted from 10v, the poet watches the slumbering clouds "from hour to hour") and their vision of clouds in the stasis of "island quiet," check the forward movement, the urgency and bold assertiveness of the poem with moments of calm and distanced contemplation.

The gradual weakening of what might have stood as an epic invocation continues with the addition of a coda to the poem, first drafted on 11r–12r of DC MS. 65 and incorporated in later versions.[11] The first fair copy had ended with a vision of intellectual strength, a blazing shower of "beatitude and light." A more timid poet now proclaims his self-consciousness:

If sympathizing Bards in this late
May gain permission so to speak [11r]

and introduces qualifications:

Visions with all but beatific light
Enrichd.... [12r]

[11]The drafting on 11r–12r leads directly to Mary Wordsworth's fair copy in DC MS. 143 and is probably contemporary with it.

The poem that began as a celebration and welcoming of the energetic transience of the clouds turns, finally, to a lament for that very transience and the inadequate powers of memory "To keep the fleeting treasure, unimpaired" (DC MS. 65, $12^r$). In the last line of the poem, the poet turns to the only imaginable consolation, "the bosom of eternal things."

## IV

Like *To the Clouds, The Tuft of Primroses* began as a more confident work than it was to become. The first discrete stage of the poem's composition, the 57 consecutive lines of rapid fair copy on $13^v$–$15^v$ in DC MS. 18, does not ignore the vulnerability of the primrose, the troubles of "those who droop / Sick poor or weary or disconsolate," or the danger of a female friend's illness. But these very real evils are overbalanced by "pleasure," "new gladness," "delight," "mild assurances," and, finally, the "surpassing joy" with which the fragment comes to a triumphant close.

Significantly, Wordsworth appears to have taken great pains with the transitional passage that links the first 57 lines to the rest of the poem in DC MS. 65. First entered at the foot of $32^r$ and top of $33^r$, the passage is completely redrafted at least four separate times before reaching its fifth and final state on $29^v$ (the four intermediate stages of revision occur on $32^v$ and $30^v$; fresh starts in two of these stages and in the base text on $33^r$ might be counted as separate drafts, for a total of seven). This careful attention to the passage might have stemmed from several causes. First, to preserve the unity of the poem, the primrose lines (ll. 1–61 in the reading text—essentially the same as the first 57 lines in DC MS. 18) had to be linked to the lines on the desecration of Grasmere (ll. 70–129). This task may have seemed easy enough: the primrose, even the thought of it, had provided other consolations at other times. In the first version of the lines, this notion is somewhat vague; the poet will not forget the "ancient claims" of the primrose in its "pure self":

> no surely had the stream
> Risen only to its old accustomed height
> Thy reappearance could not have inspired
> A faint emotion. [DC MS. 65, $33^r$]

The vagueness and the strength of this early version lie in the entirely metaphorical stream that has flooded the poet's heart. But by mid-page on $30^v$, the image is dropped in favor of a much clearer transition; the "dear thoughts" (l. 63) with which the poem begins are linked to other thoughts in other seasons (ll. 67–70).

Yet even though the literal sense of the transitional lines becomes clearer, they remain at least potentially troubling. Wordsworth's evident intention was to base a thematic connection on the joyful hopes associated with the "happy Flower" (l. 62), but his challenge was to maintain the buoyant confidence of the opening of the poem in face of the tragic episodes he was about to introduce. The flood of undifferentiated emotion that clouds the first version of the transition (33$^r$) is carefully resolved, in the final version (29$^v$), into three parts: "Dear thoughts" of the recovery of a "Friend" (l. 63); the "pleasure" inspired by the appearance of the flower "In its pure self" (l. 67); and thoughts of the flower in other seasons, when its blooms are hidden from view (ll. 67–70).

The primrose appears once more, and for the last time in the poem, in lines 235–250, immediately after the description of the desecration of Grasmere and the story of Joseph Sympson and his family. The poet's focus on the Sympsons' garden flowers, now all "sullied and disgrac'd" (l. 230), allows him to return naturally to his own "little Primrose" that "Remains, in sacred beauty, without taint / Of injury or decay" (ll. 236–237). The return underscores the formal unity of the poem to this point, but the primrose that was a harbinger of renewed health and vitality is now the last item in what amounts to an elegiac catalogue of the flowers in the Sympsons' abandoned garden (ll. 206–234). With the poem thus doubled back on itself, Wordsworth paused, at least temporarily. His original set of line numbers ends at mid-page on 41$^r$ with line 222 (the number, not the usual multiple of 10 or 20 lines, indicates a stopping place, as does the fresh start at the top of 42$^v$), and it is this first portion of the poem that is most aptly titled *The Tuft of Primroses.*

Sometime after completing the 222 lines of his first line count, Wordsworth returned to the story of the Sympsons and modified it in two important ways. First, he nearly doubled the length of that part of the story in which old Joseph Sympson, the "Patriarch of the Vale," lives on in solitude after all the other members of his family have died (ll. 168–199). Then, on 37$^r$, he deleted a four-line address to "Emma" (his sister Dorothy) and his wife:

> Methinks that Emma hears the murmuring song
> And the pure Ether of her Maiden soul
> Is overcast, and thy maternal eyes
> Mary, are wet, but not with tears of grief.[12]

[12]Ink offset from the box drawn around the four lines on 37$^r$ shows that they were deleted after ll. 168–192 had been entered on the facing verso.

Both changes are taken into account in Wordsworth's revised numbering of the poem and show him circling back, in the process of composition, not just to the unadorned tale of the death of a family, but to those aspects of it which concerned him most: the spare fact of an old man's solitude and, just as important, the responses of the neighbors who witnessed it. Wordsworth drops the direct address to his listeners, Mary and "Emma," but carefully incorporates his audience as participants in the expanded version of the episode, structuring it around the choral responses of their collective voice:

> "How will he face the remnant of his life,
> What will become of him?," we said, and mused
> In vain conjectures; "Shall we meet him now,
> Haunting with rod and line the rocky brooks
> And mountain-Tarns; or shall we, as we pass,
> Hear him alone, and solacing his ear
> With music? . . ."   [Ll. 175–181]

In its last appearance in the poem, the tuft of primroses is a distant comfort; it can give "one short instantaneous chear of mind" to a "stranger late in travel" (ll. 243–244),

> as I myself
> Have often seen her, when the last lone Thrush
> Had ceas'd his vesper hymn. . . .   [Ll. 244–246]

In the "gloom / Of Twilight" (ll. 246–247) the flowers shine "Like the broad Moon, with lustre somewhat dimm'd" (l. 249)—still a beautiful image, but far from inspiring the "surpassing joy" of the earliest part of the poem (DC MS. 18, 15$^{v}$). The flower first thought of as "Queen," "prophet," or "promiser" of renewed life (DC MS. 18, 15$^{v}$) proves to be an inadequate consolation for the desecration of Grasmere, and we hear of it no more. Instead, the poet's grief prompts him to frame a prayer that he knows must go unanswered:

> Oh for some band of guardian Spirits, prompt
> As were those human ministers of old,
> Who, daily, nightly, under various names,
> With various service stood or walk'd their rounds
> Through the wide forest, to protect from harm
> The wild Beast with her young
>
> . . .
>
> Continual and firm peace, from outrage safe
> And all annoyance, till the sovereign comes

Heading his train, and through that franchise high
Urges the chase with clamorous hound and horn.
[Ll. 251–256, 261–264]

The pastoral vision may interpose a little ease, but its artificiality is no match for the real tragedy of Grasmere. When the prayer gives way to questions:

Have not th'incumbent Mountain looks of awe
In which this mandate may be read, the streams
A voice that pleads, beseeches, and implores?
[ll. 272–274, first entered on 42$^{r}$]

composition breaks off. Only after starting over, on the top of 42$^{v}$, from the last appearance of the primrose, did Wordsworth come finally to an unqualified statement of his sense of loss, his last direct reference in the poem to Grasmere:

the deafness of the world is here,
Even here, and all too many of the haunts
Of Fancy's choicest pastime, and the best
And Dearest resting places of the heart
Vanish beneath an unrelenting doom. [Ll. 275–279]

What follows is the transitional passage in which Wordsworth explains that the "Hermit" of old time sought a life of seclusion not primarily as a retreat from the troubles of the world, but "for its absolute self, a life of peace, / Stability without regret or fear, / That hath been, is, and shall be ever more" (ll. 291–293). The passage stands as a preface to the story of St. Basil, his sister Macrina, and his friend Gregory Nazianzen—figures who present interesting parallels to Wordsworth, Dorothy Wordsworth, and Coleridge.

St. Basil, the founder of Eastern monasticism, had, as a young man, fled the "vain felicities of Athens" (l. 312) to live in a mountainous retreat not unlike Wordsworth's Grasmere. Like Wordsworth, he had been influenced by his sister, a "pious Maid, most beautiful / And in the gentleness of woman wise" (ll. 321–322). Having established himself in his "Pontic solitude," Basil implored his friend Gregory—another father of the Eastern church and "the man he held most dear" (l. 360)—to join him, promising a life of fruitful labor and bodily health:

So shall thy frame be strong thy spirits light
Thy own endeavour fill thy temperate board. . . . [DC MS. 65, 53$^{r}$]

As he wrote these lines, Wordsworth must have thought of Coleridge, whom he had left perhaps no more than a few weeks earlier, ailing and unproductive in London.

The ultimate sources for the story of Basil and Gregory are their letters. The first translation to be published in English was John Henry Newman's;[13] it shows that Wordsworth may have been translating directly from Basil's letter XIV, thirty years earlier, in lines 330–429 of *The Tuft of Primroses.* Mary Moorman speculates that it was during the trip to London in the spring of 1808, while visiting his brother Christopher, that Wordsworth saw an edition of St. Basil's letters (Moorman, II, 133); an edition of Gregory's works was in his Rydal Mount library at his death.[14]

But the scrap of *Tuft of Primroses* drafting now at Trinity College, Dublin, is kept in an envelope bearing the scrawled notation "Fragment of Wordsworth MS.S found in W's copy of Cave's lives"—making it seem likely that Wordsworth took most, if not all, of the details of Basil's life from William Cave's *Ecclesiastici,* printed together with his *Apostolici* in the folio edition (1716) that he owned.[15] Cave's *Life of St. Basil* (pp. 470–508 in the 1716 folio), based on loose translations from the letters of Basil and Gregory, contains so many clear parallels to Wordsworth's account that it is worth quoting at some length:

But wearied at length with the troublesome Interruptions of Society, he withdrew into the adjacent Wilderness, where he fix'd his Station in the Mountainous Parts, near the Bank of the River *Iris,* a famous River, which arising in the Mountains of *Armenia,* runs through the Middle of *Pontus,* and empties itself into the *Euxine* Sea. The place he made choice of, was naturally fitted for all the Advantages of Solitude and Contemplation; it was a high Mountain, cloth'd with a thick shady Wood, and watered on the North with cool and Crystal Springs that issued from it. At the Foot of the Hill was a fruitful Valley, the Verdure and Fertility whereof, was not a little owing to those benign Streams that flowed from the neighbouring Hills; as for its Quietness and Security, it was beholden to the Woods, variegated with all Sorts of pleasant Trees that encompass'd it. Nature had form'd it into a kind of *Peninsula,* and fortified it with Bulwarks on every Side; two Parts of it were secured by deep and unapproachable Valleys; a Third by the River, which, falling from a Precipice, was a sure Wall on that side: On the other was a ragged and naked Rock, which, joining to the Valley, cut off all Avenues that Way. There was but one Passage to it, and that too

[13]In *The Church of the Fathers* (London, 1840); Basil's letter XIV is at pp. 59–60. Newman had published a shorter, early version of the story of Basil and Gregory in *The British Magazine,* 6 (1834), 42–49.

[14]Chester L. Shaver and Alice C. Shaver, *Wordsworth's Library: A Catalogue* (New York, 1979), p. 109.

[15]Ibid., p. 49; the present location of Wordsworth's copy is not known.

secur'd by those who liv'd within. It was on the most prominent Part of this Mountain that S. *Basil* fix'd his Cell, whence there was an easy and delightful Prospect both into the Valley below, and upon the neighbour River, which flowing with a quick rapid Stream, and dashing it self against the Rocks that opposed its Passage, at once gratified both the Eye and Ear. Nor wanted there other Divertisements to those, who were desirous to entertain themselves with innocent Pleasures. For as the River afforded plenty of excellent Fish, and the adjoining Hills conveniency for Sport and Game; so the Birds from the Woods charm'd the Ear with untaught Music, while the Eye was ravish'd to look down and behold the Plains overspread with a natural Tapestry of Herbs and Flowers. But the greatest Advantage of the Place, was its Solitude, being perfectly remote from all Company, not a Man seen that way, unless when Hunting by chance brought them thither, and that not in quest of Beasts of prey, Wolves, Lions, &c. (for with such the Place was not infested) but of Deer, wild Goats, and such-like peaceable and harmless Creatures.

IV. THE good Man was infinitely satisfied with the Place of his Retirement, and wanted nothing to complete his Happiness, but the Company of his dear Friend *Nazianzen,* whom he oft invited to come thither to him; in one of his Letters he elegantly describes his fortunate Islands (as *Nazianzen* calls them) laying before him all the wild inartificial Pleasures of the Place, and the great Advantages it ministered to Piety and Contemplation. Which *Nazianzen* in his Answer with a great deal of witty Eloquence retorts upon him, turning all the Passages of his Letter into Sport and Merriment. But having after some time broken loose from those Affairs that detain'd him, over he goes to him, and joyful, we may be sure, was the Meeting of those two dear Companions, whose Inclinations, Studies, and Way of Life ran both in the same Channel. But though so mutually conversant with each other, yet they liv'd apart in different Cells, as is plain from *Nazianzen's* Epistle to *Amphilochius,* one of the pious Inhabitants of that Place. Indeed *Basil's* company and Course of Life quickly drew others into those Parts, who flying from the Noise and Troubles of the World, did after his Example, give up themselves to the Severities and Mortifications of a retired Life. He had in his Travels, with great Complacency, observ'd the Strictness practis'd by the Monks and Anchorets in *Egypt* and *Palestine,* whose Rules and Institutions he resolv'd to set on foot at his Return. And meeting at *Cæsarea,* with some ready dispos'd to a Monastic Life, he joyn'd himself to them, till being forc'd thence, he now again reviv'd the Design, in a Place much more opportune and convenient for it. Great numbers flocking thither, they soon grew up into Religious Societies, spending their Time in singing Psalms, in fervent Prayers, devout Meditations, reading and expounding the holy Scriptures, and the constant Exercises of piety and vertue. And what Hours were borrowed from the Offices of Religion, were laid out in bodily Labours, felling Wood, or digging Stones, in setting Trees, planting and watering Gardens, an Imployment which at once afforded both Maintenance and Recreation. And because no Course of Life can be managed without some fix'd Laws and Constitutions, he advis'd with *Nazianzen* about drawing up particular Orders to be observ'd in the monastick State, which they form'd into Rules and Canons and for the benefit of Posterity as well as the present Age, committed and consign'd to Writing. Some such Thing he had been hammering at his first coming into the Wilderness, as appears by his Letter to *Nazianzen* upon that Subject, wherein he acutely ballances the

Advantages and Disadvantages both of a civil and retired Life, and gives many excellent Directions necessary to be observ'd by those who embrace a solitary and ascetick Life. These were the first Rules of monastick Discipline that were establish'd in the *Eastern* Church, and from hence were deriv'd the several Constitutions of all those Religious Orders that afterwards over-ran the Church. [Pp. 477–479; footnotes omitted]

Several other debts to Cave are recorded in the notes to the reading text of *The Tuft of Primroses* and the note to drafts on the back of the letter from Francis Wrangham to Wordsworth of May 7, 1808, now DC MS. 172.

Newman's summary of the Basil–Gregory relationship, built around translations of the correspondence that Wordsworth may have read, shows parallels to the friendship of Wordsworth and Coleridge that could hardly be clearer. The close early partnership described by Gregory, when

> each of us was bold to trust in each,
> Unto the emptying of our deepest hearts,[16]

would have been familiar to the poet who had written "The poem to Coleridge." Both Coleridge's exaggerated regard for "The Giant Wordsworth" (*STCL,* I, 391) and Wordsworth's dependence on Coleridge's guidance ("I am very anxious to have your notes for The Recluse. I cannot say how much importance I attach to this" [*EY,* p. 452]) correspond to much in Gregory's letters:

> Do you, however, come to me, and revive my virtue, and work with me; and, whatever benefit we once gained together, preserve for me by your prayers, lest otherwise I fade away by little and little, as a shadow, while the day declines. For you are my breath, more than the air, and so far only do I live, as I am in your company, either present, or, if absent, by your image. [Newman, p. 130]

Even Newman's evaluation of the characters of Basil and Gregory, "the one with deep feelings, the other with acute and warm" (p. 119), sounds familiar to readers of a letter to Coleridge, written in a month that may well have seen the bulk of *Tuft of Primroses* composition:

> Each of our dispositions has in this its habits and character. I am not fond of making myself hastily beloved and admired, you take more delight in it than a wise man ought. I am naturally slow to love and to cease loving. . . . It often surprized me to see you fallen at once into a long trot of sympathy with persons whose faces you hardly

---

[16]Newman, *Church of the Fathers,* p. 119. Throughout, the second edition of 1842, more widely available than the first edition, is quoted.

knew; you perhaps are equally surprised at my [*end of draft*] [May or June 1808; *MY*, I, 245]

After entering a first draft of Basil's letter to Gregory in DC MS. 65, Wordsworth came to another significant stopping place in his composition of the poem: the 375 lines of his revised line count, which ends on 53$^{r}$. Wordsworth may have begun the story of St. Basil as a separate poem. Early jottings toward the description of Basil's retreat and his address to Gregory are found on the back of a letter from Francis Wrangham to Wordsworth, dated May 7, 1808, DC MS. 172. Other letters, with additional drafting for the St. Basil passage on their versos, seem to have existed;[17] the fragment of manuscript now at Trinity College, Dublin (MS. 5901), may be part of one of them. But once incorporated in *The Tuft of Primroses,* the St. Basil episode, and especially the address to Gregory, continued to expand. The first version—from "Come O Friend" on 50$^{r}$ to the last line on 53$^{r}$—is complete in under 40 lines; the second, on 54$^{r}$–56$^{r}$, has 52 lines. In its third and final form, the letter has grown to a length of 71 lines (ll. 358–429, on 58$^{r}$–59$^{v}$).

In its first form, the letter emphasizes the positive aspects of life in what St. Basil calls "This blest Arcadia . . . these purer fields / Than those which Pagan superstition feigned / For mansions of the happy dead" (51$^{r}$). But in the second version, this exaggerated promise is dropped, along with a simple line on Basil's personal emotions—"I feel that wanting Thee I am alone" (51$^{r}$)—and two of the lines that had underscored the Gregory/Coleridge parallel:

> So shall thy frame be strong thy spirits light
> Thy own endeavour fill thy temperate board. [53$^{r}$]

What Wordsworth added, on 54$^{r}$–55$^{r}$, was a sober passage of 15 lines, in which St. Basil details the "sterner duties" and extreme solitude of his retreat:

> when thou wouldst assume
> The burthen and the seasonable yoke
> [ ] by our frail Nature, woulds be [ ]
> By vigils abstinence and prayer with tears
> What place so fit?—a deeper solitude
> Thebais, or the Syrian wilderness,
> Contains not, in its dry & barren round. [55$^{r}$]

If the simple, unclouded happiness of the first version of the letter is qualified by this vision of requirements and limits, it is almost entirely lost in

[17]See the headnote to the transcription of the lines on this letter, below.

the third version, expanded with no fewer than four new passages that center on decay, uncertainty, and "vain disquietude" (ll. 365–370, 373–376, 389–397, 404–406). In effect, St. Basil now makes a persuasive case for the hermit's life as "a refuge from distress or pain" (both of which he so eloquently describes), "A breathing time, vacation, or a truce" (ll. 289–290)—exactly the motives Wordsworth himself had taken pains to discount only a few pages earlier (ll. 280–308, on $44^{r}$–$45^{r}$).

St. Basil's consoling vision of "these fortunate Isles" ($51^{r}$) gives way, through Wordsworth's revisions, to an intrusive desolation:

> What if the Roses and the flowers of Kings,
> Princes and Emperors, and the crowns and palms
> Of all the great are blasted, or decay . . . ? [Ll. 365–367]

The grand scale of the language, so removed from the personal simplicity of the deleted line, "I feel that wanting Thee I am alone" ($51^{r}$), is of a piece with Wordsworth's intention to broaden the scope of his poem with what amounts to an extended historical analogy.[18] It is hardly necessary to list the many similarities, in detail and phrasing, between Grasmere vale and St. Basil's retreat: the cottages in both are situated "aloft" in the mountains (l. 135; $47^{r}$); both are surrounded by woods (l. 214; l. 341) and by "gay" shrubs and flowers (l. 208; $48^{r}$); both are graced with the song of "murmuring streams" (l. 124; l. 357). Finally, even the memory of St. Basil, which "hung through many an age, / In bright remembrance, like a shining cloud" (ll. 472–473), recalls our parting glimpse of the primrose, "boldly hung as if in air, / Like the broad Moon, with lustre somewhat dimm'd" (ll. 248–249).

After a false start (on $64^{r}$–$65^{r}$), in which Wordsworth rejects the idea of following the boisterous adventures of Robin Hood in favor of some quieter activity, he adds, in a new ink and in a slightly different hand, a second extended analogy to the desecration of Grasmere: the destruction of the Grande Chartreuse during the French Revolution. Returning to autobiography and a meditative pattern established in the crossing-the-Alps passage in Book VI of *The Prelude,* Wordsworth interrupts his story of past events at the monastery just at the moment when they stir present feelings: "Yes I was moved and to this hour am moved" (l. 526). For a while at least, the poet's state of mind as he writes is identical to what it was during the episode he describes, and an early failure of the French Revolution is linked to the failure of Wordsworth's poetic revolution at Grasmere. He announces a new episode:

---

[18]Ll. 365–367 were translated by Wordsworth from the foundation charter of the Abbey of St. Mary's, Furness; see the note to these lines in the reading text.

> the unwearied Song will lead
> Into a lonely Vale, the mild abode
> Of female Votaries [ll. 570–572]

but after 20 lines that characterize the "chosen Spot" as undefended, lowly, and unassuming, *The Tuft of Primroses* breaks off with the telltale repetition of a phrase—"tilth and vineyard"—that had been used before, in line 486. Wordsworth may have sensed that his poem was moving in circles, that another analogy to life in the vale of Grasmere was unnecessary.

As handwriting and ink color suggest, the lines on St. Paul's, already completed in DC MS. 18, had been entered at the back of DC MS. 65 during or just before the first stages of work on *The Tuft of Primroses.* When Wordsworth went on to extend his long poem, he was, physically at least, working through the notebook toward a visionary spot of time, perhaps with the idea that it would serve as a fitting coda to the whole. The pattern had been tried once before, in the early months of 1804, when Wordsworth briefly fixed the design of a five-book *Prelude* that was to have closed, similarly, with "spots of time" (Jonathan Wordsworth and Stephen Gill have attempted a reconstruction in "The Five-Book *Prelude* of Early Spring 1804," *Journal of English and Germanic Philology,* 76 [1977], 1–25).

*To the Clouds,* with its final "Vision of beatitude and light," anticipates at least four passages in *The Tuft of Primroses,* each of which recapitulates the movement of *St. Paul's* from trouble to security. In the first of these passages, the "stranger late in travel" looks up to receive an "instantaneous chear of mind" from a sublimated vision of the primrose, "Lonely and bright and as the Moon secure" (ll. 243–250). In the second, St. Basil's monastic example hovers over the history of the Eastern church "In bright remembrance, like a shining cloud" (l. 473). In the third passage, Fountains Abbey stands

> glorious in decay,
> Before the pious Traveller's lifted eye,
> Threatening to outlive the ravages of Time,
> And bear the cross till Christ shall come again. [Ll. 493–496]

Finally, three lines from the Chartreuse episode summarize the pattern:

> To struggle,—to be lost within himself
> In trepidation,—from the dim abyss
> To look with bodily eyes, and be consoled. [Ll. 565–567]

The lines might stand as a summary of *St. Paul's.* It should not be forgotten that the "huge majestic Temple of St. Paul" is surmounted by a cross, and that Wordsworth had been impressed by "The cross . . . / By angels planted on the aëreal rock," seen frequently in the valleys surrounding the Grande Chartreuse (*Descriptive Sketches,* ll. 70–71).

Wordsworth never completed *The Tuft of Primroses.* Like St. Basil, he felt an "urgent summons" (l. 460) to engage in more worldly affairs, and his next project was an extended political essay, *The Convention of Cintra* (*Prose,* I, 221–366)—the pamphlet that Coleridge described, perhaps more accurately than he knew, as "almost a self-robbery from some great philosophical poem" (*STCL,* III, 214). *The Tuft of Primroses,* as a whole, may not have soared to the "high dogmatic Eloquence" and "oracular [tone]" that Coleridge set as standards for "impassioned Blank Verse" (*STCL,* III, 214), but Wordsworth later returned to substantial portions of it, extracting and revising them for use in *The Excursion* and *The Prelude.* The tragedy of the Sympson family (ll. 135–199), along with the "What if the Roses and the flowers of Kings" passage from St. Basil's address to Nazianzen (ll. 365–370), were taken into Book VII of *The Excursion.* The "What impulse drove the Hermit to his Cell" lines (280–308) found their way first into Book V (l. 16, *apparatus criticus; PW,* V, 153) and then into Book III (ll. 367–405; *PW,* V, 86–87). In 1815, Wordsworth quoted a version of lines 549–551, part of the Chartreuse episode, in his *Essay, Supplementary to the Preface* of the new edition of his poems (*Prose,* III, 84). Finally, the entire Chartreuse episode was fitted into its proper chronological place in the poet's life, to become the only passage of significant length added to *The Prelude* during all of Wordsworth's extensive revisions of the poem, from 1805 until his death (*Prel.,* pp. 198–203). Clearly, Wordsworth never entirely abandoned *The Tuft of Primroses,* but came back to those parts of it that were most congenial to his poetic temperament—the simple tragedy of the Sympsons and the autobiographical crisis at the Chartreuse. It seems reasonable to suggest that, in a way, Wordsworth was finally able to finish the poem by knitting its fragments back into the larger fabric of *The Excursion* and *The Prelude,* where for him "despondency" could be more effectively "corrected."

## V

Unlike *The Tuft of Primroses, Composed when a probability existed* . . . is a finished work. In fact, Wordsworth seems to have been particularly satisfied with its ending. The final lines of the poem, taken over unrevised from the earliest manuscripts and pasted into MS. A, remained virtually untouched as the poem grew from a length of 101 to 182 and finally 202 lines. Throughout this evolution, the structure of the poem remained essentially what it had been in MS. A. Bidding farewell to his favorite spring, the poet imagines how it will appear to others ("What loiterer now . . ."; l. 22, early reading text). An extended meditation on visions in the fountain brings him to a declaration of faith:

> to the idealizing soul,
> Time wears the colors of Eternity,
> And Nature deepens into Nature's God.— [Ll. 68–70]

After reflecting, briefly, on the historical "idolatry" of streams, the poet blesses those who will come after him ("Peace to the Matron . . .", l. 83), and the "evening uproar" of a "cloud of rooks" signals the end of the "protracted strain" (ll. 88–90). Not only this overall movement—the poet's sense of loss, his imaginative vision of what others will see at a beloved spot, his benediction, the rooks that signal the end of both poems—but a number of specific parallels of phrasing and detail mark the poem as a late, if perhaps not very remarkable, successor to one of Coleridge's "conversation poems": *This Lime-Tree Bower My Prison.*

What is remarkable is that Wordsworth thought of *Composed when a probability existed* . . . as an "introduction to a portion" of *The Recluse* and expanded it accordingly. When he remarked to Henry Crabb Robinson that this portion of his great poem was to contain "a poetical view of water as an *element* in the composition of our globe,"[19] Wordsworth seems to have been thinking about the kind of grand epic scheme Coleridge had formulated by 1796 as a series of "Hymns to the Sun, the Moon, and the Elements"—one of which, of course, was water.[20] It was perhaps with such a project in mind that Wordsworth added three new passages to the 101-line poem in MS. A: the lines on Narcissus and his "watery Duplicate," on the muses at Castaly and Hippocrene, and on Joan of Arc's vision at "the Fountain of the Fairies" (late reading text, ll. 68–81, 145–162, 163–189); a fourth passage, containing humbler characters—a "dear friend," a man waiting for a ship, a "simple child"—was included in MS. B ($4^r$, ll. 66–79), but only its first lines were retained in the final fair copy of the poem (ll. 82–89). These extended analogies to the poet's own situation, apparently meant to lend the poem mythic and historical weight, almost double its length. Interestingly, the most important of them, the story of Joan of Arc's transformation from rustic visionary to political prophet, owes a significant debt to Southey's

---

[19]*Robinson on Books,* ed. Morley, I, 339.

[20]*STCNB,* I, entry 174. John Livingston Lowes traced the "prenatal history" of Coleridge's Hymn to Water, suggesting that preparation for the unwritten poem may have played a significant role in the gestation of *The Rime of the Ancient Mariner* (*The Road to Xanadu* [Boston, 1930], pp. 75–78); as late as 1816, Coleridge wrote that he hoped to complete "Seven Hymns with a large preface or prose commentary to each—1. to the Sun. 2. Moon. 3. Earth. 4. Air. 5. Water. 6. Fire. 7. God" (*STCL,* IV, 687).

early epic, *Joan of Arc,* published in 1796 (see note to ll. 163–189, late reading text). And in Southey's lines on Joan's vision at a secluded well, Coleridge had found a model for the "still roaring dell" in *This Lime-Tree Bower My Prison,* echoed throughout *Composed when a probability existed. . . .* Once again, as in *The Tuft of Primroses,* Wordsworth's poem had moved from a humble domestic beginning to larger historical issues, and once again the last significant addition to the poem was, like the Chartreuse episode, an attempt to come to terms with a central symbol of the French Revolution.[21]

The Joan of Arc lines, then, can be identified as Wordsworth's last sustained effort at *Recluse* composition, and they might stand as a symbol for the failure of the whole, a failure or inability to move beyond autobiographical meditation to epic narrative, or to the even more remote authority of a great "Philosophical poem." Joan's story, like the history of St. Basil in *The Tuft of Primroses,* allows Wordsworth to rewrite a portion of his own life, thinly veiled in historical or mythic detail. The peculiar compound echoes in the Joan of Arc lines—the details from Southey and from Coleridge—betray an uneasy synthesis of narrative matter and meditative method. The "Fountain of the Fairies" inspires Southey's Joan to exploits that fill thousands of lines; Coleridge's "still roaring dell" is central to an imaginative redemption of his own solitude.[22] In *Composed when a probability existed . . . ,* Wordsworth strains the framework of Coleridge's conversation poem to accommodate Joan's story. In 1826, with his poetic powers failing him, Wordsworth still hoped to show that the failure of the most important political revolution in modern history could be subsumed in a triumph of the imagination.

---

[21]Coincidentally, the phrase "tilth and vineyard"—used twice in *The Tuft of Primroses* (ll. 486, 592)—occurs in a canceled draft line for the Joan of Arc episode: DC MS. 105, MS. A(1), 2ʳ.

[22]Coleridge would have been thoroughly familiar with the "Fountain of the Fairies" episode at the end of bk. I of *Joan of Arc;* he himself wrote the first 450 lines of bk. II, as Southey acknowledged in the preface to the first edition (Bristol, 1796). See note to ll. 163–189 of the late reading text of *Composed when a probability existed of our being obliged to quit Rydal Mount as a Residence.*

# Editorial Procedure

Like other volumes in this series, this edition provides two kinds of texts: (1) "reading texts," from which all complexities and variant readings have been stripped away, and (2) transcriptions of manuscripts, with facing photographic reproductions of the manuscripts if those manuscripts are complex and difficult to read. Editorial procedures have been adapted to the different aims of these two styles of presentation.

In this volume, the 1808 reading text of *To the Clouds,* based on Wordsworth's first complete fair copy of the poem, on $3^r$–$7^r$ of DC MS. 65, faces the text of the poem as it was published in *Poems, Chiefly of Early and Late Years,* in 1842. Variants from the two final fair copies (DC MSS. 151/3 and 151/6) and from the editions of 1845, 1846, and 1849 are contained in an *apparatus criticus* to the 1842 text. No complete fair copy of *The Tuft of Primroses* exists, and the reading text here is therefore constructed from the latest recoverable readings in Wordsworth's fullest draft of the poem, in DC MS. 65. Where the latest readings are incomplete or illegible, penultimate readings have been adopted. The result is, perforce, a conjectural reconstruction that shows what the poem would have looked like had Wordsworth ordered a fair copy made before abandoning *The Tuft of Primroses* as a separate work. The reading text of *St. Paul's* is based on Wordsworth's fair copy in DC MS. 65, $119^r$–$120^r$. The early reading text of *Composed when a probability existed of our being obliged to quit Rydal Mount as a Residence* is based on the earliest complete form of the poem that can now be recovered, the patched-together fair copy in DC MS. 105, MS. A, incorporating only corrections that appear to have been made by the copyist in the process of transcription. The late reading text, on facing pages, is based on the final fair copy, as revised by Wordsworth and his clerk John Carter, in the Pierpont Morgan Library. An *apparatus criticus* to the late reading text contains variants from the Pierpont Morgan manuscript found in DC MS. 89 and MS. B(2) of DC MS. 105.

All the reading texts attempt to preserve the punctuation, spelling, and capitalization of the manuscripts on which they are based, but a few obvious errors and misspellings have been corrected, ampersands have been expanded, and capitalization and punctuation have been modified, sparingly, where the sense requires it. In each *apparatus,* two sorts of variant are regularly omitted: those that involve only the substitution of the ampersand for "and" and those that involve no more than single-letter miswritings corrected by the copyist. Further details about editorial procedure will be found in the headnote to each reading text.

The other main sort of text, transcription of a manuscript, is more complicated. Here the aim is to show with reasonable typographic accuracy everything in the manuscript which could be helpful to a study of the poem's growth and development. Even false starts and corrected letters can sometimes reveal the writer's intention, and they are here recorded, though reinforced letters and random marks are normally not. Passages in Wordsworth's hand are discriminated from those in the hands of his amanuenses by printing his in roman type, theirs in italic with footnotes identifying the copyist, though identification of hands must sometimes be conjectural, especially in the case of scattered words or parts of words. Revisions are shown in type of reduced size just above or below the line to which they pertain, and an effort has been made to show spacing and other such physical features so that they resemble those of the manuscript itself, though some minor adjustments have been made in the interest of clarity; doubled-back lines are shown approximately as they appear in the manuscript. Since the primary purpose of the transcriptions is to provide easy reading of the manuscripts, they do not show the large deleting X's or vertical strokes or enclosing boxes or other such devices visible in facing photographs. Where the transcriptions are not faced with photographs, these devices are described in footnotes. The transcriptions do, however, show horizontal cross-out lines and single-letter erasures or deletions, since these frequently help the reader to follow the process of composition. Line numbers correspond to those of the reading text to which each manuscript contributes, except for the transcription of DC MS. 105, MS. B, in which lines have been numbered serially, as explained in the headnote to DC MS. 105.

The following symbols are used in both reading texts and transcriptions:

| | |
|---|---|
| [ ] | Gap or blank in the manuscript. |
| [?peace] | Conjectural reading. |
| [ ? ? ] | Illegible word or words; each question mark represents one word. |

The following symbols are used in transcriptions and in the *apparatus criticus*:

| | |
|---|---|
| Y{ou / e} | An overwriting: original reading, "Ye," converted to "You" by writing "ou" upon the "e." |

| | |
|---|---|
| ;} | A short addition, sometimes only a mark of punctuation. |
| [ ? ? ] | Deleted and illegible word or words. |
| That more | Word or words written over an erasure. |
| 161a, 161b | The first and second halves, respectively, of a line of verse. |

The following abbreviations are used in the *apparatus criticus*:

| | |
|---|---|
| *alt* | Alternate reading; the original reading is not deleted. |
| *del* | Reading deleted. |
| *del to* | Reading changed to another reading; the original is deleted. |
| *eras* | Erased. |
| *punct* | Punctuation. |
| *rev* | Revised. |

# Reading Texts

*The Tuft of Primroses* (1808)
*St. Paul's* (1808)
*To the Clouds* (1808 and 1842)

*Composed when a probability existed of our being obliged to quit Rydal Mount as a Residence* (1826),
Earliest and Latest Versions

# *The Tuft of Primroses* (1808)

*The Tuft of Primroses* was abandoned in DC MS. 65 as a series of verse passages, many beginning as fair copy and degenerating into drafting. Most of the passages are overlapping; virtually all of them contain further revision and drafting. Since there is no complete fair copy of the poem, a reading text has to be constructed from Wordsworth's latest revisions or alternate readings; where such revisions are incomplete or illegible, penultimate readings have been adopted. As an editorial reconstruction, this reading text is what would have resulted if, before abandoning his poem, Wordsworth had asked for a fair copy incorporating his latest carefully written entries.

In the reading text that follows, a horizontal rule indicates a point at which blocks of fair copy, separated in the manuscript by drafting or intermediate fair-copy stages, have been editorially joined together. Footnotes report passages that were entered as alternate versions of the text, generally on versos and often facing the uncanceled fair-copy lines to which they correspond. Shorter alternate versions, as of a word or phrase, are also reported in footnotes, along with the uncanceled original readings. These alternate versions, as the latest readings, have uniformly been incorporated in the reading text, although Wordsworth's intentions regarding them are not always clear. Throughout, Wordsworth's spelling and capitalization have been retained, but obvious errors and inconsistencies have been silently mended and punctuation has been sparingly modernized. The reader may refer to the transcriptions and textual notes for a complete account of earlier readings, emended readings, and the few later readings that are too fragmentary to be included in the reading text.

The list below indicates the leaves of DC MS. 65 from which each portion of the reading text has been taken.

| *Reading text lines* | *Leaves of DC MS. 65* | *Reading text lines* | *Leaves of DC MS. 65* |
|---|---|---|---|
| 1–41 | $30^{r}$, $31^{r}$, $32^{r}$ | 126–134 | $35^{v}$ |
| 42–43 | $31^{v}$ | 135–142 | $34^{v}$ |
| 44–47 | $32^{r}$ | 143–144 | $35^{v}$ |
| 48–51 | $31^{v}$ | 145–167 | $36^{r}$, $37^{r}$ |
| 52–61 | $32^{r}$ | 168–192 | $36^{v}$ |
| 62–70 | $29^{v}$ | 193–197a | $38^{r}$ |
| 71–115 | $33^{r}$, $34^{r}$, $35^{r}$ | 197b–199a | $37^{v}$ |
| 116–118 | $34^{v}$ | 199b–225 | $38^{r}$, $39^{r}$ |
| 119–125 | $35^{r}$ | 226 | $38^{v}$ |

| *Reading text lines* | *Leaves of DC MS. 65* |
|---|---|
| 227–243 | 40$^{r}$ |
| 244–275 | 42$^{v}$, 43$^{r}$ |
| 276–279 | 43$^{v}$ |
| 280–325a | 44$^{r}$, 45$^{r}$, 46$^{r}$, 47$^{r}$ |
| 325b–329 | 46$^{v}$ |
| 330–358a | 49$^{r}$, 50$^{r}$ |
| 358b–433 | 58$^{r}$, 58$^{v}$, 59$^{r}$, 59$^{v}$ |
| 434–440 | 57$^{r}$ |
| 441–468a | 60$^{r}$, 61$^{r}$ |
| 468b–472 | 60$^{v}$ |
| 473–477 | 61$^{r}$, 62$^{r}$ |
| 478–483 | 63$^{r}$ |
| 484 | 62$^{v}$ |
| 485–502 | 63$^{r}$, 64$^{r}$ |
| 503 | 63$^{v}$ |
| 504–507a | 64$^{r}$ |
| 507b–546 | 65$^{r}$, 66$^{r}$, 67$^{r}$ |
| 547 | 66$^{v}$ |
| 548–592 | 67$^{r}$, 68$^{r}$, 69$^{r}$, 70$^{r}$ |

# The Tuft of Primroses

Once more I welcome Thee, and Thou, fair Plant,
Fair Primrose, hast put forth thy radiant Flowers,
All eager to be welcomed once again.
O pity if the faithful Spring, beguiled
By her accustomed hopes, had come to breathe
Upon the bosom of this barren crag
And found thee not; but Thou art here, reviv'd,
And beautiful as ever, like a Queen
Smiling from thy imperishable throne,
And so shalt keep for ages yet untold,
Frail as Thou art, if the prophetic Muse
Be rightly trusted, so shalt Thou maintain
Conspicuously thy solitary state,
In splendour unimpaired. For Thou art safe
From most adventurous bound of mountain sheep
By keenest hunger press'd, and from approach
Of the wild Goat still bolder, nor more cause,
Though in that sunny and obtrusive [?seat],
Hast thou to dread the desolating grasp
Of Child or school boy, and though hand, perchance,
Of taller Passenger may want not power
To win thee, yet a thought would intervene,
Though Thou be tempting, and that thought of love
Would hold him back, check'd in the first conceit
And impulse of such rapine. A benign,

---

1 The echo of the opening line of *Lycidas* is clearer in the earliest draft version of this line, in DC MS. 18, 30v.

2 In a note (dictated to Isabella Fenwick in 1843) to a later poem, *The Primrose of the Rock* (1831), WW identified the location of the tuft of primroses: "It stands on the right hand a little way leading up the middle road from Rydal to Grasmere. We have been in the habit of calling it the Glow-worm Rock from the number of glow-worms we have often seen hanging on it as described. The tuft of primrose has, I fear, been washed away by the heavy rains" (DC MS. 153).

7–19 WW intended to drop his direct address to the primrose and refer to it instead in the third person, but his revisions were not carried beyond l. 19, and are therefore not included in the reading text.

20 The word "roaming" was entered as an alternate above the line, evidently to replace "perchance" at the end of the line, but the revision was not carried through.

21 The word "may" was entered as an alternate to "might," left uncanceled.

A condescending ordonnance as might [?calm],
Hath guarded long and still shall guard thy flowers,
Less for thy beauty's sake, though that might claim
All favour, than for pleasure which Thou shed'st,
Down-looking, and far-looking all day long,
Upon the Travellers that do hourly climb
This steep, new gladness yielding to the glad,
And genial promises to those who droop,
Sick, poor, or weary, or disconsolate,
Brightening at once the winter of their souls.
—I have a Friend whom seasons as they pass'd
All pleased; they in her bosom damp'd no joy
And from her light step took no liberty,
When suddenly as lightning from a cloud
Came danger with disease; came suddenly
And linger'd long, and this commanding Hill,
Which with its rocky chambers heretofore
Had been to her a range of dear resort,
The palace of her freedom, now, sad doom!
Was interdicted ground—a place of fear
For her, a melancholy Hill for us,
Constrain'd to think and ponder for her sake.
Fair primrose, lonely and distinguished Flower,
Well worthy of that honourable place
That holds thy beauty up to public view,
For ever parted from all neighbourhood,
In a calm course of meditative years,
Oft have I hail'd thee with serene delight,
—This greeting is far more—it is the voice
Of a surpassing joyance!—She herself
With her own eyes shall bless thee ere Thou fade;
The Prisoner shall come forth, and all the toil
And labours of this sharp ascent shall melt
Before thy mild assurances, and pain
And weakness shall pass from her like a sleep

27 See transcription for undeleted earlier readings.

36–61 Sara Hutchinson was seriously ill in March and April of 1808 (*MY*, I, 200–228).

42–43 See transcription for undeleted earlier readings.

44 The word "doom" was entered as an alternate to "change," left uncanceled.

48–51 See transcription for undeleted earlier readings.

51 In DC MS. 65, 31[v], the line begins "From"—an obvious error for "For," which is restored here from prior versions of the line on 32[r] and 31[v].

58 The word "sharp" was entered as an alternate to "steep," left uncanceled.

Chas'd by a bright glimpse of the morning sun.
Farewell! yet turning from thee, happy Flower,
With these Dear thoughts, not therefore are old claims
Unrecognized—not therefore is the sense
Less vivid of that pleasure which to me
Thy punctual reappearance would have given
In its pure self. For often when I pass
This Rock, while Thou art in thy winter sleep,
Or the rank summer hides thy flower-like leaf,
I have a thought for thee. Alas how much,
Since I beheld and loved Thee first, how much
Is gone, though thou be left; I would not speak
Of best Friends dead, or other deep heart loss
Bewail'd with weeping, but by River sides
And in broad fields how many gentle loves,
How many mute memorials pass'd away.
Stately herself, though of a lowly kind,
That little Flower remains and has survived
The lofty band of Firs that overtopp'd
Their antient Neighbour, the old Steeple Tower;
That consecrated Train which had so oft
Swung in the blast, mingling their solemn strain
Of music with the one determined voice
From the slow funeral bell, a symphony
Most awful and affecting to the ear
Of him who pass'd beneath: or had dealt forth
Soft murmurs like the cooing of a Dove
Ere first distinguishably heard, and cast
Their dancing shadows on the flowery turf,
While through the Churchyard tripp'd the bridal train
In festive Ribbands deck'd; and those same trees,
By moonlight, in their stillness and repose,
Deepen'd the silence of a hundred graves.
Ah, what a welcome! when from absence long
Returning, on the centre of the Vale

---

62–70 See transcription for undeleted earlier readings.

73–74 The poet's brother John had died in 1805.

79–114 "All the trees in Bainriggs are cut down, and even worse, the giant sycamore near the parsonage house, and all the finest firtrees that overtopped the steeple tower." (DW to Catherine Clarkson, July 19, 1807, in *MY*, I, 159); see Introduction, above.

81 The word "Train" was entered as an alternate to "File," left uncanceled.

94–95 The Wordsworths had been living at Coleorton since October 1806, and they returned to Grasmere on July 10, 1807 (*Chronology: MY*, p. 358).

I look'd a first glad look and saw them not.
Was it a dream! the aerial grove, no more
Right in the centre of the lovely vale
Suspended like a stationary cloud,
Had vanish'd like a cloud—yet say not so,
For here and there a straggling Tree was left
To mourn in blanc and monumental grief,
To pine and wither for its fellows gone.
—Ill word that laid them low—unfeeling Heart
Had He who could endure that they should fall,
Who spared not them nor spar'd that sycamore high,
The universal glory of the Vale,
And did not spare the little avenue
Of lightly stirring Ash-trees, that sufficed
To dim the glare of summer, and to blunt
The strong Wind turn'd into a gentle breeze,
Whose freshness cheared the paved walk beneath,
That antient walk which from the Vicar's door
Led to the Church-yard gate. Then, Grasmere, then
Thy sabbath mornings had a holy grace,
That incommunicable sanctity
Which Time and nature only can bestow,
When from his venerable [?home] the Priest
Did issue forth glistening in best attire,
And down that consecrated visto paced
Towards the Churchyard where his ready Flock
Were gathered round in sunshine or in shade,
While Trees and mountains echoed to the Voice
Of the glad bells, and all the murmuring streams
United their soft chorus with the song.
Now stands the Steeple naked and forlorn,
And from the spot of sacred ground, the home
To which all change conducts the thought, looks round
Upon the changes of this peaceful Vale.
What sees the old grey Tower through high or low

---

100 "Had" was entered as an alternate to "Was," uncanceled.

111 The word "gentle" was entered as an alternate to "favouring," apparently uncanceled.

116–118 See transcription for undeleted earlier readings.

120 The phrase "that consecrated" was entered as an alternate to "through that domestic," left uncanceled.

126–134 See transcription for undeleted earlier readings.

130 The word "high," left out of the final version on 35v, is supplied from an earlier version on 36r, facing.

Of his domain, what injury doth he note
Beyond what he himself hath undergone,
What other profanation or despoil
Of fairest things that calls for more regret
Than that small cottage? There it is aloft,
And nearest to the flying clouds of three,
Perch'd each above the other on the side
Of the vale's northern outlet—from below
And from afar, yet say not from afar,
For all things in this little world of ours
Are in one bosom of close neighbourhood,
The hoary steeple now beholds that roof
Laid open to the glare of common day,
And marks five graves beneath his feet, in which,
Divided by a breadth of smooth green space
From all the other hillocks which like waves
Heave close together, they who were erewhile
The Inmates of that Cottage are at rest.
Death to the happy House in which they dwelt
Had given a long reprieve of forty years;
Suddenly then they disappeared—not twice
Had Summer scorch'd the fields, not twice had fallen
The first white snow upon Helvellyn's top,
Before the greedy visiting was closed
And the long-priviledg'd House left empty, swept
As by a plague; yet no rapacious plague
Had been among them, all was gentle death,
One after one, with intervals of peace,
A Consummation and divine accord,

---

132 A revised version of the second half of this line, not fully legible in the manuscript (DC MS. 65, 35v) is not included in the reading text.

135 Capitalization and punctuation of this line, left in draft on DC MS. 65, 34v, have been emended to accord with earlier versions on 35v and 36r.

135–234 The Reverend Joseph Sympson (1715–1807) and his family lived at High Broadrain, a farmhouse near Dunmail Raise, on the road to Keswick. They were close friends of the Wordsworths and are often mentioned by DW and WW in letters of 1800–1804 and in DW's journals. The deaths of "old Mr. Sympson" and "his son the parson" are mentioned by DW in a letter of July 19, 1807 (*MY*, I, 158).

146–147 The words "all . . . together" were entered as alternates, expanding a single phrase left uncanceled: "From nearest neighbourhood."

148 "The inmates of my cottage all at rest"—Coleridge's *Frost at Midnight*, l. 4.

149–197 These lines were later revised, beginning on DC MS. 65, 36v–38v, for inclusion in *The Excursion* (1814), VII, 261–310 (1850: VII, 242–291).

159 The phrase "divine accord" was entered as an alternate to "a harmony," left uncanceled.

Though fram'd of sad and melancholy notes,
Sweet, perfect, to be wish'd for, save that here
Was something sounding to our mortal sense
Like harshness, that the old greyheaded Sire,
The Oldest, he was taken last, survived
When the dear Partner of his manhood's prime,
His Son, and Daughter, then a blooming Wife,
And little smiling Grandchild were no more.
'Twas but a little patience and his term
Of solitude was spent.—The aged one,
(He was our first in eminence of years
The Patriarch of the Vale,—a busy Hand,
Yea more, a Burning palm, a flashing eye,
A restless foot, a head that beat at nights
Upon his pillow with a thousand schemes)
"How will he face the remnant of his life,
What will become of him?," we said, and mused
In vain conjectures; "Shall we meet him now,
Haunting with rod and line the rocky brooks
And mountain-Tarns; or shall we, as we pass,
Hear him alone, and solacing his ear
With music?," for he, in the fitful hours
Of his tranquillity, had not ceas'd to touch
The harp or viol which himself had framed
And fitted to their tasks with perfect skill.
"What Titles will he keep, will he remain
Musician, Gardener, Builder, Mechanist,
A Planter and a Rearer from the seed,
A man of hope and forward-looking mind,
Even to the last?"—such was he unsubdued.
But Heaven was gracious; yet a little while,
And this old Man, he and his chearful throng
Of open schemes, and all his inward hoard
Of unsunn'd griefs, too many and too keen,
Fell with the body into gentle sleep
In one blest moment, and the family,
By yet a higher privilege, once more

162 The word "something" stands as a revision of "somewhat," left uncanceled.

168–192 See transcription for undeleted earlier readings.

197 Capitalization and punctuation have been emended to join the two halves of the line on 38r and 37v of DC MS. 65.

Were gathered to each other where they sleep,
For they were strangers, in the realm of death
Divided from all neighbourhood. Yet I own,
Though I can look on their associate graves
With nothing but still thought, that I repine,
It costs me something like a pain to feel
That after them so many of their works,
Which round that Dwelling covertly preserv'd
The History of their unambitious lives,
Have perish'd, and so soon!—The Cottage-Court,
Spread with blue gravel from the torrent's side
And gay with shrubs, the garden, bed and walk
His own creation, that embattled Host
Of garish tulips, fruit trees chosen and rare,
And roses of all colours, which he sought
Most curiously, as generously dispers'd
Their kinds, to beautify his neighbours' grounds;
Trees of the forest, too, a stately fence
Planted for Shelter in his manhood's prime,
And Small Flowers watered by his wrinkled hand,
That all are ravaged;—that his Daughter's Bower
Is creeping into shapelessness, self-lost
In the wild wood, like a neglected image
Or fancy which hath ceased to be recalled.
The jasmine, her own charge, which she had trained
To deck the wall, and of one flowery spray
Had made an Inmate, luring it from sun
And breezes, and from its fellows, to pervade
The inside of her chamber with its sweet,
And be the Comrade of her loneliest thought,—
I grieve to see that Jasmine on the ground
Stretching its desolate length, mourn that these works
Of love and diligence and innocent care
Are sullied and disgrac'd; or that a gulf
Hath swallowed them which renders nothing back;
That they, so quickly, in a cave are hidden
Which cannot be unlock'd; upon their bloom
That a perpetual winter should have fallen.
Meanwhile the little Primrose of the rock

---

198 The word "realm" was entered as an alternate for "world," left uncanceled.
224 The word "pervade" was entered as an alternate for "caress," left uncanceled.

Remains, in sacred beauty, without taint
Of injury or decay, lives to proclaim
Her charter in the blaze of noon; salutes
Not unobserved the early Shepherd Swain,
Or Labourer plodding at th'accustomed hour
Home to his distant hearth; and may be seen,
Long as the fullness of her bloom endures,
With one short instantaneous chear of mind,

---

By stranger late in travel, as I myself
Have often seen her, when the last lone Thrush
Had ceas'd his vesper hymn, piercing the gloom
Of Twilight with the vigor of a star,
Say rather, boldly hung as if in air,
Like the broad Moon, with lustre somewhat dimm'd,
Lonely and bright and as the Moon secure.
  Oh for some band of guardian Spirits, prompt
As were those human ministers of old,
Who, daily, nightly, under various names,
With various service stood or walk'd their rounds
Through the wide forest, to protect from harm
The wild Beast with her young, and from the touch
Of waste the green-leav'd Thicket to defend,
Their secret couch, and cool umbrageous trees,
Their canopy, and berry-bearing shrub
And grassy lawn, their pasture's open range;
Continual and firm peace, from outrage safe
And all annoyance, till the sovereign comes
Heading his train, and through that franchise high
Urges the Chase with clamorous hound and horn.
O grant some wardenship of spirits pure,
As duteous in their office to maintain
Inviolate for nobler purposes
These individual precincts, to protect,
Here, if here only, from despoil and wrong
All growth of nature and all frame of Art

---

256 The manuscript reading, "Beasts," is here emended to accord with WW's revision of the line on 42ᵛ of DC MS. 65.

267 The reading of the manuscript is "purpose" but Wordsworth must have intended the plural to make the line scan.

By, and in which, the blissful pleasures live.
Have not th'incumbent Mountains looks of awe
In which this mandate may be read, the streams
A voice that pleads, beseeches, and implores?
In vain—the deafness of the world is here,
Even here, and all too many of the haunts
Of Fancy's choicest pastime, and the best
And Dearest resting places of the heart
Vanish beneath an unrelenting doom.
  What impulse drove the Hermit to his Cell
And what detain'd him there his whole life long
Fast anchored in the desart? Not alone
Dread of the persecuting sword, remorse,
Love with despair, or grief in agony;
Not always from intolerable pangs
He fled; but in the height of pleasure sigh'd
For independent happiness, craving peace,
The central feeling of all happiness,
Not as a refuge from distress or pain,
A breathing time, vacation, or a truce,
But for its absolute self, a life of peace,
Stability without regret or fear,
That hath been, is, and shall be ever more.
Therefore on few external things his heart
Was set, and those his own, or if not his,
Subsisting under Nature's stedfast law.
What other yearning was the master tie
Of the monastic brotherhood, upon rock
Aerial or in green secluded vale,
One after one collected from afar,
An undissolving fellowship? What but this,
The universal instinct of repose,
The longing for confirm'd tranquillity,
Inward and outward, humble and sublime,
The life where hope and memory are as one,
Earth quiet and unchanged, the human soul
Consistent in self rule, and heaven revealed

---

276–279 See transcription for undeleted earlier readings.

280–308 WW first adapted this passage for inclusion at the beginning of bk. V of *The Excursion* (see *PW*, V, 153), then included a later version of it in bk. III of 1814, ll. 374–410 (1850: III, 367–405). Work toward the *Excursion* text begins on DC MS. 65, $43^{v}$–$45^{r}$.

To meditation in that quietness.
  Thus tempted, thus inspired, St. Basil left
(Man as he was of noble blood, high-born,
High-station'd, and elaborately taught)
The vain felicities of Athens, left
Her throng of Sophists glorying in their snares,
Her Poets, and conflicting Orators,
Relinquish'd Alexandria's splendid Halls,
Antioch and Cesarea, and withdrew
To his delicious Pontic solitude,
Remembering with deep thankfulness meanwhile
Those exhortations of a female voice
Pathetically urg'd, his Sister's voice,
Macrina, pious Maid, most beautiful
And in the gentleness of woman wise,
By whom admonish'd, He while yet a Youth
And a triumphant Scholar, had dismiss'd
That loftiness, and modestly inclined
To a strict life of virtuous privacy.
Which sequestration when he chose, erelong
He found the same beyond all promise rich
In dignity, sincere content, and joy.

---

  Mark, for the Picture to this hour remains,
With what luxuriant fondness he pourtrays

---

309–477 St. Basil, scholar and theologian born at Cesarea in A.D. 329, retired to a mountain retreat in Pontus, where he organized a monastery. WW's source for the story of Basil, Macrina, and Nazianzen is *The Life of St. Basil Bishop of Caesarea in Cappodocia,* pp. 470–508 of William Cave's *Apostolici* (1716), a book found in WW's library after his death (Chester L. Shaver and Alice C. Shaver, *Wordsworth's Library: A Catalogue* [New York, 1979], p. 49). See Introduction, p. 21.

312 Basil called Athens "*an empty and vain Felicity*" (Cave, *Apostolici,* p. 473). See Introduction, p. 20.

315 "Relinquish'd" was entered as an alternate to "Abandon'd," left uncanceled.

319–326 In Cave's *Apostolici,* p. 507, Macrina, whose "piety encreas'd with her Years, and her Beauty with both," persuades "her brother *Basil,* then newly return'd from University, to lay aside the lofty Opinion of his great Learning, and to embrace the humble and difficult way of Vertue, and to form himself to the strictness of a retired Life." See Introduction, p. 20.

325 The phrase "modestly inclined" was entered as an alternate to "and bent his dearest hopes," left uncanceled.

326–329 See transcription for uncanceled earlier readings.

330–429 The "Picture" that "to this hour remains" is Basil's letter XIV to his friend Gregory Nazianzen, from which WW's description in these lines may be drawn. It has been suggested (*Chronology: MY,* p. 379, and Moorman, II, 132–133) that WW read Basil's letter while visiting

The lineaments and image of that spot,
In which upon a Mount, sylvan and high,
And at the boldest jutting in its side,
His cell was fix'd, a Mount with Towering Hills
Fenc'd round and vallies intricate and deep,
Which, leaving one blind Entrance to a plain
Of fertile Meadow ground that lay beneath,
Fronting the cell, had from all quarters else
Forbidden all approach, by rocks abrupt,
Or rampart as effectual of huge woods
Neither austere nor gloomy to behold,
But a gay prospect lifting to the sun
Majestic beds of diverse foliage, fruits
And thousand laughing blossoms; and the plain
Stretch'd out beneath the high perch'd cell was bright
With herbs and flowers, and tufts of flowering plants,
The choicest which the lavish East pours forth,
And sober-headed Cypress interspers'd,
And grac'd with presence of a famous Stream,
The Rapid Iris, journeying from remote
Armenian Mountains to his Euxine bourne,
Sole Traveller by the guarded mount, and He,
To enter there, had leapt with thunderous Voice
Down a steep rock, and through the secret plain,
Not without many a lesser bound, advanc'd
Self-chear'd with song, to keep his onward course
Like a belated Pilgrim.

---

Come O Friend!
(Thus did St. Basil fervently break forth,
Entreated thus the man he held most dear)
Come Nazianzen to these happy fields,
To this enduring Paradise, these walks

---

his brother Christopher at Lambeth, c. March 25–April 2, 1808. But it is more likely that the primary source for the story of Basil and Gregory is Cave's *Apostolici,* which WW owned in the folio edition of 1716. See the note to the transcription of DC MS. 172, below; the notes to ll. 312 and 319–326 of this reading text; and the Introduction, p. 21.

336 "Fenc'd" was entered as an alternate to "Girt," left uncanceled.

347 The word "herbs" (in place of "herb") is supplied from a deleted version of the line.

361 WW had the works of Gregory Nazianzen in his Rydal Mount library (Shaver and Shaver, *Wordsworth's Library,* p. 109).

Of contemplation, piety, and love,
Coverts serene of bless'd mortality.
What if the Roses and the flowers of Kings,
Princes and Emperors, and the crowns and palms
Of all the great are blasted, or decay—
What if the meanest of their subjects, each
Within the narrow region of his cares,
Tremble beneath a sad uncertainty?
There is a priviledge to plead, there is,
Renounce, and thou shall find that priviledge, here.
No loss lamenting, no privation felt,
Disturb'd by no vicissitudes, unscarred
By civil faction, by religious broils
Unplagu'd, forgetting, and forgotten, here
Mayst thou possess thy own invisible nest,
Like one of those small birds that round us chaunt
In multitudes, their warbling will be thine,
And freedom to unite thy voice with theirs,
When they at morn or dewy evening praise
High heaven in sweet and solemn services.
Here mayst thou dedicate thyself to God
And acceptably fill the votive hours,
Not seldom as these Creatures of the grove
That need no rule, and live but to enjoy,
Not only lifted often to the calm
Of that entire beatitude in which
The Angels serve, but when thou must descend
From the pure vision, and thy soul admit
A salutary glow of hope and fear,
Searching in patience and humility
Among the written mysteries of faith

---

365–367 WW attached the following note to a revised version of these lines included in bk. VII of *The Excursion* (1814):

The "Transit gloria mundi" is finely expressed in the Introduction to the Foundation-Charters of some of the ancient Abbeys. Some expressions here used are taken from that of the Abbey of St. Mary's Furness, the translation of which is as follows:

"Considering every day the uncertainty of life, that the roses and flowers of Kings, Emperors, and Dukes, and the crowns and palms of all the great, wither and decay; and that all things with an uninterrupted course, tend to dissolution and death: I therefore," &c. [*PW,* V, 262, 468]

374 The manuscript reads "unscared"; "unscarred" has been restored from 51$^{r}$ of DC MS. 65.

381–382 "There entertain him all the saints above, / In solemn troops and sweet societies" (*Lycidas,* ll. 178–179); "From noon to dewy Eve" (*Paradise Lost,* I, 743).

The will divine, or when thou wouldst assume
The burthen and the seasonable yoke
Required by our frail Nature, wouldst be tamed
By vigils, abstinence, and prayer with tears,
What place so fit?—a solitude this deep
Thebais or the Syrian Wilderness
Contains not in its dry and barren round;
For not a human form is seen this way,
Unless some straggling Hunter led by chance.
Him, if the graver duties be performed,
Or overwrought with study, if the mind
Be haunted by a vain disquietude
And gladly would be taken from itself,
Or if it be the time when thoughts are blithe,
Him mayst Thou follow to the hills, or mount
Alone, as fancy prompts, equipp'd with bow
And shafts and quiver, not for perilous aim
At the gaunt wolf, the Lion, or the Pard,
These lurk not in our bounds, but Deer and Goat
And other kinds as peaceable are there
In readiness for inoffensive chase.
The River also owns his harmless tribes
And tempts thee to like sport; labour itself
Is pastime here, for generous is the Sun,
And cool airs blowing from the mountain top
Refresh the brow of him who in plain field
Or garden presses his industrious spade.
Or if a different exercise thou chuse,
And from boon nature rather wouldst receive
Food for the day; behold the fruits that hang
In the primaeval woods—the wells and springs
Have each a living garland of green herbs,
From which they to the rifling hand will yield
Ungrudgingly supply that never fails,
Bestowed as freely as their water—pure
To deck thy temperate board.—
From theme to theme
Transported in this sort by fervent zeal
That stopp'd not here, the venerable Man,

---

405 The phrase "haunted . . . disquietude" was entered as an alternate for "restless under vain disturbances," left uncanceled.

Holy and great, his invitation breathed.
And Nazianzen fashion'd a reply
Ingenious and rhetorical, with taunts
Of wit and gay good-humour'd ridicule,
Directed both against the life itself
And that strong passion for these fortunate isles,
For this Arcadia of a golden dream.
But on her inward council seat, his soul
Was mov'd, was rapt, and fill'd with seriousness;
Nor was it long ere broken out from ties
Of the world's business he the call obey'd.
And Amphilochius came, and numbers more,
Men of all tempers, qualities, estates,
Came with one spirit, like a troop of fowl
That, single or in clusters, at a sign
Given by their leader, settle on the breast
Of some broad pool, green field, or shady tree,
In harmony and undisturbed repose;
Or as a brood of eager younglings flock,
Delighted, to the mother's outspread wings
And shelter there in unity and love.
  An intellectual Champion of the faith,
Accomplish'd above all who then appeared,
Or, haply, since victoriously have stood
In opposition to the desperate course
Of Pagan rites or impious heresies,
St. Basil, after lapse of years, went forth
To a station of authority and power,
Upon an urgent summons, and resign'd,
Ah, not without regret, the heavenly Mount,
The sheltering Valley, and his lov'd Compeers.
He parted from them, but their common life,
If neither first nor singular, at least

---

433–438 Gregory Nazianzen's reply is his Epistle IV. See Introduction, sec. IV.

435 The manuscript's "gay-good humord" has been emended.

437 The word "isles," singular on 57r, is supplied from 60r of DC MS. 65.

438 The word "dream," not present on 57r, is here supplied from 60r of DC MS. 65.

443 Amphilochius, bishop of Iconium, was regarded as the foremost member of the Eastern church, after his friends Basil of Cesarea and Gregory of Nazianzus. See Introduction, sec. IV.

448 The word "leaf" in this line on 60r is apparently a mistake; "field" has been restored from 57r.

458–462 Basil was called from his Pontic retreat to an important council at Constantinople, and in 370 he was made bishop of Cesarea. See Introduction, sec. IV.

More beautiful than any of like frame
That hitherto had been conceived, a life
To which by written institutes and rules
He gave a solid being, did not thence
Depart with him, nor ceas'd when he, and they
Whom he had gather'd to his peaceful Vale
In that retirement, were withdrawn from earth.
And afterwards it hung through many an age,
In bright remembrance, like a shining cloud,
O'er the vast regions of the western Church;
Whence those communities of holy men
That spread so far, to shrouded quietness
Devoted, and of saintly Virgins pure.

---

Fallen, in a thousand vales, the stately Towers
And branching windows gorgeously array'd,
And aisles and roofs magnificent that thrill'd
With halleluiahs, and the strong-ribb'd vaults
Are crush'd, and buried under weeds and earth
The cloistral avenues—they that heard the voice
Of some sequester'd brook in Gallia's Vales,
Soft murmuring among woods and olive bowers
And tilth and vineyards, and the Piles that rose
On British lawns by Severn, Thames, or Tweed
And saw their pomp reflected in the stream,
As Tintern saw; and, to this day, beholds
Her faded image in the depths of Wye.—
Of solemn port, smitten but unsubdued
She stands; nor less tenacious of her rights
Stands Fountains Abbey, glorious in decay,
Before the pious Traveller's lifted eyes,
Threatening to outlive the ravages of Time,
And bear the cross till Christ shall come again.
So cleave they to the earth, in monument
Or Revelation, nor in memory less
Of nature's pure religion, as in line

---

468–472 See transcription for undeleted earlier readings.

484 The line was entered on a verso as an alternate to, or revision of, "Of Rhone or Loire, or some sequester'd brook," which was left uncanceled.

486 The phrase "tilth and vineyard" is used at l. 592, where WW breaks off the poem.

Uninterrupted it hath travelled down
From the first man who heard a howling storm,
Or knew a troubled thought or vain desire,
A hope which had deceived, or empty came,
Or, in the very sunshine of his joy
And saddened at a perishable bliss,
Or languish'd idly under fond regrets
That might not be subdued.—

---

"And is thy doom
Pronounc'd (I said, a Stripling at that time,
Who with a Fellow-pilgrim had been driv'n
Through madding France before a joyous gale,
And to the solemn haven of Chartreuse
Repaired for timely rest) and are we twain
The last, perchance, the very last, of men
Who shall be welcom'd here, whose limbs shall find
Repose within these modest cells, whose hearts
Receive a comfort from these awful spires?
Alas for what I see, the flash of arms,
O sorrow! and yon military glare,
And hark those voices! let us hide in gloom
Profoundest of St. Bruno's wood, these sighs,

---

502 The word "knew" was entered as an alternate to "felt," left uncanceled.

507a The word "night" was entered as an alternate to "world," left uncanceled.

507a/507b At this point in DC MS. 65 ($64^r$–$65^r$) WW deleted 14 lines of fair copy on Robin Hood and his troop:

Me thinks I hear,
Not from these woods, but from some merry grove
That lies I know not where, the spritely blast
Of the clear bugle, and from thicket green
Of hollies sparkling in an April sun
Forth, in a moment, issues to the glade
A Troop of green clad Foresters in arms
Blithe Outlaws and their Chieftain:—would the[y] rouze
The Stag, dislodge the Hart; or will they keep
Their oath in presence of Maid Marian sworn
And with a cloud of shafts this day confound
The royal Officers? let them on, and yield
Even at their pleasure to the boisterous drift
Of pastime or adventure—let them on
I love them better when at ease at [?last]

507–567 WW and his friend Robert Jones visited the Grande Chartreuse during their walking tour of France and the Alps in 1790, but the monastery was not occupied by revolutionary

These whispers that pursue, or meet me, whence
[ ] are they but a common [ ]
From the two Sister Streams of Life and Death;
Or are they by the parting Genius sent,
Unheard till now, and to be heard no more?"
  Yes I was moved and to this hour am moved.
What Man would bring to nothing, if he might,
A natural power or element? and who,
If the ability were his, would dare
To kill a species of insensate life,
Or to the bird of meanest wing would say,
Thou, and thy kind, must perish.—Even so,
So consecrated, almost, might he deem
That power, that organ, that transcendent frame
Of social being.—"Stay your impious hand,"
Such was the vain injunction of that hour,
By Nature uttered from her Alpine throne,
"O leave in quiet this embodied dream,
This substance by which mortal men have clothed,
Humanly cloth'd the ghostliness of things,
In silence visible and perpetual calm.
Let this one Temple last—be this one spot
Of earth devoted to Eternity."—
I heard, or seem'd to hear, and thus the Voice
Proceeded—"honour to the Patriot's zeal,
Glory and life to new-born liberty—
All hail ye mighty passions of the Time,
The vengeance, and the transport, and the hope,
But spare, if past and present be the wings
On whose support harmoniously conjoined
Moves the great Spirit of human knowledge, spare
This House, these courts of mystery, where a step

---

soldiers until 1792. An early version of these lines was included in *Descriptive Sketches*, ll. 53–79, in 1793; a later version was added in 1816–1819 to *The Prelude*, VI, 418–488 (*Prel.*, pp. 197–203). Adaptation of the lines for *The Prelude* begins on 66v–67r of DC MS. 65.

523 The "Sister Streams of Life and Death" are, as WW's note to *Descriptive Sketches*, l. 73, points out, "Names of rivers at the Chartreuse."

524 "The parting Genius is with sighing sent" (Milton's ode *On the Morning of Christ's Nativity*, l. 186).

547 The line was entered on a verso as an alternate to "Hail to the mighty Passions of the," left incomplete but uncanceled.

549–551 WW quoted a slightly modified version of these lines in the *Essay, Supplementary to the Preface* in the 1815 edition of his *Poems* (*Prose*, III, 84).

Between the Portals of the shadowy rocks
Leaves far behind the vanities of life,
Where, if a peasant enter, or a king,
One holy thought, a single holy thought
Has power to initiate—let it be redeemed
With all its blameless priesthood—for the sake
Of Heaven-descended truth; and humbler claim
Of these majestic floods, my noblest boast;
These shining cliffs, pure as their home, the sky;
These forests unapproachable by death,
That shall endure as long as Man endures
To think, to hope, to worship, and to feel;
To struggle,—to be lost within himself
In trepidation,—from the dim abyss
To look with bodily eyes, and be consoled."
Such repetition of that [ ]
My thoughts demanded; now an humbler task
Awaits us, for the unwearied Song will lead
Into a lonely Vale, the mild abode
Of female Votaries. No [ ] plain
Blank as the Arabian wilderness defends
This chosen Spot, nor is it [ ]
By rocks like those of Caucasus, or Alps,
The untransmuted Shapes of many worlds,
Nor can it boast a massy Structure huge,
Founded and built by hands, with arch and towers,
Pillar and pinnacle and glittering spire
Sublime, as if in Emulation reared
Of the eternal Architect—these signs,
These tokens—admonitions to recall,
Curbs to restrain, or stays to lean upon,
Such food to nourish or appease the Soul
The gentle Beings who found harbour here
Required not. Them a lowly Edifice
Embrac'd by [?lowly] grounds that did not aim
To overshadow, but to screen and hide,
Contented,—and an unassuming brook
Working between these hills its aimless way
Through meadow, chestnut wood, and olive bowers
And tilth and vineyard.——

---

592 The phrase "tilth and vineyards" had been used in l. 486.

## *St. Paul's* (1808)

The reading text of *St. Paul's* is based on Wordsworth's latest fair copy, on 119$^{r}$–120$^{r}$ of DC MS. 65. Manuscript variants can be found below in the full transcriptions of *St. Paul's* work in DC MS. 18 (1$^{v}$–3$^{v}$) and DC MS. 65 (118$^{v}$–120$^{r}$).

# [*St. Paul's*]

Press'd with conflicting thoughts of love and fear,
I parted from thee, Friend! and took my way
Through the great City, pacing with an eye
Down cast, ear sleeping, and feet masterless,
That were sufficient guide unto themselves,
And step by step went pensively. Now, mark!
Not how my trouble was entirely hush'd,
(That might not be) but how by sudden gift,
Gift of Imagination's holy power!
My Soul in her uneasiness received
An anchor of stability. It chanced
That, while I thus was pacing, I raised up
My heavy eyes and instantly beheld,
Saw at a glance in that familiar spot
A visionary scene: a length of street
Laid open in its morning quietness,
Deep, hollow, unobstructed, vacant, smooth,
And white with winter's purest white, as fair,
As fresh and spotless as he ever sheds
On field or mountain. Moving Form was none,
Save here and there a shadowy Passenger,
Slow, shadowy, silent, dusky, and beyond
And high above this winding length of street,
This noiseless and unpeopled avenue,
Pure, silent, solemn, beautiful, was seen
The huge majestic Temple of St. Paul
In awful sequestration, through a veil,
Through its own sacred veil of falling snow.

---

Title The lines were never titled by WW; de Selincourt's title is here adopted for convenience (*PW*, IV, 374).

9 This line appears to have been inadvertently omitted, then inserted in the fair copy in DC MS. 65, 119[r]; the reading here is restored from DC MS. 18, 1[v].

11b–14a WW drafted a shorter version of this passage in DC MS. 65, 118[v]:

I raised
My heavy eyes while pacing thus & saw
Saw at a glance

## *To the Clouds* (1808 and 1842)

The 1808 reading text of *To the Clouds* is based on the earliest complete fair copy of the poem, entered by Wordsworth at the beginning of DC MS. 65 ($3^r$–$7^r$). The 1842 text is here reprinted from *Poems, Chiefly of Early and Late Years,* pages 85–88; variant readings from the editions of 1845, 1846, and 1849–50 and from the two late fair copies, DC MSS. 151/3 and 151/6, are contained in an *apparatus.* Further variants can be found below, in the full transcription of *To the Clouds* work in DC MS. 18 ($4^v$–$12^v$, $23^v$, $24^v$), DC MS. 65 ($8^r$, $9^v$–$12^r$, $113^v$, $117^r$), and DC MS. 143. The bracketed line numbers in the 1842 reading text indicate corresponding lines in the 1808 reading text.

DC MS. 151 consists largely of portions of the printer's copy for *Poems, Chiefly of Early and Late Years.* Folders 3 and 6 are made from sheets of paper folded once to form pages about 20 centimeters wide by 25.2 centimeters high; there are no watermarks or chain lines. The fair copy in folder 3 is in Mary Wordsworth's hand; the fair copy in folder 6, in Dora Wordsworth's hand, was apparently made necessary by Wordsworth's late revisions in folder 3.

## To the Clouds

Army of clouds, what would ye? Flight of Clouds,
Ascending from behind the motionless brow
Of this tall Rock as from a hidden world,
O whither in this eagerness of speed?
What seek ye? or what shun ye? of the Wind
Companions, fear ye to be left behind,
Or racing on your blue ætherial field
Contend ye with each other? of the Sea,
Children, bright Children of the distant sea,
Thus post Ye over dale and mountain height
To sink upon your Mother's joyous lap?
Or were Ye rightlier hail'd when first mine eyes

---

The note dictated by WW to Isabella Fenwick in 1843 reads as follows: "These verses were suggested while I was walking on the foot-road between Rydal Mount and Grasmere. The clouds were driving over the top of Nab Scar across the vale; they set my thoughts agoing, and the rest followed almost immediately" (DC MS. 153).

1 The phrase "what would ye?" is supplied from DC MS. 18, $4^v$ and $6^v$, to fill the blank left in WW's fair copy in DC MS. 65.

9 The word "bright" is supplied from DC MS. 18, $4^v$ and $6^v$, to fill the blank left in WW's fair copy in DC MS. 65.

## ADDRESS TO THE CLOUDS.

Army of Clouds! ye winged Host in troops
Ascending from behind the motionless brow
Of that tall rock, as from a hidden world,
O whither with such eagerness of speed?
[5] What seek ye, or what shun ye? of the gale
Companions, fear ye to be left behind,
Or racing o'er your blue ethereal field
Contend ye with each other? of the sea
Children, thus post ye over vale and height
To sink upon your mother's lap—and rest?
[12] Or were ye rightlier hailed, when first mine eyes
Beheld in your impetuous march the likeness
Of a wide army pressing on to meet
Or overtake some unknown enemy?—
But your smooth motions suit a peaceful aim;

---

ADDRESS TO THE CLOUDS.] *no title, MS. 151/3* Address to the Clouds— *in WW's hand, MS. 151/6* To the Clouds. *1845–49*

1 Army] Army *MSS. 151/3, 151/6* ye winged Host in troops] equestrian host on wings *MS. 151/3* equestrian host on wings *del by WW to* ye winged Host in troops *MS. 151/6, with* out *(WW) del at beginning of line* wingèd *1845–49*

2 the] yon *del to* the *MS. 151/3*

3 *no commas, MS. 151/3*

4 O] Oh *overwritten* O *MS. 151/6* speed?] speed *MS. 151/3* speed, *rev to* speed *MS. 151/6*

5 or what] or, *with* what *inserted, MS. 151/3* ye?] ye! *rev to* ye? *MS. 151/6*

7 oer . . . etherial *MSS. 151/3, 151/6*

8 Of the Sea *MSS. 151/3, 151/6*

9 *no comma MS. 151/3*

10 mother's lap—and rest?] Mother's lap, & rest. *MS. 151/3* Mother's lap and rest *MS. 151/6, then punct added*

11 hailed,] hailed *MS. 151/3*

13 Army *MSS. 151/3, 151/6*

14 enemy? *MS. 151/3*

15–17 *original readings in MS. 151/3, with revisions in WW's hand, then entire passage del:*

though
But smooth your motion, smooth ~~as~~ keen & fleet
And ye may not unaptly be compared
~~Compared~~ with things in character & aim
Even now with things of peaceful character & aim
~~Peaceful~~ a ~~never ending~~ flight of Birds
~~A flight~~

*WW then entered and canceled* But smooth your motion *in margin, followed by ll. 15–17 unpunctuated but otherwise as in PELY except for l. 15* motion suits *and l. 17* Birds

I lifted, for Ye still are sweeping on
Like a wide Army in impetuous march,
Or like a never-ending Flight of Birds
Aerial, upon due migration bound,
Embodied Travellers not blindly led
To milder climes? or rather do ye urge
In caravan your hasty pilgrimage,
With hope to pause at last upon the tops
Of some remoter mountains more belov'd
Than these, and utter your devotion there
With thunderous voice? or are ye jubilant,
And would ye tracking your proud Lord, the Sun,
Be present at his setting? or the pomp
Of Indian mornings would ye fill, and stand,
Yourselves apparell'd in the virgin garb
Of radiance yet unknown, transcendent hues?
O whence, Ye clouds, this eagerness of speed?
Sheer o'er the Rock's gigantic brow Ye cut
Your way, each thirsting to reveal himself, athirst,
The coming and the going, to secure
Each for himself an unbelated course?
Ye clouds, the very blood within my veins
Is quickened to your pace, a thousand thoughts,
Ten thousand winged Fancies have Ye rais'd,
And not a Thought which is not fleet as Ye are.
Speak, silent Creatures! they are gone, are fled,
All buried in yon mighty mass of gloom
That loads the middle heaven, and clear and bright
And vacant does the region of the east
Appear, a calm descent of sky that leads
Down to some unapproachable abyss,
Down to the hidden world from which they came.

And Fancy, not less aptly pleased, compares
Your squadrons to an endless flight of birds
[16] Aerial, upon due migration bound
To milder climes; or rather do ye urge
In caravan your hasty pilgrimage
To pause at last on more aspiring heights
[22] Than these, and utter your devotion there
With thunderous voice? Or are ye jubilant,
And would ye, tracking your proud lord the Sun,
[25] Be present at his setting; or the pomp
Of Persian mornings would ye fill, and stand
Poising your splendors high above the heads
Of worshippers kneeling to their up-risen God?
[29] Whence, whence, ye Clouds! this eagerness of speed?
[38] Speak, silent creatures—They are gone, are fled,
Buried together in yon gloomy mass
[40] That loads the middle heaven; and clear and bright
And vacant doth the region which they thronged
Appear; a calm descent of sky conducting
Down to the unapproachable abyss,
[44] Down to that hidden gulf from which they rose
To vanish—fleet as days and months and years,
Fleet as the generations of mankind,
Power, glory, empire, as the world itself,
The lingering world, when time hath ceased to be.

---

17 Birds *MS. 151/6*
18 Aerial,] Aerial *MS. 151/3*
19 climes— . . . Ye *MS. 151/3*
22 these,] these *MS. 151/6*
23 Voice *MSS. 151/3, 151/6* jubilant,] jubulant *MS. 151/3*
24 Lord *MSS. 151/3, 151/6*
26 fill,] fill *MS. 151/3*
27 Poizing *MSS. 151/3, 151/6* splendours *MS. 151/6* splending *rev to* splendours *MS. 151/3*
28 worshippers *rev to* Worshippers *MS. 151/3* Worshippers *MS. 151/6*
29 Whence, whence Ye Clouds this eagerness of speed *MS. 151/3*
30 Speak silent Creatures—they are gone, are fled *MS. 151/3* Creatures *MS. 151/6*
33 Region *MSS. 151/3, 151/6*
34 Appear, *MS. 151/6*
35 abyss,] abyss *MS. 151/3*
36 gulf] gulph *MSS. 151/3, 151/6*
37 *no punct MS. 151/3*
38 *no comma MS. 151/3*
39 itself,] itself *MS. 151/3* World *MS. 151/6*
40 World *MS. 151/6*

But the Wind roars, and toss the rooted Trees
As if impatient of yon lofty seat
On which they are enthralled from year to year.
But Lo, the pageant is renew'd, behold,
Another bright Precursor of a band
Perhaps as numerous, from behind the Rock
Mounting, the steady Rock that in its pomp
Of sullenness refuses to partake
Of the wild impulse; from a fount of life
Invisible, the long Procession streams,
A rapid multitude of glorious Shapes,
Glorious or darksome. Welcome to the Vale
Which they are entering, welcome to mine eye
That sees them, to my Soul that owns in them
And in the bosom of the Firmament
Wherein they move, by which they are contained,
An Image, a reflection palpable
Of her capacious self, of what she is
With all her restless Offspring, what she is
And what she doth possess!—
An humble walk
Here is my Body doomed to tread, this Path,
A little hoary line and faintly traced,
Work shall I call it of the Shepherd's foot,
Or of his sheep?—joint vestige of them both;
I pace it unrepining, for my thoughts
See what they will and through their own wide world
Go with the perfect freedom which is theirs.
Where is the Orphean Lyre or Druid Harp
To accompany the Song? the mountain Wind
Shall be our hand of music! it shall sweep
The rocks and quivering trees and billowy lake,
And search the fibres of the inner caves, and they

---

51 The word "its" (covered by a blot in DC. MS. 65, $5^r$) is supplied from DC MS. 18, $9^v$.

But the winds roar, shaking the rooted trees,
And see! a bright precursor to a train
[50] Perchance as numerous, overpeers the rock
That sullenly refuses to partake
[53] Of the wild impulse. From a fount of life
Invisible, the long procession moves
Luminous or gloomy, welcome to the vale
[57] Which they are entering, welcome to mine eye
That sees them, to my soul that owns in them,
And in the bosom of the firmament
O'er which they move, wherein they are contained,
A type of her capacious self and all
Her restless progeny.
A humble walk
[65] Here is my body doomed to tread, this path,
A little hoary line and faintly traced,
Work, shall we call it, of the shepherd's foot
Or of his flock?—joint vestige of them both.
[69] I pace it unrepining, for my thoughts
Admit no bondage and my words have wings.
Where is the Orphean lyre, or Druid harp,
To accompany the verse? The mountain blast
Shall be our *hand* of music; he shall sweep
[75] The rocks, and quivering trees, and billowy lake,
And search the fibres of the caves, and they

---

41 roar,] roar *MSS. 151/3, 151/6* trees,] trees *MS. 151/3*
42 *no punct MS. 151/3*
43 *no punct MS. 151/6*
45 impulse. From] impulse; from *MS. 151/3, and* impulse from *MS. 151/6, both rev to* impulse. From life, *MS. 151/3*
47 Luminous] Radient *rev to* Radiant *then* luminous *inserted by WW as alternate, MS. 151/3* gloomy, welcome] *rev to* gloomy. Welcome *MS. 151/3*
49 soul that owns in them,] Soul that in them owns *with* owns *and* in them *marked for transposition, MS. 151/3* Soul *MS. 151/6*
51 O'er . . . contained,] Oer . . . contained *MS. 151/3*
53 *no period MS. 151/3*
54 my] the *del to* my *MS. 151/3* path,] path *MS. 151/3*
55 *no punct MS. 151/3*
56 Shepherd's *and no commas MSS. 151/3, 151/6*
57 flock?—] Flock, *MS. 151/3* Flock, *rev to* Flock?— *MS. 151/6* both, *rev to* both. *MS. 151/6*
58 *no comma MS. 151/3*
59 bondage, *MSS. 151/3, 151/6*
60 Lyre *MSS. 151/3, 151/6* harp,] Harp *MS. 151/3* Harp, *MS. 151/6*
61 Verse *MS. 151/3* Mountain *MSS. 151/3, 151/6*
62 *hand*] *band rev to hand MS. 151/6* music, *MS. 151/3*

Shall answer: for our Song is of the Clouds,
And the Wind loves them, and the gentle gales
Love them, and every idle breeze in heav'n
Bends to that favorite burthen; and the Sun
(That is the daily source of joyous thought,
And Type of Man's far-darting reason, He
Who therefore was esteemed in antient times
The God of Verse, and stood before men's eyes
A blazing intellectual Deity)
Loves his own glory in their looks, the Sun
Showers on that unsubstantial Brotherhood
A Vision of beatitude and light.

Shall answer, for our song is of the Clouds
[78] And the wind loves them; and the gentle gales—
Which by their aid re-clothe the naked lawn
With annual verdure, and revive the woods,
And moisten the parched lips of thirsty flowers—
[79] Love them; and every idle breeze of air
Bends to the favourite burthen. Moon and stars
Keep their most solemn vigils when the Clouds
Watch also, shifting peaceably their place
Like bands of ministering Spirits, or when they lie,
As if some Protean art the change had wrought,
In listless quiet o'er the ethereal deep
Scattered, a Cyclades of various shapes
And all degrees of beauty. O ye Lightnings!
Ye are their perilous offspring; and the Sun—
Source inexhaustible of life and joy,
[82] And type of man's far-darting reason, therefore
In old time worshipped as the god of verse,
[85] A blazing intellectual deity—
Loves his own glory in their looks, and showers
Upon that unsubstantial brotherhood
Visions with all but beatific light

---

63 trees, . . . lake,] trees . . . lake *MS. 151/3*
65 Song *MSS. 151/3, 151/6*
66 them;] them, *MS. 151/3* them, *rev to* them; *MS. 151/6* gales—] gales *MS. 151/3*
68 *no commas MS. 151/3*
69 *no punct MS. 151/3*
70 them,—*MS. 151/3*
71 favorite . . . Stars *MS. 151/6*
72 cloud *MSS. 151/3, 151/6*
74 ministring *MSS. 151/3, 151/6* lie,] lie *MS. 151/3*
75 protean *rev to* Protean *MS. 151/6* *no comma MS. 151/3*
76 oer *MS. 151/3* etherial *MSS. 151/3, 151/6*
78 Lightnings] lightenings *MS. 151/3* Lightenings *rev to* Lightnings *MS. 151/6*
79 *no punct MS. 151/3*
80 inhaustible *MS. 151/3* *no comma MSS. 151/3, 151/6*
81 *no hyphen,* reason *over erasure, and* thence *rev to* therefore *as alternate by* WW, *MS. 151/3* Man's *MSS. 151/3, 151/6*
82 God *MSS. 151/3, 151/6* verse,] Verse *MS. 151/3* Verse, *MS. 151/6*
83 *no punct MS. 151/3*
84 showers, *MS. 151/6*
85 brotherhood, *MS. 151/6*

Enriched—too transient were they not renewed
From age to age, and did not, while we gaze
In silent rapture, credulous desire
Nourish the hope that memory lacks not power
To keep the treasure unimpaired. Vain thought!
Yet why repine, created as we are
For joy and rest, albeit to find them only
Lodged in the bosom of eternal things?

---

87 Enriched, *MS. 151/6*
88 not,] not *MS. 151/3*
89 desire] desire, *PELY (1842); printer's error corrected 1845–1849*
91 Vain] vain *rev to* Vain *MS. 151/3*
92 *no comma MS. 151/3*
94 eternal] enduring *with* eternal *entered as alternate MS. 151/3* things?] things *rev to* things? *MS. 151/6*
94 *below the line in MS. 151/3 MW entered the line count* 107 *probably taking it over by mistake from DC MS. 143*

## *Composed when a probability existed of our being obliged to quit Rydal Mount as a Residence* (1826)

### Earliest and Latest Versions

A reading text based on the earliest complete version of the poem, reconstructed from DC MS. 105, MS. A, is here presented on left-hand pages, facing a late reading text drawn from Mary Wordsworth's final fair copy of the poem, preserved in the Pierpont Morgan Library. Bracketed line numbers in the late reading text indicate corresponding lines in the early reading text. The early text incorporates revisions made by the copyist in the course of transcription, as well as a few passages that survive within MS. A from an even earlier stage of composition; full details can be found in the transcription of DC MS. 105, MS. A, below. Beneath the late text is an *apparatus criticus* that records variants in the Morgan manuscript (where that manuscript is obviously defective, other manuscripts are used to establish the reading text), in the penultimate fair copy of the poem in DC MS. 89, and in Wordsworth's fair copy of the first half of the poem in DC MS. 105, MS. B(2). Other variants can be seen, below, in the full transcriptions of partial and subordinate versions preserved in MSS. A(1), B, B(1), and C—all from DC MS. 105.

The Morgan manuscript consists of five consecutive bifolia; leaves of wove paper measure approximately 20.7 by 25.4 centimeters. Mary Wordsworth's fair copy begins on $1^r$ and ends at the top of $10^r$; versos are blank, except for $10^v$, which became the outside cover when the entire manuscript was folded in half. On the top portion of $10^v$ Wordsworth's clerk John Carter entered the title: "Verses / on / Nab Well / 1826." A strip of paper approximately 4.5 centimeters wide has been cut away from the foot of the same leaf. Morgan manuscript variants recorded in the *apparatus criticus* are in Mary Wordsworth's hand unless otherwise noted.

DC MS. 89 is a leather-bound folio volume that was in use at Rydal Mount from the 1820s onward. It contains miscellaneous late work, in various hands, ranging from a fair copy of *Airey Force Valley* on $2^r$ to a remedy for blistered feet on $226^r$. The book appears to have contained a total of 238 leaves, in 21 gatherings (4 sixteens, 8 twelves, 7 eights, 1 six, and one more probably of sixteen, now reduced to four); 201 of these leaves survive, two of them partially cut away, and there are 25 stubs. The book as originally bound contains two kinds of paper, one watermarked with a fleur-de-lis over a large, diagonally striped medallion and countermarked PR, the other with a fleur-de-lis over a similar but smaller medallion, countermarked RC. The leaves measure approximately 28 by 43.8 centimeters; chain lines run vertically at intervals of 2.7 centimeters. There are three paste-overs, one of blue-tinted wove stock and two of cream wove stock. The folio album is alphabetically thumb-indexed, and on $92^{v}$, facing the letter N on $93^{r}$, a fair copy of *Composed when a probability existed* . . . was begun by Dora Wordsworth; presumably the poem was thought of as "Verses on Nab Well"—the title used by John Carter on the outside of the Morgan manuscript and by Christopher Wordsworth in *Memoirs,* I, 23n. The fair copy continues on $93^{r}$ and $93^{v}$, where, after a total of 119 lines (from l. 117 of the late reading text) John Carter entered the remaining 82 lines. The presence of drafting toward *The unremitting voice of mountain streams* on $94^{v}$ obliged Carter to crowd the last ten lines of his poem into the outer margin of $94^{r}$. DC MS. 89 variants recorded in the *apparatus criticus* are in the hand of the copyist (that is, Dora for ll. 1–117, John Carter for ll. 118–202) unless otherwise noted.

DC MS. 105, MS. B(2), a single sheet folded to form two leaves, each measuring approximately 18.2 by 22.7 centimeters, contains a fair copy of the first half of the poem, through line 91 of the late reading text. The paper is watermarked PINE & DAVIS over the date 1823; chain lines are at intervals of 2.5 centimeters. All entries in the manuscript are in Wordsworth's hand.

## [*Composed when a probability existed of our being obliged to quit Rydal Mount as a Residence*]

Pellucid Spring! unknown beyond the verge
Of a small Hamlet, there, from ancient time,
Not undistinguished; (for of Wells that ooze
Or Founts that gurgle from the moss-grown side
And craggy forehead of this cloud-capp'd hill,
Their common Sire, thou only bear'st his Name)
One of my last fond looks is fix'd on Thee;
Who with the comforts of my daily meal
Hast blended, thro' the space of twice seven years,
Beverage as choice as ever Hermit prized,
That Persian Kings might envy; and whose pure
And gentle aspect oft has minister'd
To finer uses. They for me must cease;

1–13 Christopher Wordsworth identified the spring at Rydal Mount as "the Nab Well" (*Memoirs,* I, 23); see n. 2 to Introduction, above. The "craggy forehead" is Nab Scar; the "neighbouring Stream" mentioned in DC MS. 105 (MS. A, 1$^v$, top paste-over, recto; MS. B2; 2$^r$; MS. B(1), 1$^v$) is Rydal Beck, described in *An Evening Walk* (1793), ll. 71–88.

# Composed when a probability existed of our being obliged to quit Rydal Mount as a Residence.

---

The doubt to which a wavering hope had clung
Is fled; we must depart, willing or not,
Sky-piercing Hills! must bid farewell to you
And all that Ye look down upon with pride,
With tenderness embosom; to your paths,
And pleasant dwellings, to familiar trees
And wild flowers known as well as if our hands
Had tended them: and O pellucid Spring!
Insensibly the foretaste of this parting
Hath ruled my steps, and seals me to thy side,
Mindful that Thou (ah wherefore by my Muse
So long unthanked) hast cheared a simple board
With beverage pure as ever fixed the choice

---

*title* *added by WW, MS. 89 (with no period); not present in MS. B(2)*

2 fled;— *MS. 89, MS. B(2)* not,] not; *MS. 89* not; *rev to* not, *Morgan MS.*

4 ye *MS. 89* *no comma MS. 89, MS. B(2)*

5 tenderness, *Morgan MS.* imbosom; *MS. 89, MS. B(2)* paths,] paths *MS. 89, MS. B(2)*

6 dwellings,] Dwellings *MS. 89, MS. B(2)*

7 Flowers *MS. B(2)* hands] hand *MS. 89*

8 tended] planted *del to* tended *Morgan MS.* them; *MS. 89, MS. B(2)* O] Thou, *del to* O! *then to* O *(WW) MS. 89* Thou, *MS. B(2)*

8/9 *the following lines are marked for deletion in the Morgan MS.:*

Unheard of, save in one small Hamlet, here
N} {ed,
&}ot undistinguish{able for of Wells that ooze
Or founts that gurgle from yon craggy Steep,
Their common Sire, thou only bears't his name.

*in MSS. 89 and B(2) the lines, enclosed in parens, are also marked for deletion, with the following variants:* ooze] ouze *MS. 89* Steep,] Steep *MS. 89* founts] fonts *MS. B(2)* yon] a *del to* yon *MS. B(2)* craggy Steep,] craggys steep *then* steep *capitalized MS. B(2)* of,] of *both MSS* Hamlet,] hamlet, *both MSS* Not undistinguish'd, *both MSS* bears't] bear'st *both MSS*

10 steps,] steps *MS. 89, MS. B(2)* to] at *MS. 89, MS. B(2)* side,] side; *MS. 89* side *MS. B(2)*

11 thou *rev to* Thou *MS. 89* my] thy *MS. 89* the MS. B(2)

12 unthank'd *MS. 89, MS. B(2)* cheared] che[ ? ] *del to* cheared *Morgan MS.*

13 pure] as pure *then* as *del Morgan MS.* fix'd *MS. 89, MS. B(2)*

Days shall pass on, and months revolve, and years
Fade, and the moralizing mind derive
No lesson from thy presence, Gracious Power,
By the inconstant nature *we* inherit
Unmatch'd in delicate beneficence;
For neither unremitting rains avail
To swell thee into voice, nor hottest drought
Can stint thy bounty, nor thy beauty mar.

Of Hermit, dubious where to scoop his Cell;
[11] Which Persian Kings might envy; and thy meek
And gentle aspect oft has ministered
To finer uses. They for me must cease;
Days will pass on, the year, if years be given,
[15] Fade,—and the moralizing mind derive
No lesson from the presence of a Power
By the inconstant nature we inherit
Unmatched in delicate beneficence;
For neither unremitting rains avail
[20] To swell Thee into voice; nor longest drought
Thy bounty stints, nor can thy beauty mar,
Beauty not therefore wanting change to stir
The fancy, pleased by spectacles unlooked for.
  Not yet, perchance, translucent Spring! had tolled

---

14 *no comma MS. 89, MS. B(2)* dubious] doubtful *del to* dubious *MS. B(2)* where] when *MS. B(2)* Cell;] cell, *MS. 89* cell *MS. B(2)*

15 envy: *MS. B(2)*

16 has] have *Morgan MS., MS. 89* ministre'd *Morgan MS.* ministr'd *MS. 89* minister'd *MS. B(2)*

17 uses] ones *del to* uses *(WW) MS. 89* they *rev to* They *MS. 89*

18 *no commas MS. B(2)* given,] given *MS. 89*

19 Fade— *MS. 89, MS. B(2)*

20 power *rev (WW) to* Power *MS. 89*

22 Unmatched] Nor, match *rev to* Unmatched *Morgan MS.* Unmatches *rev to* Unmatch *MS. 89* Unmatch *MS. B(2)* benificence; *rev to* beneficence; *(WW) MS. 89*

24 Thee] thee *rev to* Thee *MS. B(2)* The *rev to* Thee *MS. 89* voice;] voice, *rev to* voice; *Morgan MS.* voice, *MS. 89* voce, *MS. B(2)* longet droughts *rev (WW) to* longest drought *MS. 89* largest drouth *rev to* longest drouth *MS. B(2)*

25 beauty mar,] beauty mar; *MS. 89* beautty mar. *MS. B(2)*

26 stir] please *del to* stir *Morgan MS.* *in MS. 89, l. 26 was inserted by WW at ll. 25/28, with* stir] pleas X, *the* X *serving as link to a passage in margin in WW's hand:*

> Beauty not therefore wanting change to ~~please~~ stir
> The fancy, pleased by spectacles unlook'd for
> And transformations silently fulfill'd:
> No witch craft, meek Enchantress! equals thine.—

*earlier work toward the passage, in WW's hand in pencil, is found in opposite margin:* nor that beauty mar / Which wants not change to please *followed by work in ink:*

> to please
> The fancy for in spectacles unlooked for
> And transformations silently fulfill'd
> What withcraft, meek Enchantress! equals thine

*ll. 26–27 are missing from MS. B(2)*

27 *inserted, with no comma, Morgan MS. and linked to the following lines in margin, deleted (the second, a version of l. 90):*

> And transformations silently fulfilled:
> No witchcraft meek Enchantress equals thine!

28 Not] Nor *Morgan MS.* yet,] yet *MS. 89, MS. B(2)* Spring, *rev to* Spring! *Morgan MS.* toll'd *MS. 89, MS. B(2)*

What Loiterer now, with aid of sloping beams
From summer suns, that countenance will peruse,
Pleas'd to detect the dimpling stir of life,
The breathing faculty with which thou yield'st,
Tho' a mere goblet to the careless eye,
Boons inexhaustible? Who, hurrying on
With a step quickened by November-cold,
Shall pause, the skill admiring that can work
Upon thy chance-defilements—wither'd twigs
That, lodg'd within thy crystal depths, grow bright
As if they from a silver tree had fallen;
And oaken leaves, that, driven by whirling blasts
Into thy cell, have sunk and rested there,
Till, the more perishable parts consumed,
Thou, by a crust of liquid beads, hast turned
The Skeletons to brilliant ornaments?

The Norman curfew bell when human hands
First offered help that the deficient rock
Might overarch Thee, from pernicious heat
Defended, and appropriate to Man's need.
Such ties will not be severed: but, when We
Are gone, what summer Loiterer with regard
Inquisitive, thy countenance will peruse,
[24] Pleased to detect the dimpling stir of life,
The breathing faculty with which thou yield'st
(Tho' a mere goblet to the careless eye)
Boons inexhaustible? Who, hurrying on
With a step quickened by November's cold,
Shall pause, the skill admiring that can work
[30] Upon thy chance-defilements—withered twigs
That, lodged within thy chrystal depths, seem bright
As if they from a silver tree had fallen—
[33] And oaken leaves that, driven by whirling blasts,
Sunk down, and lay immersed in dead repose
For Time's invisible tooth to prey upon—
Unsightly objects and uncoveted,

---

30 offer'd *MS. 89, MS. B(2)* deficiant *rev to* deficient *MS. 89*
31 thee, *MS. 89, MS. B(2)*
32 mans *MS. 89* man's *MS. B(2)*
33 sever'd but *rev to* sever'd; but, *MS. 89 (WW)* sever'd, but *rev to* sever'd;—but, *MS. B(2)*
34 with regard] will regard, *Morgan MS.*
35 countenance, *Morgan MS.*
36 Pleasd *MS. B(2)* *no comma MS. 89, MS. B(2)*
37 yeildest *rev to* yeild'st *MS. 89*
38 *parens added Morgan MS.* Tho'] Though *MS. 89, MS. B(2)* eye, *rev to* eye *Morgan MS.*
39 inexaustible *MS. 89* *no comma MS. 89, MS. B(2)*
40 quickened *rev to* quicken'd *MS. 89 (WW)* quicken'd *MS. B(2)* November *rev to* November's *Morgan MS.* *no comma MS. 89, MS. B(2)*
41 admiring] admitting *rev to* admiring *Morgan MS.* admireing *rev to* admiring *MS. 89*
42 thy] the *rev to* thy *MS. 89* chance-defilements; *MS. 89* chance defilements; *MS. B(2)* wither'd *MS. 89, MS. B(2)*
43 That] That *rev to* That, *Morgan MS.* lodged *rev to* lodg'd *(WW) MS. 89* lodg'd *MS. B(2)* cristal *rev to* crystal *(WW) MS. 89* crystal *MS. B(2)* depths,] depths *inserted with caret (WW) MS. 89* depths *MS. B(2)* seem] see *rev to* seem *MS. 89* seen *rev to* seem *MS. B(2)* *at end of line* as *erased MS. 89*
44 they *and* a *inserted with carets Morgan MS.* fallen; *MS. 89, MS. B(2)*
45 driv'n *and no commas MS. 89, MS. B(2)*
46 Sunk down, and lay] Sunk down, and lay'n *MS. 89* Have sunk, and lain *rev in pencil to* Fell—sank and lay *then in ink to* Sank down, and lay *MS. B(2)* immers'd . . . repose, *MS. 89, MS. B(2)*
47–50 *Morgan MS.:*

For Time's invisible tooth to prey upon
Unsightly objects & uncovet/ed, ~~till Thou~~

*continued on p. 81*

But should a luckless hand, from off the floor
On which the gleaming relics lie, uplift them,
However gently, into vulgar air,
At once their tender brightness disappears,
And the rash intermeddler steals away,
Chiding his folly. Thus (I feel the truth)
Thus with the fibers of these thoughts it fares;

Till thou with crystal bead-drops didst encrust
[37] Their skeletons turned to brilliant ornaments.
But, from thy bosom, should some venturous hand
Abstract those gleaming relics, and uplift them,
[40] However gently, toward the vulgar air,
At once their tender brightness disappears,
Leaving the Intermeddler to upbraid
His folly. —Thus (I feel it while I speak)
Thus, with the fibres of these thoughts it fares;

---

crystal
~~encrusting~~ { ~~liquid~~
Till thou with { chrystal bead-drops didst ~~turn~~
∧ encrust
turned
k } o }
Their sh } eletu } ns∧to brilliant ornaments.

*with* crystal *and* encrust *and* turned *in JC's hand; MS. 89, which omitted ll. 47–48, was revised by WW as follows:*

Unsightly and uncoveted till Thou
Till thou, with crust of liquid beads, did'st turn
Encrusting them with liquid pearls
Their skeletons to brilliant ornaments.
ut venturous
B∧from thy bosom would some covetous hand

*then all but last line del to the following passage in margin (WW):*

in dead repose.
For time's invisible tooth to prey upon
Unsightly objects & uncoveted
{ st
Thou did {
Till with crystal bead-drops ~~dost~~ encrust
{ '
Their skeletons turn { ~~e~~d to brilliant ornaments.
some { ous
But from thy bosom would ~~some~~ ventur { ing hand

*with* 'Till thy crystalline bead drops did encrust *as alternate in margin (WW); MS. B(2) contains only ll. 49–50:*

didst
'Till Thou, with crust of liquid beads, ~~hast~~ turn'~~d~~
Their skeletons to brilliant ornaments.

51 *readings of MS. 89 shown in transcriptions, above; no comma MS. B(2)* should] would *MS. B(2)* venturous] covetous *MS. B(2)* covetous *del to* venturous *Morgan MS. (JC)*

52 Relics, *MS. 89, MS. B(2)*

53 towar'd *Morgan MS.* tow'rd *MS. 89* tow'rd~~s~~ *MS. B(2)*

54 disappear, *rev to* disappears, *(WW) MS. 89*

55 Intemeddler *rev to* Intermeddler *(WW) MS. 89*

56 folly.—This *rev to* folly.—Thus *Morgan MS.* follies. This *rev to* folly. Thus *MS. 89 (WW)* folly. Thus *MS. B(2)*

57 Thus,] This, *rev to* Thus, *Morgan MS.* This *rev to* Thus *MS. 89 (WW)* Thus *MS. B(2)* *last two words of line over erasure MS. 89*

And O how much of all that Love creates
Or beautifies like changes undergoes,
Suffers like loss when drawn out of the Soul,
Its silent laboratory. Words should say,
Could they but paint the wonders of thy cell,
How often I have mark'd a plumy fern,
Bending an apex towards its paler self,
Reflected all in perfect lineaments,
Shadow and substance kissing, point to point.

---

47 MW's revision of "&" to "when" is incorporated for the sake of sense.

[45] And oh! how much, of all that love creates
Or beautifies, like changes undergoes,
Suffers like loss when drawn out of the Soul,
Its silent laboratory! Words should say
(Could they depict the marvels of thy cell)
[50] How often I have marked a plumy fern
From the live rock with grace inimitable
Bending its apex toward a paler self
Reflected all in perfect lineaments—
[53] Shadow and substance kissing point to point
In mutual stillness; or, if some faint breeze
Entering the Cell gave restlessness to one,
The other, glassed in thy unruffled breast,
Partook of every motion, met, retired,
And met again, such playful sympathy,
Such delicate caress as in the shape
Of this green Plant had aptly recompensed,

---

58 And] An *rev to* And *Morgan MS. (WW)* oh!] Oh *MS. 89, MS. B(2)* *no comma MS. 89, MS. B(2)* loves create *rev to* love creates, *MS. 89*

59 beautiful *rev to* beautifies *Morgan MS., MS. 89 (WW)* undergoes,] undergoes, *with final* s *del then restored (JC) then del Morgan MS.* undergoes *MS. 89, MS. B(2)*

60 Soul,] soul *Morgan MS., MS. 89, MS. B(2)*

61 laboratory!— *MS. 89, MS. B(2)*

62 *parens added Morgan MS.* depict] define *del to* depict *Morgan MS. (JC)* depart *rev to* depict *MS. 89 (WW)* marvels] features *with alternate* marvels *in pencil and ink MS. B(2)*

63 mark'd *MS. 89, MS. B(2)* plumy fern] pleasing form *del to* plumy fern *MS. 89 (WW)*

64 inimitable *rev to* inimitible *Morgan MS.*

65 tow'rd *MS. 89, MS. B(2)*

66 lineaments, *MS. 89, MS. B(2)*

67 shadow] shadows *with* s *eras MS. 89* to point, *then comma eras MS. B(2)*

68 *no comma MS. 89, MS. B(2)* faint] bold *del to* faint *MS. B(2)*

69 Enterig *MS. B(2)* Cell] cell, *MS. 89, MS. B(2)* one,] One *MS. 89* one *rev to* One *MS. B(2)*

70 other glassed *rev to* Other glass'd *MS. 89 (WW)* Other glass'd *MS. B(2)* breast,] breast *MS. 89, MS. B(2)*

71 retired,] retired *MS. 89*

72 again; *MS. 89, MS. B(2)* sympathy,] sympathy *Morgan MS. MS. 89, MS. B(2)*

73 in] if *rev to* in *Morgan MS.*

74 Plant] plant *rev to* Plant *Morgan MS. (WW)* recompensed,] recompens'd *MS. 89, MS. B(2)*

---

63–67 These lines contain the first of a considerable number of echoes in this poem of Coleridge's *This Lime-Tree Bower My Prison:*

the ferny rock
Whose plumy ferns for ever nod and drip
Spray'd by the waterfall.

(*The Poetical Works of Samuel Taylor Coleridge,* ed. Ernest Hartley Coleridge [2 vols.; Oxford, 1912], I, 178n).

A subtler operation may withdraw
From sight the solid floor that limited
The nice communion, but that barrier gone,

For baffled lips and disappointed arms
And hopeless pangs, the Spirit of that Youth,
The fair Narcissus, by some pitying God
Changed to a crimson Flower, when he, whose pride
Provoked a retribution too severe,
Had pined; upon his watery Duplicate
Wasting that love the Nymphs implored in vain.
  Thus while my Fancy wanders, Thou, clear Spring—
Moved (shall I say?) like a dear friend who meets
A parting moment with her loveliest look
And seemingly her happiest, look so fair
It frustrates its own purpose, and recalls
The grieved One whom it meant to send away—
Dost tempt me by disclosure exquisite
To linger, bending over Thee; for now,
What witchcraft, mild Enchantress, may with thine
Compare! thy earthy bed a moment past
Palpable unto sight as the dry ground,
Eludes perception, not by rippling air
Concealed, nor through effect of some impure
Upstirring; but, abstracted by a charm

---

75 lip, . . . arms, *MS. B(2)*

76 pangs,] prays *rev to* pangs *MS. 89 (WW)* *no commas MS. 89, MS. B(2)*

78 Changed *rev to* Chang'd *MS. 89 (WW)* Chang'd *MS. B(2)* he,] he *MS. 89, MS. B(2)* whose] when *rev to* whose *MS. 89 (WW)*

79 *no comma Morgan MS.*

80 Upon a *false start del MS. B(2)* pined;] pin'd; *MS. 89* pin'd, *MS. B(2)* his] a *del to* his *del, then restored MS. 89 (WW)* a *MS. B(2)* watery] watry *rev to* watery *Morgan MS.* wattry *rev to* watry *MS. 89 (WW)* watry *MS. B(2)*

81 Nymph's *Morgan MS.* Nyphs *rev to* Nymphs *MS. 89 (WW)*

82 thou, *rev to* Thou *Morgan MS.* Spring—] Spring *MS. 89, MS. B(2)*

83 *question mark inserted Morgan MS. (JC)* (Mov'd) (shall I say?) *MS. 89* (Mov'd (shall I say?) *MS. B(2)* Friend *MS. 89, MS. B(2)*

84 moment, *Morgan MS.*

86 purpose,] purposing, *rev to* purpose *MS. B(2)* recals *rev to* recalls *Morgan MS.*

87 griev'd *MS. 89, MS. B(2)* One] one *rev to* One *Morgan MS., MS. 89 (WW)* away—] away) *MS. 89, MS. B(2)*

89 linger,] linger *MS. 89* thee *rev to* Thee *MS. 89* now,] now *MS. 89, MS. B(2)*

90 thine] thee *Morgan MS.*

90–91
    What witchcraft meek Enchantress can with thine
~~Thy earthy bed a little moment past~~
    Compare? thy earthy bed a moment past
~~Thy bed with pebbles strewn~~

*MS. B(2), which ends at this point*

92 unto] to *Morgan MS.*

94 Concealed, *rev to* Concealed *Morgan MS.*

90–99 *MS. 89:*

~~(What witchcraft meek Enchantress may compare with thine)~~
    ~~compare~~
  pebbly {T  pebbly
~~With thine~~) {thy ~~earthy~~ bed a moment past
Palpable uto sight as the dry ground

Nought checks nor intercepts the downward shew
Created for the moment: flowrets, plants,
And the whole body of grey wall they deck,
Reflected, but not there diminutive,
There of etherial texture, and, thro' scale
Of vision less and less distinct, descending
To gloom impenetrable. So, in moods
Of thought pervaded by supernal grace,

Of thy own cunning, earth mysteriously
From under thee hath vanished, and slant beams,
The silent inquest of a western sun,
Assisting, lucid Well-Spring! Thou revealest
Communion without check of herbs and flowers,
And the vault's hoary sides to which they cling,
Imaged in downward shew; the flowrets, herbs—
*These* not of earthly texture, and the Vault
Not *there* diminutive, but, through a scale
[62] Of vision less and less distinct, descending
To gloom impenetrable. So (if Truths
The highest condescend to be set forth
By processes minute) even so—when thought

---

Eludes perception not by rippling airs ~~co~~
Concealed nor through effect of some impure
e|i
Upstirring, but abstracted by a sli|ght feat
mysteriously
Of thy own cunning earth ~~from under Thee~~
From under thee
Has vanish'd, and slant beams ~~of W piercing light~~
The silent inquest of a western Sun
We| |S
Assisting lucid wi|ll-|spring! thou reveal'st

*with revisions, overwritings, and the word* feat *in WW's hand; JC then entered ll. 90–97 in margin as in reading text, above, except: no punct ll. 90, 95* Compare—*l. 91* unto *l. 92* Upstirring but *l. 93* air] airs *l. 93* Of thy own cunning. Earth from under thee/Has vanished, and slant beams of piercing light *ll. 96–97.*

96 thy] my *Morgan MS.*

98 inquest *inserted in gap Morgan MS. (JC)* sun,] cloud *del to* sun, *Morgan MS.*

100 *no comma MS. 89*

101 vault's . . . cling,] Vault's: . . . clung *MS. 89*

102 Imag'd *MS. 89* shew] show *MS. 89* flowrets, herbs—] flower, the herbs *with* the *del to* its *Morgan MS. (JC)* flower its herbs, *MS. 89*

103 vault *MS. 89*

104 scale of *with* of *del MS. 89*

105 vision less] Visionary *rev to* Visionless *MS. 89 (WW)* *no comma MS. 89*

106 impenetrable] imperishable *Morgan MS.* impenitrable *rev to* impenetrable *MS. 89* if] for *del to* when *del to* if *Morgan MS. (JC)* for *del in pencil to* when *with* So if *in margin in pencil MS. 89 (WW)*

107 condescendant *with* ant *eras MS. 89*

108 processes] processor *rev to* processes *MS. 89* *right paren inserted over comma MS. 89* even so—when] even so,— *then* can *added, then all del to* even so—when *Morgan MS. (JC)* even so if *rev in ink and pencil to* ev'n so when *MS. 89 (WW)* Thought *MS. 89*

---

97–98 *This Lime-Tree Bower My Prison,* ll. 32–35:

Ah! slowly sink
Behind the western ridge, thou glorious Sun!
Shine in the slant beams of the sinking orb,
Ye purple heath-flowers! richlier burn, ye clouds!

Is the firm base of ordinary sense
Supplanted, and the residues of flesh
Are linked with spirit; shallow life is lost
In being; to the idealizing soul,
Time wears the colors of Eternity,
And Nature deepens into Nature's God.—
  Millions of kneeling Hindoos at this day
Bow to the watery element adored
In their vast stream; and if an age hath been,
As books and haply votive Altars vouch,
When British floods were worshipped, some faint trace
Of that idolatry, thro' Monkish rites
Transmitted even to living memory,
Might wait on Thee—a bashful little one,

Wins help from something greater than herself—
[65] Is the firm basis of habitual sense
Supplanted, not for treacherous vacancy
And blank dissociation from a world
We love, but that the Residues of flesh,
Mirrored, yet not too strictly, may refine
[68] To Spirit; for the idealizing Soul
Time wear the features of Eternity;
[70] And Nature deepen into Nature's God.
  Millions of Kneeling Hindoos at this day
Bow to the watery Element, adored
In their vast Stream, and if an age hath been
(As Books and haply votive Altars vouch)
[75] When British Floods were worshipped, some faint trace
Of that Idolatry, through Monkish rites
Transmitted far as living memory,
Might wait on Thee, a silent monitor,

---

109 Wins] With *del to* Wins *Morgan MS. (JC)* With *del to* Win *then* Wins *entered in margin, pencil and ink, MS. 89 (WW)* herself—] herself *MS. 89*

110 *entire line inserted Morgan MS. (JC)* firm basis] coarse texture *with* firm basis *entered as alternate (WW) and fuller alternate entered in margin (WW) MS. 89:* Are the fond aims

111 supplant'd; *rev to* supplanted; *MS. 89 (WW)* *in margin, possibly alternates for* treacherous *WW entered* finite *and* tangible *MS. 89*

112 from a world] but that the Residues of flesh *del to* from a world *Morgan MS.* blank] black *rev to* blank *MS. 89 (WW)*

113 love, . . . flesh,] love; . . . flesh *MS. 89*

114 Mirror'd *MS. 89* *no commas MS. 89*

115 Spirit: *MS. 89* Idealizing soul *MS. 89*

116 weaken *del to* wear *Morgan MS. (JC)* Eternity, *MS. 89*

117 deeper *rev to* deepen *MS. 89* Natures *MS. 89*

119 element, *rev to* Element *Morgan MS.*

120 stream, *rev to* Stream, *Morgan MS.* Stream; *MS. 89*

122 floods *MS. 89*

123 Idolatry,] idolatry *MS. 89*

124 Memory, *MS. 89*

124–126 *in margin, MS. 89, WW drafted alternates*

still on thee Pellucid Spring
Attends, on thee a bashful little one

125 Thee,] thee *rev to* Thee *MS. 89* silent monitor,] bashful Little One *del to* silent monitor, *Morgan MS.* silent Monitor *MS. 89*

---

108–117 *This Lime-Tree Bower My Prison,* ll. 37–43:

So my friend
Struck with deep joy may stand, as I have stood,
Silent with swimming sense; yea, gazing round
On the wide landscape, gaze till all doth seem
Less gross than bodily; and of such hues
As veil the Almighty Spirit, when yet he makes
Spirits perceive his presence.

Yet, to the measure of thy promises,
Strict as the mightiest; on thee, sequestered
For meditation, nor inopportune
For social interests such as I have shared.
—Peace to the Matron who shall bend to dip
Her pitcher in the favourite lymph, by me
No longer greeted; to the blushing Girl,
Oft tempted here to linger when waylaid
By her Betrothed, joy and happiness.

---

80 MW's revision of "on" to "upon" is not incorporated, though it may have been made in the course of transcription.

83 MW repeated "To dip" at the beginning of the line, then when she deleted the phrase was obliged to add "by me" at the end; her corrections have been incorporated.

On Thee, bright Spring, a bashful little One,
Yet to the measure of thy promises
True, as the mightiest; upon Thee, sequestered
For meditation, nor inopportune
For social interest such as I have shared.—
[83] Peace to the sober Matron who shall dip
Her pitcher here at early dawn, by me
No longer greeted—to the tottering Sire,
For whom like service, now and then his choice,
Relieves the tedious holiday of age,
Thoughts raised above the Earth while here he sits
[85] Feeding on sunshine—to the blushing Girl
Who here forgets her errand, nothing loth
To be waylaid by her Betrothed, peace
And pleasure sobered down to happiness!
  But should these Hills be ranged by One whose Soul,
Scorning love-whispers, shrinks from love itself
As Fancy's snare for female vanity,
Here may the Aspirant find a trysting place
For loftier intercourse. The Muses, crowned
With wreaths that have not faded to this hour,
Sprung from high Jove, of sage Mnemosyne

---

126 Thee,] thee *rev to* Thee *MS. 89* Little-one *MS. 89*
128 True,] True *entered in blank left in fair copy MS. 89 (WW)* mightiest; upon Thee,] mightier if thee, *rev to* mightiest; upon Thee *Morgan MS.* mightiest, upon thee *MS. 89* sequestered, *MS. 89*
129 inopportune] inappropriate *del to* inopportune *Morgan MS. (JC)*
130 interest] interests *with* s *eras Morgan MS.* shared— *MS. 89*
131 Peace] —Bene *with alternate* —Peace *MS. 89 (WW)*
132 Pitcher *MS. 89*
134 choice,] choice *MS. 89*
135 *no comma Morgan MS.*
136 Thoughts] Thought *rev to* Thoughts *Morgan MS. (JC)* earth *MS. 89*
137 sunshine; *MS. 89*
139 betrothed, *rev to* Betrothed, *MS. 89 (JC)*
140 And] Peace & *del to* And *Morgan MS. (JC)* to] by *del to* to *Morgan MS. (JC)*
141 hills . . . one *MS. 89* *no comma Morgan MS., MS. 89*
142 *no comma Morgan MS., MS. 89* shrinks] should *del to* shrinks *Morgan MS. (JC)*
145 *no comma Morgan MS., MS. 89*
146 wreaths] wreathes *MS. 89* hour,] hour *Morgan MS.* Hour *MS. 89*
147 Sprung] Sprang *rev to* Sprung *MS. 89 (WW)* *no comma MS. 89*

---

131–140 *This Lime-Tree Bower My Prison,* ll. 64–67:

and sometimes
'Tis well to be bereft of promis'd good
That we may lift the soul, and contemplate
With lively joy the joys we cannot share.

Enamoured, so the fable runs; but they
Certes were self-taught Damsels, scattered Births
Of many a Grecian Vale, who sought not praise
And heedless ever of Listeners, warbled out
Their own emotions, given to mountain air
In notes which mountain echoes would take up
Boldly and bear away to softer life;
Hence deified as Sisters they were bound
Together in a never-dying choir;
Who, with their Hippocrene and grottoed fount
Of Castaly, attest that woman's heart
Was in the limpid age of this stained World
The most assured seat of fine ecstasy,
And new-born Waters deemed the happiest source
Of Inspiration for the conscious lyre.
  Lured by the crystal element in times

---

148 Enamour'd, *MS. 89*
149 Certies *rev to* Certes *Morgan MS. (JC)*
150 grecian *rev to* Grecian *(WW), with last three letters over erasure MS. 89*
151 listeners *MS. 89* *no comma MS. 89* out] oer *rev to* out *Morgan MS.*
152 *no comma Morgan MS., MS. 89*
155 deified] dressed *del to* deified *MS. 89 (WW)*
156 never-dying] never dying *MS. 89*
157 *no comma Morgan MS., MS. 89*
158 Woman's *MS. 89*
159 limpid *entered by WW in blank, MS. 89* world *MS. 89*
160 fine ecstasy,] *missing in Morgan MS.* fine ectasy *entered by WW in blank, MS. 89*
161 Waters, *Morgan MS.* *in MS. 89 the line reads as follows, with revisions by WW, along with the second* waters *entered in blank:*

{— deem'd source
And ~~waters~~ new{ly born waters the happiest service

162 conscious *entered by WW in blank MS. 89*

---

163–189 Wordsworth's source for this passage is the second edition of Robert Southey's *Joan of Arc, An Epic Poem* (2 vols.; Bristol, 1798). Joan's inspirational vision at the "Fountain of the Fairies" (bk. I, pp. 126–130)—mentioned only briefly in Southey's first edition (Bristol, 1796)—anticipates much of the language and many of the details in WW's lines (see sec. V of the Introduction, above). Wordsworth approved of portions of Southey's poem that he saw in manuscript in 1795, but after reading the first edition in 1796, he pronounced Southey "a coxcomb" (*EY*, pp. 153–154, 163, 169). Wordsworth and Coleridge consulted the second edition together soon after it appeared (*STCL*, I, 412). In 1837, WW and MW read Southey's latest edition of the poem and MW, writing to Dora Wordsworth, explained that they were "much pleased. . . . In many parts I was reminded of favourite bits of Father—and he could not but perceive the like—tho' he does not charge himself with being an imitation . . .": *The Letters of Mary Wordsworth, 1800–1855*, ed. Mary E. Burton (Oxford, 1958), p. 198.

Stormy and fierce, the Maid of Arc withdrew
From human converse to frequent alone
The Fountain of the Fairies. What to her,
Smooth summer dreams, old favours of the place,
Pageants and revels of blithe Elves—to her
Whose country groaned under a foreign scourge?
She pondered murmurs that attuned her ear
For the reception of far other sounds
Than their too happy minstrelsy,—a Voice
Reached her with supernatural mandates charged,
More awful than the chambers of dark earth
Have virtue to send forth. Upon the marge
Of the benignant fountain, while she stood
Gazing intensely, the translucent lymph
Darkened beneath the shadow of her thoughts
As if swift clouds swept over it, or caught
War's tincture, mid the forest green and still,
Turned into blood before her heart-sick eye.
Erelong, forsaking all her natural haunts,
All her accustomed offices and cares
Relinquishing, but treasuring every law
And grace of feminine humanity,
The chosen Rustic urged a war-like Steed
Toward the beleagured City, in the might

---

164 *no comma Morgan MS., MS. 89*

166 fountain *MS. 89* fairies *rev to* Fairies *MS. 89 (WW)* *no comma MS. 89*

167 favors *MS. 89* place,] place *MS. 89*

168 Pageants] Pageant *Morgan MS.* blithe] the *del to* blithe *MS. 89 (WW)* Elves *entered by WW in blank, MS. 89*

169 country— *Morgan MS.* groaned] ground *rev to* groan'd *Morgan MS.* *question mark added Morgan MS. (JC)*

172 too-happy *MS. 89*

173 *no comma Morgan MS., MS. 89*

175 virtue to *entered by WW in blank, MS. 89* Marge *MS. 89*

176 *no comma MS. 89*

177 intently *del to* intensely, *Morgan MS.*

180 War's] Wars *Morgan MS., MS. 89* forest] firns *rev to* forest *Morgan MS.* still,] still *MS. 89*

182 haunts,] haunts *MS. 89*

184 law] line *del to* law *MS. 89 (WW)*

185 *no comma Morgan MS.*

186 war-like] warlike *MS. 89*

187 Toward] For *del to* Tow'rd *MS. 89 (WW)* beleagured] dist *del to* belligerent *del by JC to* beleagured *Morgan MS.* beleagur'd *MS. 89* *no comma MS. 89*

The cloud of rooks descending from mid air
Softens its evening uproar towards a close
Near and more near, for this protracted strain
A warning not unwelcome—Fare thee well,
Emblem of equanimity and truth,
Farewell—if thy composure be not ours,
Yet if thou still, when we are gone, will keep
Thy living chaplet of moist fern and flowers
Cherished in shade tho' peeped at by the Sun,
So shall our bosoms feed a covert growth
Of grateful recollections, tribute due,
(Not less than to wide lake and foaming rill)
To thy obscure and modest attributes,
To thee, clear Spring! and all-sustaining Heaven.

94–95 SH revised "if" to "as" and reversed the positions of "fern" and "flower" by the superscription of numerals ("2" and "1"); her revisions have not been incorporated, though they may have been made before the scrap containing ll. 94–101 was pasted on to complete the text.

Of prophesy, accoutred to fulfil,
At the sword's point, visions conceived in love.
[88] The cloud of Rooks descending through mid air
Softens its evening uproar towards a close
[90] Near and more near; for this protracted strain
A warning not unwelcome. Fare thee well!
Emblem of equanimity and truth,
Farewell!—if thy composure be not ours,
Yet as Thou still when we are gone wilt keep
[95] Thy living chaplet of fresh flowers and fern,
Cherished in shade though peeped at by the sun;
So shall our bosoms feel a covert growth
Of grateful recollections, tribute due
[100] To thy obscure and modest attributes,
To thee clear Spring, and all-sustaining Heaven!

1826

---

188 prophecy, *MS. 89* accoutred] mounted *del to* accoutred *Morgan MS. (JC)* fulfil,] fulfil *MS. 89*
190 through] in *del to* through *MS. 89*
192 near.— *MS. 89* this protracted strain *entered by WW in blank, MS. 89*
193 a *overwritten* A *MS. 89 (WW)* unwelcome. *MS. 89* well!] well *MS. 89*
194 truth. *MS. 89*
195 Farewell.— *MS. 89* *no comma MS. 89*
196 thou *rev to* Thou *MS. 89 (WW)* wilt] will *rev to* wilt *Morgan MS.*
197 Chaplet *MS. 89* *no comma MS. 89*
198 tho' . . . sun;— *MS. 89*
199 bosoms] bosom *rev to* bosoms *MS. 89 (WW)*
200 recollections] recollection *rev to* recollections *Morgan MS.*
201 *no comma Morgan MS., MS. 89*
202 all-sustaining] all sustaining *MS. 89* 1826] 1826. *MS. 89*

---

190–192 *This Lime-Tree Bower My Prison*, ll. 68–70:

when the last rook
Beat its straight path along the dusky air
Homewards, I blest it!

# Transcriptions and Photographic Reproductions

# DC MS. 18: Drafting toward *St. Paul's, To the Clouds,* and *The Tuft of Primroses.*

DC MS. 18 (formerly MS. Verse 34), the first extant manuscript of *Peter Bell,* now consists of 27 leaves (two of them partially cut away) and five stubs, all but one with some writing visible. The leaves, measuring approximately 12.5 centimeters wide by 20.5 centimeters high, seem once to have been gathered in eights. The paper is watermarked with a small fleur-de-lis and countermarked B over the date 1795; chain lines, running vertically, are approximately 2.6 centimeters apart. The same paper makes up MS. B of *The Ruined Cottage* (see *"The Ruined Cottage" and "The Pedlar" by William Wordsworth,* ed. James Butler [Ithaca, 1979], p. 130).

The manuscript apparently assumed its present fragmentary state during early work on *Peter Bell.* What survives is essentially the scrap of notebook to which Wordsworth turned in 1808 to begin drafting the blank-verse lines that were to become *St. Paul's, To the Clouds,* and *The Tuft of Primroses.* Leaves 2 and 7, now only stubs, were torn away some time after their use in 1808. Bracketed numbers at the top of each page of transcription indicate the reading-text lines to which that page contributes. Full transcription of the *Peter Bell* material may be found in John E. Jordan's edition of that poem for this series (Ithaca, 1985), pp. 157–223.

2 Press'd by conflicting thoughts of love and fear
I parted from thee, Friend! and took my way
Through the great City, walking with an eye
Downcast, ear sleeping, and feet masterless,
That were sufficient guide unto themselves
And step by step went pensively. Now mark,
Not how my trouble was entirely hush'd
That might not be, but how by sudden gift
Gift of Imagination's holy power,
My Soul in her uneasiness received
An anchor of security.—It chanced
That, while I thus was pacing, I raised up
My heavy eyes, and instantly beheld
Saw at a glance in that familiar place
A visionary scene: a length of street
Laid open in its morning quietness
Deep, hollow, unobstructed, vacant, smooth
And white with winter's purest white, as fresh
And fair and spotless as he ever sheds
On field or mountain.—Moving form was none
Save here & there a dusky Passenger
Slow, shadowy, silent, soundless, dusky: and beyond
And high above this winding length of street
This soundless noiseless and unpeopled avenue
Pure silent, solemn, beautiful, was seen
The Huge majestic Temple of St Paul
In awful sequestration, through a veil
Through its own sacred veil of fallen snow.

[DC MS. 18, 1v] [*St. Paul's*, ll. 1–27]

Press'd by conflicting thoughts of love and
fear
I parted from thee, Friend! and took my way
Through the great City, walking with an eye
Downcast, ear sleeping, and feet masterless,
That were sufficient guide unto themselves
And step by step went pensively. Now mark,
Not how my trouble was entirely hush'd
That might not be, but how my sudden gift
Gift of Imagination's holy power!
My Soul in her uneasiness received
An anchor of security.—It chanc'd
That, While I thus was pacing, I rais'd up
My heavy eyes, and instantly beheld
Saw at a glance in that familiar place
{s
A visionary scene: a length of {Street
Laid open in its morning quietness
Deep, hollow, unobstructed, vacant, smooth
And white with Winter's purest white, as fresh
And fair and spotless as he ever sheds
On field or mountain.—Moving form was none
Save here & there a dusky Passenger
silent
Slow, shadowy, soundless, dusky: and beyond
And high above this winding lengh of street
soundless un}
This noiseless and [?]} peopled avenue
Pure silent, solemn, beautiful, was seen
The Huge Majestic Temple of St Paul
In awful sequestration, through a veil
Through its own sacred veil of falling
snow.

---

The fair copy on this page leads to the final fair copy of *St. Paul's* in DC MS. 65 ($119^r$–$120^r$). The penciled 2 visible in the upper left corner of the photograph is part of a recent numbering of the pages of this manuscript, made when its leaves were not in their original order; this numbering continues throughout the manuscript

The ends of five words ("r"; "treet"; "een"; "l"; "l") are visible on $2^v$, now only a stub, indicating the entry of some version of at least ll. 21–27 of *St. Paul's.* The position of the lines at the middle of the stub suggests that $2^v$ was used for drafting intermediate between $3^v$ and $1^v$.

Oppressed with heavy thoughts of love and fear
I parted from the friend and took my way
Through the great City walking with downcast eye
ear sleeping and feet masterless
And feet that were guide unto themselves
And step by step went pensive Now mark
How in that mood of grief I overcame
How my uneasy mind received at once
An arc
Laid open in its morning quietness
And white with white as pure as winter lays
On field or mountain. Entirely of all [illegible] Moving form was none
All present was this long and hollow walk
Save here and there a dusky passenger
Slow shadows, soundless, dusky and beyond
And high above this winding length of street
This noiseless and unpeopled avenue
Not how my sorrow was entirely hushed
That might not be but how by sudden
My soul in her uneasiness received
An anchor of stability.

[DC MS. 18, 3v] [*St. Paul's,* ll. 1–11, 15–23]

Oppressd with heavy thoughts of Love and fear
I parted from thee friend and took my way
Lai walkd, {d
Through the great City, ~~with~~ with {eowncast
Ears sleeping and feet masterles eyes
And feet that were guide unto themselves
And step by step went pensivel now mark
How in that mood of sorrow I received
How my [?unease] of mind received at once
An anc

Laid open in its morning quietness
And white with white as pure as Winter lays
Throng there was none
On field or mountain. Empty of all voice
moving form was none
All presence was this long and hollow walk
Save here and there a dusky passenger
Slow shadowd, soundless, dusky and beyond
length of street
And high above this winding ~~avenue~~
This noiselss and unpeopled avenue

how trouble
Not my sorrow was entirely hushd
{s
That might not be but how by {[?]udden
My Soul in her uneasiness receivd
An anchor of stability.

---

The work on this page is the earliest *St. Paul's* drafting.

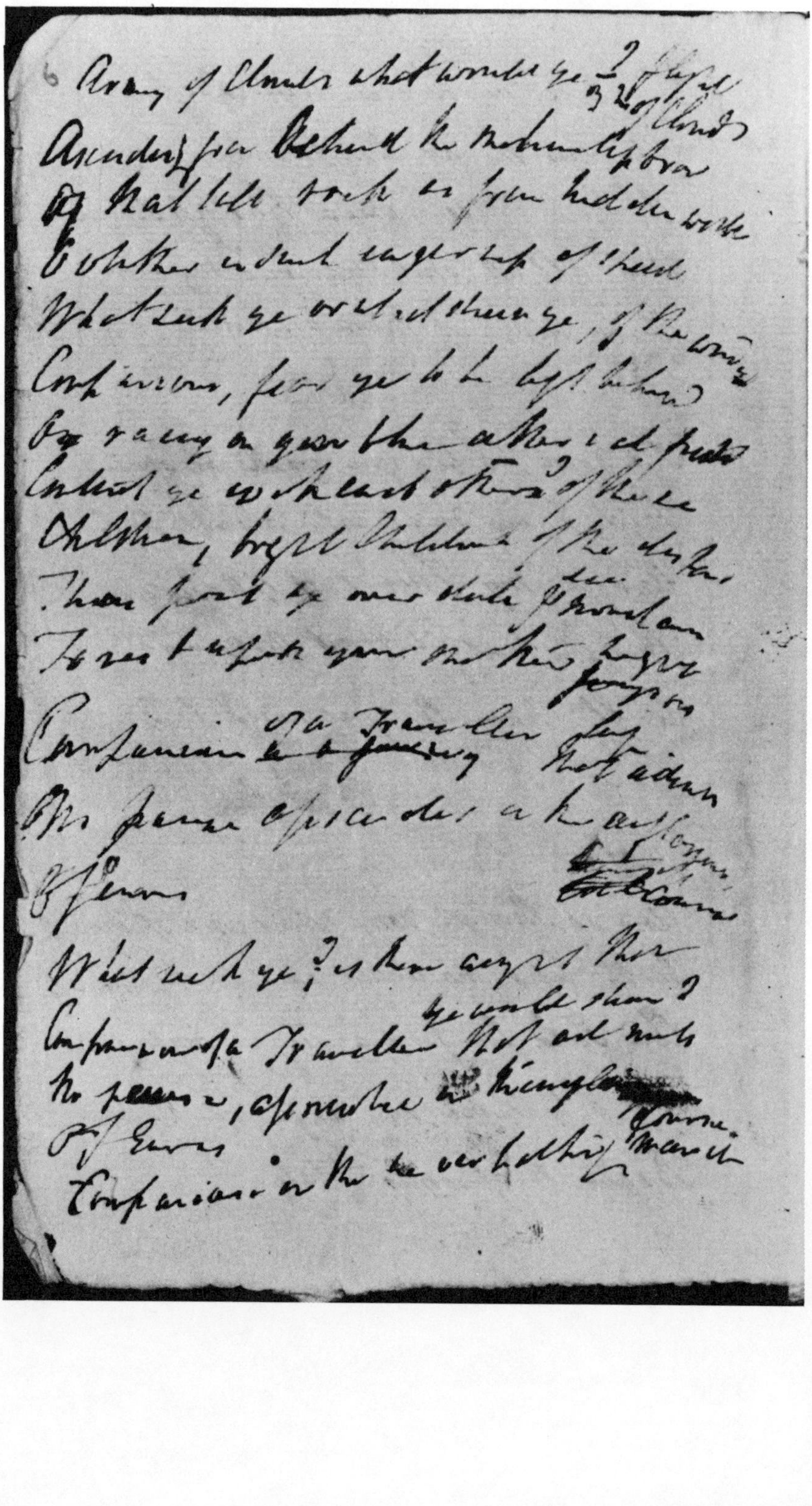

[DC MS. 18, 4$^{v}$] [*To the Clouds,* ll. 1–11]

Army of Clouds what would ye—? flight
be} 32 of Clouds
Ascending from the}hind the motionless brow
{Of
{As that tall rock as from hidden world
O whither in such eagerness of speed
What seek ye or what shun ye, of the winds
Companions, fear ye to be left behind
{r {ur
O{n racing on yo{n blue atherial field
—?
Contend ye with each other of the se
Children, bright Children of the distant
sea
Thus post ye over dale & mountain
height
To rest upon your mothers joyous
of a Traveller lap.
Companions ~~on a journey~~ that admits
{No
{Of pause [?associates] in the [?unflagging]
~~march~~
~~toil~~ course
Of Eurus

What seek ye? is there aught that
ye would shun?
Companions of a Traveller that admits
No pause, [?associates] in [?th'unflagging]
[ ? ]
course
Of Eurus
Companions in the never halting march

---

Drafting on this page and at the top of 5$^{v}$ is the earliest work on *To the Clouds.* The 32 after the first line on the page may be a line count, but it cannot be explained, though it is tempting to speculate that the 28 lines of *St. Paul's* may have been linked, perhaps with 3 lines that could have been entered on the lower half of 2$^{v}$, to the first line on this page, to yield a count of 32 lines.

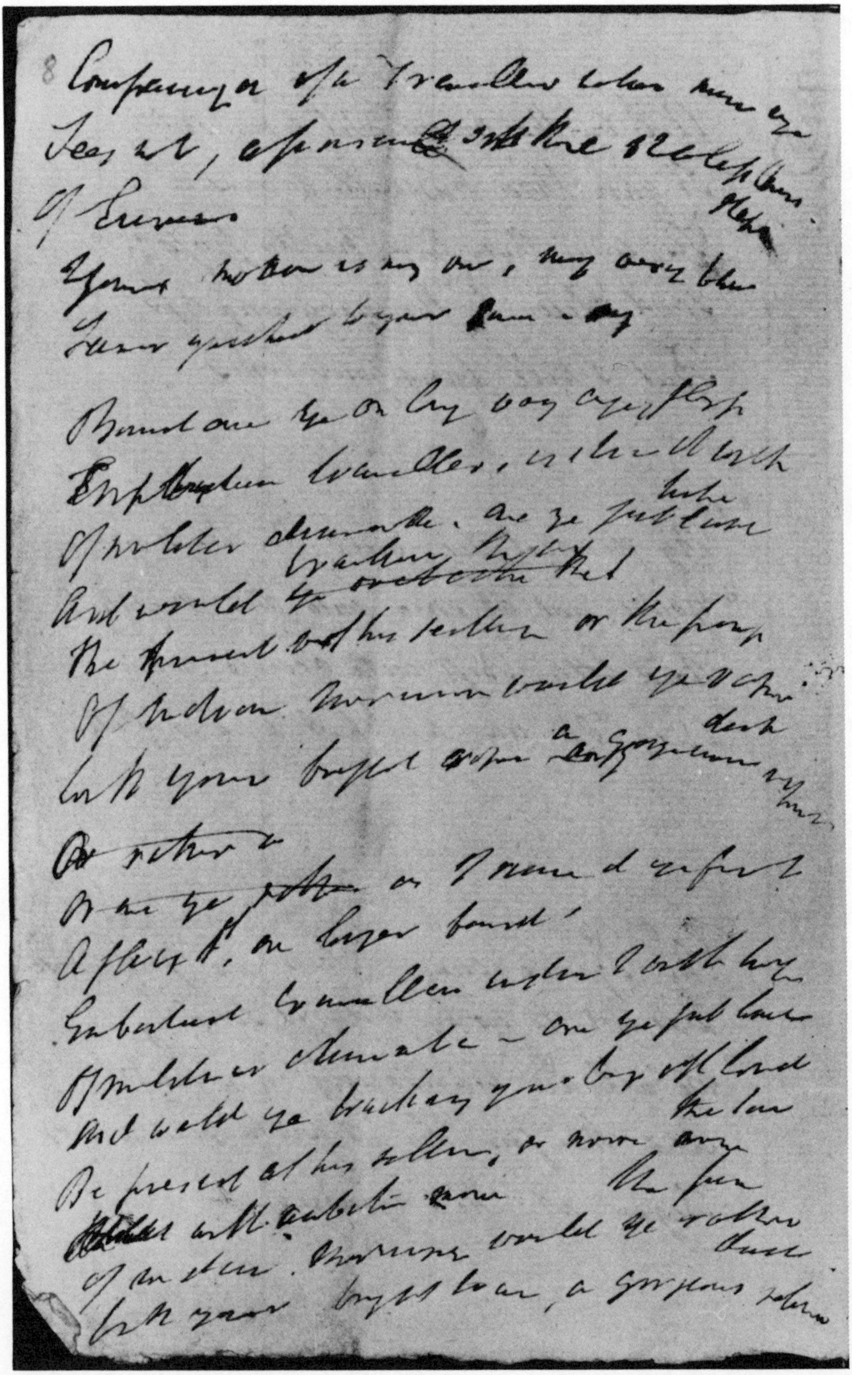

[DC MS. 18, $5^v$] [*To the Clouds,* ll. 17–18, 34–35, 23–28]

Companyons of a Traveller whom mine eye
[?]
Sees not, associates} [?] the [?viewless] [ ? ]
steps
Of [?Eurus]
Your motion is my own, my very blood
[?Seems] quickend to your pace—my

Bound are ye on long voyages flock
[ ? ] travellers instinct with
hope
Of milder climate. are ye jubilant
tracking their
And would ~~ye overtake the~~ S
{at
Be present {be his setting or the pomp
Of Indian mornin would ye rather
deck
a gorgeous retinue
With your bright robes ~~an~~ g
~~Or rather a~~
~~Or are ye rather~~ as I named ye first
of
A flight, on larger bound
Embodied travellers instinct with hopes
Of milder climate—are ye jubilant
And would ye tracking your bright lord
the Sun
Be present at his setting, or more [ ? ]
the pom
{[ ? ]
{[ ? ] with [ ? ? ]
Of indian mornings would ye rather
deck
With your bright train, a gorgeous retinue

---

Drafting at the top of this page runs on from $4^v$; the rest of the drafting on the page leads to further work entered on the bottom half of $7^v$.

10 Army of Clouds what would ye? Flight of Clouds
Ascending from behind the motionless brow
Of that tall Rock as from a hidden world
O whither in such eagerness of speed?
What seek ye? or what shun ye?—of the Wind
Companions fear ye to be left behind
Or racing on your blue aerial field
Contend ye with each other?—of the Sea
Children, bright Children of the distant Sea
Thus post ye over Dale and mountain height
To rest upon your Mothers joyous lap?
Your motion is my own; my very blood
Is quickened to your pace—a thousand
thoughts
Ten thousand winged Fancies have ye raised
And not a thought that is not fleet as
ye are.
Speak, silent Creatures!—they are gone, are
fled
All buried in yon mighty mass of gloom
That loads the middle heaven: and clear
blue
And vacant doth the region of the South
Appear the enchanted South from which
they came

[DC MS. 18, 6v] [*To the Clouds,* ll. 1–11, 34–44]

Army of Clouds ?{w}hat would Ye? Flight of Clouds
Ascending from behind the motionless brow
Of that tall Rock as from a hidden world
O whither in such eagerness of speed?
What seek ye? or what shun ye?—{O / of} the Wind
Companions fear ye to be left behind
Or racing in your blue etherial field
Contend ye with each other?—of the Sea
Children, bright Children of the distant Sea
Thus post ye over Dale and mountain height
To rest upon your Mothers joyous lap?
Your motion is my own; my very blood
Is quickened to your pace—a thousand thoughts
Ten thousand winged Fancies have ye raised
And not a thought which is not fleet as ye are.
Speak, silent Creatures!—they are gone—are fled
All buried in yon mighty mass of gloom
That loads the middle heaven: and clear & blue
And vacant does the region of the south
Appear th'exhausted South from which they came

---

The space at the foot of the page suggests that WW paused after entering a discrete block of *To the Clouds* fair copy here and before resuming composition on 7v.

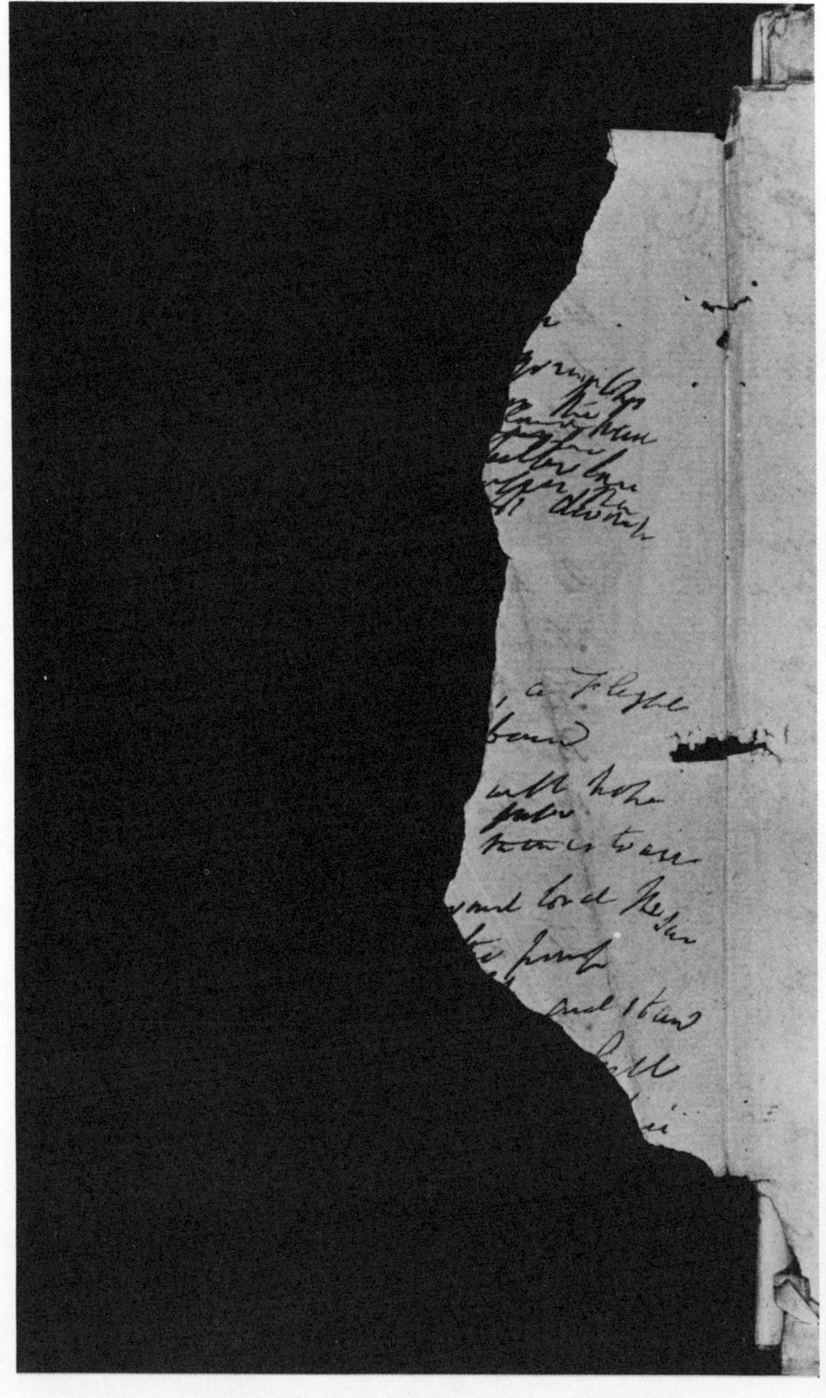

[DC MS. 18, 7v] [*To the Clouds,* ll. 15–28]

[ ? ]
[ ? ? ]
[ ? ] the
land [ ? ]
[ ? ? ]
[?better love]
[ ? ? ]
[ ? ] [?divine]

], a Flight
]bound
]with hope
jubi
~~[ ? ]~~ track
]roud lord the Sun
]the pomp
[?]
] and stand
]light
]es

---

Line endings visible at the top of the stub indicate the presence of some eight lines of drafting. Line endings at the bottom of the stub indicate drafting leading to the last ten lines on 8v and the first four lines on 9v.

18

Flight of Clouds

Ascending from behind the motionless brow
Of that tall rock, as from a hidden world
O whither in such eagerness of speed
What seek ye? or what shun ye? of the wind
Companions, fear ye to be left behind
Or racing on your blue ethereal field
Contend ye with each other? — of the sea
Children, bright children of the distant sea
Thus post ye, over dale and down
To sink upon your Mothers joyous lap Then keep
Or come ye, as I named hailed you first a flight the
Aerial on a due migration bound,
Embodied Travellers not breathing bird
To milder climes, or rather do ye urge
Your Caravan your hasty pilgrimage
With whom to pause at last upon the top
Of some remoter mountains more beloved
Than these, and utter your devotion there
With thunderous voice? or are ye jubilant
& would ye tracking your proud
Lord the Sun,

[DC MS. 18, 8v] [*To the Clouds,* ll. 1–24]

Flight of Clouds
Ascending from behind the motionless brow
Of that tall rock, as from a hidden world
O whither in such eagerness of speed
What seek ye? or what shun ye? of the
wind
Companions, fear ye to be left behind
e}
Or racing on your blue ae thieral field
Contend ye with each other?—of the sea
Children, bright Children of the distant
sea
Thus post ye, over dale and moun
tain height
To sink upon your Mothers joyous lap
hailed
Or come ye, as I ~~named~~ you first, a Flight
Aerial on a due migration bound,
Embodied Travellers not blindly led
To milder climes, or rather do ye urge
Your Caravan your hasty pilgrimage
With hope to pause at last upon the top
Of some remoter mountains more belovd
Than these, and utter your devotion there
With thunderous voice—? or are ye jubilant
And would ye tracking your proud
Lord, the Sun,

---

The second fair-copy beginning of *To the Clouds* starts on this page; it is continued on 9v and ends on 10v. The last two letters of "jubilant" (in the second line from the foot of the page) are hidden by a tear and fold in the manuscript.

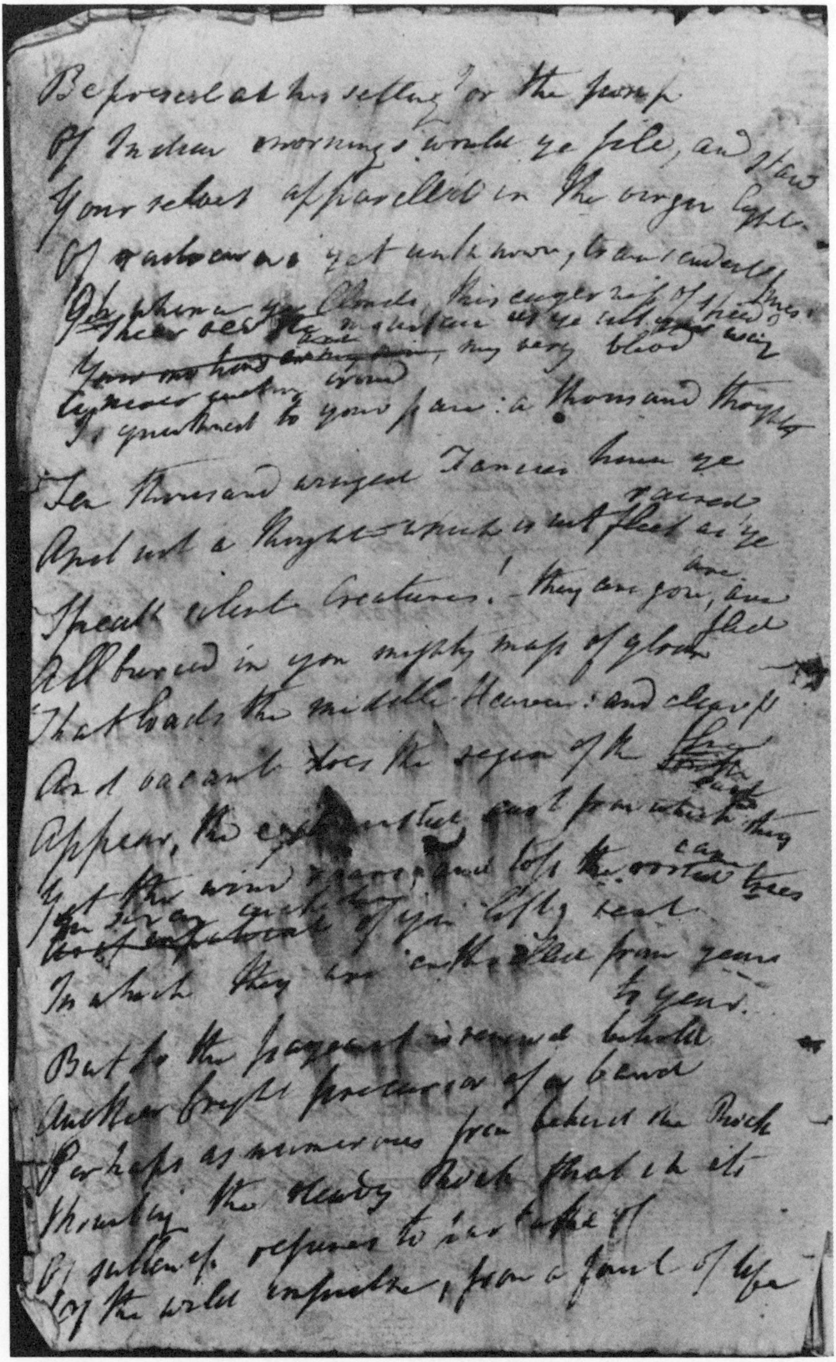

[DC MS. 18, 9v] [*To the Clouds,* ll. 25–53]

Be present at his setting? or the pomp
Of Indian mornings would ye fill, and stand
Yourselves apparell'd in the virgin light
Of radiance yet unknown, transcendent
{Oh hues
{Ye whence, ye Clouds, this eagerness of speed?
Sheer oer the mountain as ye cut your way
{s {~~are~~
~~Your motion{ — {is my own,~~ my very blood
A never ending croud
Is quickned to your pace: a thousand thoughts
Ten thousand winged Fancies have ye
raised,
And not a thought which is not fleet as Ye
are.
Speak silent Creatures!—they are gone, are
fled
All buried in yon mighty mass of gloom
That loads the middle Heaven: and clear &
blue
And vacant does the region of the ~~south~~

---

*To the Clouds* fair copy begun on 8v continues on this page and ends on 10v. In the second line from the foot of the page, "of" is deleted by erasure.

Revisions entered on 10r, facing, continue work begun on 9v and lead to 11v, where WW makes a fresh start, going back to the last line on 8v. A photograph of the page is provided in John Jordan's edition of *Peter Bell* in this series (Ithaca, 1985), p. 174. The entries on 10r were made in the following order:

left margin:

As ye go forward away when first seen
{e tall rocks
She{ar oer that ~~mountain~~ crest ye cut your way
A never ending croud
As trembling to be forward & first se

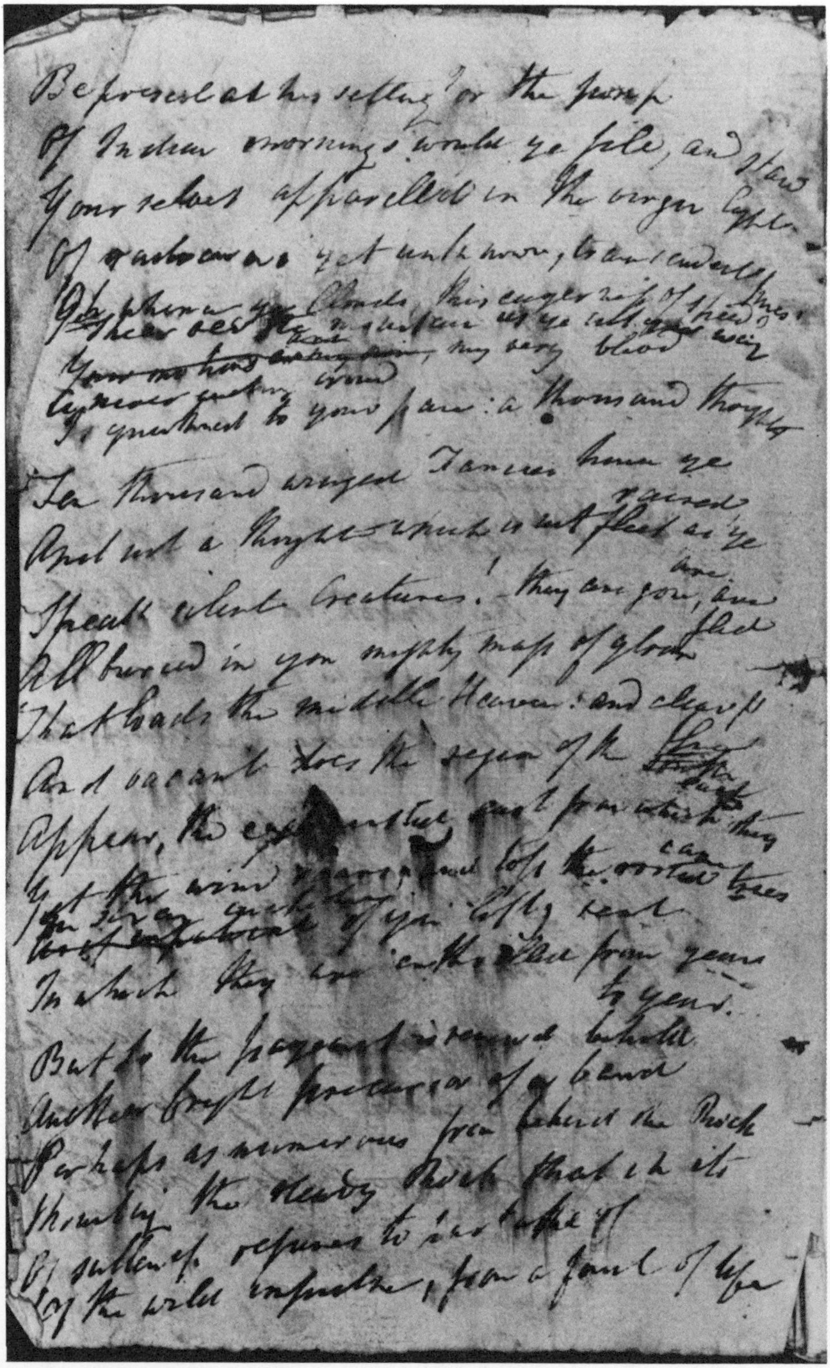

[DC MS. 18, 9$^{v}$, cont.] [*To the Clouds,* ll. 25–53]

east
Appear, the exhausted east from which they
came
Yet the wind roars, and toss the rooted trees
In strong impatience
~~As if impatient~~ of yon lofty seat
In which they are enthralled from yearr
to year.
But Lo the pageant is renewd behold
Another bright precursor of a band
Perhaps as numerous from behind the Rock
Mounting the steady Rock that in its
Of sulleness refuses to partake ~~of~~
Of the wild impulse, from a font of life

---

mid-page:

as thirstin

lower half of the page:

As thirsting to be forward, to be seen
Sheer or the talls rocks cret ye cut
way
An never ending croud

mid-page:

{S
{[?]heer oer the rocks gigantic brow
ye cut

14

Beneath the long procession stream
I rested upon the bulk of glorious shapes
Glorious or darksome. welcome to the eye
What they are called my, welcome to mine [eye]
That sees them, to my Soul, which owns
An Image, a reflection [higher than] visible
Of her capacious self, of what she is
With all her restless offspring, that she is
And what she doth possess.

[DC MS. 18, 10ᵛ] [*To the Clouds,* ll. 54–64]

Invisible the long procession streams
m} {s
A rapid of}ultitude of glorious {Shapes
Glorious or darksome. welcome to the vale
Which they are entering, welcome to mine eye
eye
That sees them, to my Soul, which owns
in them
palpable
An Image, a reflection visible
Of her capacious self, of what she is
With all her restless offspring what she
is
And what she doth possess.

---

*To the Clouds* fair copy begun on 8ᵛ and continued on 9ᵛ ends on this page.

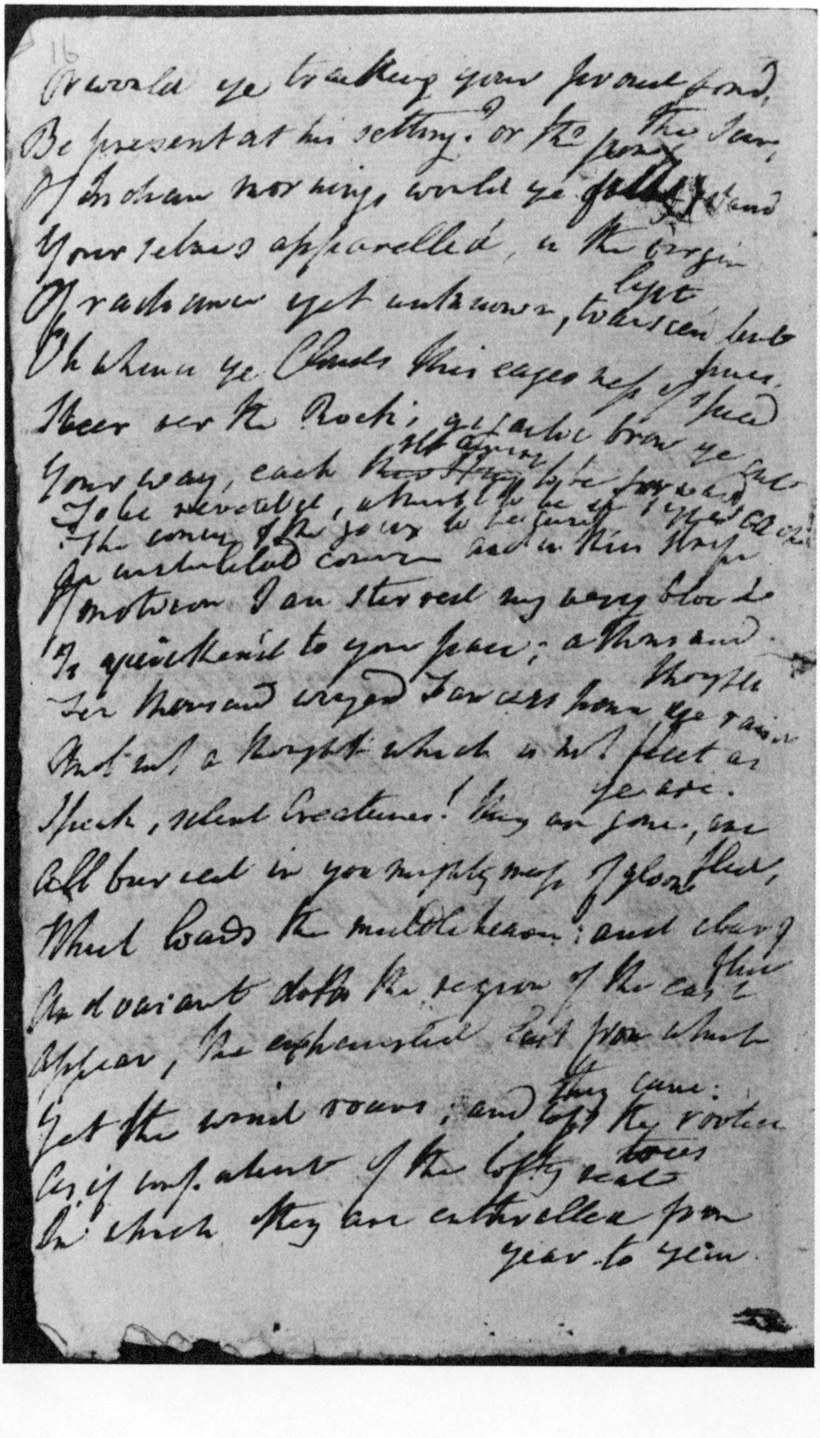

[DC MS. 18, 11v] [*To the Clouds,* ll. 24–47]

Or would ye tracking your proud Lord,
the Sun,
Be present at his setting? or the pomp
{ fill
Of Indian mornings would ye {[?deck] & stand
Yourselves apparelled, in the virgin
light
Of radiance yet unknown, transcendent
hues.
Oh whence ye Clouds this eagerness of speed
Sheer oer the Rock's gigantic brow ye cut
straining
Your way, each ~~thirsting~~ to be forward, each
To be reveald, athirst to be in sight
The coming & the going to secure
An unbelated course and in this strife
Of motion I am stirred my very blood
Is quicken'd to your pace; a thousand
thoughts
Ten thousand winged Fancies have ye rais'd
And not a thought which is not fleet as
ye are.
Speak, silent Creatures! they are gone, are
fled,
All buried in yon mighty mass of gloom
Which loads the middle heaven: and clear &
blue
And vacant doth the region of the east
Appear, the exhausted East from which
they came:
Yet the wind roars; and toss the rooted
{ t
{[?]rees
As if impatient of the lofty seat
On which they are enthralled from
year to year

---

The fair copy on this page represents a fresh start at the passage beginning with the last line on 8v and continued on 9v. The revision lines at mid-page, entered in a gap left in the fair copy, lead to further revisions on 12v.

The following revisions, on 12r, facing, lead from the first line at the top of 11v to the first two lines at the top of 24v:

Of Kingly state, and [ ? ? ? ]

or must [ ? ? ]
or rather must ye, [?lack ?or]

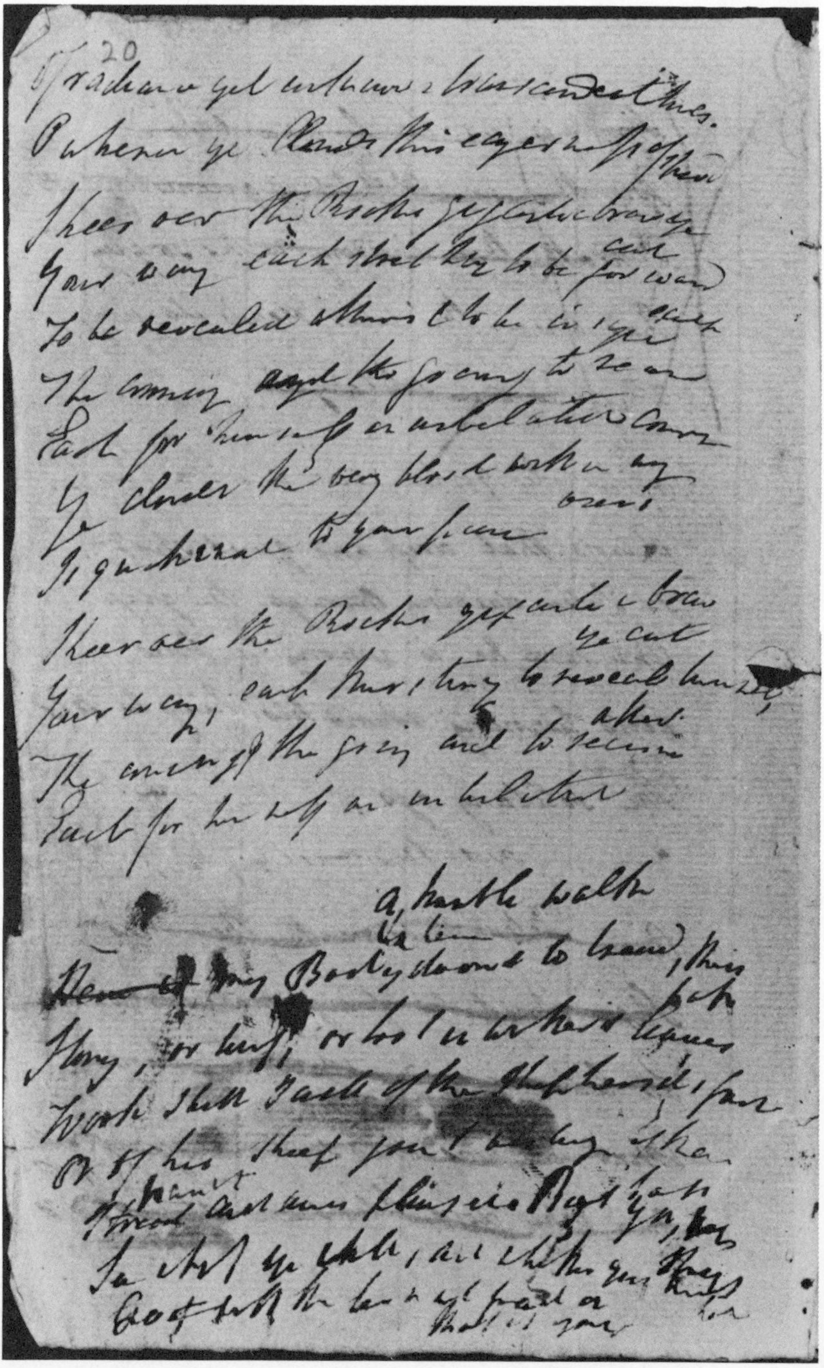

[DC MS. 18, 12v] [*To the Clouds,* ll. 28–35, 64–71]

Of radiance yet unknown transcendent hues.
O whence ye Clouds this eagerness of speed
Sheer oer the Rocks gigantic brow ye
cut
Your way each stretching to be forward
each
To be revealed athirst to be in sight
an
The coming [?]d the going to secure
Each for himself an unbelated course
Ye clouds the very blood within my
viens
Is quickened to your pace

Sheer oer the Rocks gigantic brow
ye cut
Your way, each thirsting to reveal himself,
athir
The coming & the going and to secure
Each for himself an unbelated

a humble walk
is here
~~Here is~~ my Body doomd to tread, this
path
Stony, or turf, or lost in wither'd leaves
Work shall I ask of the Shepheard's foot
Or of his sheep joint vestige of them
pace it both
I tread and know [?pleasure] But you, my
thoughts
See what ye will, and whither you might
Go & with the [?perfect] freedom
that is yours

---

The blocks of revision at the top and middle of the page continue revisions entered at mid-page on 11v. The block of drafting at the foot of the page is the earliest version of ll. 64–71 (DC MS. 65, 6r).

Once more I live to welcome thee once more and thou
Once more Welcome thee and thou fair Flower
Fair primrose tuft hast put forth thy bright
And liberal to be welcomed once again Flow
O [illegible] if the faithful Mary had come
With her accustomed hopes had come to breathe
Upon the bosom of this barren ~~rock~~ crag
And found [illegible] thee her [illegible] pains
So often found, but thou art here Fair Flower
And [illegible] as ever like a Queen
Smiling from thy imperishable throne:
And so shalt sit for ages yet unborn
Frail as thou art: if the prophetic Muse
Be rightly trusted so shalt sit & keep
Conspicuously thy solitary state
[illegible] upon the bare & [illegible] So thou are safe
In splendour unimpaired: [illegible] bare
Protected from the most adventurous hand
Of the boldest mountain sheep and from the approach
Of the wild Goat still bolder, nor more [illegible]
That thou to tread [illegible]

He pulled the creature did not move
Upon his back then Peter leapt
And with his staff and heels he plied
The little ass on either side
But still the ass his station kept

[DC MS. 18, 13v] [*The Tuft of Primroses,* ll. 1–19]

~~Once more~~ I live to welcome thee once more and thou
Once more I welcome thee and Thou fair Flower
Fair primrose tuft has put forth thy bright
Flow
And livest to be welcomed once again
O Pity if the faithful Spring had come
With her accustomed hopes had come to breathe
crag
Upon the bosom of this barren ~~rock~~
not
And found ~~not~~ thee her individual joy
{F
So often found, but thou are here Fair {flower
l }
And beautiful as ever [?]}ike a Queen
Smiling from thy imperishable throne:
And so shalt sit for ages yet unborn
Frail as thou art: if the prophetic Muse
Be rightly trusted so shal sit & keep
Conspicuously thy solitary state
Midway upon that bare & upright rock
In splendour unimpaird. For thou are safe
Pro} [?st]
This}tected from the most adventurous band
[?]
Of the bold mountain sheep and from ~~the~~ approach
Of the wild Goat, still bolder, nor more cause
eager }
Hast thou to tread thinstinctive [ ? ]}ness

---

On this page WW begins fair copy of what will later be titled *The Tuft of Primroses*; the fair copy, developed from drafts on 30v and 20v, continues on 14v and breaks off on 15v. The lines visible at the foot of the photograph are a stanza of *Peter Bell.*

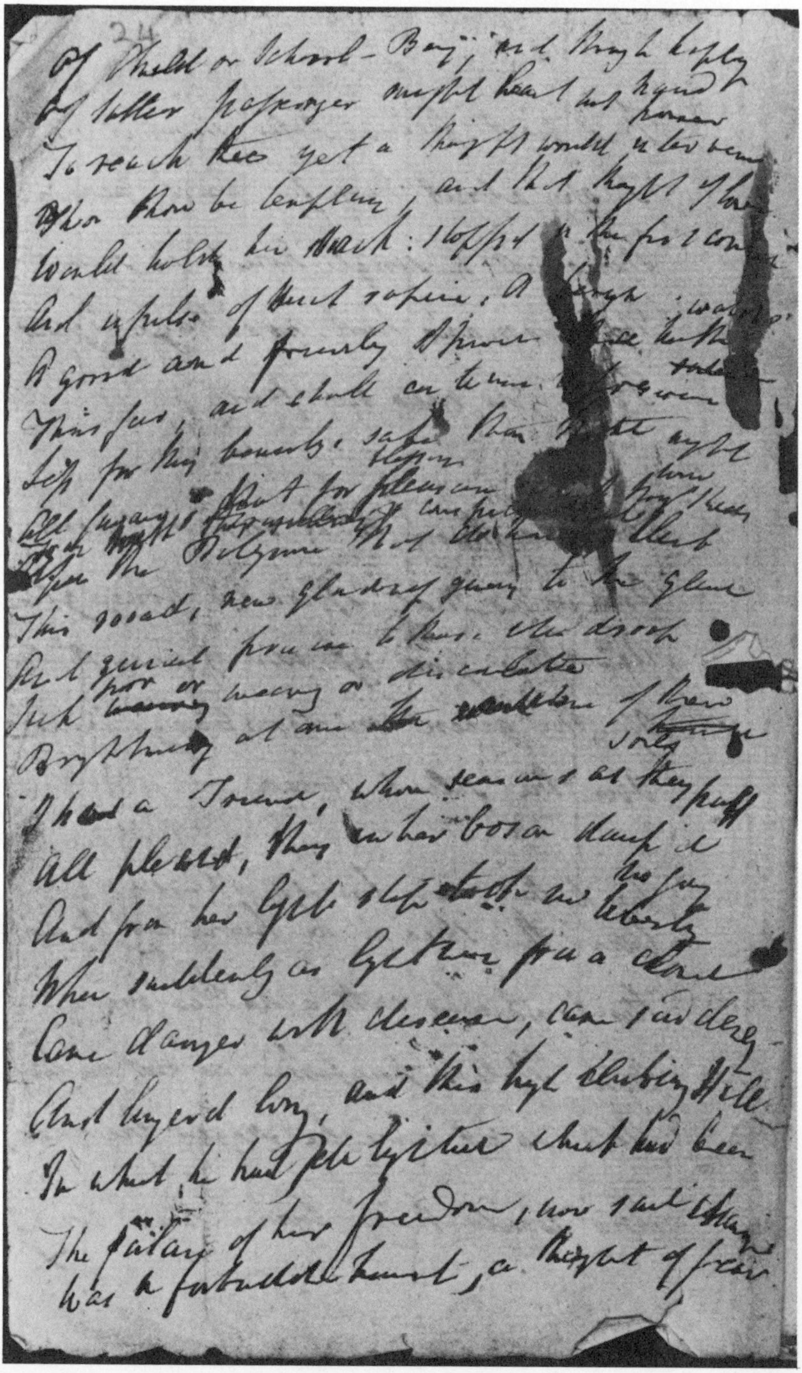

[DC MS. 18, 14v] [*The Tuft of Primroses,* ll. 20–46]

Of Child or School-Boy, and though haply
hand
{want
Of taller passenger might {[?have] not power
To reach thee yet a thought would intervene
T}
A}ho thou be tempting, and that thought of love
{back:}
Would hold his {[?sto]} stoppd in the first conceit
{such
And impulse of {his rapine. A bengn
watchd
A goood and friendly Spirit thee hath
~~[?saved]~~
Thus far, and shall continue to preserve
Less for thy beautys sake thou that might
win
b} blessing
All favour, [?]}ut for pleasure which thou sheds
{that
From {thy thy sunny & conspicuous seat
Travellers
Upon the Pilgrims that do hourly climb
This rooad, new gladness giving to the glad
And genial promise to those who droop
poor or
Sick ~~weary~~ weary or disconsolate
{winter}
Brightning at once the {[ ? ]} time of their
~~hearts~~
{had souls {d
I {[?have] a Friend, whom seasons as they pass{
{d
All pleas{e, they in her bosom damp'd
no joy
And from her light step took no liberty
When suddenly as lightning from a cloud
Came danger with disease, came suddenly
And linger'd long, and this high climbing Hill
In which he had delighted which had been
The palace of her freedom, now sad change
Was a forbidden haunt, a thought of fear

---

Fair copy of *The Tuft of Primroses,* begun on 13v, continues here. Two lines drafted on 15r, facing,

Down looking & far looking all day long
From that thy sunny & conspicuous throne

were meant for insertion ten lines from the top of 14v.

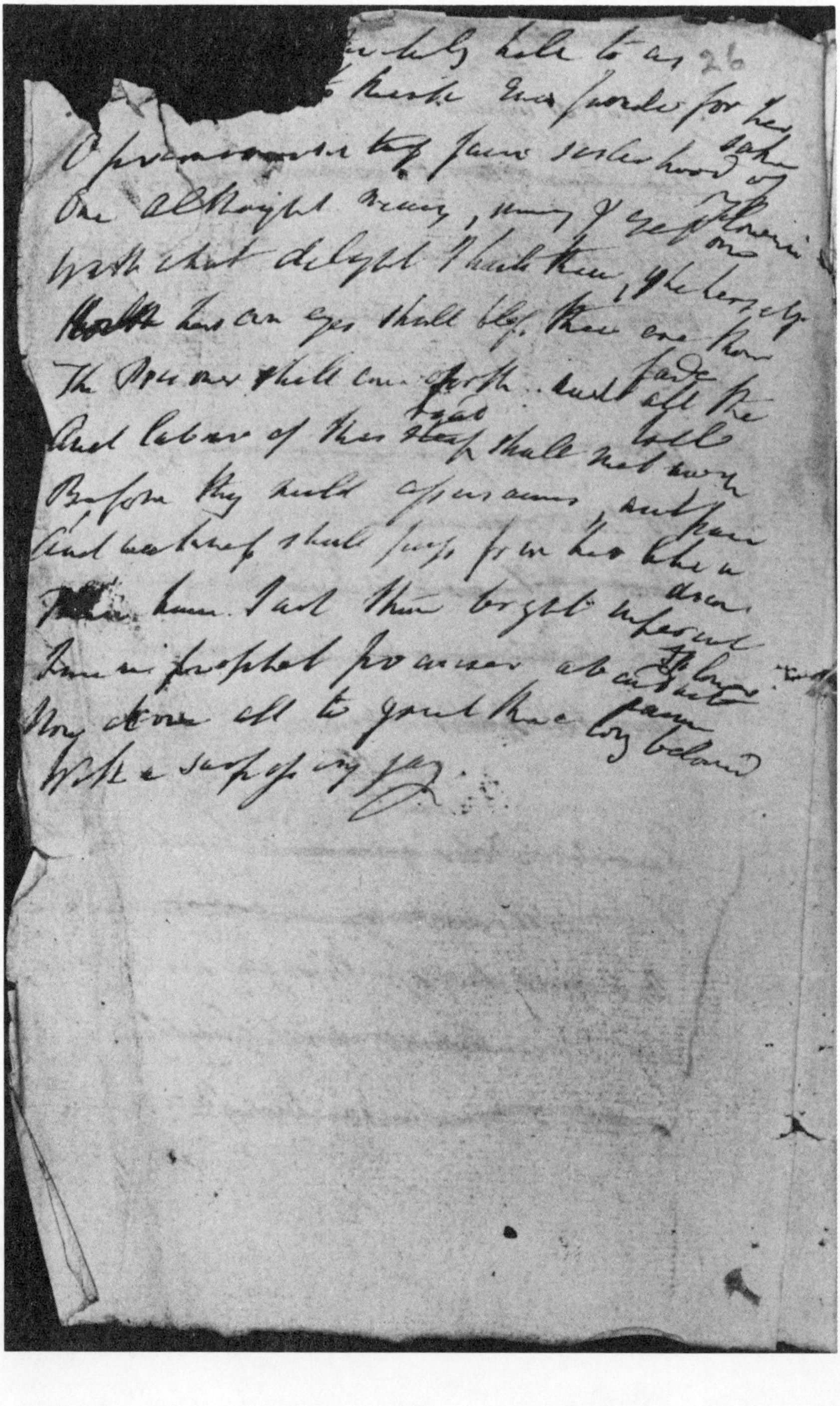

[DC MS. 18, 15v] [*The Tuft of Primroses*, ll. 47–52]

[ ]ncholy hill to us
[ ]s[ ] to think and ponder for her
sake
O primrose tuft fair sisterhood of
Flowers
One although many, many & yet one
With what delight I hail thee, she herself
{With
{Hails her own eyes shall bless thee ere thou
{forth fade
The Prisoner shall come {[?of] and all the
road toil
And labour of this ~~steep~~ shall met away
Before thy mild assurances, and pain
And weakness shall pass from her like a
dream
Then here I ask thee bright imperial
Flower
Queen prophet promiser abundant
{above [ ? ]
Now {[ ? ] all to greet [?thee] long beloved
With a surpassing joy.

---

The fair copy of *The Tuft of Primroses* begun on 13v and continued on 14v breaks off here. Revision of the last four lines continues on the fragment of manuscript at Trinity College, Dublin (MS. 5901).

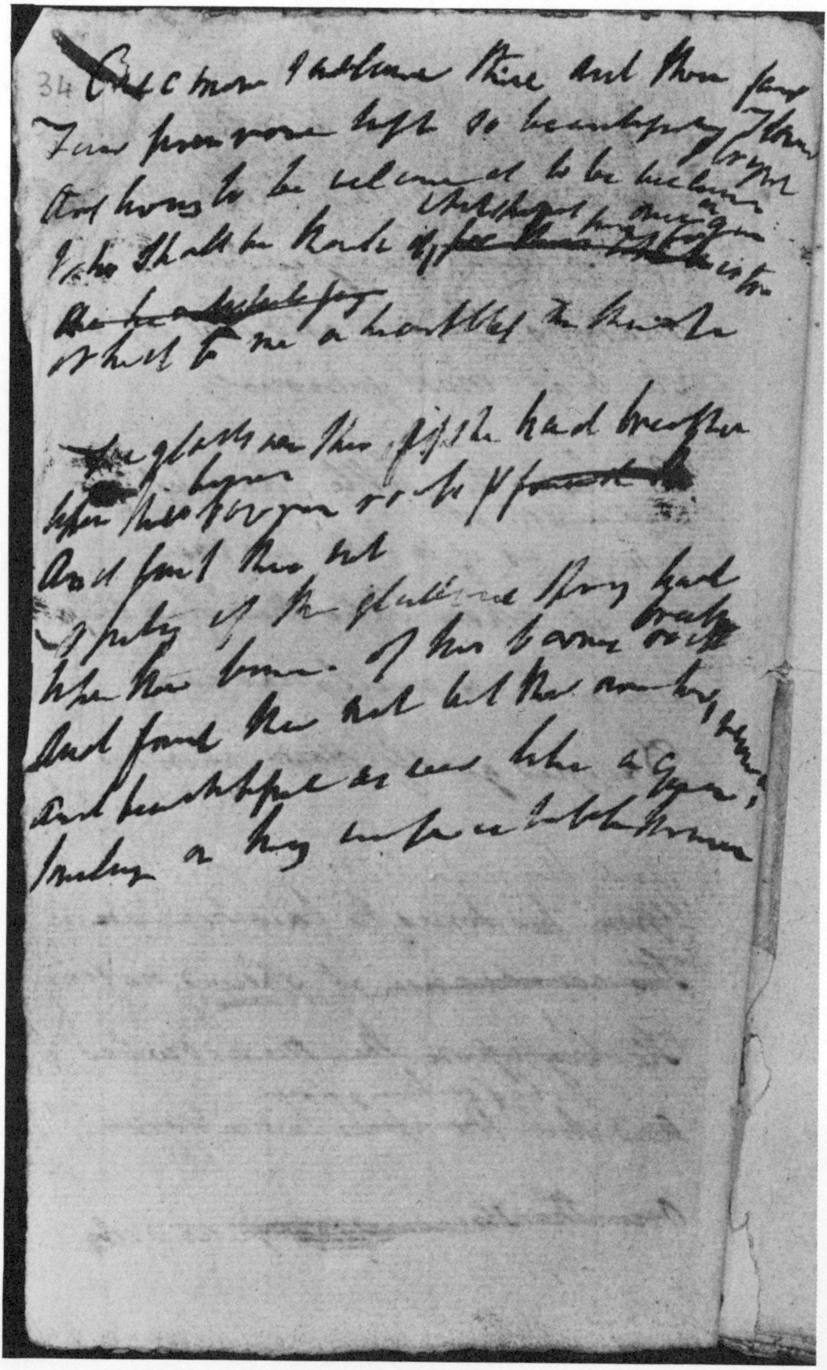

[DC MS. 18, 20v] [*The Tuft of Primroses*, ll. 1–9]

Once more I welcome thee and thou fair
Flower
Fair primrose tuft so beautiful & bright
Art living to be welcomed to be welcomd
a
once gain
[?what ?hopes ?here ?for]
Who Shall he thank if, ~~for this which~~ is to
{~~the~~
{~~A heartfelt joy~~
Which to me a heartfelt [?the] thanks

{ if }
The glad[?some] [?Spring] {of sp} she had breathd
{is barren
Upon th{e bosom rock & ~~found the~~
And found thee not
O pity if the gladsome Spring had
breath
Upon the bosom of this barren rock
And found thee not but thou are here, revivd,
And beautiful as ever like a Queen
Smiling on thy imperishable throne

---

Drafting on this page follows from work on 30v and leads to the opening lines of *The Tuft of Primroses* on 13v.

42

Or come ye, as should you first, a Flight
Aerial upon due migration bound
Embodied Travellers not blindly led
To milder climes: or, rightlier are ye named
A Caravan in hasty pilgrimage
With hope to pause at last upon the top
Of some remoter mountains more beloved
Than these, and utter your devotion
there

[DC MS. 18, 23v] [*To the Clouds*, ll. 12–22]

Or come ye, as I haild you first, a Flight
Aerial upon due migration bound
Embodied Travellers not blindly led
To milder climes: or, rightlier are ye named
A Caravan in hasty pilgrimage
With hope to pause at last upon the tops
Of some remoter mountains more belov'd
Than these, and utter your devotion
there

---

Here WW makes a fresh start at the passage of *To the Clouds* beginning ten lines from the foot of 8v; the position of the lines toward the bottom of the page matches their position on 8v.

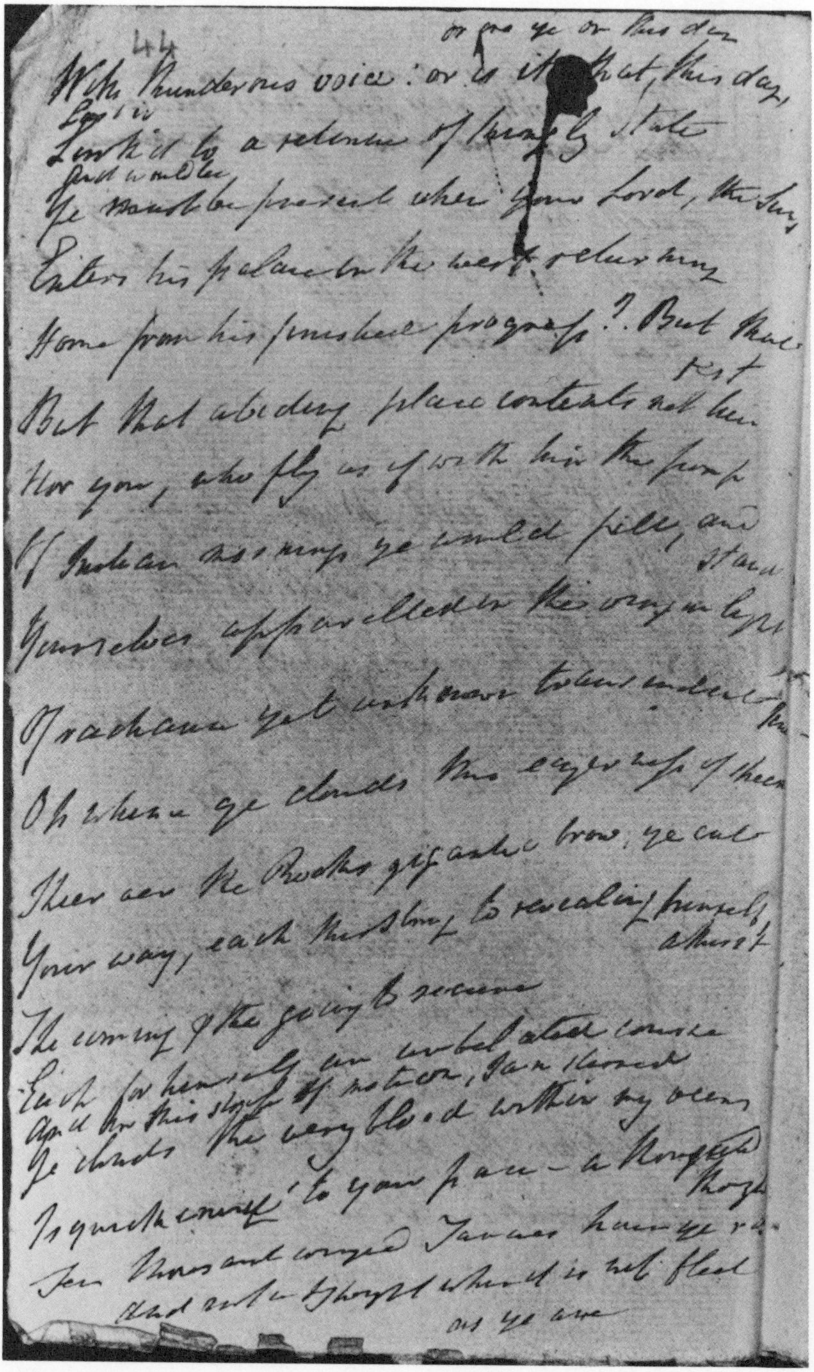

[DC MS. 18, 24ᵛ] [*To the Clouds*, ll. 23–37]

or are ye on this day
With thunderous voice: or is it that, this day,
Last in
Link'd to a retinue of kingly state
And would be
Ye must be present when your Lord, the Sun,
Enters his palace in the west returning
Home from his finished progress? But that
rest
But that abiding place contents not him
Nor you, who fly as if with him the pomp
Of Indian mornings ye would fill, and
stand
Yourselves apparelled in the virgin light
Of radiance yet unknown transcendent hues
Oh whence ye clouds this eagerness of speed
Sheer oer the Rocks gigantic brow, ye cut
Your way, each thirsting to revealing himself,
athirst
The coming & the going to secure
Each for himself an unbelated course
And in this strife of motion, I am stirred
Ye clouds the very blood within my veins
Is quickenin{d/g} to your pace—a thou{sand/ght}
thoughts
Ten thousand winged Fancies have ye raisd
And not a Thought which is not fleet
as ye are

---

The fair copy is continued from 23ᵛ. Drafting leading to the second line on the page is on 12ʳ; see note to 11ᵛ.

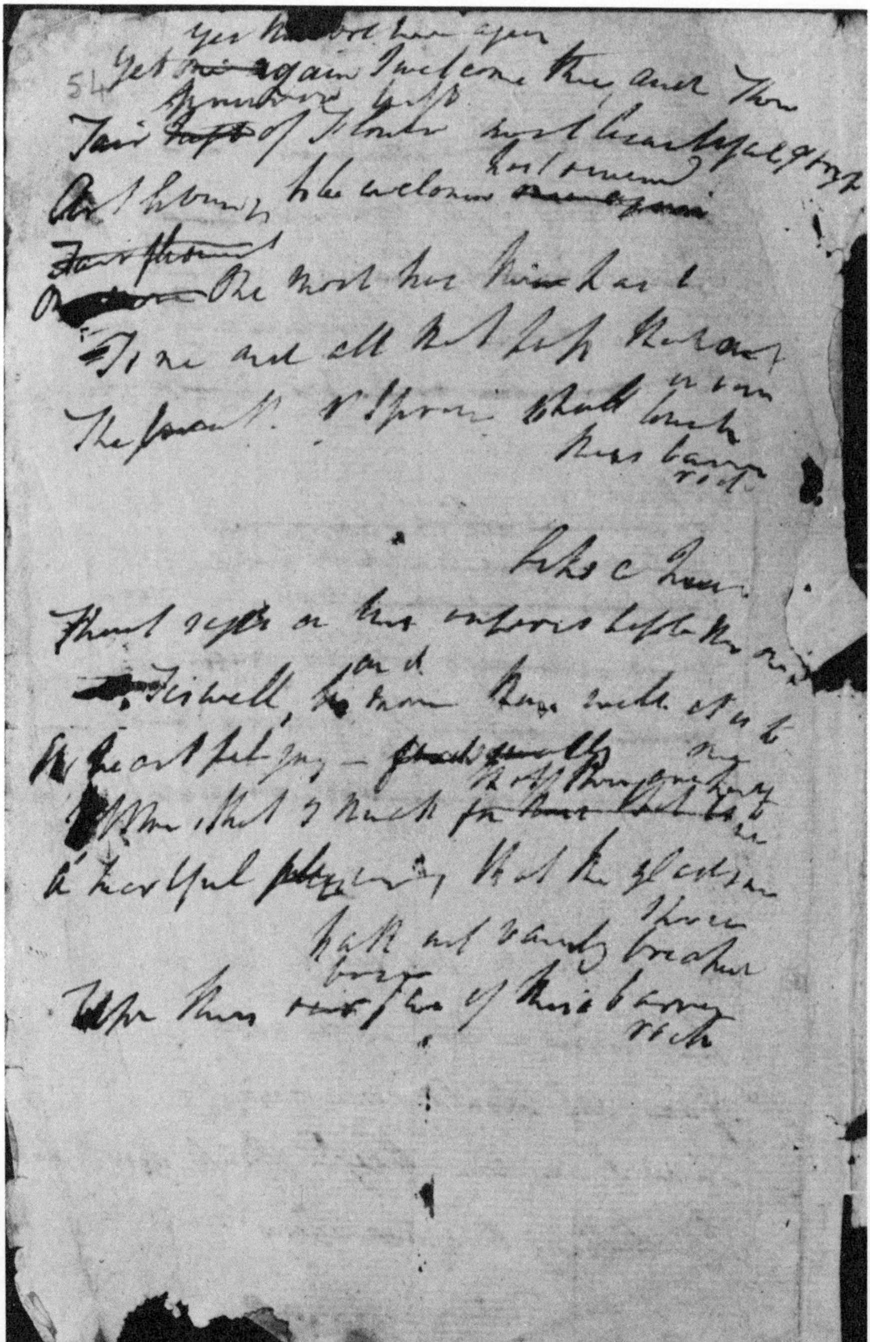

[DC MS. 18, 30$^{v}$] [*The Tuft of Primroses,* ll. 1–9]

yes tho[ ]art here again
Yet ~~once a~~gain I welcome thee, and Thou
primrose tuft
Fair ~~tuft~~ of Flowers most beautiful, & bright
hast renewed
Art living to be welcomd ~~once again~~
~~Fair flowers~~
~~Once more~~ One most [ ? ] [?thou] hast
To me and all that pass that [?way]
in vain
The breath of Spring shall touch
this barren
rock

Like a Queen
That sists on her imperishable throne
and
Tis well, ~~tis~~ more than well it is to
me
{[?each ?severally]}
A heartfelt joy—{[ ? ? ]}
that thou are here
[?]Who that of much ~~for that that is~~ to
me
ple}
A heartful joy}asure that the gladsome
Spring
hath not vainly breathed
{U bosom
{[?]pon this ~~rock~~ [?] of this barren
rock

---

This page contains the earliest drafting for the opening of *The Tuft of Primroses* and leads to further drafting on 20$^{v}$.

# DC MS. 172
# (Letter from Wrangham to Wordsworth, May 7, 1808): Drafting toward *The Tuft of Primroses*

Francis Wrangham's letter is written on one side of a single sheet, approximately 18.6 centimeters wide by 22.8 centimeters high; the paper is watermarked JN and chain lines are at intervals of 2.5 centimeters. The letter was folded in half to form a bifolium, and needle holes show that it was stitched into some other manuscript, where its verso formed two blank pages. These pages were used by Wordsworth for early drafting of parts of *The Tuft of Primroses,* lines 331–346, 358–426. Ink offset on the face of the letter (1$^{v}$ of the bifolium) shows that additional leaves, probably bearing further *Tuft of Primroses* drafting, once existed. The Gordon Graham Wordsworth note accompanying DC MS. 65 at the Wordsworth Library in Grasmere refers to "the stitched up scraps of letters, all bearing a date early in 1808 and having fragments of the verses on St. Basil written on their reverse." The letter from Wrangham must be one of the "scraps" that Gordon Wordsworth saw; the fragment of manuscript preserved at Trinity College, Dublin (MS. 5901), may be another.

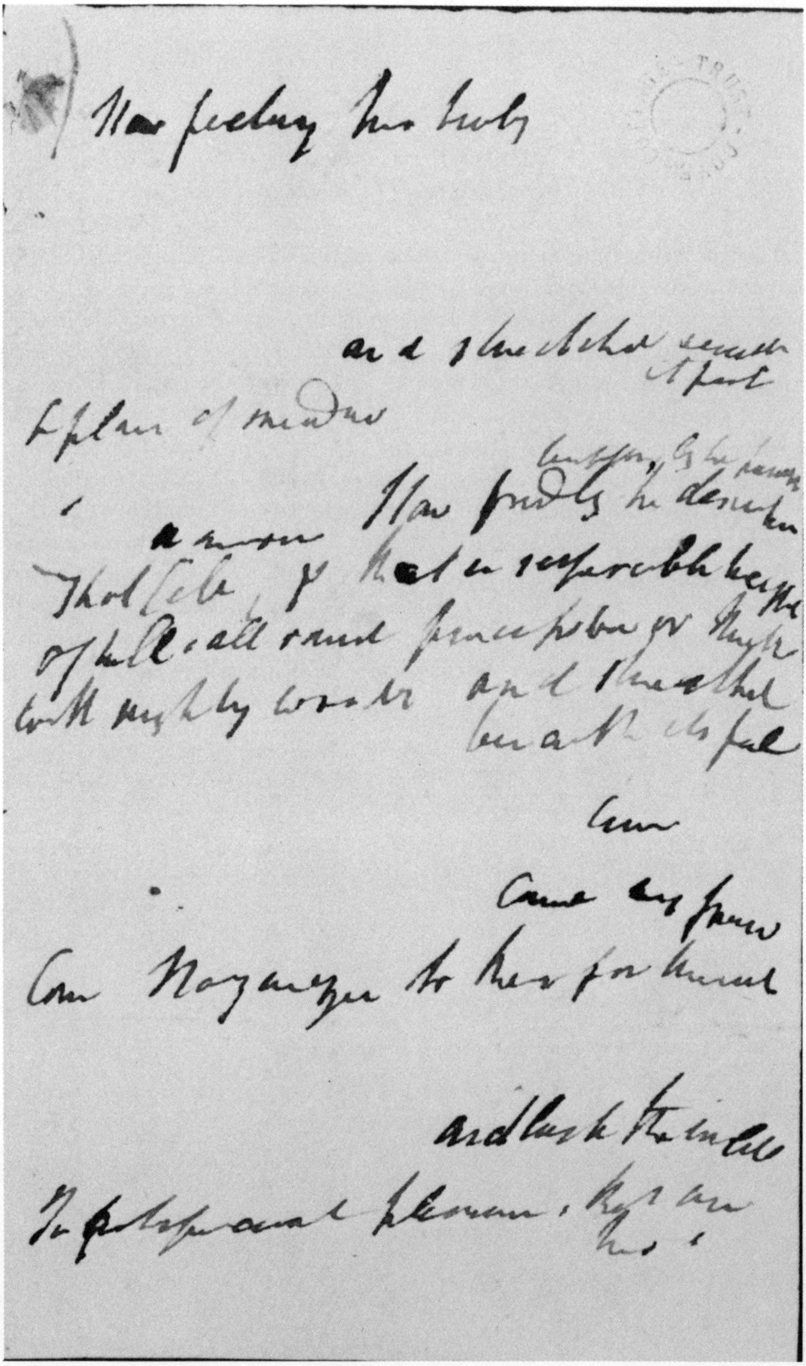

## [DC MS. 172: *The Tuft of Primroses*]

### [1r]

How feeling his [?holy]

and stretchd beneath
it feet
A place of meadow

[?tenderly] he [?pourtrays]
[?a] [ ? ] How fondly he describes
That Cell, & that insuperable height
Of hills all round precipice or Rock
With mighty woods and strecthd
beneath its feet

Come
Come my friend
Come Nazianzen to this fortunate

and taste the wild
Inartificial pleasures that are
here

---

The top half of this page contains early drafting toward ll. 330–341 of *The Tuft of Primroses.* Drafting toward the foot of the page, beginning with the word "Come," contributes to further drafting at the top of 2v. For the phrase "wild / Inartificial pleasures" see note to 2v.

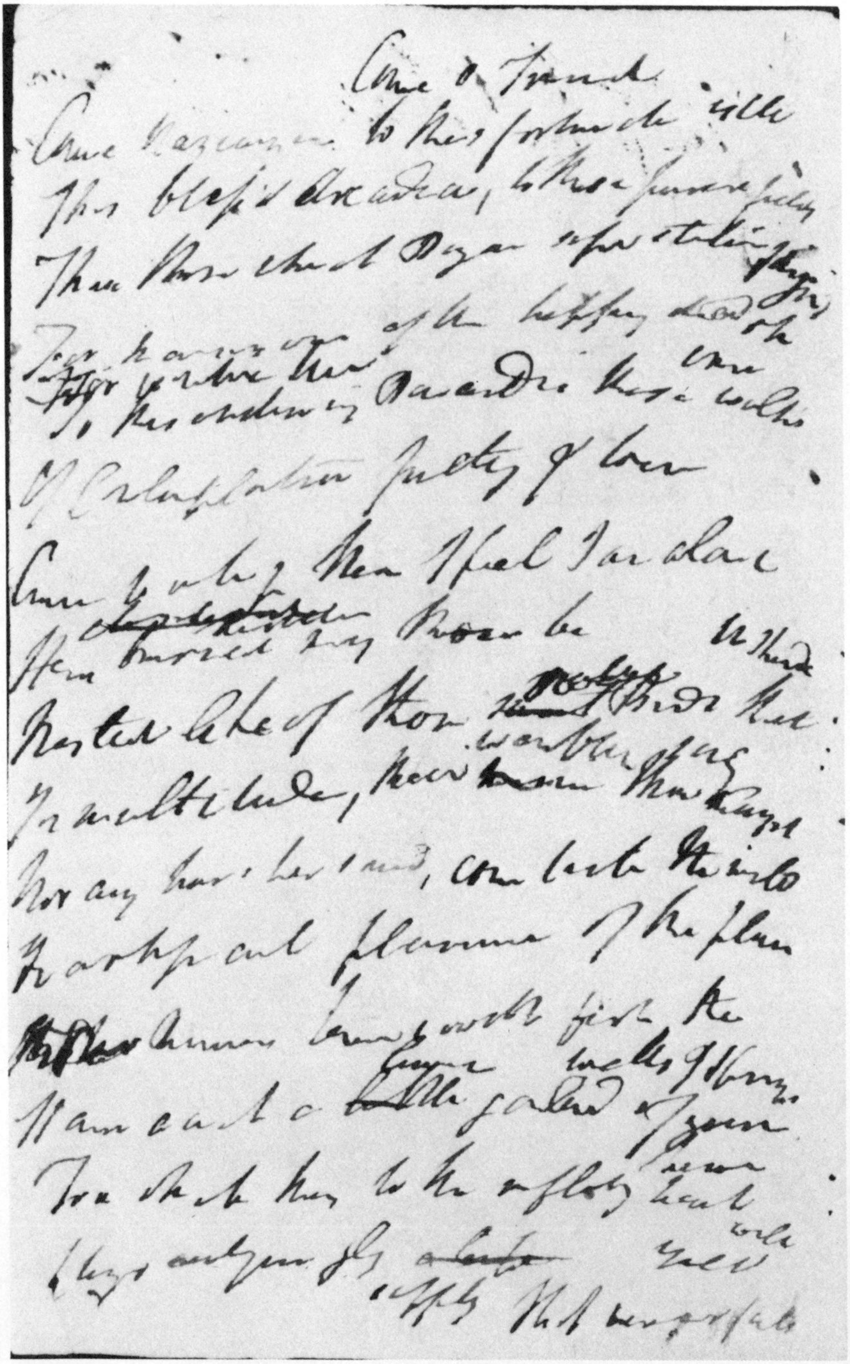

[2v]

Come O Friend
Come Nazianzen to this fortunate isle
This bless'd Arcadia, to these purer fields
Than those which Pagan superstition feignd
For mansions of the happy dead oh
{For come
{To wanting thee
To this enduring Paradise these walks
Of Contemplation piety & love
Come to [?wanting] thee I feel I am alone
~~desolated~~
hidden {ou
Here buried may th{ee be in shade
{sweet
{[ ? ]
Nested like of those ~~sweet~~ Birds that
warbling sing
In multitude, their ~~music~~ thou mayst
Nor any harsher sound, come taste the wild
Inartificial pleasure of the place
{ The
{[ ? ] Rivers teem with fish the
living wells & springs
Have each a ~~little~~ garland of green
herbs
Fro which they to the rifling hand
will
yield
Ungrudgingly ~~a large~~
supply that never fals

---

This page contains early drafting toward scattered passages between ll. 358 and 427 of *The Tuft of Primroses.* The phrase "the wild / Inartificial pleasure of the place" and the related phrase at the foot of 1r are taken from William Cave's *Apostolici* (1716), p. 478. See Introduction, sec. iv.

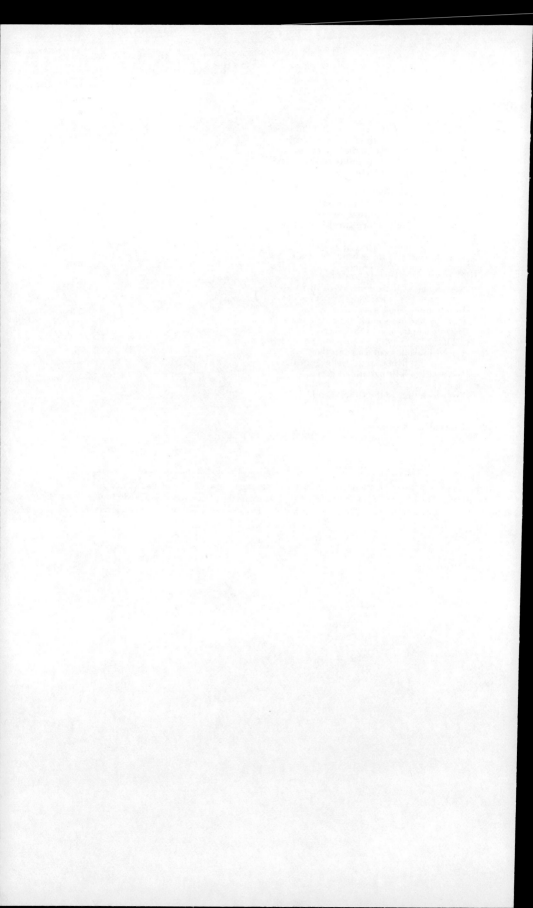

# Trinity College (Dublin) MS. 5901
## Drafting toward *The Tuft of Primroses*

The drafting on this small fragment of paper, early work toward lines 62–67 of *The Tuft of Primroses,* is intermediate between the last four lines on 15$^{v}$ of DC MS. 18 and further drafting in DC MS. 65, starting with the last line at the foot of 32$^{r}$ and continuing at the top of 33$^{r}$. MS. 5901 is a roughly triangular scrap, evidently torn from the corner of a page, measuring 15.3 centimeters wide by 4.8 centimeters high (at the long edge). The paper is laid, with chain lines 2.4 centimeters apart. A trace of sealing wax, at the upper left-hand corner of the recto, may show that the fragment was torn from what was originally a letter, perhaps one of the "stitched up scraps" described by Gordon Graham Wordsworth in his note accompanying DC MS. 65 (see headnote to the transcription of draft lines on the verso of the letter from Wrangham to Wordsworth, May 7, 1808—DC MS. 172—above). The envelope containing MS. 5901 at Trinity College identifies it as a "Fragment of Wordsworth MS.S found in W's copy of Cave's lives"—a work contained in Wordsworth's Rydal Mount Library.

The passage on the recto is crossed out with a large X.

# [Trinity College (Dublin) MS. 5901: *The Tuft of Primroses*]

[Recto]

~~Yet not~~
Yet not for this thou bright Imperial Flower
though summoned
now
Queen prophet Promiser (~~do I lose sight~~
above all to greet thee long beloved
[?passing] joy do I lose sight
woulds have been, to me
[?isely] if the stream
[? ? ?]

---

[Verso]

Farewell, yet leaving there with such firm hopes
{f
Bright {Flower so gladly greeted not for [?]
Have I forgotten what thou art to [?m]
For [?thy] pure self—no surely [?]
Of Gratitude which [?]
[ ? ]

# DC MS. 65: *To the Clouds,* *The Tuft of Primroses, St. Paul's*

DC MS. 65 (formerly MS. Verse 54) is a small, commercially manufactured notebook in marbled boards. It contains 8 gatherings of 16 leaves, for a total of 128 leaves, the first and last of which are pasted-down inside covers. Three leaves (114, 115, 116) have been cut or torn from the notebook and are now missing; two others (2 and 3) have been partially burned away. Each leaf measures approximately 12.2 centimeters wide by 20 centimeters high. The paper is watermarked with a fleur-de-lis and countermarked 1802; chain lines are vertical at intervals of 2.5 centimeters.

Most work in DC MS. 65 dates from 1808, when Wordsworth entered *To the Clouds* at the beginning of the notebook ($3^{r}$–$7^{r}$), *The Tuft of Primroses* at the middle ($29^{v}$–$70^{r}$), and *St. Paul's* near the end ($118^{v}$–$120^{r}$). Further work on two passages from *The Tuft of Primroses*—the tale of Joseph Sympson ($36^{r}$–$38^{v}$) and the "What impulse drove the Hermit to his Cell" lines ($43^{v}$–$45^{r}$)—took place when they were adapted for use in *The Excursion* in 1809/1812, and some revision of the Grande Chartreuse passage ($65^{r}$–$70^{r}$) is probably related to its inclusion in Book VI of *The Prelude* in 1816/1819. Extensive draft revision (on $1^{v}$–$7^{r}$) and two late fair copies of *To the Clouds*—one begun by Wordsworth on $113^{v}$ and probably continued on leaves 114–116, now missing ($117^{r}$ contains draft revisions), the other in Mary Wordsworth's hand on $8^{r}$–$10^{v}$—may have been entered in 1826, when Wordsworth seems to have considered publishing the poem (see Introduction, above), or later, when it was being readied for inclusion in the 1842 volume, *Poems, Chiefly of Early and Late Years.* Further revision of Mary Wordsworth's fair copy, extending onto $11^{r}$–$12^{r}$, was incorporated in the fair copy of the poem entered in DC MS. 143. Large portions of the notebook—$12^{v}$–$29^{r}$, $70^{v}$–$113^{r}$, and $120^{v}$–$128^{r}$—remain blank.

In the transcriptions, editorial numbers in the left-hand margins of $3^{r}$–$7^{r}$ correspond to lines in the 1808 reading text of *To the Clouds.* Numbers in the left-hand margins of $8^{r}$–$12^{r}$ and $113^{v}$ correspond to lines in *To the Clouds* as published in 1842. For $11^{r}$, line numbers have been assigned serially in the right-hand margin for ease of reference. Editorial numbers in the left-hand margins of $29^{v}$–$70^{r}$ and $119^{r}$–$120^{r}$ indicate lines that make up the reading texts of *The Tuft of Primroses* and *St. Paul's.*

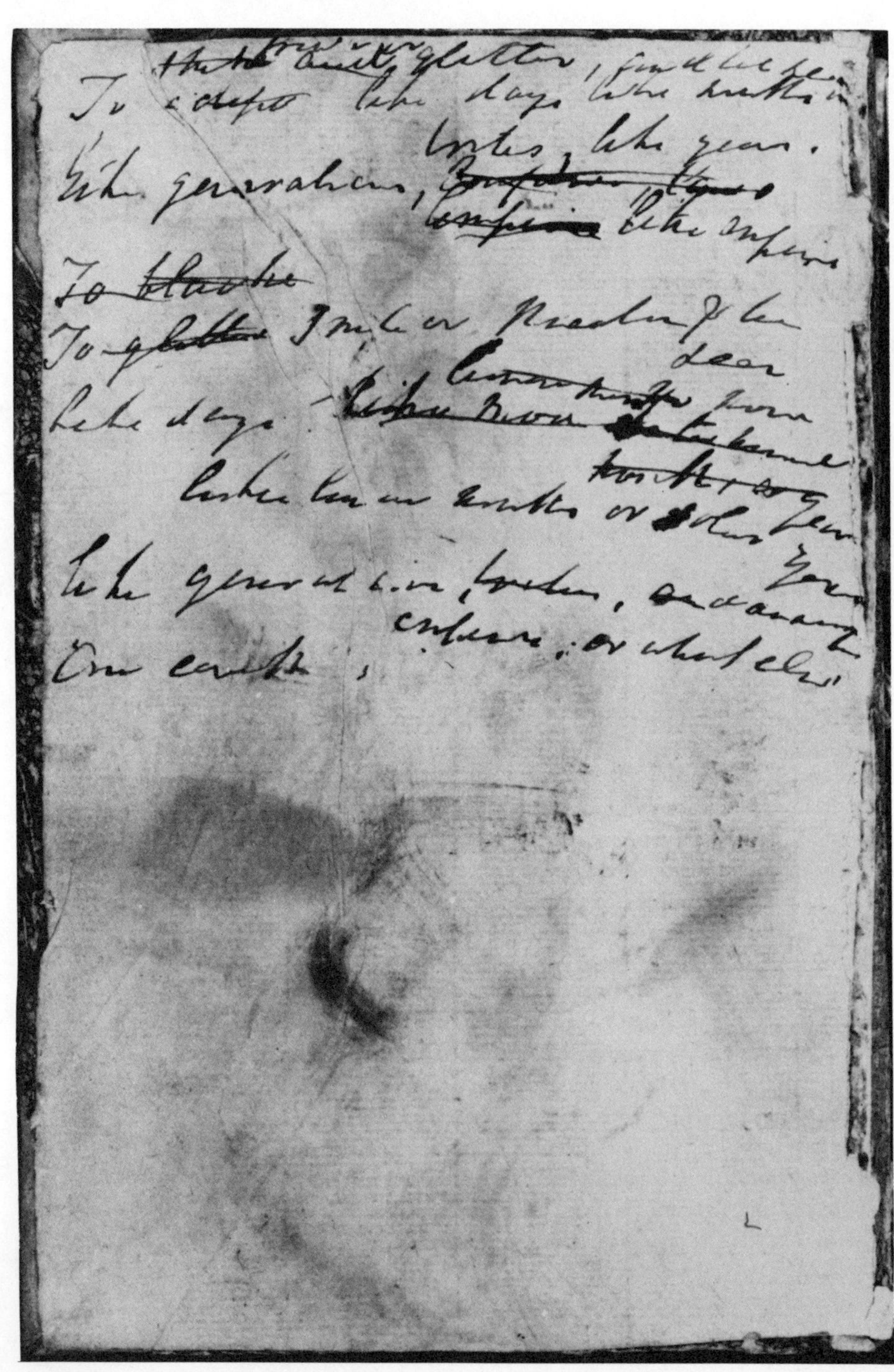

[DC MS. 65, 1$^{v}$] [*To the Clouds*]

[ ? ]
~~shake and~~ glitter, and be seen
To ~~accept~~ like days like months [ ? ]
like years
tribes
Like generations, ~~Empires, [ ? ]~~
~~Empire~~ like empires
~~To bla[ ? ]~~
To ~~glitter~~ smile or [?threaten] & be
seen
~~lunar months~~ [?moon]
Like days— ~~like moon determined~~
~~months or year~~
like lunar months or solar years
Like generations, ~~tribes~~ [?~~an~~d among]
empires, or what else
Our earth

---

The *To the Clouds* drafting on this page ( a pasted-down endpaper) leads to further drafting on 2$^{v}$ and the top of 3$^{v}$, contributing to ll. 38–40 on 9$^{v}$.

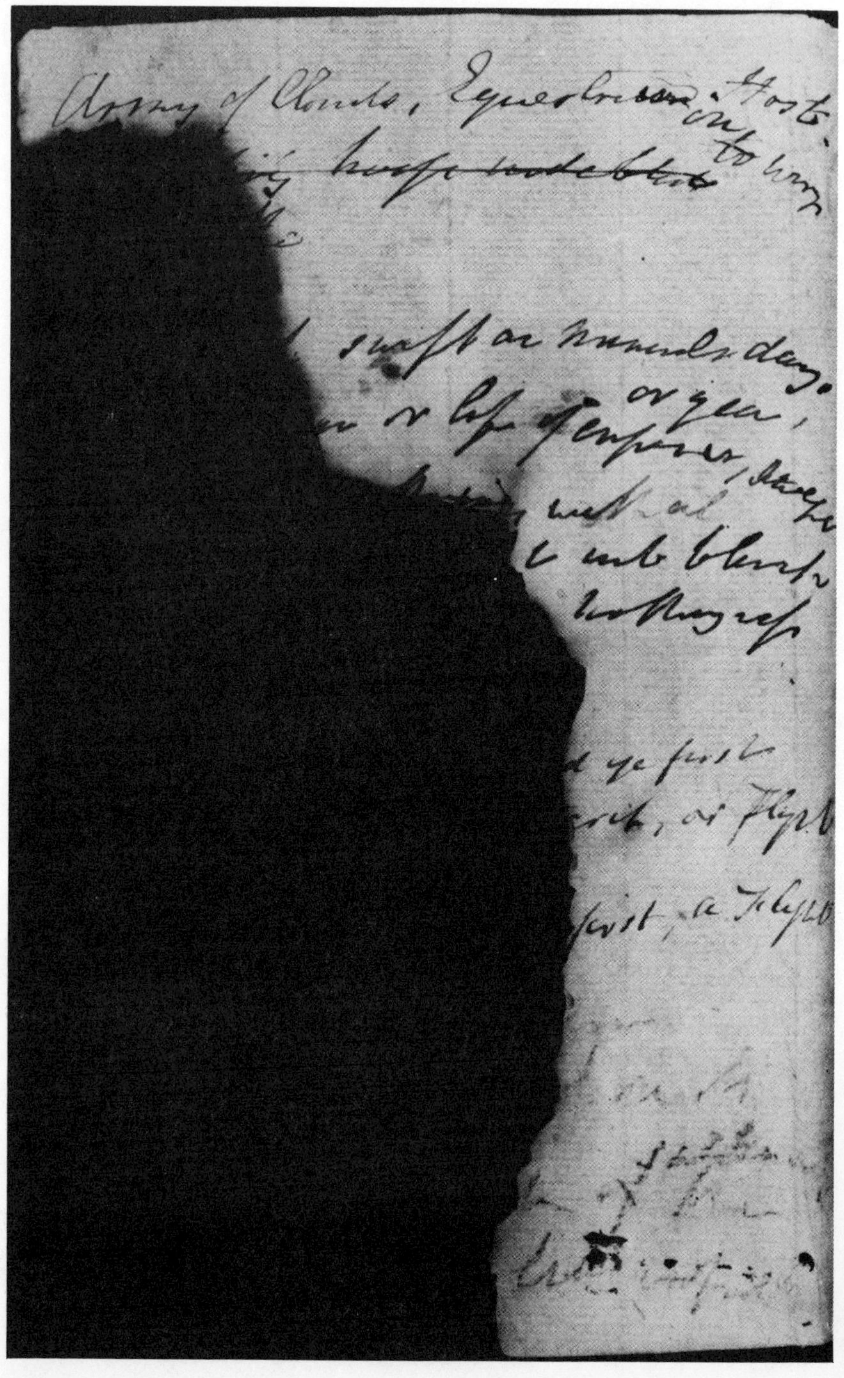

[DC MS. 65, 2$^{v}$] [*To the Clouds*]

Army of Clouds, Equestrian Host
on
~~to~~ wings
]~~king huge [?wide] [?blest]~~
]the

] swift as [?seconds] days,
or years
] or life of empires, swift
] [ ? ] withal
] [?and ?blank]
] nothingness

]d ye first
]arch, or Flight
]first, a Flight

] [ ? ]
]clouds
] [ ? ]
] [ ? ] of the
] like empire

---

About half of this page has been burned away. The first line at the top of the page incorporates one of the revisions of l. 1 on 3$^{r}$ and becomes l. 1 in DC MS. 143. The canceled line is apparently an alternate version of l. 2 on 3$^{r}$.

The block of five lines of drafting at mid-page is related to the drafting on 1$^{v}$ and the top of 3$^{v}$, which contributes to ll. 38–40 on 9$^{v}$. The next group, of three lines, at mid-page represents draft revision of ll. 12–15 on 3$^{r}$. The drafting at the foot of the page, in faint pencil, is related to the block of five lines of drafting at mid-page.

To the Clouds

19

Army of Clouds Flight of Clouds

Ascending from behind the motionless brow
Of that tall Rock as from a hidden world
O whither in such eagerness of speed?
What seek ye? or what shun ye? of the Gale
Companions fear ye to be left behind
Or racing on your blue aetherial field
Contend ye with each other? of the Sea
Children thus post ye over vale and height
Children of the distant sea
To sink upon your Mother's joyous lap?
Or were ye rightlier hailed when first mine eyes
Beheld, for ye still are sweeping on
Like a wide Army in impetuous march
Or like a never-ending Flight of Birds
Aerial, upon due migration bound
Travellers not blindly led

[DC MS. 65, 3r] [*To the Clouds*]

To the Clouds

in squadrons
Army of clouds∧ e } Flight of Clouds
[?]} questrian host on
Ascending from behind the motionless brow
{at
Of th{is tall Rock as from a hidden world
such
O whither in ~~this~~∧eagerness of speed?
gale
What seek ye? or what shun ye? of the ~~Wind~~
Companions fear ye to be left behind
Or racing on your blue ætherial field
Contend ye with each other? of the Sea
thus post ye over vale and h[
Children, Children of the distant sea
Your privilege of [ ? ] [?view] [ ? ]
~~Thus post Ye over dale and mountain height~~
To sink upon your Mothers joyous lap?
{ere
Or w{he Ye rightlier hail'd when first mine eyes
I lifted, for Ye still are sweeping on
Like a wide Army in impetuous march
Or like a never-ending Flight of Birds
Aerial, upon due migration bound
[~~?Embodied~~]
~~Embodied Travellers not blindly led~~

---

1 The caret and insertions above and below the line are in pencil.
9/10 In pencil.

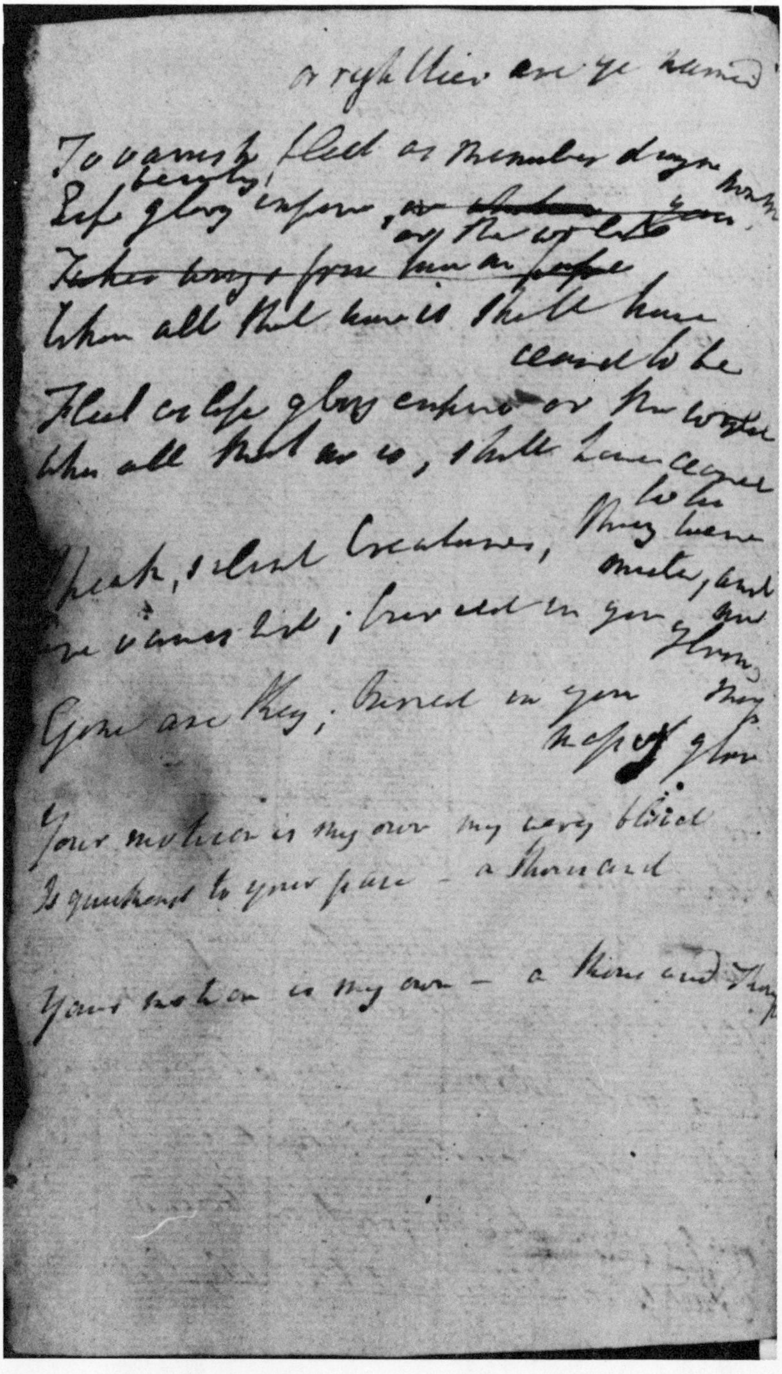

[DC MS. 65, $3^{v}$] [*To the Clouds*]

or rightlier are ye named
To vanish fleet as minutes days or months
beauty
Life glory empire, ~~or whateer your~~
or the world
~~Takes wings from human [ ? ]~~
When all that now is shall have
ceasd to be
Fleet as life glory empire or the world
When all that now is, shall have ceasd
to be

Speak, silent Creatures, they were
mute, and
now
Are vanish'd; buried in yon gloomy
mass
Gone are they; Buried in yon
mass of gloom

Your motion is my own my very blood
Is quickend to your pace—a thousand

Your motion is my own—a thousand Thoughts

---

The drafting at the top of the page follows from drafting on $1^{v}$ and $2^{v}$ and contributes to ll. 38–40 on $9^{v}$. The three lines of drafting at mid-page are alternates for ll. 38–39 on $5^{r}$. The last three lines on the page are related to revision of ll. 34–35 on $4^{r}$.

To milder climes? or rather do ye urge
In caravan your hasty pilgrimage
With hope to pause at last upon the tops
Of some remoter mountains more belov'd
Than these, and utter your devotion there
With thunderous voice? or are ye jubilant
And would ye, tracking your proud lord, the Sun,
Be present at his setting? or the pomp
Of Indian mornings would ye fill, and stand
Yourselves apparell'd in the virgin garb
Of radiance yet unknown transcendent hues
O whence, ye Clouds this eagerness of speed?
Pass o'er the Rock's gigantic brow ye come
Your way, each striving to reveal himself first
The coming and the going to secure
Each for himself an unbelated course?
Ye Clouds the very blood within my veins
Your motion is my own
Is quickened to your pace, a thousand things
Ten thousand winged fancies have ye
raised

[DC MS. 65, 4r] [*To the Clouds*]

To milder climes? or rather do ye urge
In caravan your hasty pilgrimage
With hope to pause at last upon the tops
Of some remoter mountains more belov'd
Than these, and utter your devotion there
With thunderous voice? or are ye jubilant
And would ye tracking your proud Lord, the
Sun,
Be present at his setting? or the pomp
Of Indian mornings would ye fill, and stand
{g
Yourselves apparell'd in the virgin {larb
Of radiance yet unknown transcendent hues
O whence, Ye Clouds this eagerness of speed?
{Y
Sheer oer the Rock's gigantic brow {ye cut
Your way, each thirsting to reveal himself, athirst
The coming and the going to secure
Each for himself an unbelated course?
Ye clouds the very blood within my veins
Your motion is my own
Is quickened to your pace, a thousand thoughts
Ten thousand winged Fancies have Ye
rais'd

---

The box drawn around ll. 30–34 and then extended to include ll. 35–36 here and l. 37 on 5r marked these lines for deletion during the preparation of the fair copy that starts on 8r.

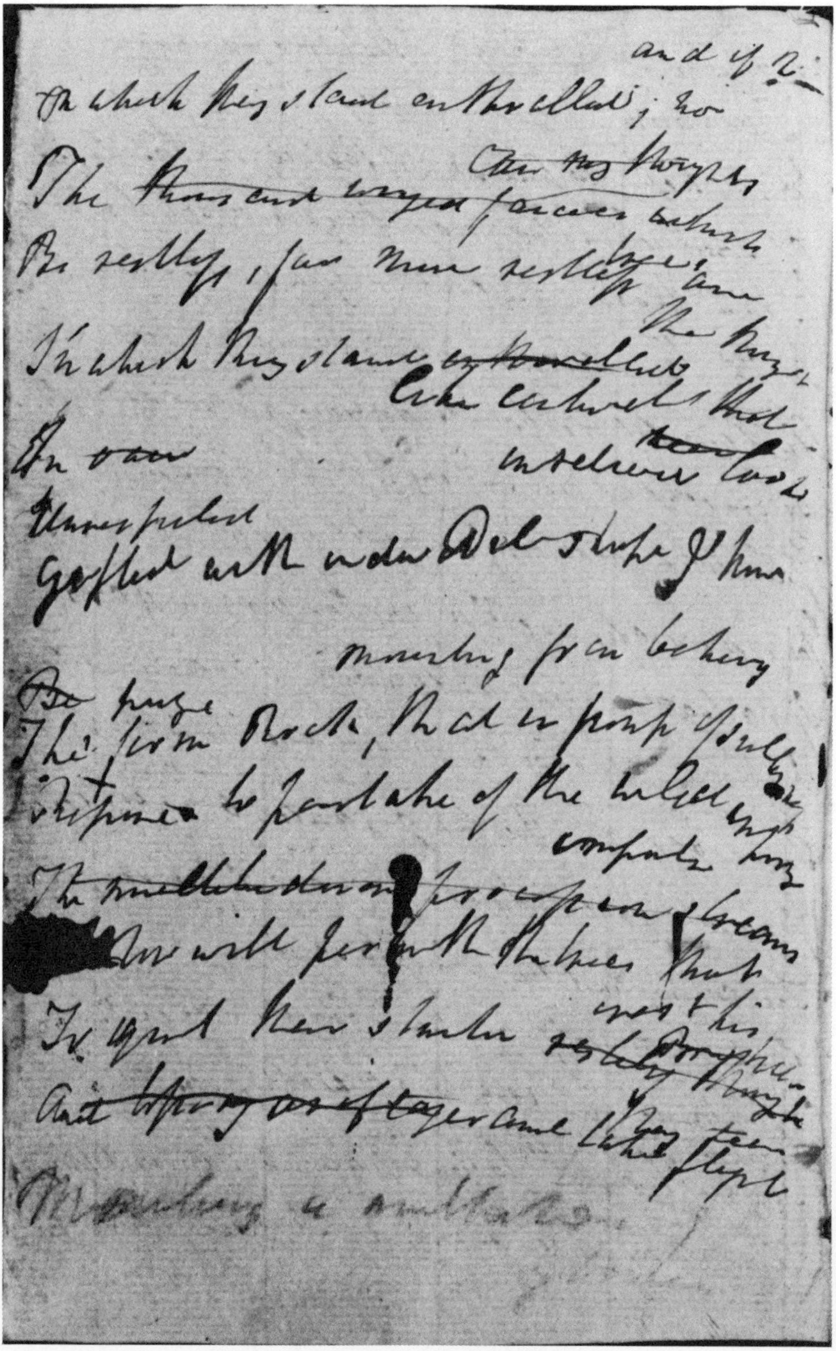

[DC MS. 65, 4$^v$] [*To the Clouds*]

and if [?]
On which they stand enthralled; nor
~~can my thoughts~~
The ~~thousand winged fancies~~ which
trees
Be restless, far more restless are
the thoughts
In which they stand ~~enthralled~~
like cataracts ~~that~~
~~seem~~
In ~~vain~~ unrelievd look
Unexpected

Gifted with individual shape & hue

mounting from behing
~~Be~~ huge
The firm Rock, that in pomp of sullenness
Refuses to partake of the wild impulse
impulse
~~The multitudinous procession streams~~
[ ? ] will [ ? ? ] the trees that
crest his
~~Brow~~ [ ? ]
To quit their station ~~restless though~~
they seem
~~And tossing as if eager~~ and take flight

Mounting a multitude of
glorious

---

The drafting at the top of the page is related to ll. 36–37 on 4$^r$–5$^r$. The line at mid-page appears to be further description of the "rapid multitude" of l. 55 on 5$^r$. The drafting on the bottom half of the page is related to ll. 50–54 on 5$^r$. The last line on the page is in pencil.

And not a thought which is not fleet as ye are

Speak silent Creatures. They are gone, are fled,

All buried in yon mighty mass of gloom

That loads the middle heaven, and clear & bright

And vacant doth the region of the east

Appear, a calm descent of sky that leads

Down to some unapproachable abyss

Down to the hidden cavern from which they came

But the wind roars and [illegible] the vortex [illegible]

As if impatient of yon lofty ~~seat~~ ridge

On which they ~~are~~ stood enthralled from year to year.

~~But~~ And lo the pageant is renewd, behold

Another bright Precursor of a band

Perhaps as numerous, from behind [illegible]

Mounting the steady Porch that [illegible]

Of sullen rest refuses to partake

Of the [illegible] impulse; from a fount of life

Invisible the long Procession streams

A rapid multitude of glorious Shapes

[DC MS. 65, $5^r$] [*To the Clouds*]

And not a Thought which is not fleet as Ye are
Speak silent Creatures! they are gone, are fled,
All buried in yon mighty mass of gloom
X X X X
That loads the middle heaven, and clear & bright
And vacant does the region of the east
Appear, a calm descent of sky that leads
Down to some unapproachable abyss
Down to the hidden world from which they came
But the Wind roars and toss the rooted Trees
that ridge
As if impatient of yon lofty ~~seat~~
stand
On which they ~~are~~ enthralled from year to year
And
~~But~~ Lo the pageant is renew'd, behold
But see Precur} to pomp
Another bright process}sor ~~of~~ a band
Perhaps as numerous, from behind the Rock
Mounting the steady Rock that in [?its] pomp
Of sullenness refuses to partake
Of the wild impulse; from a fount of life
Invisible the long Procession streams
A rapid multitude of glorious Shapes

---

37 The box drawn around this line is continued from the one around ll. 30–36 on $4^r$, marking the passage for deletion during the preparation of the fair copy that starts on $8^r$.

39/40 The four X's may signal the revision of ll. 38–39 at mid-page on $3^v$.

46–47 The marks drawn over the beginnings of these lines show that they were to be deleted in the fair copy that starts on $8^r$. Other marks and blots scattered through ll. 44–54 are ink offset from $4^v$.

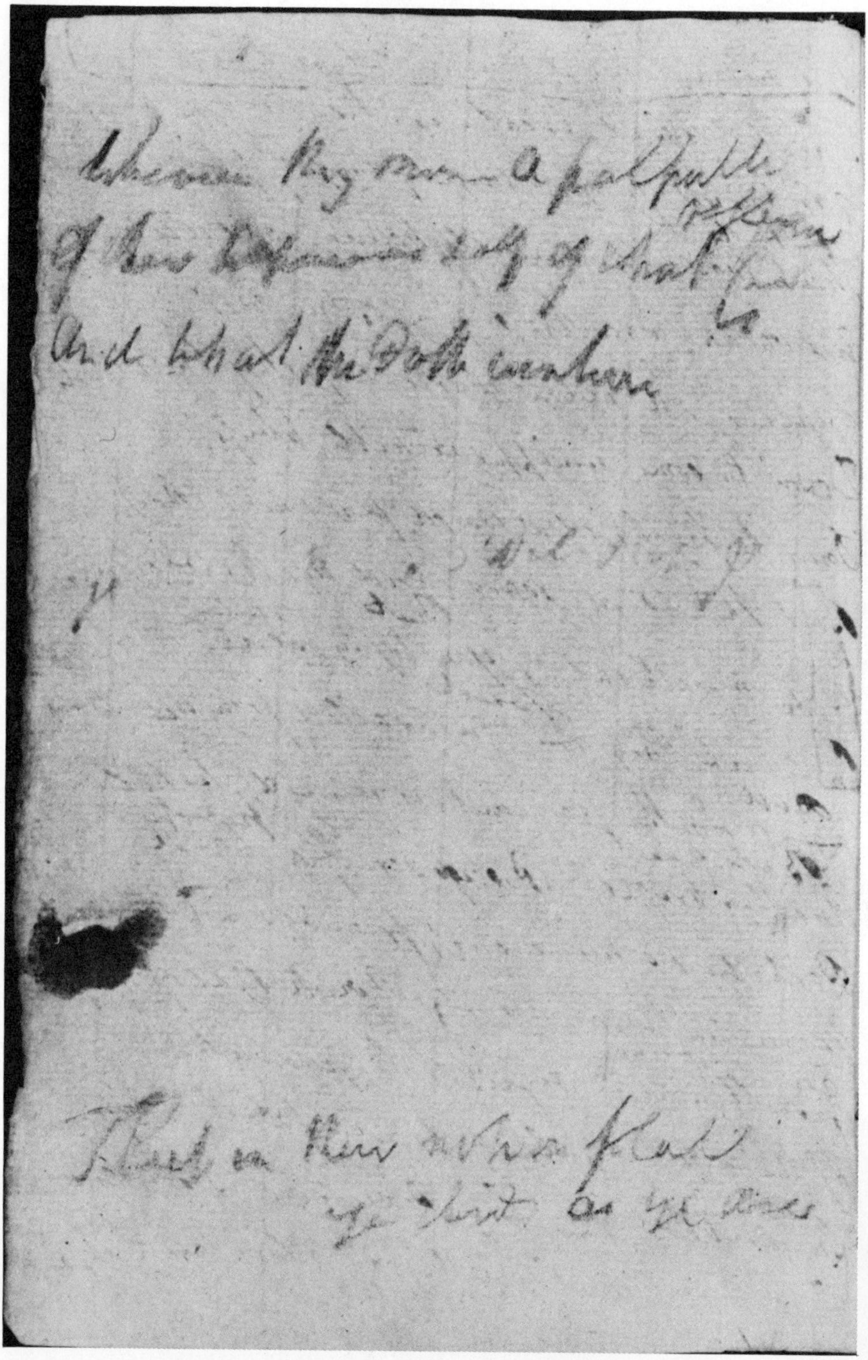

[DC MS. 65, 5v] *[To the Clouds]*

Wherein they move a palpable
reflexion
Of her capacious self of what she
is
And what she doth contain

That in their motion fleet
ye clouds O ye clouds

All entries on this page are in pencil. The three lines at the top of the page are related to ll. 60–64 on 6r. The line at the foot of the page is probably related to the passage it faces on 6r, ll. 69–71.

Glorious or darksome. Welcome to the Vale
Which they are entering, welcome to mine eye
That sees them, to my Soul that owns in
them
And in the bosom of the firmament
Wherein they move by which they are
contained
An Image, a reflection palpable
Of her capacious self of what she is
With all her restless Offspring, what she is
And what she doth possess! —

An humble walk
Here is my Body doomed to tread, this Path
A little hoary line and faintly traced
Work shall I call it of the Shepherds foot
Flock
Or of his sheep joint vestige of them both.
I pace it unrepining for my thoughts
See what they will & through their own
wide world
Go with the perfect freedom which is theirs.
Where is the Orphean Lyre or Druid Harp
To accompany the Song? the mountain wind

[DC MS. 65, 6r] [*To the Clouds*]

Glorious or darksome. Welcome to the Vale
Which they are entering, welcome to mine eye
That sees them, to my Soul that owns in
{d {the them
An{ Im{age bosom of the Firmament
{in
Where{er they move by which they are
contained
An Image a reflection palpable
Of her capacious self of what she is
{O
With all her restless {offspring, what she is
And what she doth possess!—
An humble walk
Here is my Body doomed to tread, this Path
A little hoary line and faintly traced
Work shall I call it of the Shepherds foot
flock
Or of his sheep joint vestige of them both
{[?ning]
I pace it unrepi{[ ? ] for my thoughts
See what they will & through their own
wide world
Go with the perfect freedom which is theirs.
Where is the Orphean Lyre or Druid Harp
To accompany the Song? the mountain Wind

---

67/68 In pencil.
6v is blank.

Shall be our hand of music: it shall sweep
The rocks & quivering trees & billowy lakes
And search the fibres of the inner caves & they
Shall answer: for our song is of the Clouds
And the wind loves them, and the gentle gales
Love them, and every idle breeze in heaven
Bends to that favorite burthen; and the Sun
That is the daily source of joyous thought
And Type of Man's far darting reason, He
Who therefore was esteemed in antient times
The God of verse, and stood before mens eyes
A blazing intellectual Deity
Loves his own glory in their looks, the Sun
Showers on that unsubstantial Brotherhood
A vision of beatitude & light.

[DC MS. 65, 7r] *[To the Clouds]*

74 Shall be our hand of music! it shall sweep
75 The rocks & quivering trees & billowy lake,
& search
76 And search the fibres of the inner caves & they
77 Shall answer: for our Song is of the Clouds
78 And the Wind loves them, and the gentle gales
79 Love them, and every idle breeze in heav'n
80 Bends to that favorite burthen; and the Sun
81 (That is the daily source of joyous thought
{M
82 And Type of {man's far darting reason, He
83 Who therefore was esteemed in antient times
84 The God of Verse, and stood before men's
sight
~~eyes~~
85 A blazing intellectual Deity)
86 Loves his own glory in their looks, the Sun
87 Showers on that unsubstantial Brotherhood
88 A Vision of beatitude & light.

---

The fair copy of *To the Clouds* begun on 3r ends here.

~~Army of~~ Ye ye winged Powers that
~~Legions~~ of Clouds ~~army of~~ [illegible]
Ye Clouds [illegible] like [illegible] host
~~Ascending~~ from behind the motionless brow
Of yon tall rock as from an ~~hidden~~ unknown world
O whither hurrying with such eager ~~flight~~ speed ?
~~[illegible] What seek ye wings~~
in ~~What seek~~ ye, ~~or what~~ shun ye? Of the Powers ~~gale~~
Companions fear ye to be left behind?
Or racing o'er the blue etherial field
Contend ye with each other? Of the Sea
Children, thus post ye over vale & height
~~Each panting for the foremost place to sink~~
To sink Upon your ~~[illegible]~~ Mother's joyous lap?
Or rightlier were ye named when first mine eyes
I lifted; for ye still are sweeping on
Like a wide army in impetuous march,
Or like a never-ending flight of birds
Aerial, upon due migration bound
To milder climes. Or rather do ye urge
In caravan your hasty pilgrimage
~~With hope to pause at last upon the tops~~
To pause at last on more aspiring heights
~~Of some remoter mountains more beloved~~
Than these & utter your devotion there
With thunderous voice? Or are ye jubilant
And would ye tracking your proud lord the Sun

[DC MS. 65, 8r] [*To the Clouds*]

{Y
{ye Ye winged Powers that
~~Army of~~ ~~in~~ mount
1 ~~*Legions of*~~ *Clouds* ~~*army of Earth & Air*~~
{C Host
Ye {clouds in squadrons like a winged
In Army
2 ~~*Ascending*~~ *from behind the motionless brow*
{R n} unknown
3 *Of yon tall* {*rock as from a* }~~*hidden*~~ *world*
speed
4 *O whither hurrying with such eager* ~~*flight?*~~
~~*Still still they mount—what seek ye winged*~~
{ ~~*What seek ye, or what*~~ } {O ~~*Powers*~~
5 in {~~*Winged Powers what seek*~~} ~~*shun ye?*~~ {~~*of the gale*~~
Wind
6 *Companions fear ye to be left behind,*
7 *Or racing oer the blue etherial field*
8 *Contend ye with each other. Of the Sea*
9 *Children, thus post ye over Vale & height*
~~*Each panting for the foremost place to sink*~~
To sink
10 *Upon your* ~~*distant*~~ *Mother's joyous lap?*
{ier
11 *Or rightl*{*y were ye named when first mine*
*eyes*
*I lifted; for ye still are sweeping on*
*Like a wide army in impetuous march,*
*Or like a never-ending flight of birds*
18 *Aerial, upon due migration bound*
19 *To milder climes. Or rather do ye urge*
20 *In caravan your hasty pilgrimage*
~~*With hope to pause at last upon the tops*~~
21 To pause at last on more aspiring Heights
~~*Of some remoter mountains more beloved*~~
22 *Than these & utter your devotion there*
{O
23 *With thunderous voice?* {*or are ye Jubilant*
24 *And would ye tracking your proud lord the*
*Sun*

---

The fair copy beginning on this page is in the hand of MW. At the top of 7v, facing, WW drafted two lines in pencil, related to revision of ll. 1–2:

[?Compact] of sublest elements unfit
aught
[ ? ] aught be deemed for ~~conflicts~~ &
~~[ ? ] or for strife~~
and [?friendly] [ ? ]

1 Revisions above the line, except for "{Y {ye" and "in" (which presumably signals restoration of canceled text) are in pencil; the first words in the line are canceled in pencil and ink, the last phrase in pencil.

2 Revision and cancellation are in pencil.

5 Canceled in ink and in pencil.

Be present at his setting or the pomp
Of Indian mornings would ye fill [illegible]
Thronging like Cherubim what time they cower
Before the insufferable throne of light
With wings advanced to veil their [illegible] eyes
O whence ye clouds this eagerness of speed
Speak, silent Creatures! They are gone are fled
Are fled All buried in yon mighty mass of gloom
That loads the middle heaven, & clear & bright
And vacant doth the region of the East
Appear, a calm descent of sky that leads
Down to that unapproachable abyss
From which they rose [illegible] gulph
Down to that hidden gulph from which they rose
To vanish fleet as days & months & years
Fleet as the Generations of mankind
[illegible] glory empire as the world itself
The lingering world when time hath ceased to be.
But the winds roar & toss the rooted trees
And lo! the [illegible] renewed behold
and see [illegible]
Another bright precursor to a train
Perchance as numerous overspreads the rock
That sullenly refuses to partake
Of the wild impulse from a fount of life
Invisible the long procession streams

[DC MS. 65, 9v] [*To the Clouds*]

25 *Be present at his setting or the pomp*
or speak
26 *Of Indian mornings would ye fill ~~& stand~~*
serve
*~~Thronging like Cherubim what time they cower~~*
out
With cowering wings before the
*~~Before the insufferable Throne of light~~*
And
*~~With wings advanced to veil their timid eyes~~*
29 *~~O whence ye clouds this eagerness of speed~~*
?} {T
30 *Speak, silent Creatures* } {*they are gone*—*are fled*
{*A*
31 *~~All fled~~* {*all buried in yon mighty mass of*
*gloom*
32 *That loads the middle heaven, & clear & bright*
33 *And vacant doth the region of the East*
{ea}
34 *Appear; a calm descent of sky that l*{*oa*}*ds*
35 *Down to that unapproachable abyss*
gulph
*~~From which they rose to be~~*
36 *Down to that hidden ~~world~~ from which they rose*
37 *To vanish fleet as days & months & years*
38 Fleet as the generations of mankind
39 *~~Life~~ glory empire as the world itself*
Power
[?lands] Time
40 *The lingering world when ~~it~~ hath ceased to be.*
{s {r
41 *But the wind*{ *roa*{*rs & toss the rooted trees*
*~~And lo! the pageant is renewed behold~~*
And see a
42 *~~Another~~ bright precursor to a train*
43 *Perchance as numerous overpeers the rock*
44 *That sullenly refuses to partake*
.} {F
45 *Of the wild impulse,*} {*from a fount of life*
46 *Invisible the long procession streams*

---

8v and 9r were left blank, probably inadvertently.

26/29 Revisions are in pencil, as is the signal "out"; all three lines are canceled in ink, and "Before the insufferable" and "With" are also canceled in pencil.

35/36 The word "gulph" replaces "world" in l. 36.

39/40 The conjectural word is in pencil.

A rapid multitude of glorious shapes
Glorious or darksome welcome to the vale
Which they are entering welcome to mine eye
That sees them to my soul that owns in them
And in the bosom of the firmament
Wherein they move by which they are contained
A type of her capacious self & all
Her restless progeny. A humble walk
[illegible]
Here is my body doomed to tread this path
A little hoary line & faintly traced
Work shall I call it of the shepherd's ~~[illegible]~~ foot
Or of his ~~sheep~~ flock joint vestige of them both
I pace it unrepining for my thoughts
~~[illegible]~~
~~[illegible]~~
~~[illegible]~~
~~[illegible]~~
Admit no bondage and my words have wings
Where is the Orphean lyre or Druid harp
To accompany the verse? the mountain blast
Shall be our hand of music; he shall sweep
The rocks & quivering trees & billowy lake
And search the fibres of the caves, & they
Shall answer; for our song is of the clouds

[DC MS. 65, 10r] [*To the Clouds*]

*A rapid multitude of glorious shapes*
*e*
*Glorious or darksom* { *welcome to the Vale*
*Which they are entering welcome to mine eye*
*That sees them to my Soul that owns in them*
*And in the bosom of the firmament* ~~*by*~~
*Wherein they move by which they are contained*
*A type of her capacious self & all*
*Her restless progeny.*
*A humble walk*
Immortal, with [ ? ? ? ]
*Here is my body doomed to tread this path*
*A little hoary line & faintly traced* {t
foo{d
*Work shall I call it of the Shepherd's* ~~*flock*~~
flock
*Or of his* ~~*Sheep*~~ *joint vestige of them both*
*I pace it unrepining for my thoughts*
~~walk~~ native
*See* ~~*what they will & thro' their own wide*~~ *world*
~~Go with the perfect freedom that is theirs~~
~~*Go whatsoever errand they may chuse*~~
Prompting the [ ? ? ? ]
~~*Swifter ye travellers of the sky than years*~~—
Admit no bondage and my words have wings
Harp
*Where is the Orphean Lyre or Druid*~~*s*~~ ~~*Song*~~
*To accompany the verse? the mountain blast*
*Shall be our* <u>*hand*</u> *of music; he shall sweep*
*The rocks & quivering trees & billowy Lake*
*And search the fibres of the caves, &* <u>*they*</u>
*Shall answer; for our Song is of the clouds*

---

50 Deletion by erasure.

53/54 In pencil.

58/60 The words "walk" and "native" are in pencil, as are the deletion stroke through "own wide" and the revision line beginning "Prompting the."

60 The "s" is canceled in pencil.

62 The word "hand" is underlined in ink and in pencil.

And the [illegible] loves them & the gentle gales
Which by their aged [illegible]
Whose office is to clothe the naked lawn
With annual verdure & revive the woods
And moisten the parched lips to thirsty flowers
Love them; & every idle breeze in heaven
Bends to that favourite burthen. Moon & Stars
Keep their most solemn vigils when the clouds
Watch also changing peaceably their place
Like bands of ministering Spirits, [illegible] or when they lie
[illegible]
[illegible] from hour to hour
Dispersed in island quiet. O ye Lightnings
Ye are their perilous offspring; & the Sun
[illegible] Source of [illegible]
And type of Man's far-darting reason, he
Who therefore was esteemed in ancient times
The God of verse & stood before men's sight
A blazing intellectual Deity, loves
Loves his own glory in their looks; the Sun
Showers on that unsubstantial Brotherhood
A vision of beatitude & light.

And showers

Not without due regard [illegible]
Showers on that unsubstantial Brother[illegible]
[illegible] with beatific light

[DC MS. 65, 10v] [*To the Clouds*]

{es
66 *And the wind lov{s them & the gentle gales*
67 Which by their aid ~~refresh~~ the witherd
revive
~~*Whose office is to clothe the naked*~~ *lawn*
68 ~~*With annual verdure & revive the woods*~~
of
69 *And moisten the parched lips* ~~*with*~~ *thirsty flowers*
in
70 *Love them; & every idle breeze* ~~*of*~~ *heaven*
{—.
71 *Bends to that favourite burthen{. Moon & Stars*
72 *Keep their most solemn vigils when the clouds*
*changing*
73 *Watch also* ~~*varying*~~ *peaceably their place*
bands of ~~when they, dispers'd~~
74 *Like ministering Spirits* ~~*or from hour to hour*~~
or when they lie
{[?Slumbering]
{~~[*?Dispers'd*] *along the blue etherial*~~ *deep*
Blank forms and listless through the azure
deep
~~Along the etherial deep,~~ from hour to hour
Dispers'd
~~Slumber~~, in island quiet. O ye Lightnings
79 *Ye are their perilous offspring & the Sun*
S{ inexhaustible of life & joy
80 ~~*That is the daily*~~ *s{ource of* ~~*joyous thought*~~
81 *And Type of Man's far-darting reason, He*
*Who, therefore, was esteemed in ancient times*
*The God of verse, & stood before Men's sight*
83 *A blazing intellectual Deity,* loves
reflect
*Loves his own glory in their looks; the Sun*
*Showers on that unsubstantial Brotherhood*
*A vision of beatitude & light!*
and showers
{to human
Not with out due regard {[ ? ? ] kind
Shower on that unsubstantial Brother
Visions enriched with beatific light

---

74 The cancellation above the line is in pencil; "or from" is canceled in pencil, and the entire phrase "or from hour to hour" is canceled in ink.

83 Revisions of this and the following line are in pencil. Two lines farther on, MW's fair-copy transcription stops.

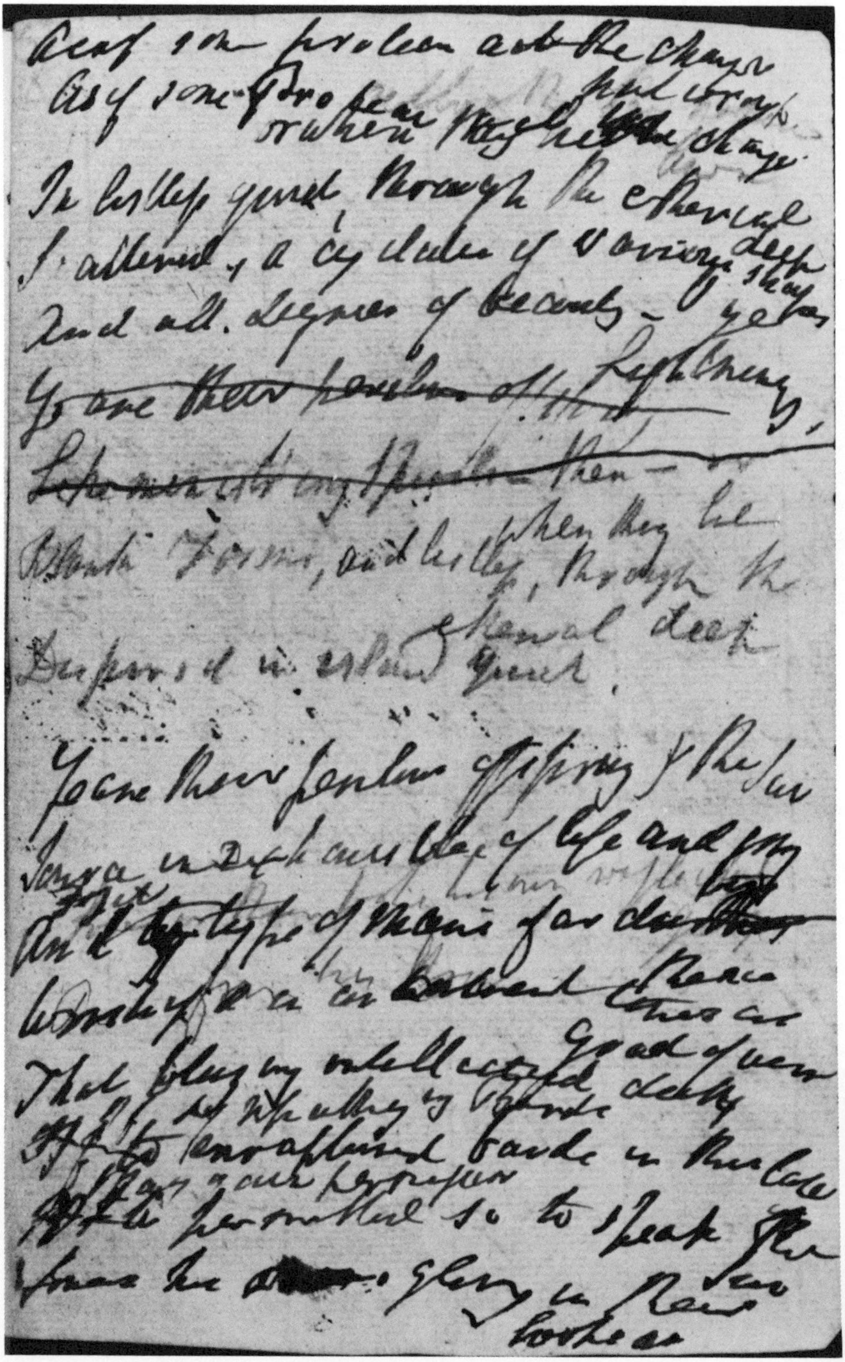

[DC MS. 65, 11r] [*To the Clouds*]

Asif some protean act the change 1
had wrought
[ ? ? ? ] 2
As if some Protean act the change 3
[ ? ]
or when they lie 4
In listless quiet, through the etherial 5
deep
So altered, a cyclades of various shapes 6
And all degrees of beauty—O ye 7
Lightnings,
~~Ye are their perilous offspring~~ 8

~~Like minist'ring Spirits—then—or~~ 9
when they lie
Blank Forms, and listless, through the 10
etherial deep
Dispersd in island quiet. 11

Ye are their perilous offspring & the Sun 12
Source inexhaustible of life and joy 13
Sees in their looks his own reflected 14
F glory
Fit [?]
And ~~ty~~ type of man's far ~~darting~~ 15
thence
And from his throne 16
Worship'd in an antient times as 17
Good of verse
That blazing intellectual deity 18
If sympathizing Bards 19
~~Iffto~~ enraptured bards in this late 20
May gain permission 21
It be permitted so to speak the 22
Sun
Loves his own glory in their 23
looks an

---

Drafting on this page continues revision of ll. 74–84 begun on 10v, and leads to further work on 11v. The lines have been numbered serially for ease of reference; ll. 2, 9–11, 14, and 16 are in pencil.

20–23 These lines are reworked at the foot of 11v.

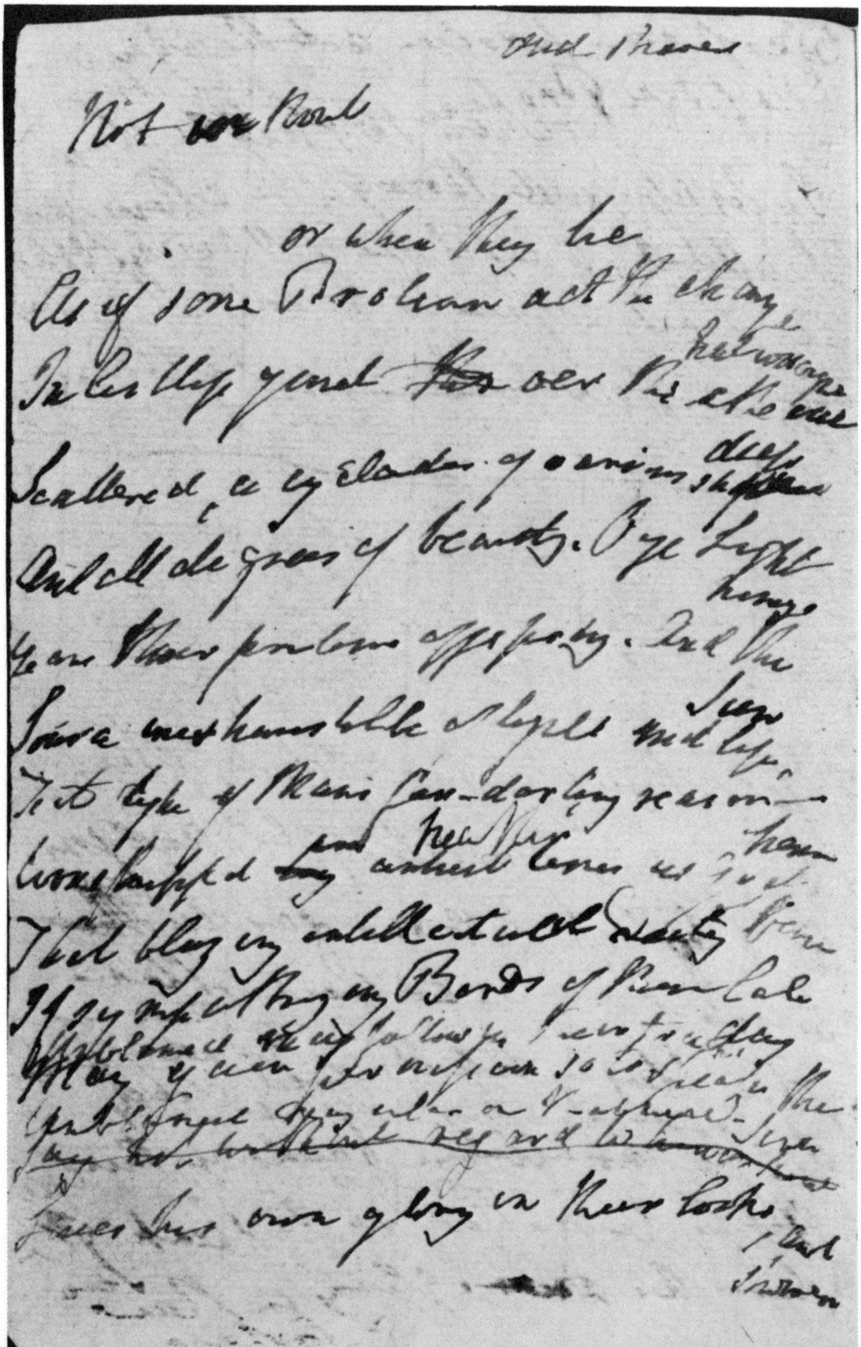

[DC MS. 65, 11^v^] [*To the Clouds*]

and showers
Not without

or when they lie
75 As if some Protean act the change
had wrought
76 In listless quiet ~~thr~~ oer the etherial
deep
{ apes
77 Scattered, a cyclades of various sh{[ ? ]
78 And all degrees of beauty. O ye Light
nings
Ye are their perilous offspring. And the
Sun
Source inexhaustible of light and life,
Fit type of Man's far-darting reason—
hence
in heathen
Worshippd ~~by~~ antient times as God
of Verse
That blazing intellectual Deity
If sympathizing Bards of their late
day
Unblamed may follow in their tracks
May gain permission so to speak the
Sun
Unblamed may enter on [ ? ? ]
~~Say not without regard to human kind~~
84 Loves his own glory in their looks, and
showers

---

Work on this page develops drafting on 11^r^.

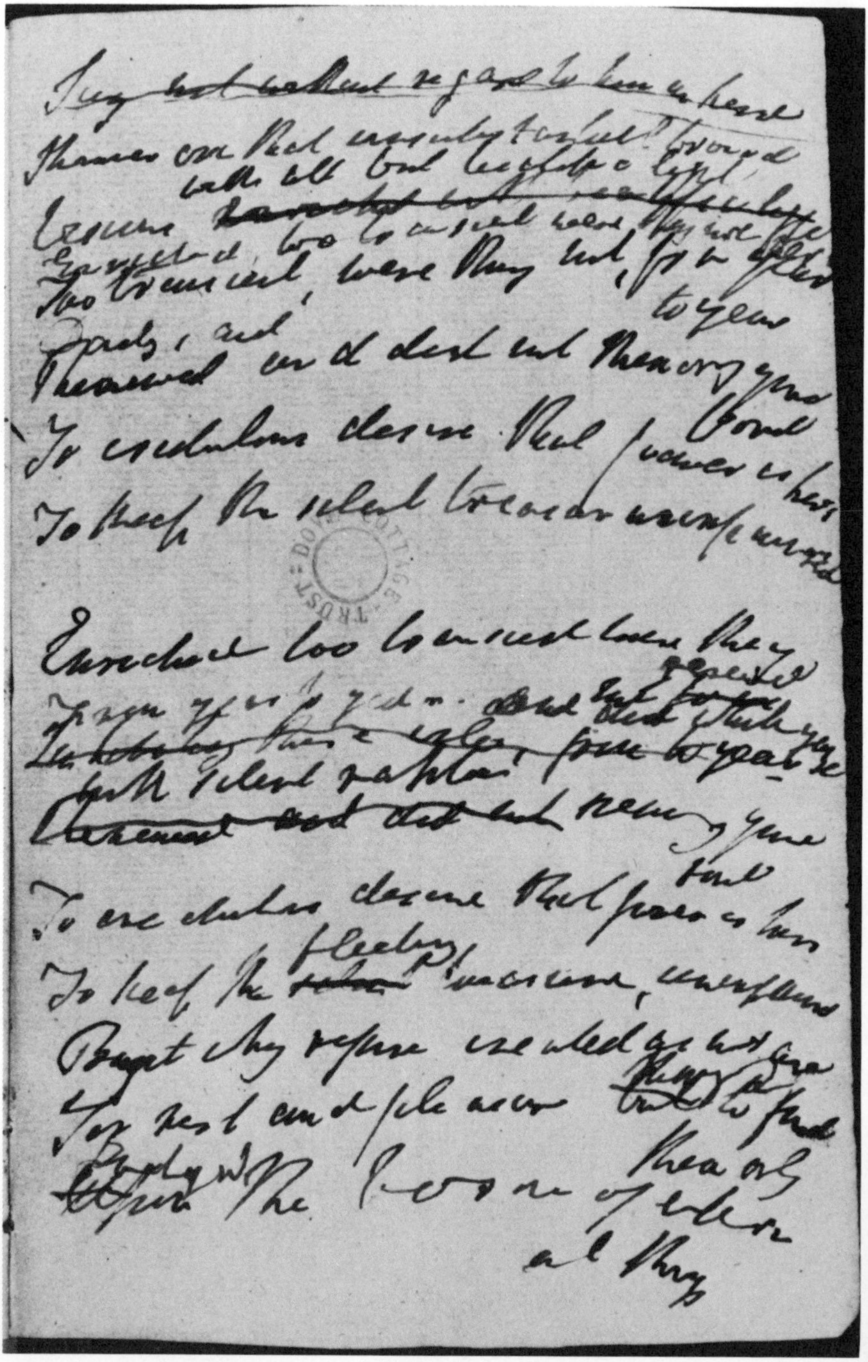

[DC MS. 65, 12r] [*To the Clouds*]

~~Say not without regard to human kind~~
Shower on that unsubstantial bro[?]d
with all but beatific light
Visions ~~enrichd with beatific light~~
Enrichd, too transient were they not renewd
Too transient, were they not, from year
to year
Daily, and
Renewed and did not Memory give
bond
To credulous desire. Real power is here
To keep the silent treasure unimpaired

87 Enriched too transient were they
renewd
{a not ~~free~~
88 From year to year {dnd did while gaze
~~In liberty these vales, from to~~ year
89 With silent rapture
~~Renewed and did not~~ memory give
soul
To credulous desire Real power is here
fleeting
91 To keep the ~~silent~~ treasure, unimpaired
Bu}
92 Ye}t why repine created as we are
though
93 For rest and pleasure ~~but~~ to find
them only
Lodged
94 ~~Up~~on the bosom of etern
al things

---

Drafting on this page continues from the foot of 11v; 12v–29r are blank.

Legions of Clouds, Armies of Earth and Air
Ascending from behind the motionless brow
Of yon tall Rock, as from a hidden world
O whither hurrying with such eager flight
Still—while they mount. What seek ye, flying,
What seek ye or what shun ye? of Power
Companions fear ye to be left behind
Or racing on your blue etherial field
Contend ye with each other? of the Sea
Children, thus post ye over Vale and Height
To sink upon your mother's joyous lap?
Or were ye rightlier hailed when first
were lifted, for ye still are sweeping on
Like a wide Army in impetuous march
Or like a never-ending flight of Birds

[DC MS. 65, 113v] [*To the Clouds*]

      {A
1 Legions of Clouds, Army of Earth and {air
2 Ascending from behind the motionless brow
3 Of yon tall Rock, as from a hidden world
4 O whithir hurrying with such eager flight?
Still—still they mount. What seek ye, winged
                    Powers,
5 What seek ye or what shun Ye? of the Gale
6 Companions fear ye to be left behind,
7 Or racing on your blue etherial Field
8 Contend ye with each other? Of the Sea
9 Children, thus post ye over Vale and
   {u                    Height
10 To~~s~~ sink {ypon your Mother's joyous lap?
          were Ye
11 Or ~~were Ye~~ rightlier hailed when first
                    mine eyes
Were lifted, for ye still are sweeping on
Like a wide Army in impetuous march
Or like a never-ending Flight of Birds

---

The fair copy of *To the Clouds* begun on this page is intermediate between those that start on 3r and on 8r. Leaves 114–116, which may have contained more of the fair copy, have been cut or torn away. In l. 10, the "s" has been deleted by erasure.

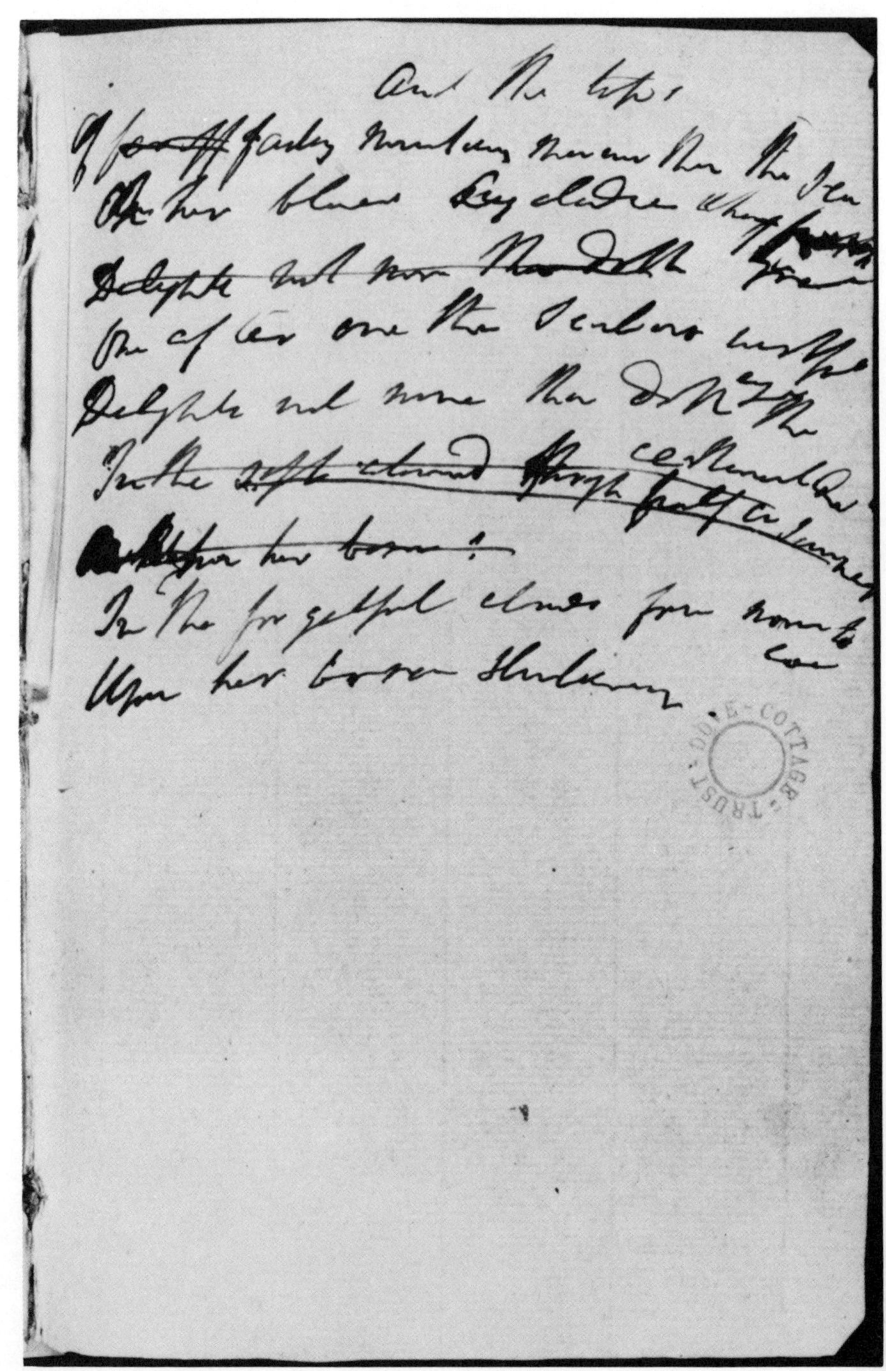
DOVE-COTTAGE-TRUST

[DC MS. 65, 117$^{r}$] [*To the Clouds*]

And the tops
Of ~~far off~~ [?fading] mountains [ ? ] than the Sea
{On {Cy
{An her blue {suclades [ ? ? ]
[ ? ]
~~Delights not more than doth~~
One after one the Sailors wistful
eye
Delights not more than doth the
aetherial [ ? ]
~~In the soft cloud through half a summer~~
~~A Upon her bosom s~~
In the forgetful climes from noon to
eve
Upon her bosom slumbering.

---

Drafting on this page, related to ll. 74/79 on 10$^{v}$, probably faced *To the Clouds* work on 116$^{v}$, now missing. Leaves 117$^{v}$–118$^{r}$ are blank.

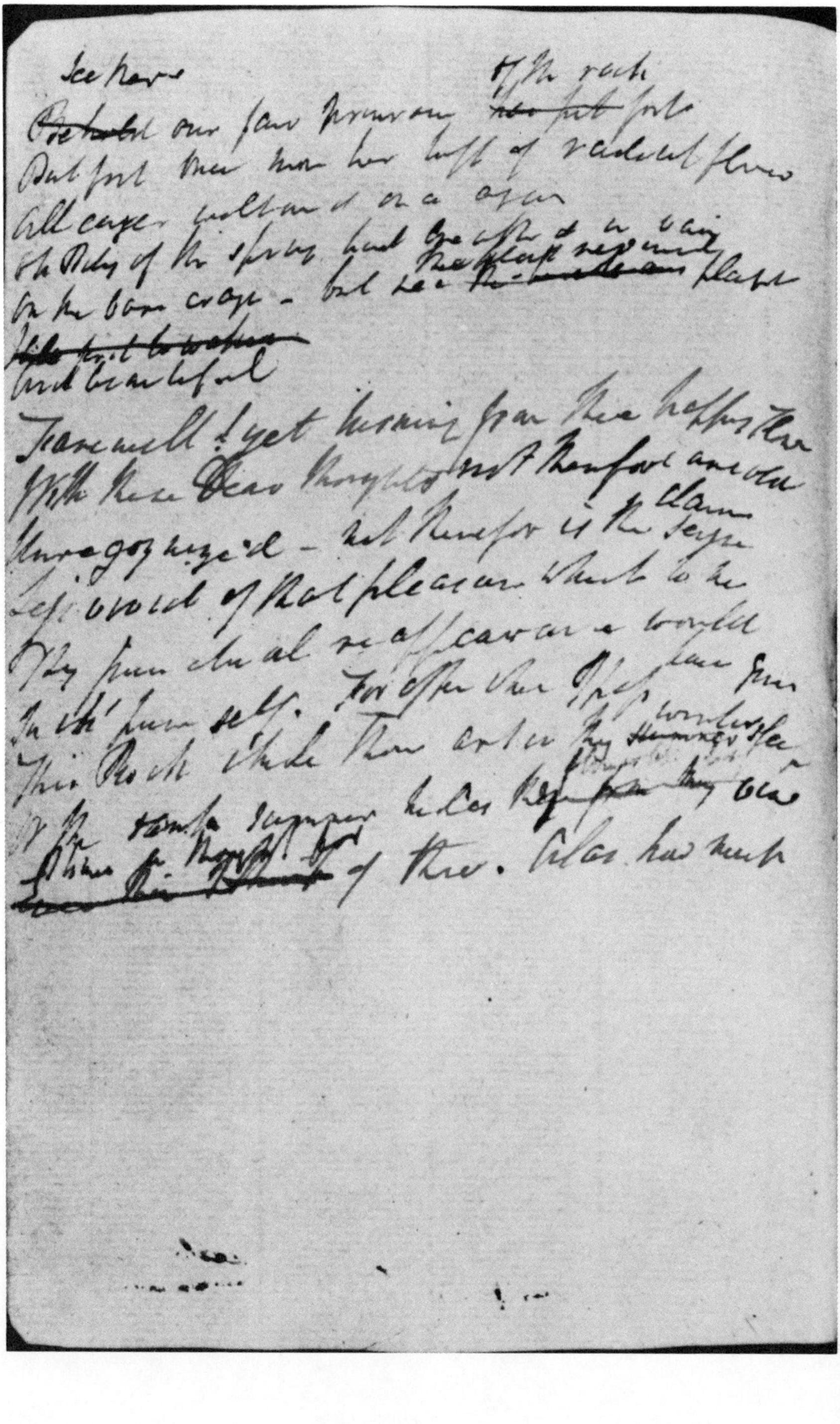

[DC MS. 65, 29v] [*The Tuft of Primroses*]

    See how                         of the rock
~~Behold~~ our fair primrose ~~has put~~ fort
Put fort once more her tuft of radiant flowers
All eager welcomd once again
Oh Pity if the spring had breathd in vain
                                the plant revives
On the bare crags—but see ~~the beauteous~~ plant
~~Still first to waken~~
And beautiful

62 Farewell! yet turning from thee happy Flower
63 With these Dear thoughts not therefore are old
                                        claims
64 Unregoznized—not therefor is the sense
65 Less vivid of that pleasure which to me
66 Thy punctual reappearance would
                                have given
67 In its' pure self. For often when I pass
                                winter
68 This Rock while Thou art in thy ~~summer~~ sleep
                                {y flower-like leaf
69 Or the rank summer hides th~~ee from my~~ view
    I have a thought for
70 ~~Even then I think~~ of thee. Alas how much

---

The rough recasting of *The Tuft of Primroses,* ll. 1–8, at the top of the page reflects WW's aborted intention (carried out in revisions of ll. 7, 9, 11, 14, 19) to drop his direct address to the primrose and refer to it, instead, in the third person.

62–70 These lines are the latest and longest revision of the passage first entered at the foot of 32r and the top of 33r and revised on 32v and then on 30v. Except for the deletions and revisions in ll. 69–70, the ink used here is the same as that used on 30v and different from that used on 32v.

The Tuft of Primroses

Once more I welcome Thee, and Thou, fair Plant
Fair Primrose hast put forth thy radiant flowers
All eager to be welcomed once again
O pity if the faithful Spring beguiled
By her accustomed hopes had come to breathe
Upon the bosom of this barren crag
And found ~~thee~~ her not; but ~~Thou art~~ there,
revived,
And beautiful as ever like a Queen
Smiling from ~~thy~~ her imperishable throne.
And so shalt keep for ages yet untold
Frail as Thou art if the prophetic Muse
Be rightly trusted, so shalt Thou maintain
Conspicuously thy solitary state
In splendour unimpaired. For ~~Thou~~ thou art safe
From most adventurous bound of mountain sheep
By keenest hunger pressed from approach
Of the wild Goat still bolder, nor more
~~Through sheltering on thy bare and~~ [illegible]
Though in that [illegible] ~~upright rock~~ [illegible]

[DC MS. 65, 30r] [*The Tuft of Primroses*]

The Tuft of Primroses

1 Once more I welcome Thee, and Thou, fair Plant
2 Fair Primrose hast put forth thy radiant Flowers
Flowers
3 All eager to be welcomed once again
4 O pity if the faithful Spring beguiled
5 By her accustomed hopes had come to breathe
6 Upon the bosom of this barren crag
her here she is she
7 And found ~~thee~~ not; but ~~Thou art~~ here,
reviv'd,
8 And beautiful as ever like a Queen
her
9 Smiling from ~~thy~~ imperishable throne
10 And so shalt keep for ages yet untold
she is
11 Frail as Thou art if the prophetic Muse
s}
12 Be rightly trusted, so ſthalt Thou maintain
13 Conspicuously thy solitary state
she is
14 In splendour unimpaired. For ~~Thou~~ art safe
15 From most adventurous bound of mountain sheep
16 By keenest hunger press'd & from approach
17 Of the wild Goat still bolder, nor more
cause
~~Thron'd midway on this bare and~~
18 Though in that sunny & obtrusive [?seat]
crag
~~upright rock~~

---

2 "Flowers" was first crowded in at the end of the line, then rewritten beneath it.
18 Entry of this line may be related to the cancellation of a similar line at ll. 30/31 on 31r.

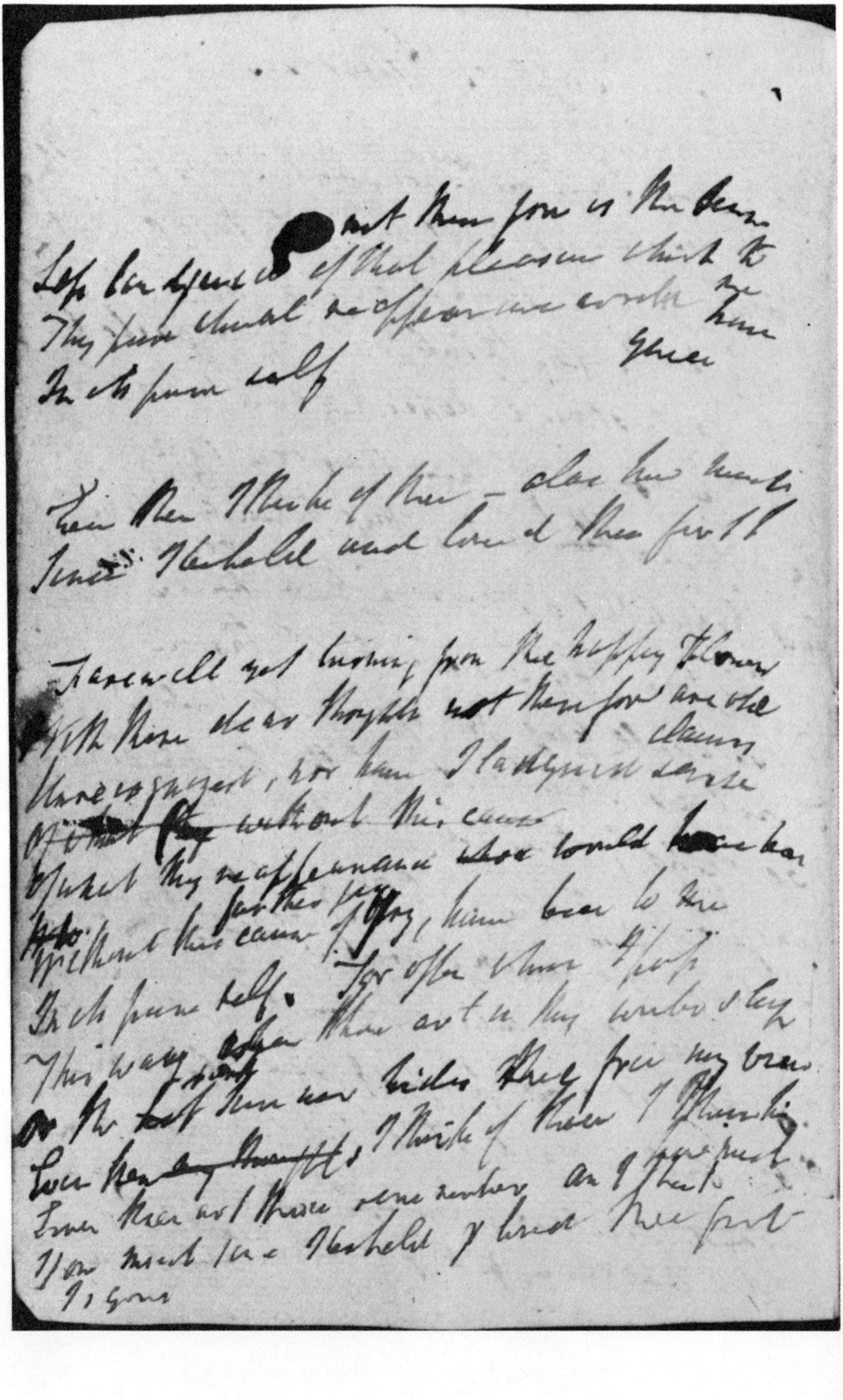

[DC MS. 65, 30$^{v}$] [*The Tuft of Primroses*]

not therefore is the Sense
Less languid of that pleasure which to
me
Thy punctual reappearance would have
given
In its pure self

Even then I think of thee—alas how much
Since I beheld and loved thee first [?I]

{F
Farewell yet turning from thee happy {flower
With these dear thoughts not therefor are old
claims
Unrecognized, nor have I languid sense
~~Of what thy without this cause~~
Of what thy reappearance ~~whou~~ would have been
~~Who~~ further joy {J
Without this cause of {joy, have been to me
In its pure self. For often when I pass
This way, when thou art in thy winter sleep
rank
Or the ~~hot~~ Summer hides thee from my view
Even then ~~my thoughts~~ I think of thee I I think
how much
Even then art thou remember an I think
How much since I beheld & loved thee first
Is gone

---

The drafting on this page is intermediate between the successive versions of ll. 62–70 on 33$^{r}$ and 32$^{v}$ and the final version on 29$^{v}$. The ink on this page is the same as that used to enter ll. 62–70 on 29$^{v}$ and different from the ink on 32$^{v}$. The two blocks of lines at the top of the page are revisions of the block of lines at the foot of the page.

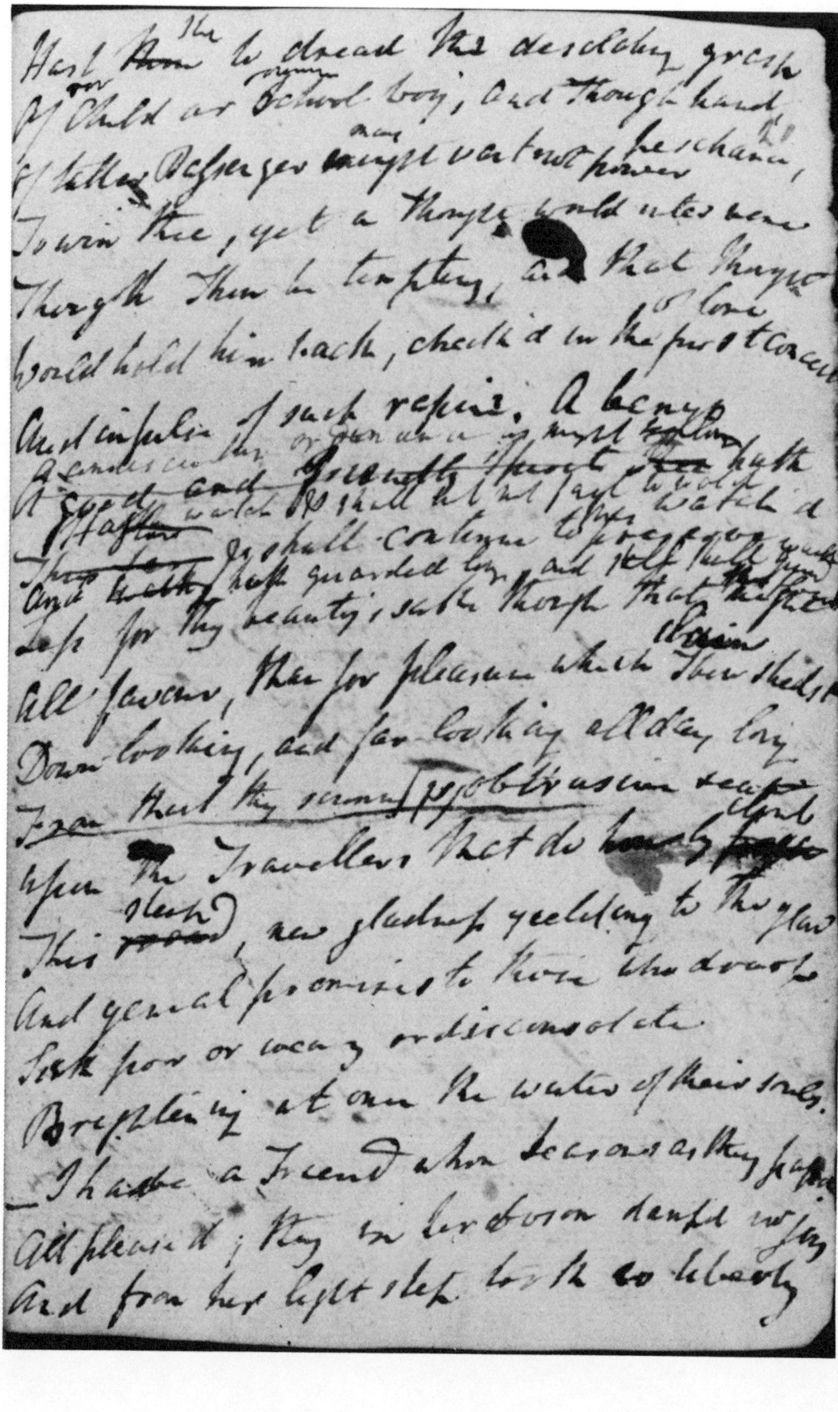

[DC MS. 65, 31r] *[The Tuft of Primroses]*

She
Hast ~~thou~~ to dread the desolating grasp
roaming
[?nor] {s {t
Of Child or {School boy, and {Though hand,
20
may perchance,
Of taller Passenger might want not power
To win thee, yet a thought would intervene
Though Thou be tempting, and that thought
of love
Would hold him back, check'd in the first conceit
And impulse of such rapine. A benign
A condescending ordonance as might [?calm]
~~A good and friendly Spirit~~ ~~Thee~~ hath
Hath watch & shall not not fail to watch
~~Stood~~ thee watch'd
~~Thus far~~, & shall continue to preserve [?watch]
And [~~?hath~~] hath guarded long and still shall guard
thy}
[?]} flowers
Less for thy beauty's sake though that might
{claim
{win
All favour, than for pleasure which Thou shedst
Down-looking, and far-looking all day long
~~From that thy sunny & obtrusive~~ seat
climb
{~~pace~~
Upon the Travellers that do hourly {~~walk~~
steep
This ~~rooad~~, new gladness yielding to the glad
And genial promises to those who droop
Sick poor or weary or disconsolate
Brightening at once the winter of their souls.
{ve {s
—I ha{d a Friend whom {Seasons as they passd
All pleased; they in her bosom dampd no joy
And from her light step took no liberty

---

The fair copy runs on from the foot of 30r.
The "20" beneath the second line at the top of the page is WW's line count to this point.
30/31 WW's cancellation of this line may be related to the entry of l. 18 on 30r, to which it is almost identical.

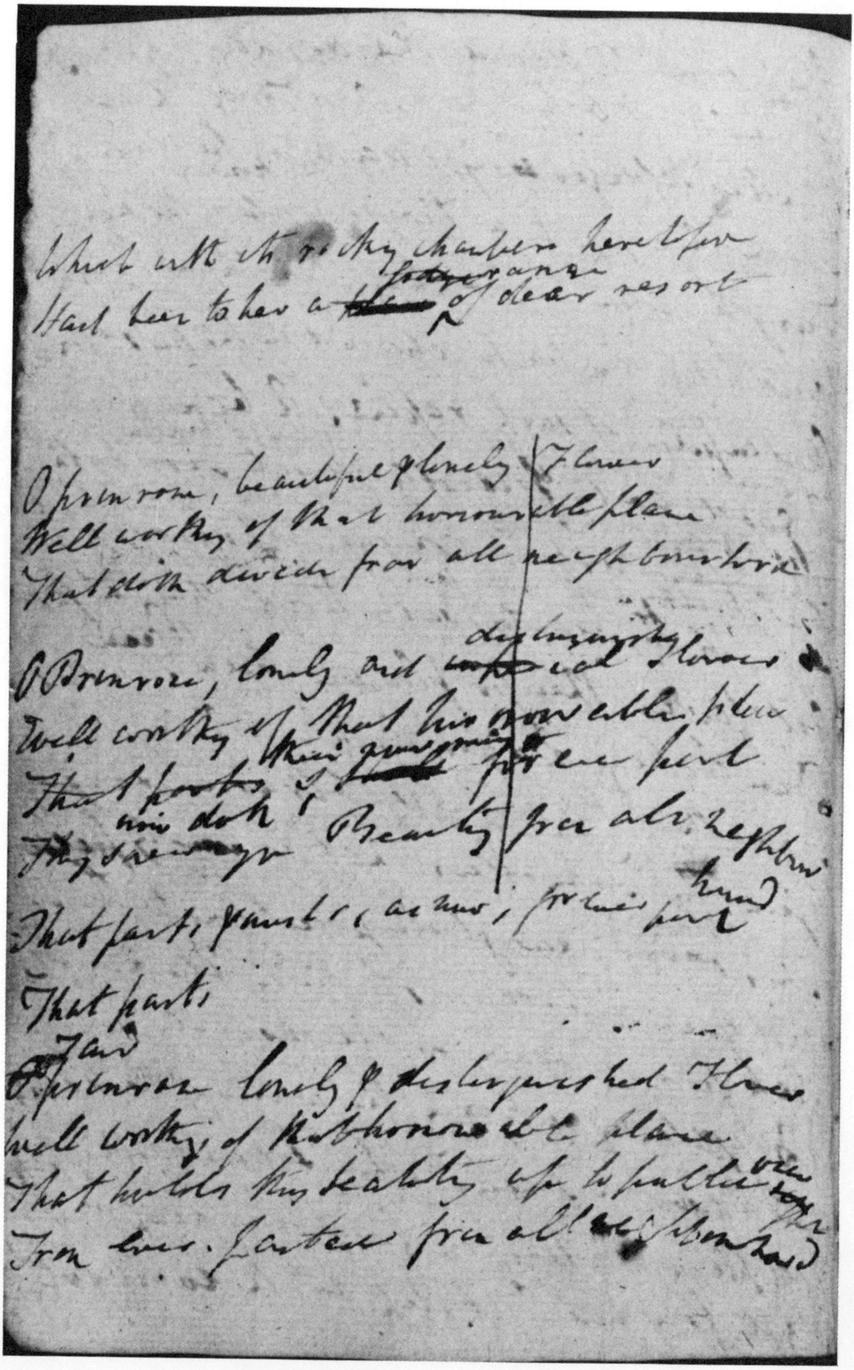

[DC MS. 65, 31ᵛ] [*The Tuft of Primroses*]

42 Which with its rocky chambers heretofore
~~lodge~~ range
43 Had been to her a ~~place~~^of dear resort

O primrose, beautiful & lonely Flower
Well worthy of that honourable place
That doth divide from all neighbourhood

distinguish
O Primrose, lonely and ~~imperial~~ Flower
Well worthy of that honourable place
their [?soverign]
~~That parts~~ & ~~shall~~ forever part
now doth
Thy soverign Beauty from all neighbour
hood
That parts & musts, as now, for ever part
That parts

Fair
48 ~~O~~ primrose lonely & distinguished Flower
49 Well worthy of that honourable place
view
50 That holds thy beauty up to public ~~sight~~
51 From ever parted from all neighbourhood

---

42–43 These lines face the point at which they are meant to be inserted on 32ʳ.

48–51 The revisions that yield this passage begin with the three-line version entered beneath ll. 42–43 at the top of the page; after redrafting on the middle of the page and interlinear revisions on 32ʳ, facing, the final version of the lines was entered at the foot of the page.

When suddenly as lightning from a cloud
Came danger with disease; came suddenly
And lingered long, and this commanding Hill
The station of her freedom, now, ~~and~~ sad change!
Was interdicted ground, a place of fear
To her, a melancholy Hill for us
Constrain'd to think of former for her sake
lovely and disregarded ye Flower
O Primrose tuft fair [illegible] of flowers
Sweet-[illegible] of that [illegible] place
And although many a time I yet and [illegible]
That [illegible] [illegible] as [illegible]
Oft in a calm course of meditative years
Oft have I hailed thee with serene delight
This greeting is far more ~~[illegible]~~ — it is the voice
Of a surpassing sorrow; of the heart [illegible]
With her own eyes shall bless thee ere
Then said
The Prisoner shall come forth shall see the tuft
And ~~fainting~~ lethargies of their sleep shall melt
Before thy mild assurances and pain
And weakness shall pass from her like a sleep
Chased by a bright glimpse of the morning sun.
Farewell! yet while I leave thee with these hopes

[DC MS. 65, 32r] [*The Tuft of Primroses*]

39 When suddenly as lightning from a cloud
40
40 Came danger with disease; came suddenly
41 And linger'd long, and this commanding Hill
~~alas~~ doom
44 The palace of her freedom, now, sad change!
45 Was interdicted ground—a place of fear
46 For her, a melancholy Hill for us
47 Constrain'd to think & ponder for her sake
lonely and distinguish'd Flower
O primrose tuft fair Sisterhood of flower
Well-worthy of that honourable place
One although many many & yet one
That parts and shall as now for ever part
Thy sover
52 ~~Oft~~ In a calm course of meditative years
53 Oft have I hail'd thee with serene delight,
far more
{ ~~far~~
54 —This greeting is { ~~[ ? ] such~~ — it is the voice
{!—}
55 Of a surpassing joyance{, S} She herself
56 With her own eyes shall bless thee ere
Thou fade
57 The Prisoner shall come forth & all the toil
sharp ascent
58 And ~~panting~~ labours of this steep shall melt
60
59 Before thy mild assurances and pain
60 And weakness shall pass from her like a
sleep
61 Chas'd by a bright glimpse of the
morning sun.
Farewell! yet while I leave thee with these
hopes

---

The fair copy runs on from the foot of 31r.

The "40" beneath the first line on the page follows from the "20" on 31r; the "60" at ll. 58/59 appears to have included ll. 42–43 and 48–51 on 31v, and if it did, it is one line off, perhaps as the result of including the uncanceled base-text line "One although many many & yet one" at the middle of this page.

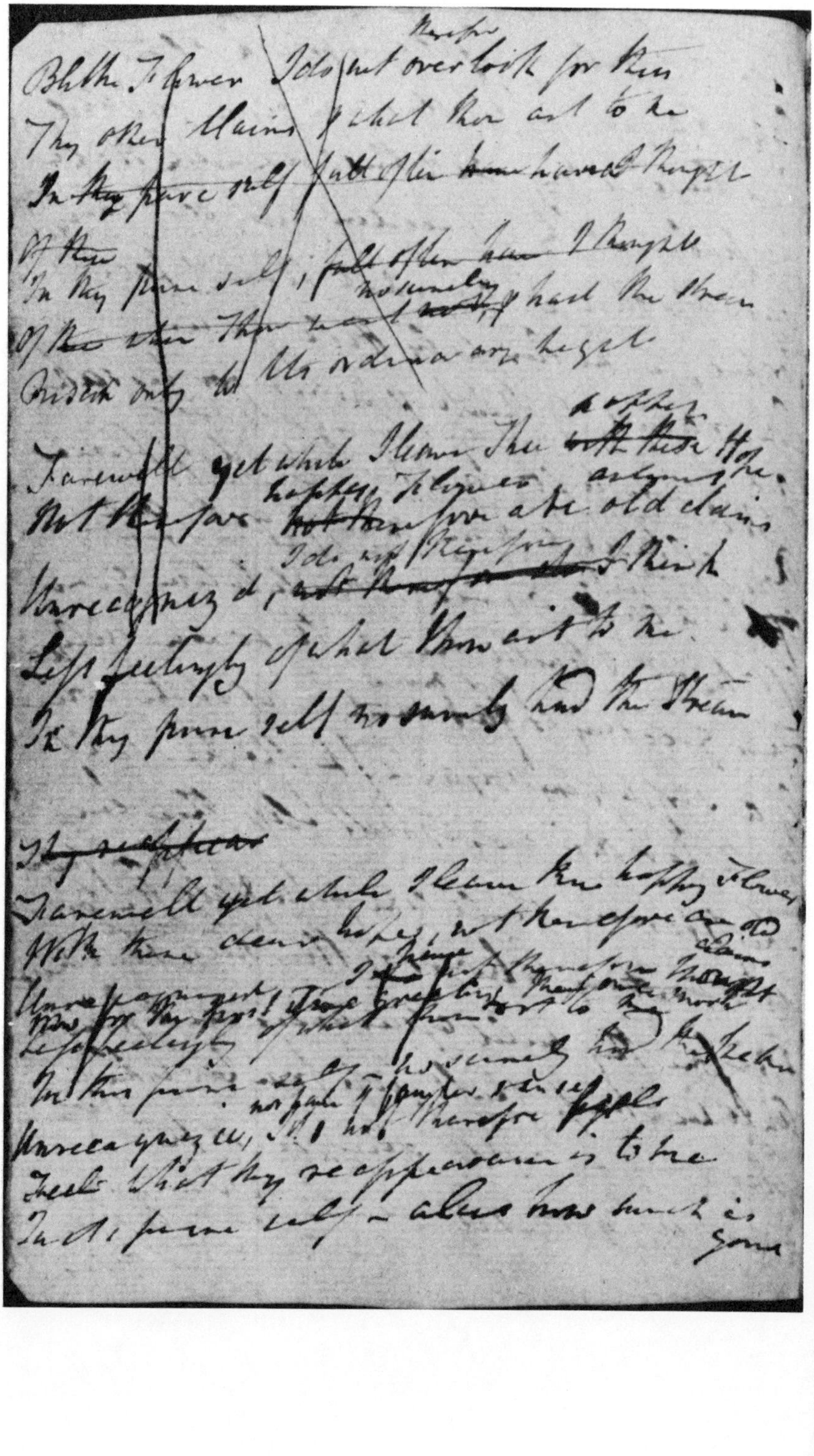

[DC MS. 65, 32v] [*The Tuft of Primroses*]

therefor
Blithe Flower I do not overlook for this
Thy other Claims & what thou art to me
I}
~~In thy pure self full often have have a} thought~~
~~Of thee~~
In thy pure self, ~~full often have I thought~~
no surely
~~Of thee when Thou wert not, &~~ had the stream
Risen only to its ordinary height

happy
Farewell yet while I leave Thee ~~with these~~ Hope
happy Flower antient
Not therefore ~~not there~~fore are old claims
I do not therefore
Unrecogniz'd, ~~not therefore do I~~ think
Less feelingly of what thou art to me
In thy pure self no surely had the Stream

~~Thy reappear~~
Farewell yet while I leave thee happy Flower
With these dear hopes, not therefore are old
claims
have {ought
Unrecognized,—I ~~do~~ not therefore th{ink
Now for the first time greeting thee once more
Less feelingly of what thou art to me
In thy pure self—no surely had the Stream
nor have I fainter sense
{feels
Unrecogniz'd, I do not therefore {less
Feels what thy reappearance is to me
In its pure self—alas how much is
gone

---

The successive versions of ll. 62–67 on this page continue revision begun at the top of 33r and lead to further drafting, in a different ink, on 30v and then to the final version of the lines, on 29v.

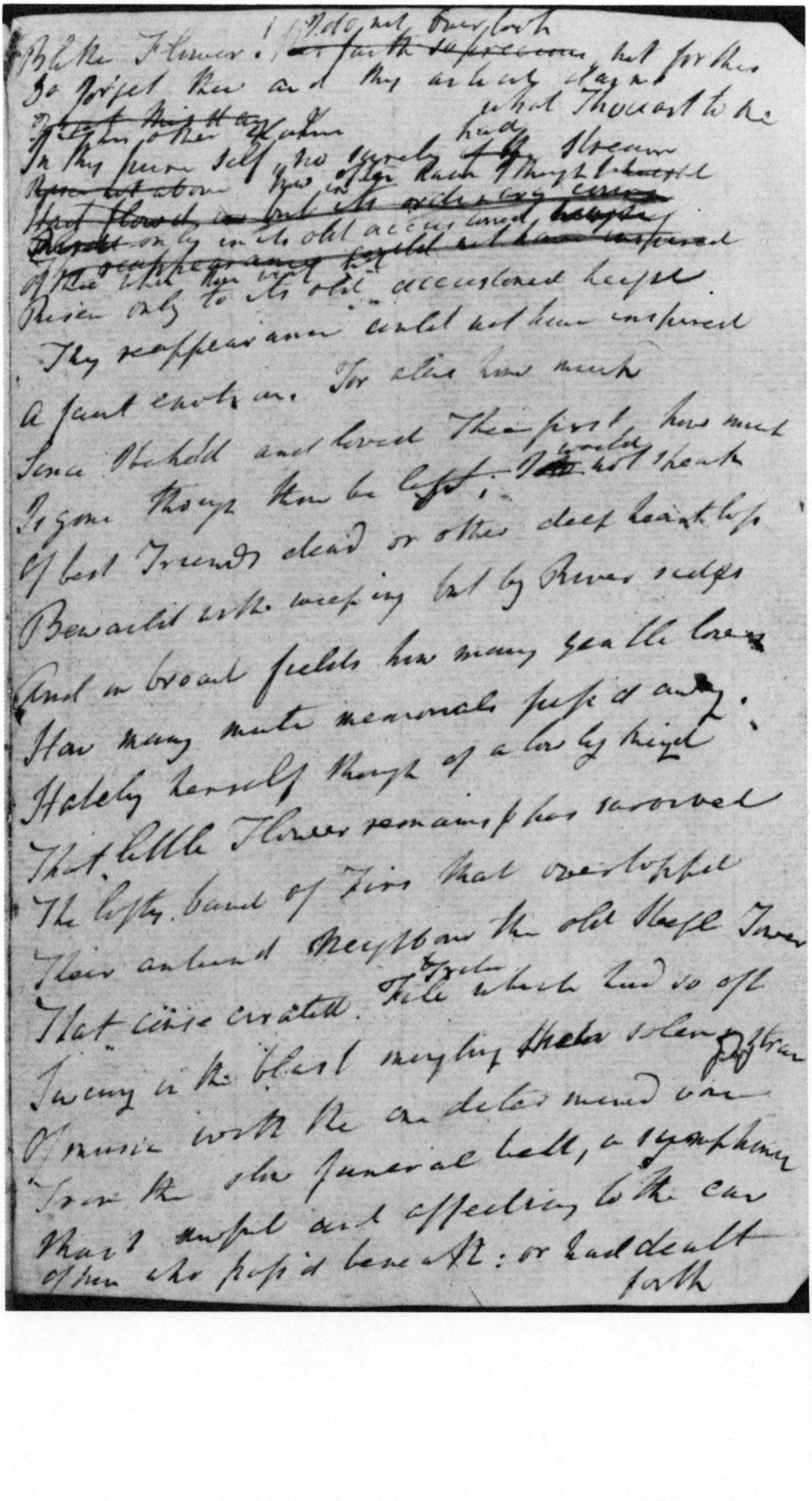

[DC MS. 65, 33r] [*The Tuft of Primroses*]

I do not overlook
Blithe Flower! ~~this faith so precious,~~ not for this
To forget thee and thy antient claims
~~Is not this day~~ & what Thou art to me
Thy other claims had
In thy pure self, no surely ~~if the~~ Stream
~~Risen not above~~ how often have I thought
in ~~height~~
~~Had flowd in but its ordinary course~~
{Risen {height
{Flowd only in its old accustomed {course
~~Thy reappearance could not have inspired~~
Of thee when thou wert not
Risen only to its old accustomed height
Thy reappearance could not have inspired
A faint emotion. For alas how much
Since I beheld and loved Thee first, how much
{ft would
Is gone though thou be le{ss; I ~~do~~ not speak
Of best Friends dead or other deep heart loss
e }
Bewail'd with weeping but by River sid[?]}s
And in broad fields how many gentle loves
How many mute memorials pass'd away.
Stately herself though of a lowly kind
That little Flower remains & has survived
The lofty band of Firs that overtoppd
Their antient Neighbour the old Steeple Tower
Train
That consecrated File which had so oft
{their
Swung in the blast mingling {a [?] solemn strain
80
Of music with the one determined voice
From the slow funeral bell, a symphony
Most awful and affecting to the ear
Of him who pass'd beneath: or had dealt
forth

---

The fair copy runs on from the foot of 32r.

Revision begun on the top half of the page is continued on 32v, facing, and, in a different ink, on 30v and 29v.

82/83 WW's count of 80 lines follows from the "60" on the preceding recto and apparently includes the five-line version of ll. 62–70 at the foot of 32v.

33v is blank.

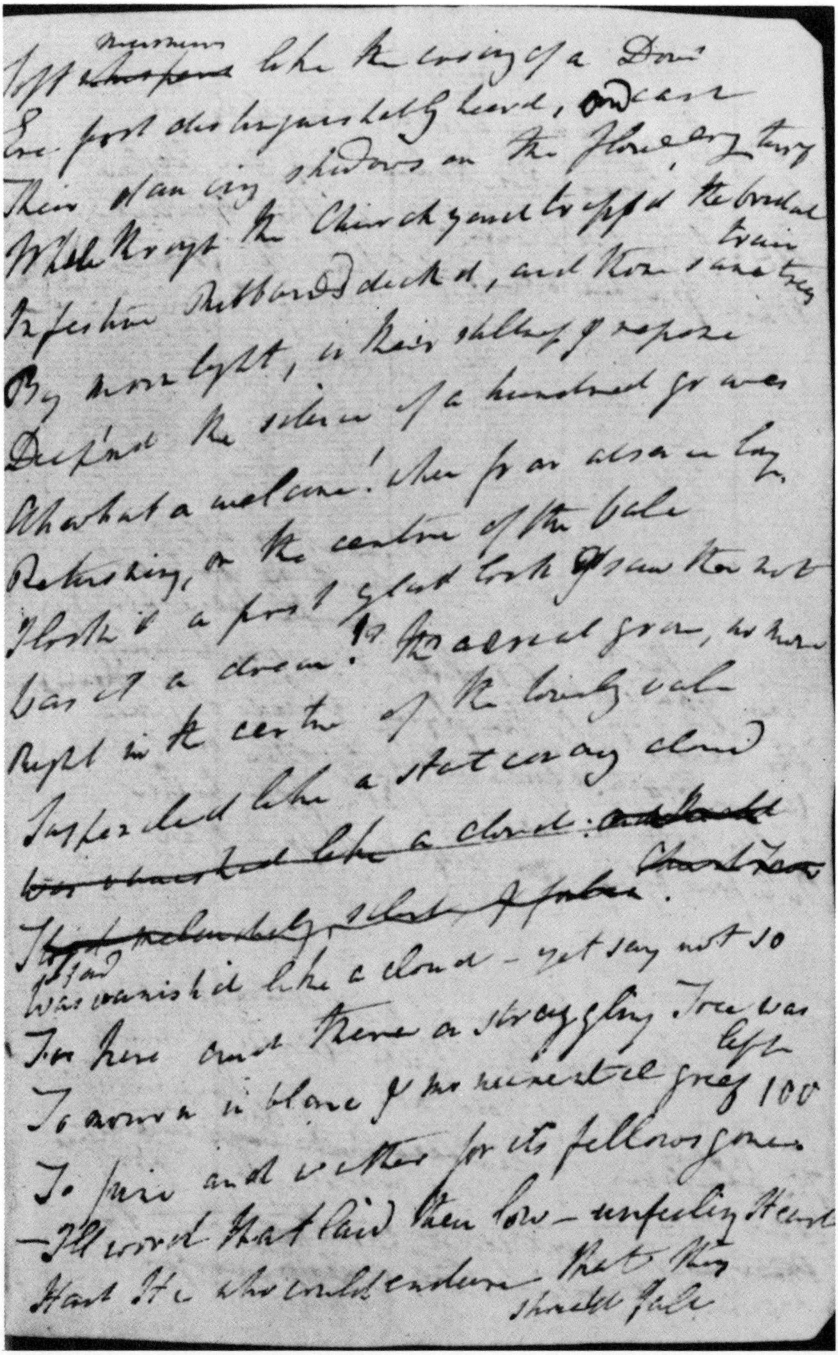

[DC MS. 65, 34r] [*The Tuft of Primroses*]

murmurs
Soft ~~whispers~~ like the cooing of a Dove
and}
Ere first distinguishably heard, or} cast
Their dancing shadows on the flowery turf
{ile
Wh{ere through the Churchyard tripp'd the bridal
train
In festive Ribbands deck'd, and those same trees
By moonlight, in their stillness & repose
Deep'nd the silence of a hundred graves
Ah what a welcome! when from absence long
Returning, on the centre of the Vale
& }
I look'd a first glad look [?I]} saw them not
!}
Was it a dream?} the aerial grove, no more
Right in the centre of the lovely vale
Suspended like a stationary cloud
~~Was vanished like a cloud: and the old~~
~~Church Tower~~
~~Stood melancholy, silent, & forlorn.~~
Had
Was vanish'd like a cloud—yet say not so
For here and there a straggling Tree was
left
To mourn in blanc & monumental grief
100
To pine and wither for its fellows gone.
—Ill word that laid them low—unfeeling Heart
Had He who could endure that they
should fall

---

The fair copy runs on from the foot of 33r.

102/103 WW's count of 100 lines, which follows from the "80" on 33r, excludes the two lines canceled on this page.

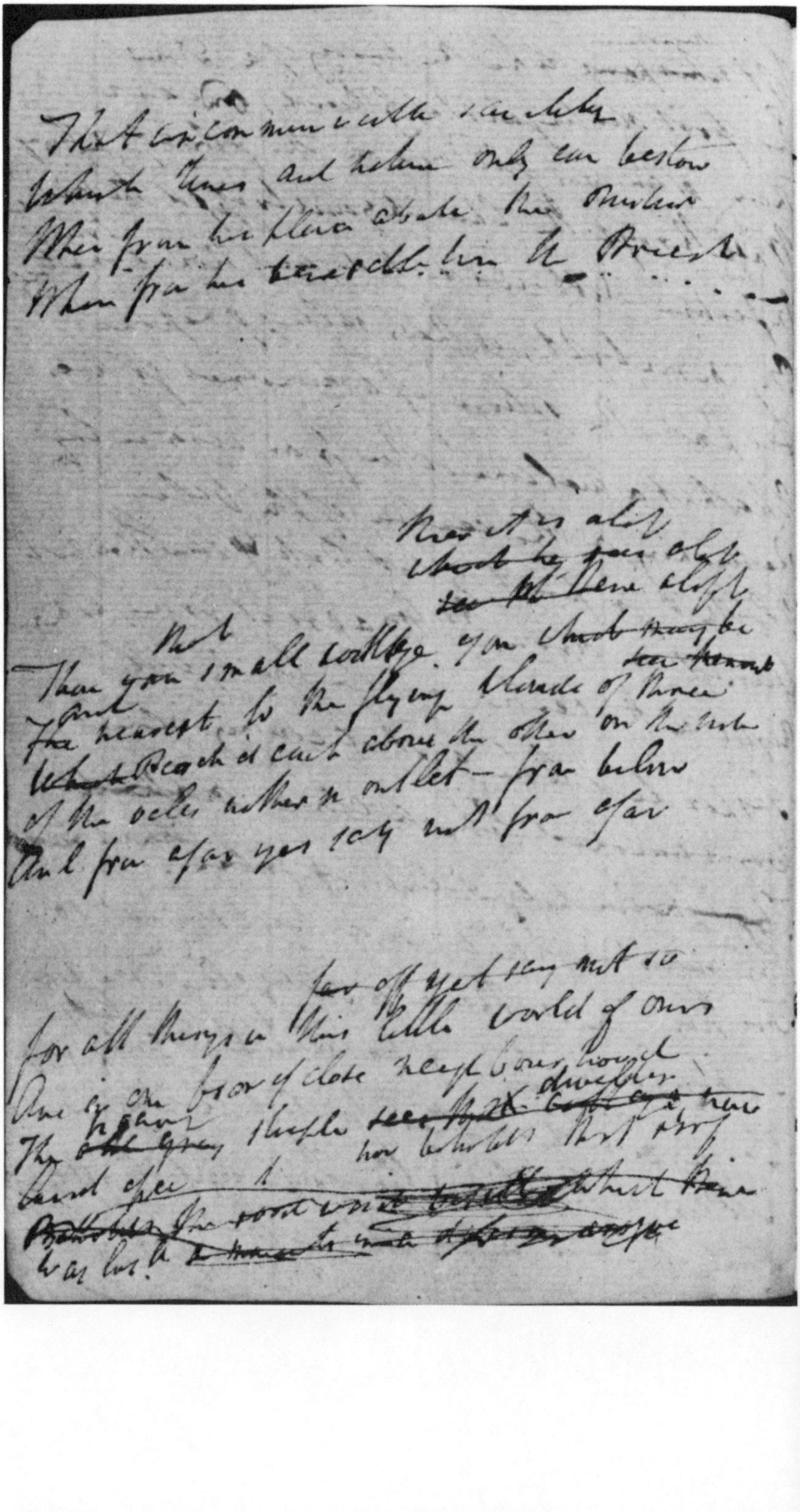

[DC MS. 65, $34^{v}$] [*The Tuft of Primroses*]

116 That incommunicable sanctity
117 Which Time and nature only can bestow
When from his plain abode the Rustic
118 When from his venerable [?home] the Priest

ther it is alof
~~which he sees~~ alof
{it
~~see {the there~~ aloft
that {t {a
135 Than ~~yon~~ small co{it{tge yon ~~which may be~~
And ~~seen [?kennd]~~
136 ~~The~~ nearest to the flying clouds of three
137 ~~Which~~ Perch'd each above the other on the side
138 Of the vales nothern outlet—from below
139 And from afar yet say not from afar

~~far off yet say not so~~
140 for all things in this little world of ours
141 Are in one bsom of close neighbourhood
hoary dwelling
142 The ~~old grey~~ steeple ~~sees that cottage, now~~
now beholds that roof
Laid open [?]
~~Beholds the [?rood work] visible which there~~
~~Was laid in moments in a [?] [?crossd]~~

---

All entries on this page are in the dark ink used in the revisions at ll. 119/120 on $35^{r}$ and ll. 131/132 on $35^{v}$, the last four lines at the foot of $35^{v}$, and the revisions at ll. 146–147 on $36^{r}$.
135–139 Developed from draft revisions on $35^{v}$.
142 The word "cottage" is canceled twice.

Who spared not them nor spar'd that sycamore high
The universal glory of the Vale
And did not spare the little avenue
Of lightly stirring ash-trees, that sufficed
To fence the glare of summer, and to blend
The strong wind turn'd into a gentle breeze
Whose freshness cheared the paved walk beneath
That ancient walk which from the Vicar's door
Led to the Church-yard gate. Then, Grasmere, then
Thy sabbath mornings had a holy grace
When from his plain abode the Vested Priest
Did issue forth glistening in best attire
And down that consecrated visto paced
Towards the Church-yard where his flock
Were gathered round in sunshine or in shade
While Trees and mountains echoed to the Voice
Of the glad bells, and all the murmuring streams
United their soft chorus with the song.

[DC MS. 65, 35r] [*The Tuft of Primroses*]

106 Who spared not them nor spar'd that sycamore
high
107 The universal glory of the Vale
108 And did not spare the little avenue
109 Of lightly stirring Ash-trees, that sufficed
~~In all as it was of unambitious length,~~ { bl
110 To dim the glare of summer, and to { [?]unt
gentle
111 The strong Wind turn'd into a favoring breeze
112 Whose freshness cheared the paved walk
beneath
113 That antient walk which from the Vacar's door
Led
114 ~~Has pav'd~~ to the Church-yard gate. Then,
Grasmere, then
115 Thy sabbath mornings had a holy grace
When from his plain abode the rustic Priest
119 Did issue forth glistening in best attire
that consecrated
120 And down through that domestic visto paced
121 Towards the ~~neighbouring~~ Churchyard
ready
where his Flock
122 Were gathered round in sunshine or in shade
123 While Trees and mountains echoed to the
Voice
124 Of the glad bells, and all the murmuring streams
120
125 United their soft chorus with the song.

---

The fair copy runs on from the foot of 34r.

119/120 For the ink used to make this revision, see note to 34v.

124/125 WW's count of 120 lines follows from the "100" on 34r and does not include any of the work on 34v.

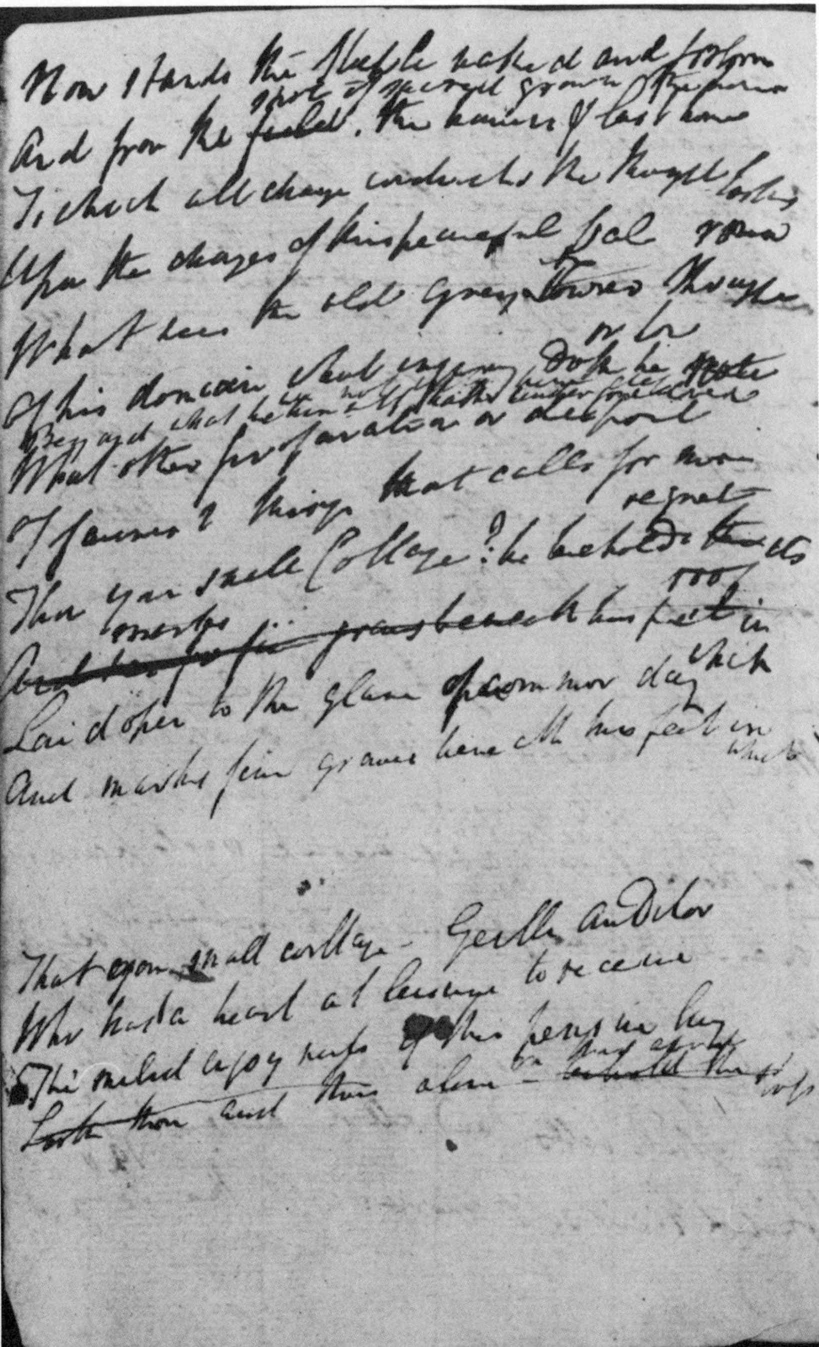

[DC MS. 65, 35v] [*The Tuft of Primroses*]

126 Now stands the Steeple naked and forlorn
spot of sacred groun the home
127 And from the ~~field~~, the haven & last home
128 To which all change conducts the thought looks
round
129 Upon the changes of this peaceful Vale
{T
130 What sees the old grey {tower through
or low
{note
131 Of his domain what injury doth he {see
are not unto him [?deprived]
132 Beyond what he himself hath undergone
133 What other profanation or despoil
134 Of fairest things that calls for more
regret
Than yon small Cottage? he beholds ~~the~~ its
roof
marks
~~And her [?fo] five graves beneath his feet in~~
which
of} {common
143 Laid open to the glare h} {er day
144 And marks five graves beneath his feet in
which

{y
That {[?]on small cottage—Gentle Auditor
t}
Who has } a heart at leisure to receive
The milid enjoyments of this pensive lay
on this abode
~~Look thou and thou~~ alone— ~~behold the [?slope~~]

---

The thirteen lines at the top of the page were meant to replace the first eight lines at the top of 36r, facing.

The four lines at the bottom of the page are developed from the lines at the top of the page and yield ll. 135–142 on 34v, where the address to a "Gentle Auditor" is dropped. For the ink used to enter the last four lines on this page and the interlinear revision at ll. 131/132, see note to 34v.

Now stands the Steeple naked & forlorn
And from the ~~[illegible]~~, the "Rural ancient House,
To which all change conducts the thought, looks round
Upon the changes of this peaceful Vale
What sees the old grey Tower, through high or low
This domain that calls for more regret
Than one small Cottage? . . .
Of grains, the five beneath its feet, in which
Divided by a breadth of smooth green space
From all the neighbourhood, they who were
The Inmates of that Cottage are at rest
Death to the happy House in which they dwelt
Had given a long reprieve of forty years.
Suddenly then they disappeared—not twice
Had Summer scorch'd the fields, not twice ~~had seen~~ had fallen
The first white ~~[illegible]~~ snow upon Helvellyn's top
Before the greedy visiting was closed
And the long-privileged House left empty, swept
As by a plague; yet no rapacious plague

140

[DC MS. 65, 36r] [*The Tuft of Primroses*]

Now stands the Steeple naked & forlorn
{haven
And from the {centre, the last central Home,
To which all change conducts the Thought, looks
round
Upon the changes of this peaceful Vale
What sees the old grey Tower, through high
or low
Of his domain that calls for more regret
Than yon small Cottage? surely not the
Of Graves, the five beneath ist feet, in which
+ {d
145 Divided by a brea{ th of smooth green space
other
146 all the hillloucks which like waves
From nearest neighbourhood, they who were
Heave close together erewhile
148 The Inmates of that Cottage are at rest
{H
149 Death to the happy {house in which they dwelt
150 Had given a long reprieve of forty years
151 Suddenly then they disappeared—not twice
152 Had Summer scorch'd the fields, not twice
had fallen
{as
snow ~~w{ere seen~~
153 The first white ~~snow~~ upon Helvellyns top
154 Before the greedy visiting was closed
155 And the long-priviledge'd House left empty,
swept
156 As by a plague; yet no rapacious plague
140

---

The fair copy runs on from the foot of 35r.

145 The X above this line marks the point at which the first block of revision at the top of 35v ends.

146–147 For the ink used to enter the revisions in these lines, see note to 34v.

156/ WW's count of 140 lines follows from the "120" on 35r and does not include revisions on 34v and 35v.

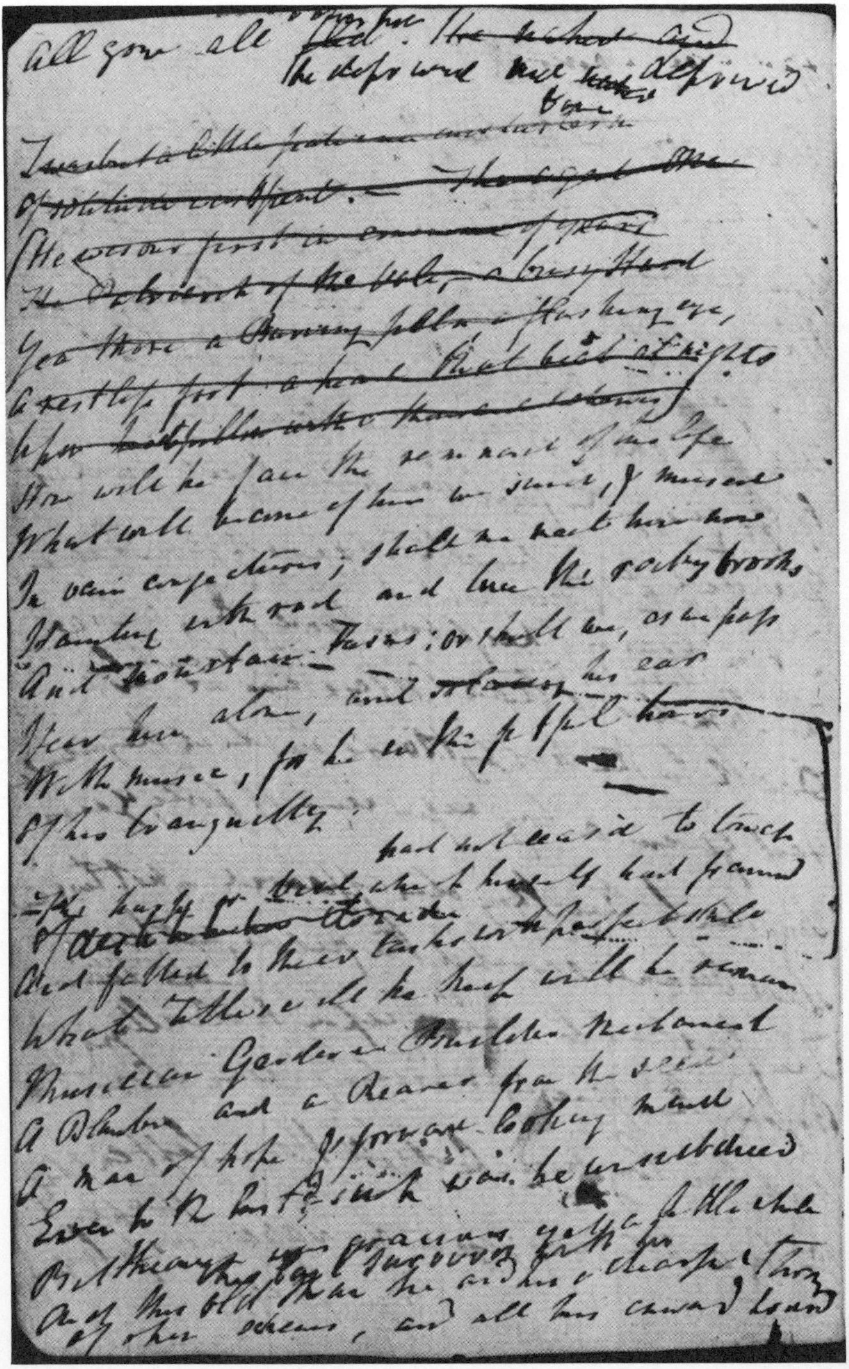

[DC MS. 65, 36v] [*The Tuft of Primroses*]

vanishd
All gone—all ~~fled. He naked and~~
deprived
he deprived and ~~naked~~
bare

168 ~~Twas but a little patience and his term~~
169 ~~Of solitude was spent.—The aged One~~
170 ~~(He was our first in eminence of years~~
171 ~~The Patriarch of the Vale,—a busy Hand~~
a{
172 ~~Yea More a Burning pl}lm, a flashing eye,~~
173 ~~A restless foot a head that beat at nights~~
174 ~~Upon his[?]pillow with a thousand schemes)~~
175 How will he face the remnant of his life
176 What will become of him we said, & mused
177 In vain conjectures; shall we meet him now
178 Haunting with rod and line the rocky brooks
{T
179 And mountain-{tarns: or shall we, as we pass
180 Hear him alone, and solacing his ear
181 With music, for he in the fitful hours
182 Of his tranquilty
had not ceas'd to touch
183 The harp or viol which himself had framed
~~Of destitution [?closed]~~
184 And fitted to their tasks with perfect skill
185 What Titles will he keep will he remain
186 Musician Gardener Builder Mechanist
187 A Planter and a Rearer from the seed
188 A man of hope & forward-looking mind
189 Even to the last?—such was he unsubdued
190 But Heaven was gracious yet a little while
this last survivor with his
191 And this old Man he and his [?] chearful throng
192 Of open schemes, and all his inward hoard

---

The numbered lines develop draft revisions on 37v and replace the passage that begins six lines from the foot of 37r, facing, and ends six lines from the top of 38r.

The slanted markings visible at mid-page in the photograph are ink offset from 37r, facing; they show that the box on 37r was drawn after the fair-copy lines were entered on this page.

The draft line at the top of the page, the deletion of ll. 168–174, and the draft insertion at ll. 190/191 are part of WW's adaptation of the story of the Sympsons to *The Excursion* (1814), VII, 261–310 (1850: VII, 242–291). The ink used to draft the line at the top of the page is the same as that used to enter the second block of lines from the top of 37v and the *Excursion* work on 38v.

182 The gap left between the halves of this line may indicate WW's intention to insert a line, or two half-lines—perhaps a version of "By blazing fire, or under shady tree" (the third line from the foot of 37v).

183/184 The deleted phrase is probably a rejected alternate for "Of solitude was spent" on the facing recto and in l. 169.

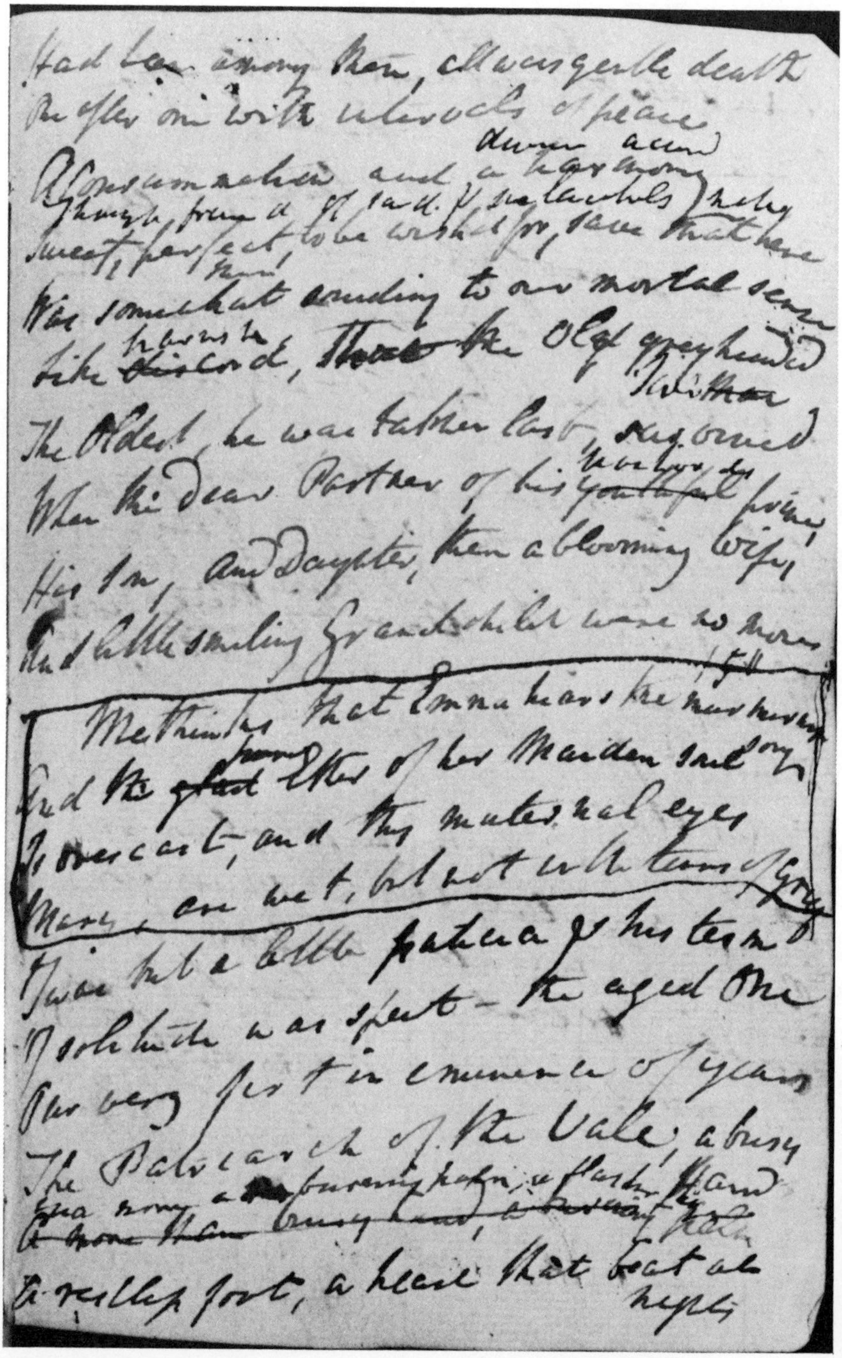

[DC MS. 65, 37r] [*The Tuft of Primroses*]

157 Had been among them, all was gentle death
158 One after one with intervals of peace
divine accord
159 A Consummation and a harmony
160 Though framd of sad & melancholy notes,
161 Sweet, perfect, to be wish'd for, save that here
thing
162 Was somewhat sounding to our mortal sense
harshness {that {d
163 Like ~~discord,~~ {[ ? ] the ol{[?] greyheaded
Sire ~~Man~~
164 The Oldest, he was taken last, survived
manhoods
165 When the dear Partner of his ~~youthful~~ prime,
166 His Son, and Daughter, then a blooming Wife,
167 And little smiling Grandchild were no more
150
Methinks that Emma hears the murmuring
pure song
And the ~~glad~~ Ether of her Maiden soul
Is overcast, and thy maternal eyes
Mary, are wet, but not with tears of grief
'Twas but a little patience & his term
Of solitude was spent—the aged One
Our very first in eminence of years
The Patriarch of the Vale, a busy
{H
{hand
Yea more, a [?] burning palm, a flashing eye
~~A more than busy hand, a burning palm~~
A restless foot, a head that beat at
nights

---

The fair copy runs on from the foot of 36r.

Interlinear revisions between ll. 158 and 165 are in the same ink as ll. 168–192 on 36v, facing.

167/ WW's count of 150 lines follows from the "140" at the bottom of 36r.

The box marks the four lines on Emma and Mary for deletion, but unlike X's or deletion lines, the box may reflect an intention to preserve the lines for later use.

The lines below the box are recopied as ll. 168–173 on 36v, facing.

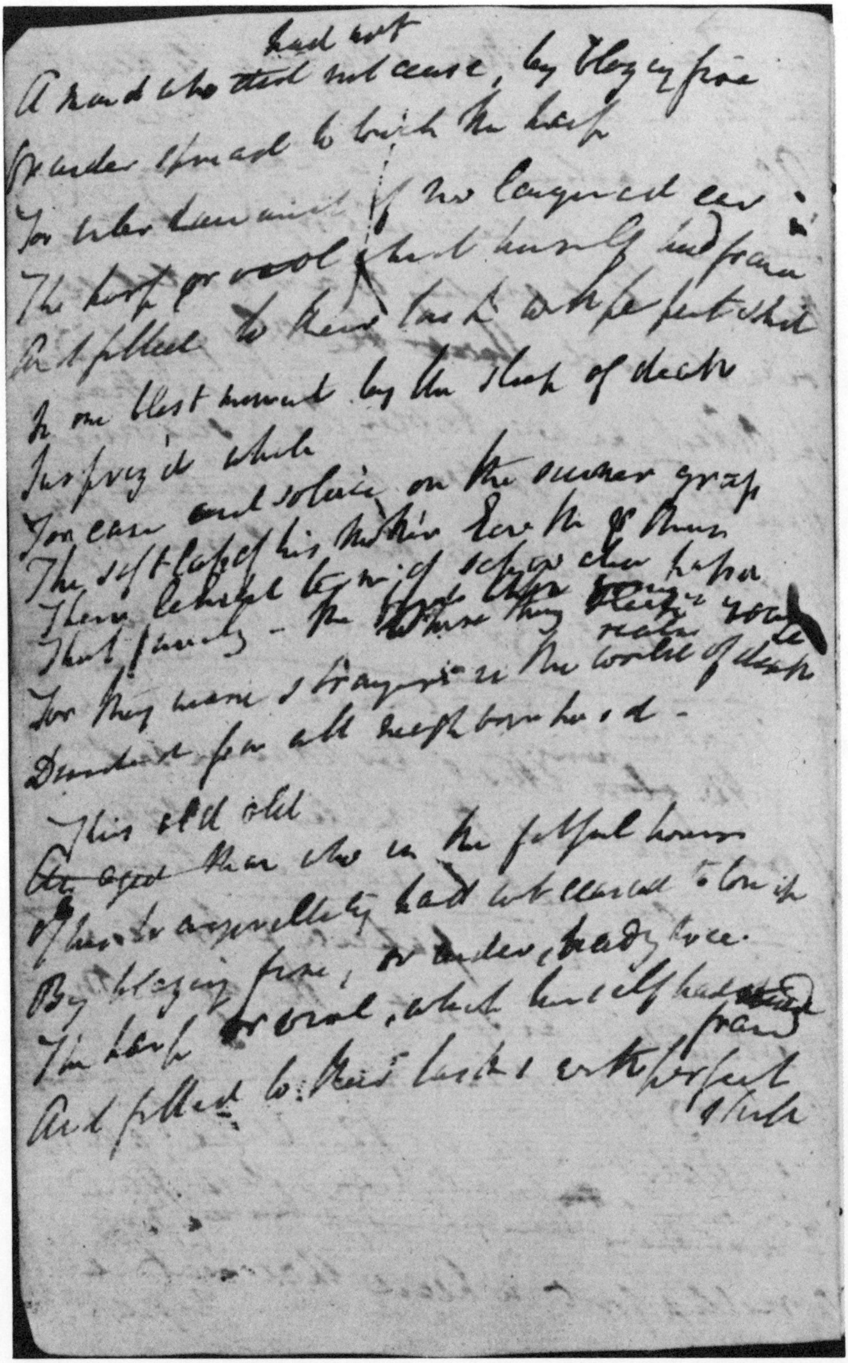

[DC MS. 65, $37^{v}$] [*The Tuft of Primroses*]

had not
A man [?d] who ~~did~~ not cease, by blazing fire
Or under spread to touch the harp
For entertainment of no languid ear
The harp or viol which himself had framd
And fitted to their task with perfect skill

In one blest moment by the sleep of death
Surpriz'd while
For ease and solace on the summer grass
The soft lap of his Mother Earth & thus
Their lenient term of separation passd
That family—the five whose graves you see

197b Where they sleep
realm
198 For they were strangers in the world of death
199a Divided from all neighbourhood—

This old old
~~An aged~~ Man who in the fitful hours
Of his tranquillity had not ceased to touch
By blazing fire, or under shady tree
The harp or viol, which himself had made
framd
And fitted to their tasks with perfect
skill

---

Vertical marks visible in the top half of the photograph are ink offset from the two large X's on $38^{r}$, facing; they suggest that the X's were entered later than any of the work on $37^{v}$.

The five lines of drafting at the top of the page expand the description of the "Patriarch of the Vale" begun at the foot of $37^{r}$ and continued at the top of $38^{r}$.

The second block of draft lines, in darker ink and entered later than the other work on the page, is part of WW's adaptation of the story of the Sympsons to *The Excursion* (1814), VII, 261–310 (1850: VII, 242-291); the lines expand ll. 194–195 on $38^{r}$, facing, and are developed in further *Excursion* work, in the same ink, at the top of $38^{v}$ (the same dark ink was used to enter the single draft line at the top of $36^{v}$).

197–199 These lines, entered opposite the point at which they are meant to be inserted on the facing recto, were probably the first work on this page; their position would have made it necessary to separate the blocks of drafting at the top and bottom of the page.

The block of lines at the bottom of the page develops the drafting at the top of the page and results in ll. 181–184 on $36^{v}$.

Upon its pillow with a thousand schemes
A Planter, and a Rearer from the seed,
Builder had been, but scanty means forbad
A Man of Hope, a forward-looking Mind
Even to the last he and his cheerful ~~store~~ throng
Of open schemes, and all his inward hoards
Of his unsured grasp to many & to heirs
Fell with the body into gentle sleep
In one blest moment, and the family
By yet a higher privilege once more
Were gathered to each other.—

Yet how 180

Though I can look on these associate
With nothing but this thought, that I repine grieve
It costs me something like a pain to ~~[illegible]~~ feel
That after them so many of these works
Which round that dwelling covertly preserve
The History of their unambitious lives
Have perished, & so soon!—the Cottage
=Court

[DC MS. 65, 38r] [*The Tuft of Primroses*]

Upon its pillow with a thousand schemes
A Planter, and a Rearer from the Seed,
Builder had been, but scanty means forbad
A Man of Hope, a forward-looking Mind
throng
Even to the last he and his chearful ~~store~~
hoard
Of open schemes, and all his inward ~~pang~~s
{Of
193 {His unsunn'd griefs, too many & to keen
194 Fell with the body into gentle sleep
195 In one blest moment, and the family
196 By yet a higher privilege once more
197a Were gathered to each other.—

199b Yet I own 180
200 Though I can look on thieir associate
graves
201 With nothing but still thought, that I repine
~~see~~
202 It costs me something like a pain to ~~think~~
feel
203 That after them so many of their works
204 Which round that Dwelling covertly
preservd
205 The History of their unambitious lives
206 Have perish'd, & so sooon!—the Cottage
{C
={court

---

The fair copy runs on from the foot of 37r.

The two large X's at the top of the page are part of WW's adaptation of ll. 168–197 to *The Excursion* (1814), VII, 261–310, 263-291 (1850: VII, 242–291); the two lines left uncanceled between the X's link the last line at the foot of 36v to the first line at the top of 38v.

The first six lines at the top of the page are developed as ll. 174, 187–188, 191–192 on 36v.

199 WW's line count, which follows from the "150" on 37r, excludes the four boxed lines on 37r and includes ll. 168–192 on 36v.

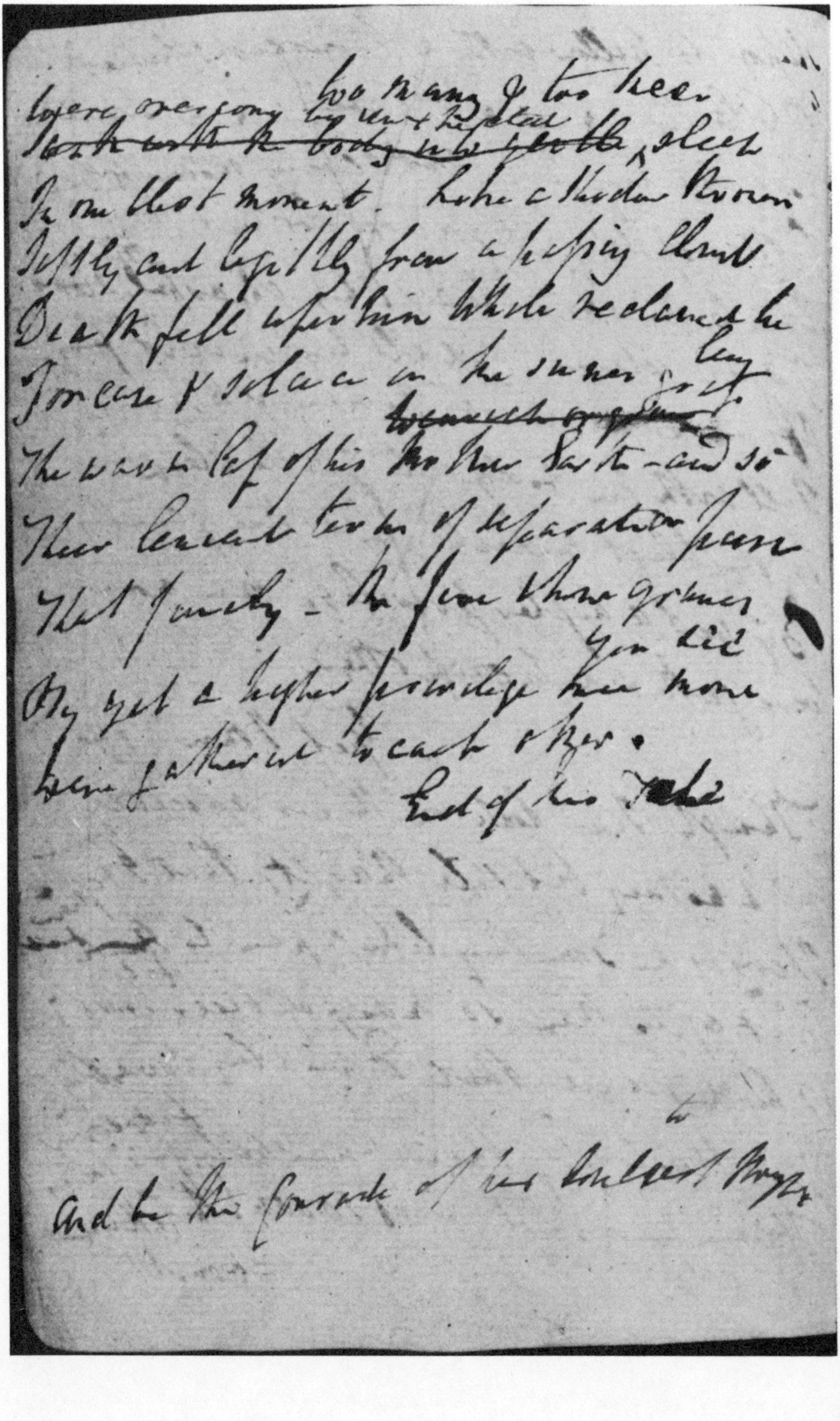

[DC MS. 65, $38^{v}$] [*The Tuft of Primroses*]

too many & too keen
Were overcome by unexpected
~~Sank with the body into gentle~~ ^ sleep
In one blest moment. Like a Shadow thrown
Softly and lightly from a passing Cloud
Death fell upon him While reclined he
lay
For ease & solace in the sumer grass
~~to enrich or grace~~
The warm lap of his Mother Earth—and so
Their lenient term of separation past
That family—the five whose graves
you see
By yet a higher privilege once more
Were gathered to each other.
End of this {Tale / [ ? ]

to
226 And be the Comrade of her lonliest thought

---

The revision of ll. 193–197 at the top of the page was intended for *The Excursion* (1814), VII, 300–310 (1850: VII, 281–291); the ink, darker than that of surrounding entries, is the same as that used to draft the single line at the top of $36^{v}$ and the second block of lines from the top of $37^{v}$.

The phrase "to enrich or grace" (below the sixth line on the page) is related to revision of l. 213 on $39^{r}$, facing; it was canceled when the *Excursion* drafting was entered over it.

226 This line is entered opposite the point at which it is meant to be inserted at the foot of $39^{r}$, facing.

Spread with blue gravel from the torrent's side
And gay with shrubs, the garden, bed & walk
Her own creation; that embattled host
Of garish tulips, fractions chosen and [illegible]
And roses of all colours, which she sought
Most curiously, as generously dispersed
~~Proud to behold them~~ in her neighbours bowers
Their kinds, to beautify grounds
Trees of the forest, too, a stately fence
Planted for shelter in the roaring winds
And small [illegible] violated by his [illegible]
That all are ravaged; that this Daughters Bower
Is creeping into the pathless, self-lost
In the wild wood, like a neglected image
Or Fancy which hath ceased to be recalled.
The promise her own choice which she had
To deck the wall and of one flowering spray
Had made an Inmate, lusing it from sun
And breeze, and from its fellows, to caress
The inside of her chamber with its sweets

[DC MS. 65, 39r] [*The Tuft of Primroses*]

Spread with blue gravel from the torrents side
And gay with shrubs, the garden, bed & walk
His own creation, that embattled Host
               {l
Of garish tu{pips, fruitrees chosen and rare
And roses of all colours, which he sought
Most curiously as generously dispersd
~~Proud to behold them in~~ his neighbours
   Their kinds, to beautify          grounds
Trees of the forest, too, a stately fence
Planted for Shelter in his manhoods
                              prime
And Small Flowers watered by his wrinkled
                                        hand
That all are ravage'd;—that his Daughters Bower
Is creeping into shapelessness, self-lost
                                        image
In the wild wood, like a neglected ~~thought~~
   {f
Or {Fancy which hath ceased to be recealled.
                                        200
The jasmine her own charge which she had
                                        trained
To deck the wall and of one flowery spray
Had made an Inmate, luring it from sun
                                        pervade
And breezes, and from its fellows, to caress
                                        {t
The inside of her chamber with its swee{p

---

The fair copy runs on from the foot of 38r.

220/221 WW's count of 200 lines, which follows from the "180" on 38r, is one line off; perhaps l. 213 appeared to have been deleted rather than revised.

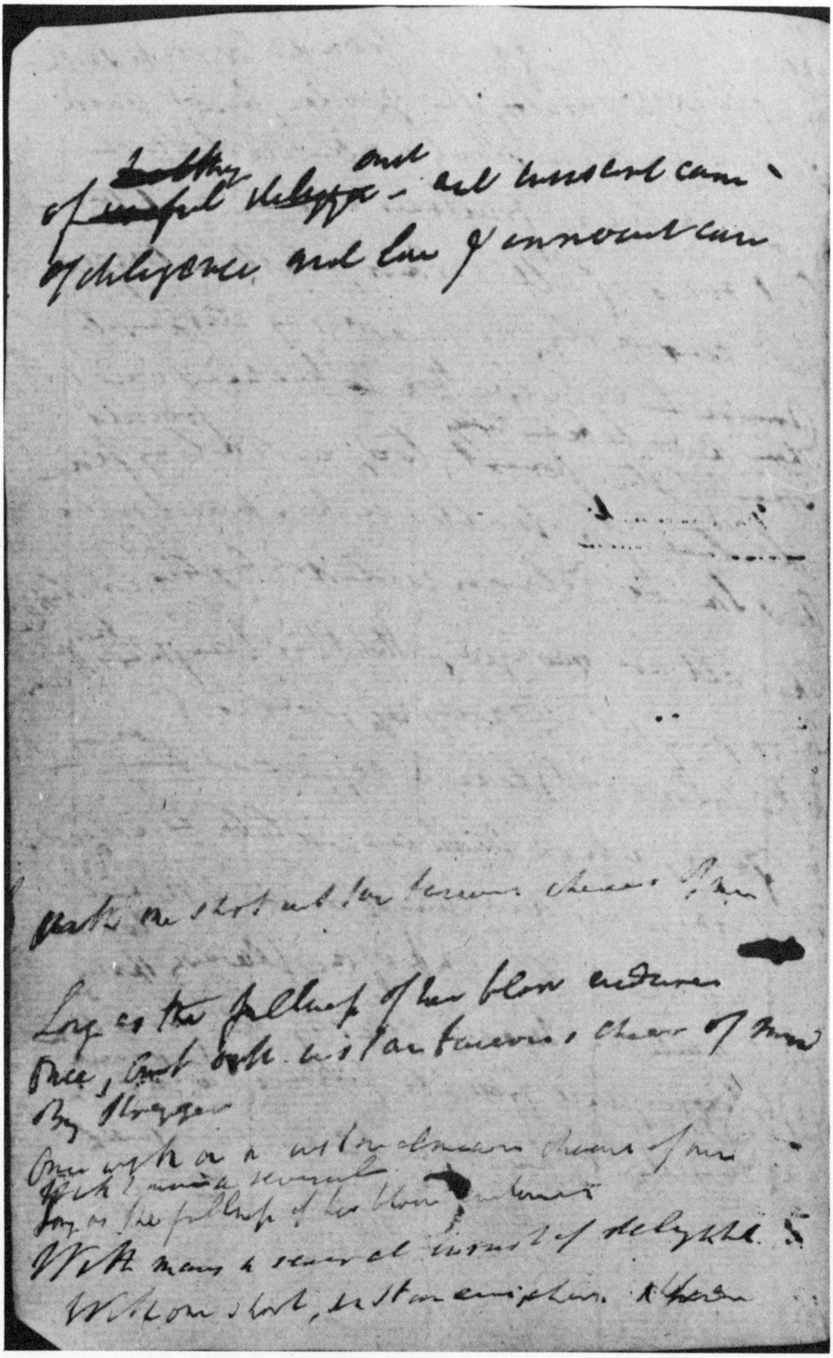

[DC MS. 65, 39v] [*The Tuft of Primroses*]

~~healthy~~ and
Of ~~useful~~ [~~?diligence~~]—and innocent care
Of diligence and love & innocent care

With one short instantaneous chear of mind

Long as the fullness of her bloom endures
Once, and with instantaneous chear of mind
By Stranger
Once with an instantaneous chear of mi
With man a several
Long as the fullness of her bloom endures
With many a several inrush of delight
With one short, instantaneous [?chear ? ]

The drafting at the top of the page results in l. 229, inserted on 40r, facing.
The drafting at the bottom of the page yields ll. 242–243, inserted at the bottom of 40r, facing.

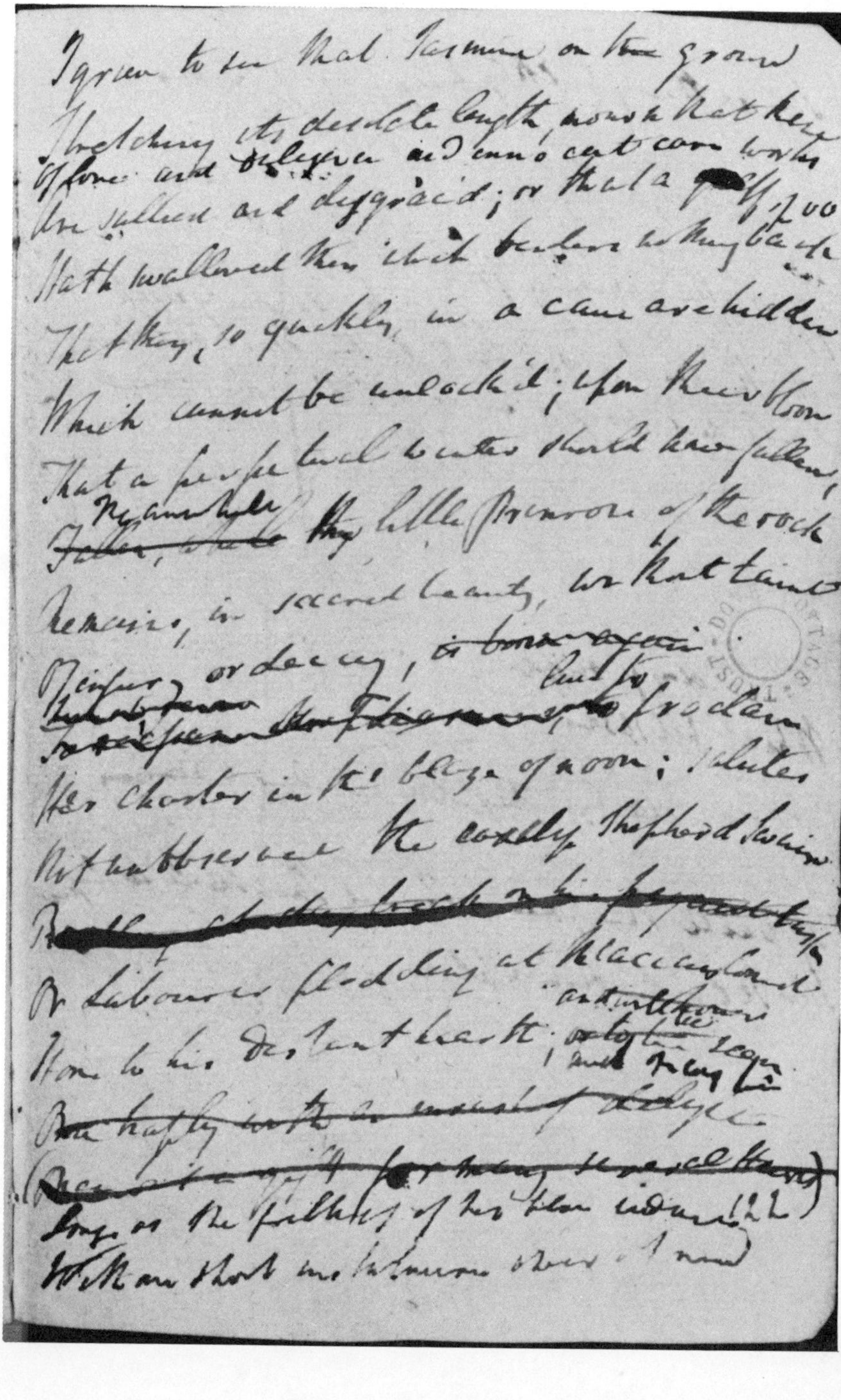

[DC MS. 65, 40r] [*The Tuft of Primroses*]

227 I grieve to see that Jasmine on the ground
228 Stretching its desolate length, mourn that these
works
229 Of love and diligence and innocent care
230 Are sullied and disgrac'd; or that a gulff
r } 200
231 Hath swallowed them which [?]}enders nothing back
232 That they, so quickly, in a cave are hidden
233 Which cannot be unlock'd; upon their bloom
234 That a perpetual winter should have fallen,
Meanwhile {the
235 ~~Fallen, while~~ {my little Primrose of the rock
236 Remains, in sacred beauty, without taint
237 Of injury or decay, ~~is born again~~
~~Lives to renew~~ lives to
~~To reap one other pleasure, to~~ proclaim
238 Her charter in the blaze of noon; salutes
{o
239 Not un{bbserved the early Shepherd Swain
~~Rambling at day break on his frequent task~~
240 Or Labourer plodding at th'accustomed
hour
~~and will be~~
241 Home to his distant hearth; ~~or to be~~ seen
and may be
~~Once haply with an inrush of delight~~
~~(Once out a gift for many several Hours)~~
242 Long as the fullness of her bloom endures 122
243 With one short instantaneous chear of mind

---

The fair copy runs on from the foot of 39r.

230/231 The line count here (abandoned with the 222 on 41r) follows from the "150" on 37r; it was made before the deletion of the four-line passage on Emma and Mary (on 37r) and the addition of the numbered lines on 36v.

241/242 The "122" is apparently a mistake for "222," the count at this point as continued from the count of 200 lines on 39r. The position of the number shows that it was probably entered before the cancellation and revision of the last two base-text lines at the foot of the page. The number, not the usual multiple of 20, indicates a stopping place in WW's count, which resumes at the top of 42v and yields the "240" at the top of 43r.

242–243 Drafting related to these lines is at the foot of 39v, facing.

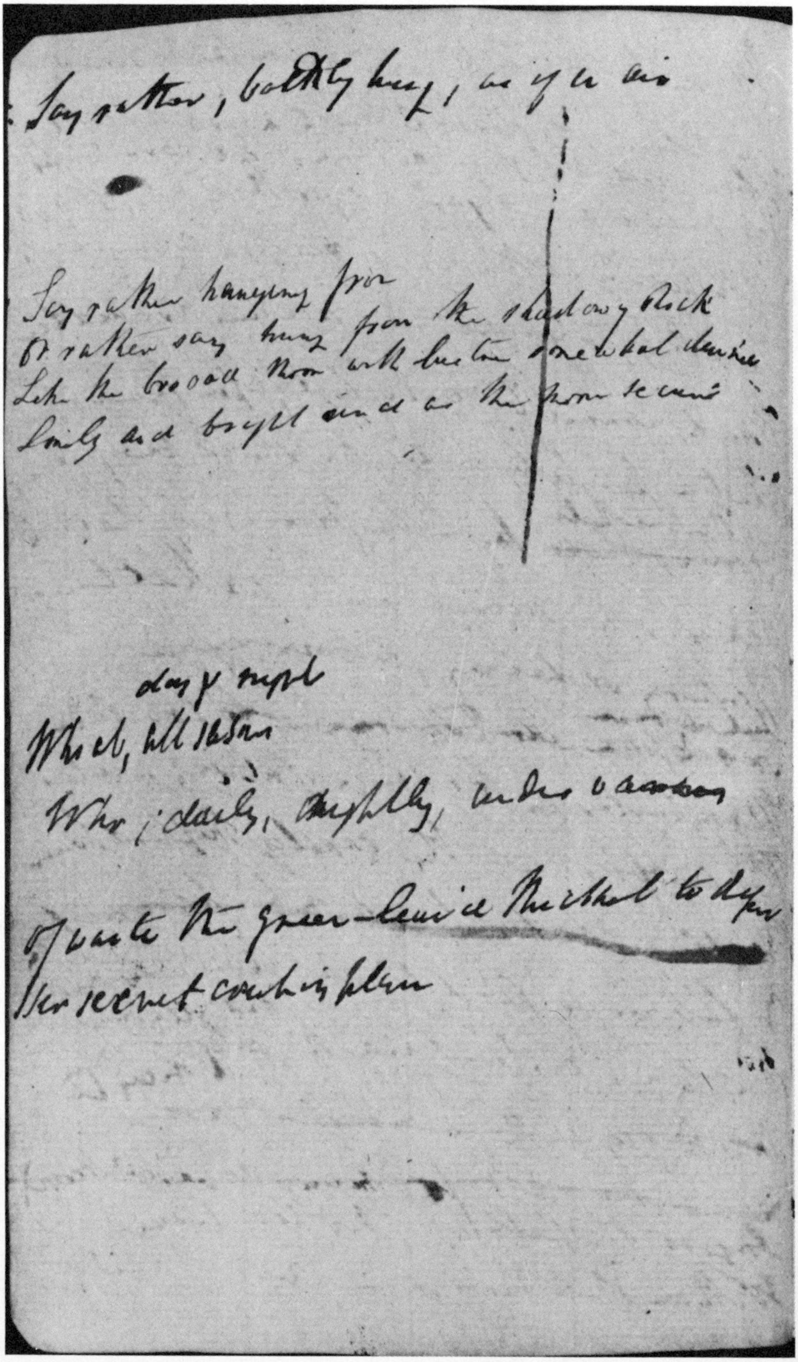

[DC MS. 65, 40v] [*The Tuft of Primroses*]

Say rather, boldly hung, as if in air

Say rather hanging from
Or rather say hung from the shadowy Rock
Like the brooad Moon with lustre somewhat dimm'd
Lonely and bright and as the Moon secure

day & night
Which, all seasons

Who, daily, nightly, under various

Of waste the green-leav'd thicket to defend
Her secret couching place

---

The drafting on this page is intermediate between passages on 41r, facing, and ll. 248–250, 253, and 257–258 on 42v. The vertical mark visible at the top half of the photograph is ink offset from 41r, facing.

By Strangers [illegible] late travel; as I myself
Have often seen her, when the last lone Thrush
Hath ceas'd her vespers, ditty piercing the gloom
Of Twilight with the vigor of a star
Say rather, standing from her station bold
Like the broad Moon, with lustre somewhat dimm'd
Large as the Moon, and as the Moon serene.
222

Oft for some band of [illegible] Guardians, grasp[illegible]
Else were those human Ministers of old
Who daily applied [illegible] under various names
With various office, strolled or walked their rounds
Through the wide Forest, to protect from harm
The [illegible] beset with her young; and from the touch
Of [illegible] wasted by green-leaf or thicket [illegible]
Her secret couching place, and stately trees
Their canopy; and berry-bearing shrub
And the grassy lawns their pasture's pleasure range
Continued & [illegible] in peace from outrage free.
And all annoyance till the Sorcerer came,

[DC MS. 65, 41r] *[The Tuft of Primroses]*

By Stranger ~~lat~~ in late travel; as I myself
Have often seen her, when the last lone Thrush
hymn,
Hath ceas'd his Vesper ^ piercing the gloom
Of Twilight with the vigor of a star
Say rather, shining from her station bold
Like the broad Moon, with lustre somewhat
{M dimm'd,
Large as the {moon, and as the Moon secure.
222

Oh for some band of viewless Guardians, prompt
As were those human Ministers of old
daily, nightly
Who ~~clad in green~~ ~~and~~ under various names
With various office, stood, or walked their rounds
{protect
Through the wide Forest, to {prevent from harm
The Wild-beast with her young; and from the
waste the green-leavd thicket to defend touch
~~Of desolation gu the leafy bower~~
Her secret couching place, and stately tree
{Their
{Her canopy, and berry-bearing shrub
{assy t} {ir
And ~~the~~ gr{een lawn }he{r pasture's pleasan
range
Continual & firm peace from outrage safe
And all annoyance till the Sovereign comes

---

The fair copy runs on from the foot of 40r.

The number "222" is the final entry in the unrevised count of base-text lines which follows from the "150" on 37r and includes the "200" at the top of 40r; as with the revised count at the foot of 40r, the number appears to indicate a stopping place in WW's transcription.

Revision begun on the bottom half of the page is continued on 40v, facing.

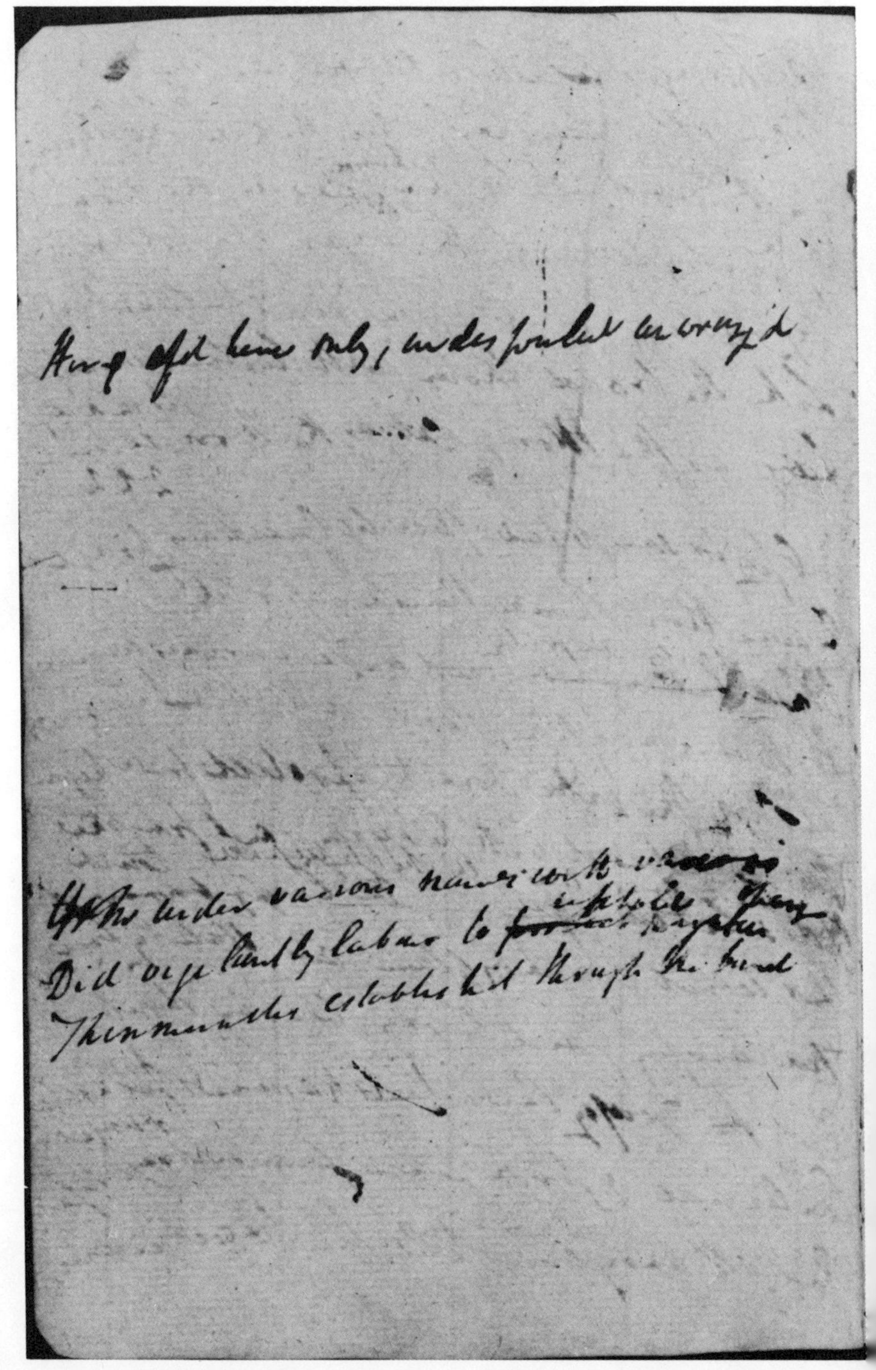

[DC MS. 65, 41$^{v}$] [*The Tuft of Primroses*]

Here {if / and} here only, undespoiled unwrong'd

{Who / The} under various names with various
charges

uphold
Did vigilantly labour to ~~protect~~ maintain
Their miracles establish'd through the land

---

The line toward the top of the page is a draft intermediate between revision on 42$^{r}$, facing, and the final version, l. 269 on 43$^{r}$.

The drafting at the bottom of the page is related to the revisions at ll. 252/253 on 42$^{v}$, which yield ll. 253–254.

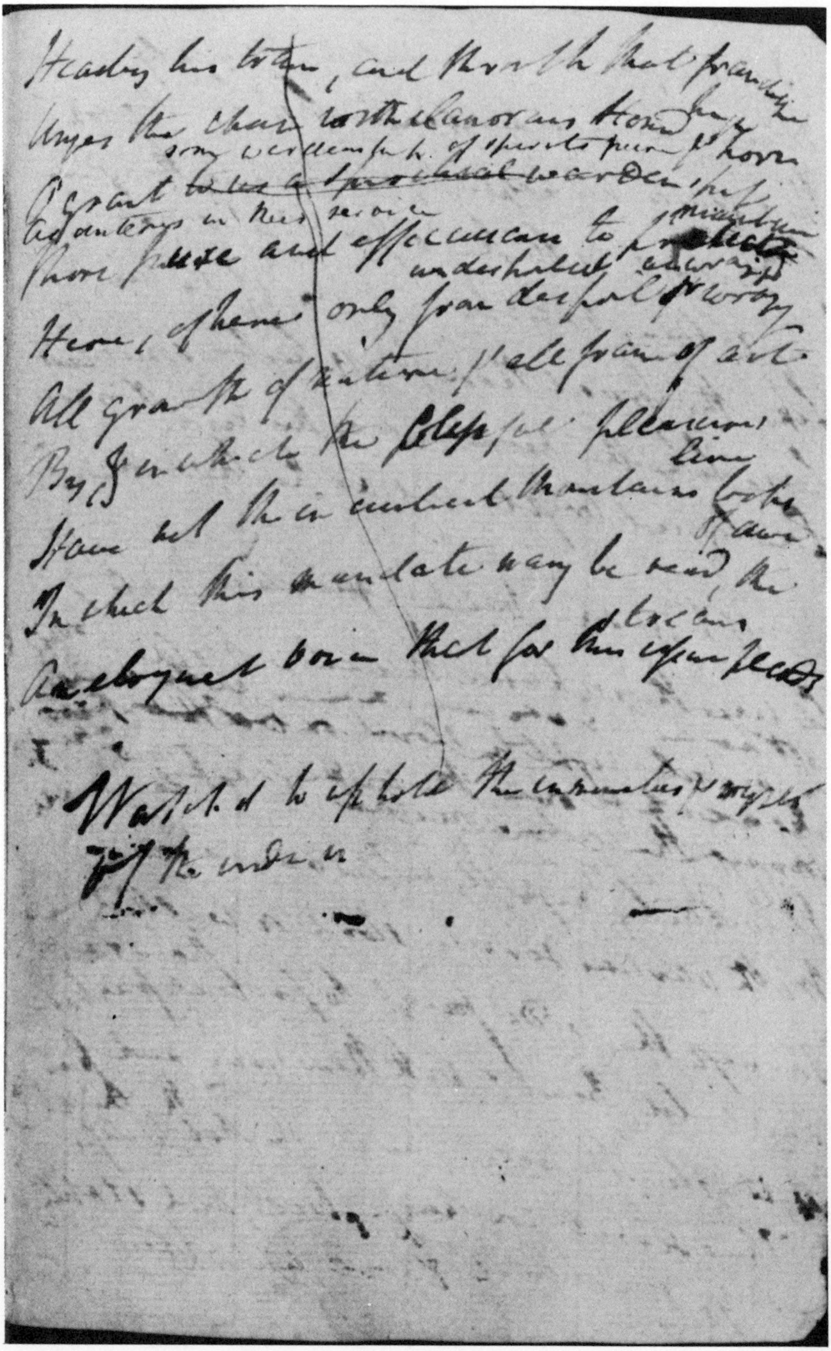

[DC MS. 65, 42r] [*The Tuft of Primroses*]

Heading his train, and through that franchise
high
Urges the chase with clamorous Hound & horn
some wardenship of spirits pure
O grant ~~to us a spiritual wardenship~~
As duteous in their service maintain
{tect
More pure and efficacious to pre{vent
undespoiled unwrong'd
{or
Here, if here only from despoil {& wrong
All growth of nature & all frame of art
bliss}
By, & in which the peace}ful pleasures
live
Have not th incumbent Mountains looks
of awe
In which this mandate may be read, the
streams
An eloquent voice that for this issue pleads

Watchd to uphold the immunities & rights
Of the endur

---

The fair copy runs on from the foot of 41r. After ten lines, WW broke off transcription and, doubling back to the passage at the top of 41r, restarted it at the top of 42v.

The one and a half lines of draft toward the bottom of the page seem to be related to the draft revision at the bottom of 41v, facing.

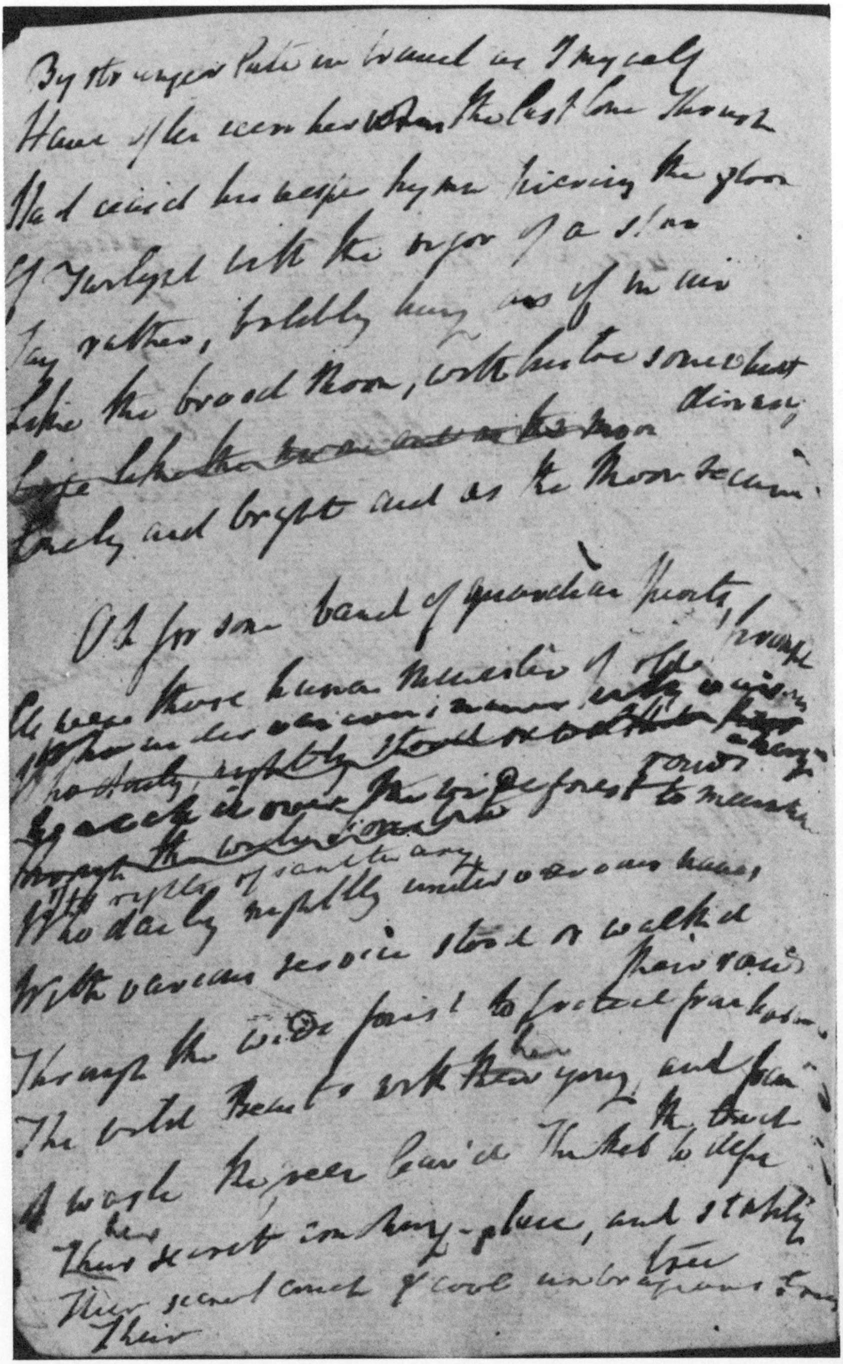

[DC MS. 65, 42v] *[The Tuft of Primroses]*

244 By stranger late in travel as I myself
{when
245 Have often seen her {of the last lone Thrush
246 Had ceas'd his vesper hymn piercing the gloom
247 Of Twilight with the vigor of a star
248 Say rather, boldly hung as if in air
249 Like the broad Moon, with lustre somewhat
dimmd,
~~Large like the Moon and as the Moon~~
250 Lonely and bright and as the Moon secure.

251 Oh for some band of guardian Spirits, prompt
252 As were those human ministers of old
Who under various names with various
~~Who daily, nightly stood or walk'd their~~
charge
rounds
Watch'd over the wide forest to maintain
~~Through the wide Forest to~~
Its rights of sanctuary,
253 Who daily nightly under various names
254 With various service stood or walkd
their rounds
255 Through the wide forest to protect from harm
her
256 The wild Beasts with ~~their~~ young, and from
the touch
257 Of waste the green leav'd Thicket to defe
her
~~Their~~ secret couching-place, and stately
tree
258 Their secret couch & cool umbrageous trees
Their

---

Here WW makes a fresh start at the passage that begins at the top of 41r and ends in the middle of 42r.

252/253 Revisions begun here and continued at the foot of 41v were abandoned when WW made a fresh start with l. 253.

256, 257/258 Deletions and revisions are in pencil.

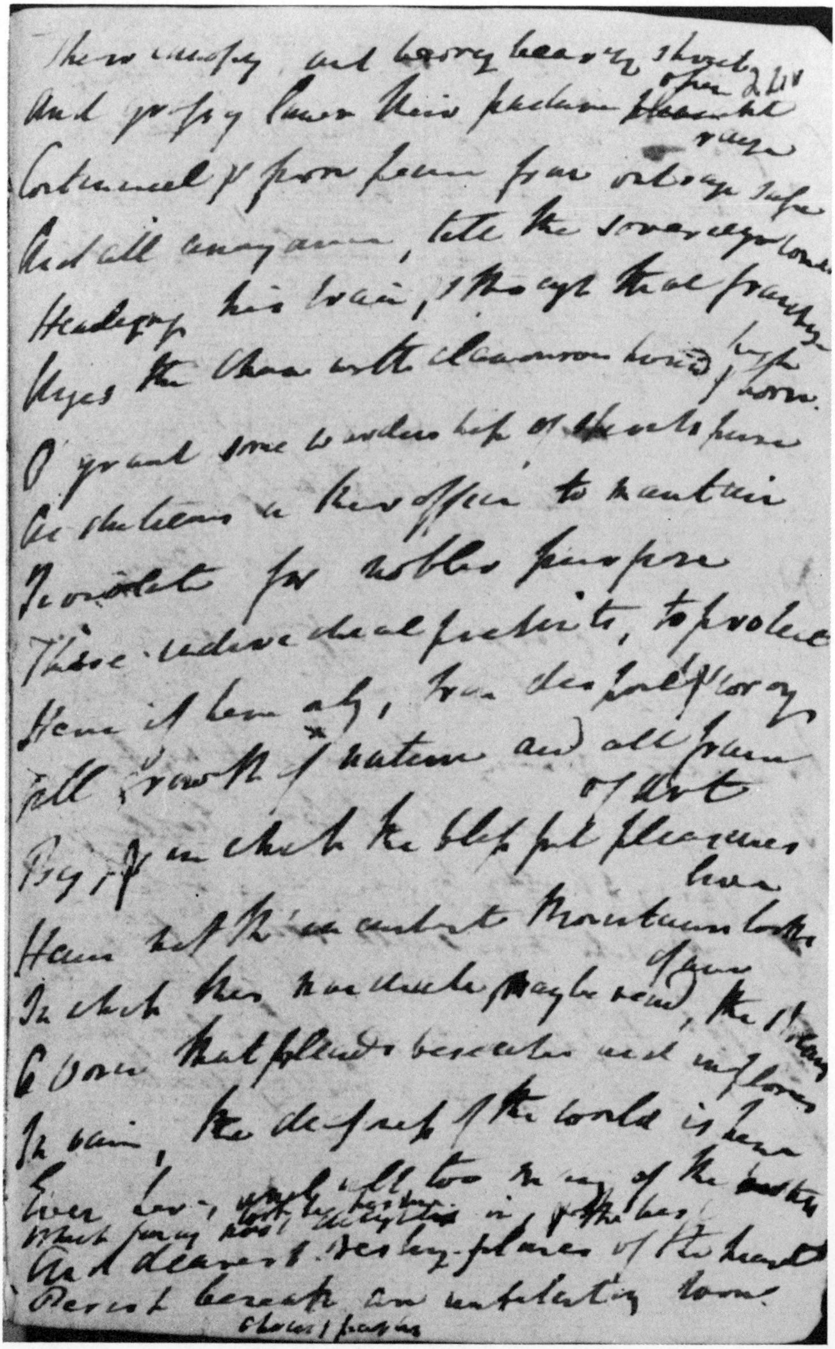

[DC MS. 65, 43r] [*The Tuft of Primroses*]

259 Their canopy, and berry bearing shrub
240
open
260 And grassy lawn their pastures ~~pleasant~~
range
261 Continual & firm peace from outrage safe
262 And all annoyance, till the sovereign comes
263 Headigng his train & through that franchise
high
264 Urges the Chase with clamorous hound & horn.
265 O grant some wardenship of spirits pure
266 As duteous in their office to maintain
267 Inviolate for nobler purpose
268 These individual precincts, to protect
269 Here if here only, from despoil & wrong
270 All growth of nature and all frame
of Art
271 By, & in which the blissful pleasures
live
272 Have not th'incumbent Mountains looks
of awe
273 In which this mandate may be read, the streams
274 A voice that pleads beseeches and implores
275 In vain, the deafness of the world is here
Even here, and all too many of the haunts
lost be pastime
Which fancy most delights in, & the best
And dearest resting-places of the heart
Perish beneath an unrelenting doom.
choicest pastime

---

The fair copy runs on from the foot of 42v, facing.

259/260 The line count, "240," follows from the "122" (a mistake for "222") at the foot of 40r and includes the lines on 42v, inadvertently counting both the revision and the fresh start of the passage beginning "Who daily nigthly . . ." on the lower half of the page.

275/ These lines are recopied at the top of 43v.

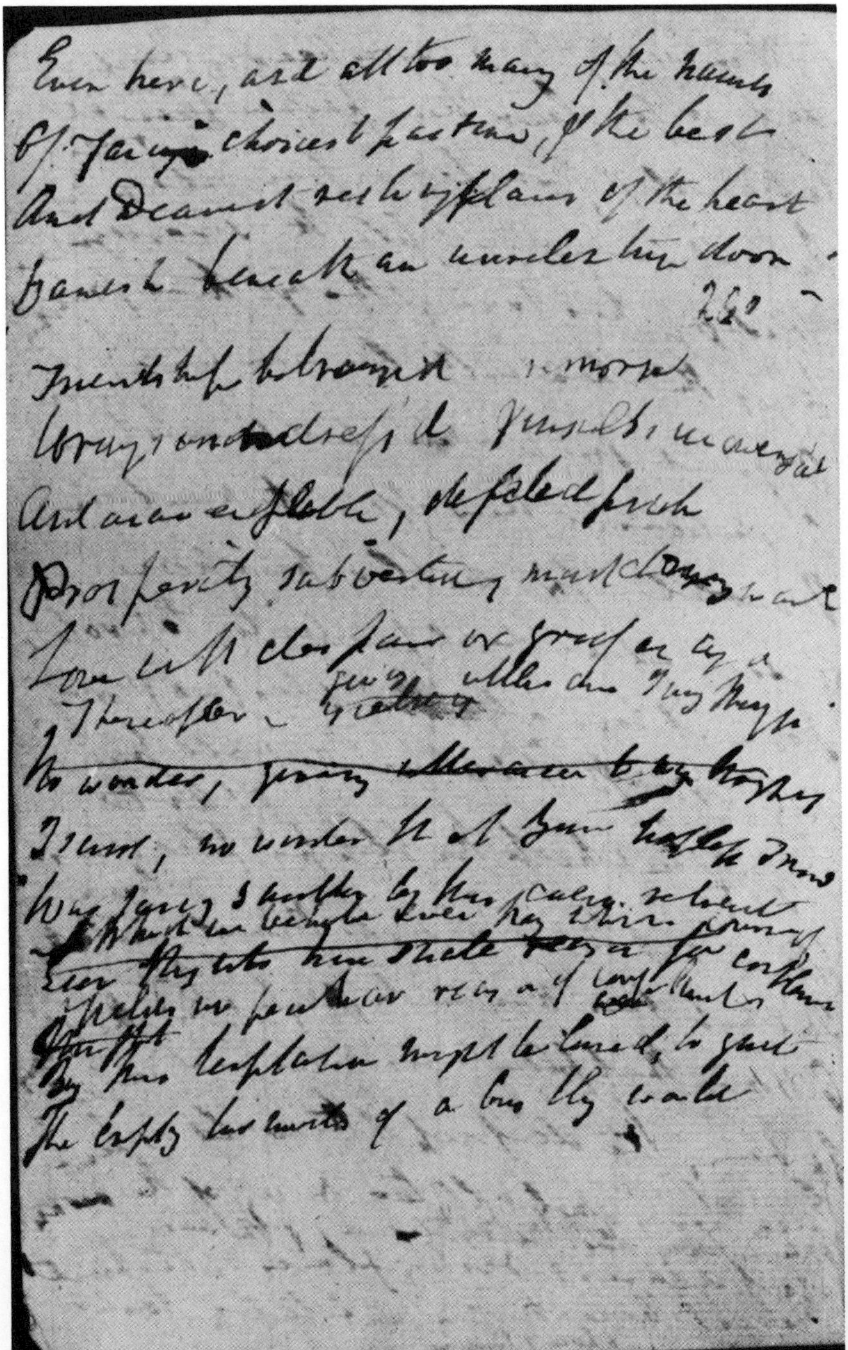

[DC MS. 65, 43v] [*The Tuft of Primroses*]

Even here, and all too many of the haunts
Of Fancy's choicest pastime, & the best
And Dearest resting places of the heart
Vanish beneath an unrelenting doom
260

Friendship betrayed remorse
Wrongs unredress'd & insults unaveng'd
And unavengeable, defeted pride
{ ening
Prosperity subverted, madd{[?ing] want
Love with despair or grief in [?agony]
giving utterance t my thoughts
Thereafter—[~~?yielding~~]
~~No wonder, giving utterance to my thoughts~~
I said, no wonder that your hapless Friend
Was fancy smitten by this calm retreat
Which we behold even they whose course of
~~Even they who have small reason for complaint~~
Yields [?no] peculiar reason of complaint
~~Might~~ ~~was~~
By this temptation might be lured, to quit
The empty turmoils of a bustling world

---

The four lines at the top of the page are a fresh copy of the last four lines at the foot of 43r.

279/ WW's line count follows from the "240" at the top of 43r. The drafting on the rest of the page is part of his adaptation of ll. 283–285 (on 44r, facing) to *The Excursion* (1814), III, 381–385 (1850: III, 374–378); the last four lines, as a result of later revision to *The Excursion*, are related to ll. 22–24 of bk. V (1814), which became V, 24–26 in 1850.

of old been
What impulse drove the Hermit to his cell
Tell age or death
And what detain'd him there ~~his whole life~~ long
till life was spent
Fast anchored in the desert? not alone
long
Dread of the persecuting sword, remorse
Love with despair or grief in agony.
Not always from intolerable pangs
compass'd round by pleasure
safe pleasures
He fled; but in ~~the height of pleasure~~ sought
quiet
For independence & ~~happiness~~, or an easy peace
The central feeling of all happiness
Not as a refuge from distress, or pain
A breathing time, vacation, or a truce
But for its absolute self, a life of peace
Stability without regret or fear
That hath been, is, & shall be evermore
Therefore on few external things his heart

[DC MS. 65, 44r] [*The Tuft of Primroses*]

of old time
What impulse drove the Hermit to his Cell
To his till age or death
And what detain'd him there ~~his whole life~~
till life was spent long
Fast anchored in the desart? not alone
Dread of the persecuting sword, remorse
Love with despair or grief in agony.
Not always from intolerable pangs
compass'd round by pleasures
life's [?deal]
He fled; but in ~~the height of pleasure~~ sigh'd
quiet
For independent ~~happiness~~, craving peace
The central feeling of all happiness
{pain
Not as a refuge from distress or {[ ? ]
A breathing time, vacation, or a truce
But for its absolute self, a life of peace
Stability without regret or fear
That hath been, is, & shall be ever more
Therefore on few external things his
heart

---

The fair copy runs on from the four lines at the top of 43v, facing. Revisions on this page are probably part of WW's adaptation of ll. 280–308 to *The Excursion* (1814), III, 374–410 (1850: III, 367–405).

Was set, and there his own, or if not his
Subsisting under natures steadfast law.
What other yearning was the master tie
Of the monastic brotherhood, upon rock
Aerial or in green secluded vale
One after one collected from afar
An undissolving fellowship? what but this
The universal instinct of repose
The longing for confirm'd tranquillity
Of small & great in or
Inward and outward, humble & sublime
The life where hope and memory are as one
Earth quiet & unchanged, the human soul
Consistent in self rule, and heaven reveal'd
To meditation in that quietness.

[DC MS. 65, 45r] [*The Tuft of Primroses*]

Was set, and those his own, or if not his
Subsisting under Natures stedfast law.
What other yearning was the master tie
Of the monastic brotherhood, upon rock
Aerial or in green secluded vale
280
One after one collected from afar
An undissolving fellowship? what but this
The universal instinct of repose
{The
{A longing for confirm'd tranquillity
In small & great in or
~~Inward and outward~~, humble & sublime
The life where hope and memory are as one
un}
Earth quiet & th}changed, the human suol
Consistent in sef rule, and heaven revealed
To meditation in that quietness.

---

The fair copy runs on from the foot of 44r.

299/300 WW's line number follows from the "260" at the top of 43v.

304 Revision of this line, in ink similar to that used on the lower part of 43v, is probably part of WW's adaptation of the line toward *The Excursion* (1814), III, 406 (1850: III, 399).

At the top of 44v, facing, WW drafted the following lines, toward bk. III of *The Excursion*:

I spoke in sympathy with him who heard
And now, upon the margin of the rock
In silence by my con

45v is blank.

Thus chasten'd thus inspired St Basil left
Man as he was of noble blood, high born,
High stationed, and elaborately taught
The vain felicities of Athens, left
Her throng of Sophists glorying in their strains
Her Poets, and conflicting Orators,
Relinquish'd
Abandon'd Alexandria's splendid Halls,
Antioch & Cesarea & withdrew
To his delicious Pontic solitude
Remembering with deep thankfulness the wise
Those exhortations of a female voice
Pathetically urg'd his Sister's voice
Macrina, pious Maid, most beautiful
And in the ~~purity~~ gentleness of women wise
By whom admonished, He while yet a Youth
And a triumphant Scholar, had dismiss'd

[DC MS. 65, 46r] [*The Tuft of Primroses*]

Thus tempted thus inspired St Basil left
(Man as he was of noble blood, high-born,
High stationd, and elaborately taught)
{A
The vain felicities of {athens, left
{S
Her throng of {sophists glorying in their snares
{O
Her Poets, and conflicting {orators,
Relinquish'd {Ha
Abandon'd Alexanndrias splendid {[?]lls
Antioch & Cesarea & withdrew
To his delicious Pontic solitude
Remembering with deep thankfulness meanwhile
Those exhortations of a female voice
300 ~~290~~
Pathetically urg'd his Sister's voice
{cr
Ma{[?]ina, pious Maid, most beautiful
gentleness
And in the ~~purity~~ of woman wise
By whom admonish'd, He while yet
a Youth
And a triumphant Scholar, had dismissd

---

The fair copy runs on from the foot of 45r.

319/320 The cancelled "290" appears to be a mistake; the "300" follows from the count of 280 lines on 45r.

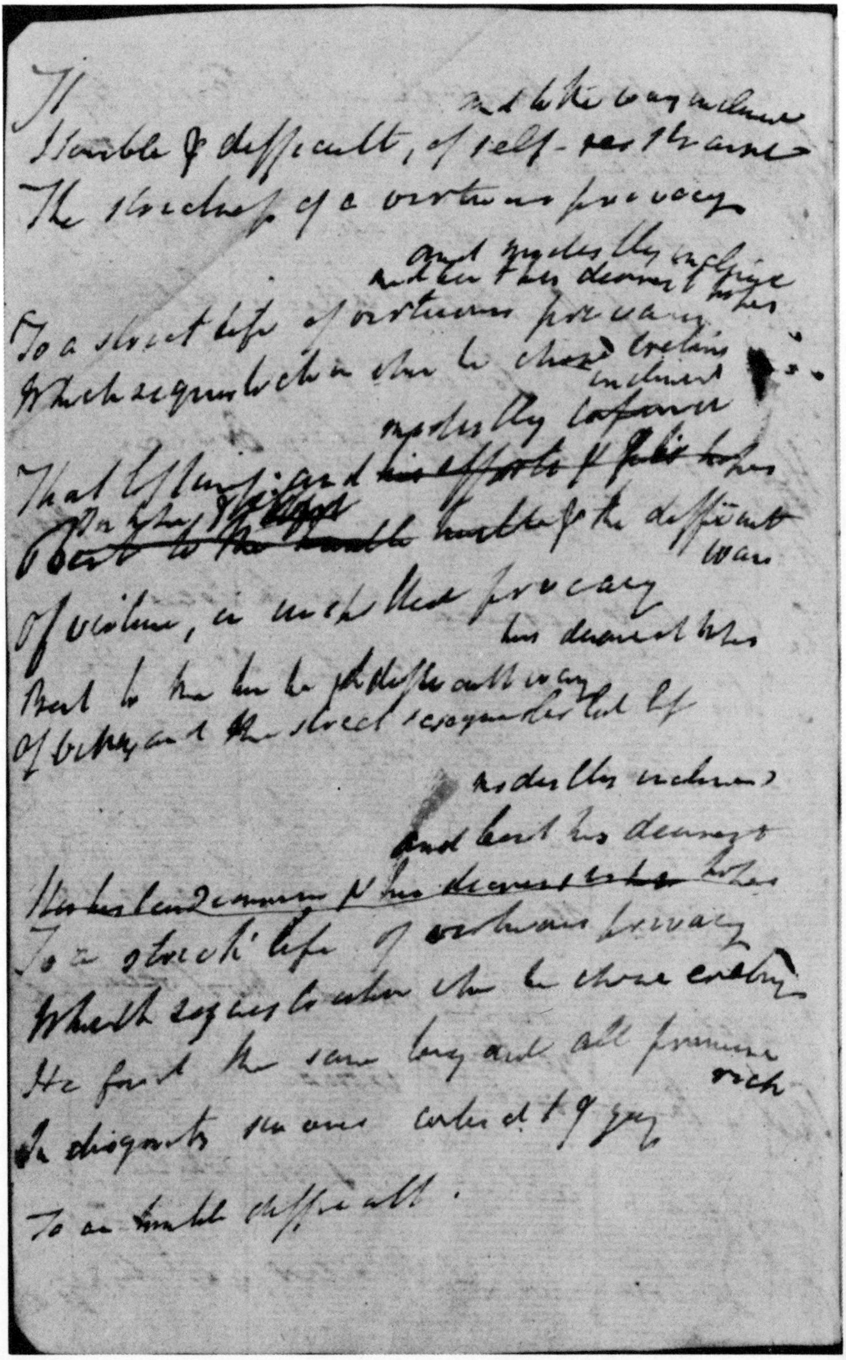

[DC MS. 65, 46$^{v}$] [*The Tuft of Primroses*]

H and to the way inclined
Humble & difficult, of self-restraint
The strictness of a virtuous privacy

and modestly inclind
and bent his dearest hopes
To a strict life of virtuous privacy
Which sequestration when he chose erelong

inclined
modestly ~~confirmd~~
{his
That loftiness: and his efforts & {[?] hopes
In hope & [?effort]
~~Bent to the humble humble~~ & the difficult
way
Of virtue, in unspotted privacy
his dearest hopes
Bent to the humble & the difficult way
Of virtue and the strict [?] sequesterted life

325b modestly inclined
and bent his dearest
hopes
~~His best endeavour & his dearest hopes~~
326 To a strict life of virtuous privacy
{ich
327 Wh{en sequestration when he chose erelong
328 He found the same beyond all promise
rich
329 In dignity sincere content & joy
To an humble difficult

---

Work on this page develops revision begun at the top of 47$^{r}$, facing, and yields ll. 325–329 at the foot of the page.

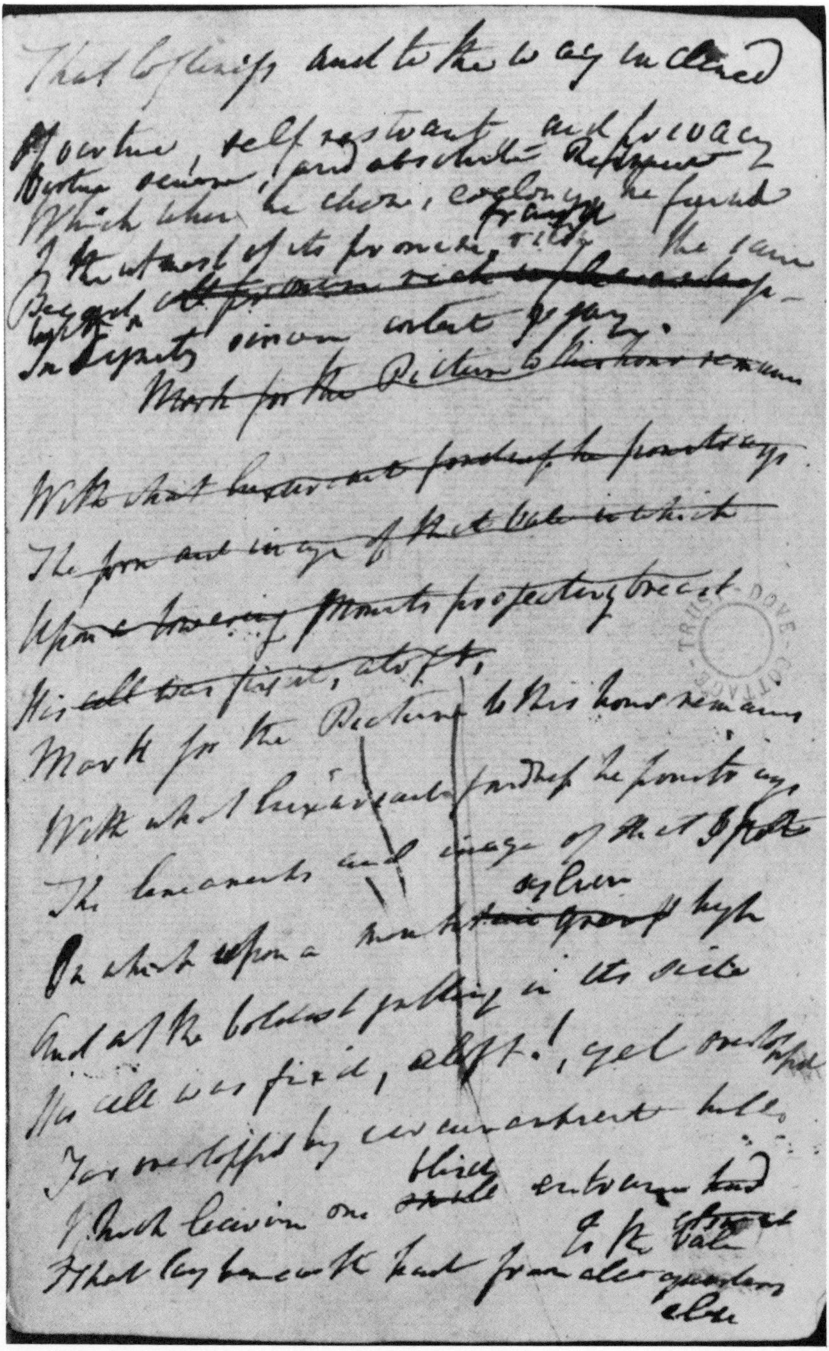

[DC MS. 65, $47^{r}$] [*The Tuft of Primroses*]

325a That loftiness and to the way inclined
Of virtue, self restraint, and privacy
Virtue severe, and absolute Restraint
Which when he chose, erelong he found
the same
fraught
T the utmost of its promise, rich
Beyond^~~all promise rich in pleasantness~~—
With
In dignity sincere content & joy.
~~Mark for the Picture to this hour remains~~
~~With what luxuriant fondness he pourtrays~~
~~The form and image of that Vale in which~~
~~Upon a towering Mounts projecting breast~~
~~His cell was fixed, aloft~~,
Mark for the Picture to this hour remains
With what luxuriant fondness he pourtrays
The lineaments and image of that {spot / vale}
sylvan
In which upon a mount~~ain green &~~ high
And at the boldest jutting in its side
His cell was fix'd, aloft!, yet overtoppd
Far overtoppd by circumambient hills
blind
Which leaving one ~~small~~ entrance ~~had~~
~~almost~~
to the vale
T That lay beneath had from all quarters
else

---

The fair copy runs on from the foot of $46^{r}$.

Revision at the top of this page is continued on $46^{v}$, facing; the canceled work on the rest of the page and on $48^{r}$ is recopied as ll. 330-358 on $49^{r}$–$50^{r}$.

$47^{v}$ is blank.

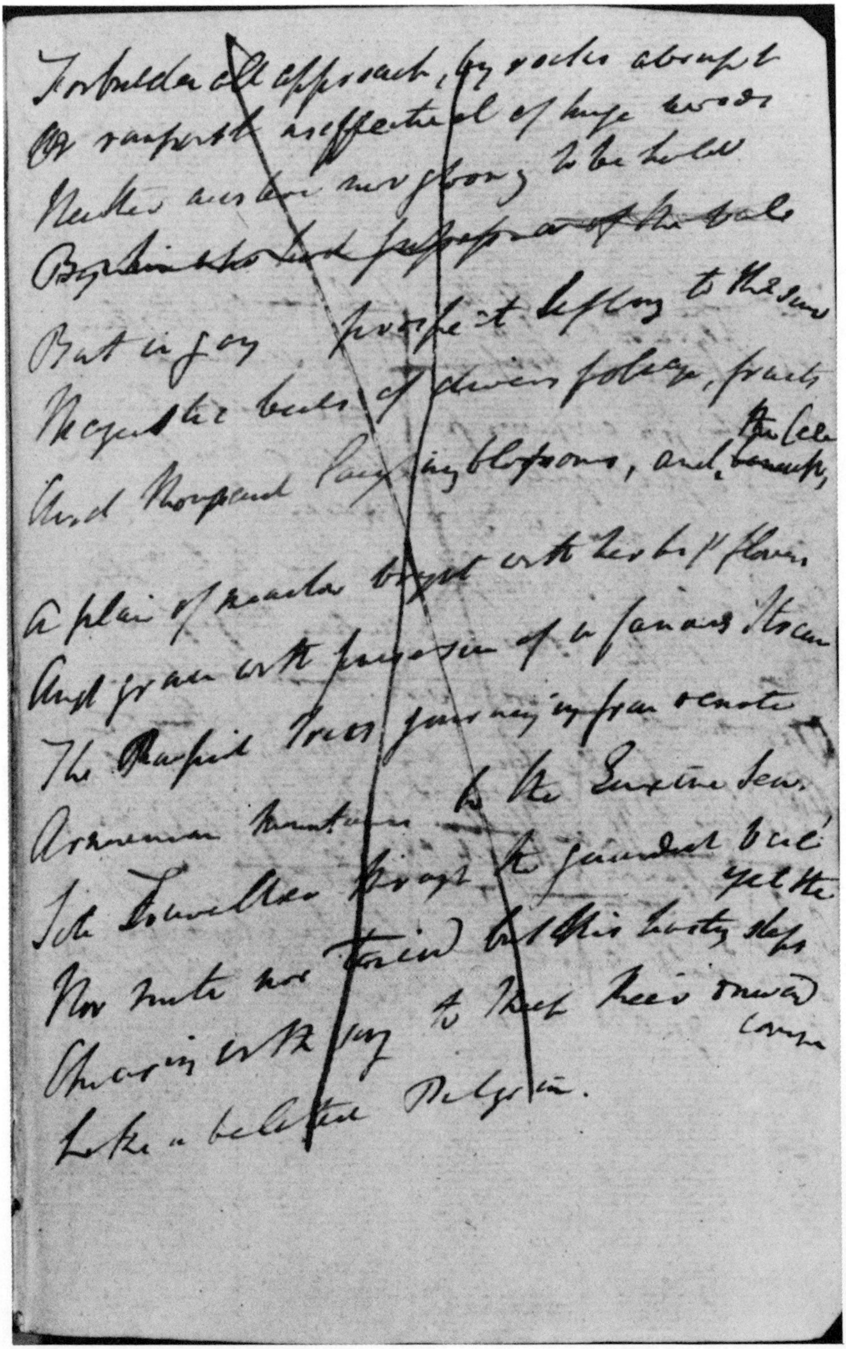

[DC MS. 65, $48^{r}$] [*The Tuft of Primroses*]

Forbidden all approach, by rocks abrupt
{Or
{As rampart as effectual of huge woods
Neither austere nor gloomy to behold
~~By him who had possession of the Vale~~
But in gay prospect lifting to the sun
Majestic beds of divers foliage, fruits
the Cell
And thousand laughing blossoms, and, ~~beneath,~~

A plain of meadow bright with herbs & flowers
And grace with presence of a famous Stream
The Rapid Iris, journeying from remote
Armenian Mountains to the Euxine Sea.
{T
Sole {traveller through the guarded Vale
yet He
Nor mute nor [?timid] but his hasty steps
Chearing with song to keep their onward
course
Like a belated Pilgrim.

---

The fair copy runs on from the foot of $47^{r}$. The passage canceled here is recopied as ll. 340–358 on $49^{r}$ and $50^{r}$.

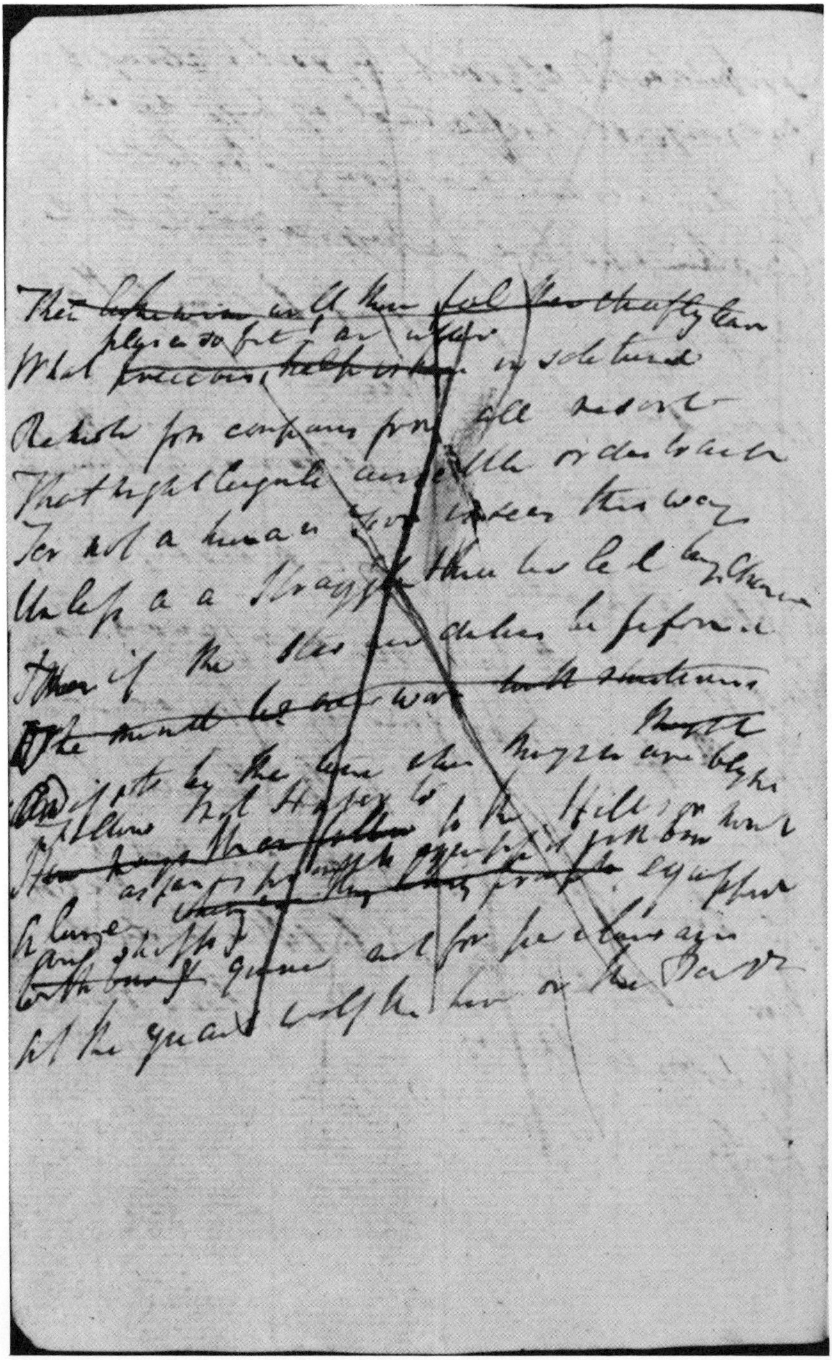

[DC MS. 65, 48$^{v}$] [*The Tuft of Primroses*]

~~Then likewise will thou feel then chiefly learn~~
        place so fit! an utter
What ~~precious help is here~~ in solituud
Remote from company from all resort
That might beguile unsettle or distract
For not a human Form is seen this way
                                    t{
Unless a a Straggler }here be led by Chance
{Then
{Him if the sterner duties be performd
{Or
{~~The mind be overworn with studious~~
                                                    ~~thought~~
{And
{Or if it be the time when thoughts are blyht
    Follow that Strager to
~~Him mayst thou follow~~ to the Hills or mount
        as fancy prompts equipp'd with bow
Alone, ~~where ere thy liking prompts,~~ equipped
    And shafts &
~~With bow &~~ quiver not for perilous aim
At the guant wolf the lion or the Pard

---

Drafting on this page, developed from earlier work on 49$^{v}$, expands and revises the lines beginning "What place so fit . . ." at the middle of 50$^{v}$ (see note to 50$^{v}$).

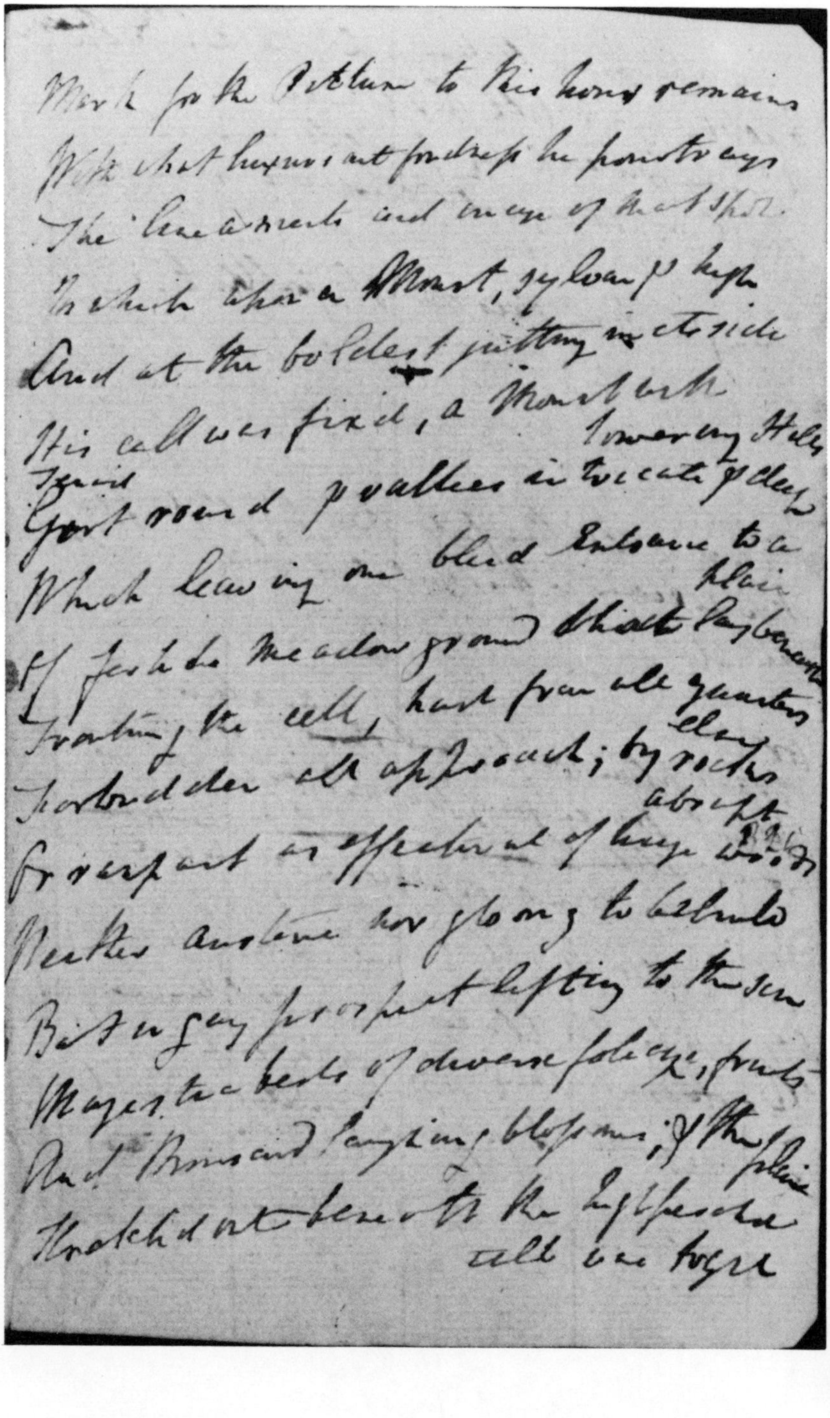

[DC MS. 65, 49r] [*The Tuft of Primroses*]

330 Mark for the Picture to this hour remains
331 With what luxuriant fondness he pourtrays
332 The lineaments and image of that spot
333 In which upon a Mount, sylvan & high
334 And at the boldest jutting in its side
335 His cell was fix'd, a Mount with
    Fenc'd                         Towering Hills
336 Girt round & vallies intricate & deep
337 Which leaving one blind Entrance to a
                                        t} {at plain
338 Of fertile Meadow ground w}h{ich lay beneath
339 Fronting the cell, had from all quarters
                                        else
340 Forbidden all approach; by rocks
                                        abrupt
                                        320
341 Or rampart as effectual of huge woods
342 Neither austere nor gloomy to behold
343 But a gay prospect lifting to the sun
344 Majestic beds of diverse foliage, fruits
345 And thousand laughing blossoms; & the plain
346 Stretch'd out beneath the high perchd
                                cell was bright

---

WW here makes a fresh start at the passage begun (then deleted) on 47r and 48r.

340/341 The count of 320 lines follows from the "300" on 46r; it does not include the revisions of ll. 325–329 on 47r and 46v.

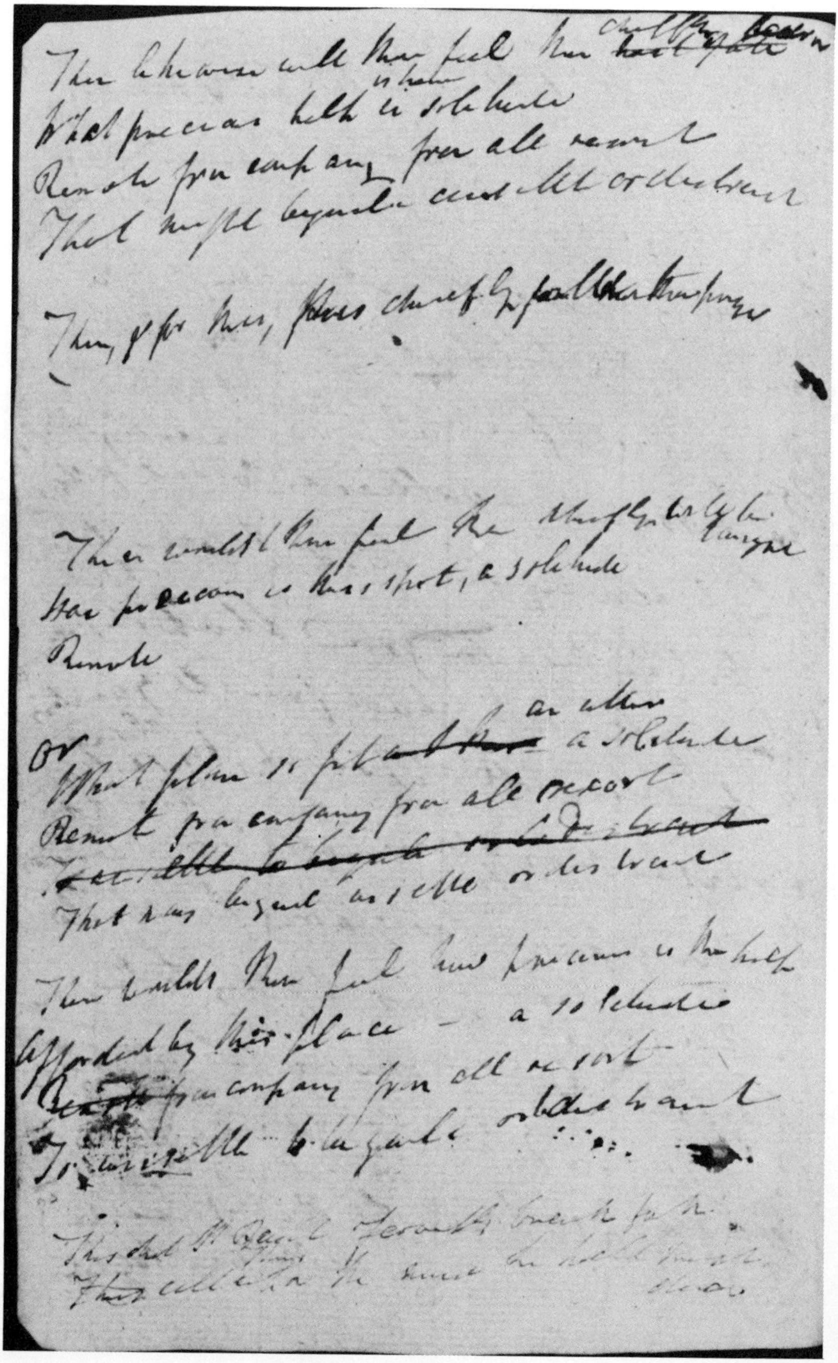

[DC MS. 65, 49$^{v}$] [*The Tuft of Primroses*]

chiefly {learn / feel}
Then likewise will thou feel then [?most] of all
is here
What precious help in solitude
Remote from company from all resort
That might beguile unsettle or distract

Then, & for this, {this / [ ? ]} chiefly {will / [ ? ? ]} thou prize

Then wouldst thou feel then chiefly will be
taught
How precious is this spot, a solitude
Remote

or an utter
What place is fit as this—a solitude
Remote from company from all resort
To unsettle to beguile or to distract
That may beguil unsettle or distract

Then woulds thou feel how precious is the help
Afforded by this place—a solitude
away
Remote from company from all resort
To unsettle to beguile or {to} distract

Thus did St Basil Fervently break forth
Thus
Thus called [?] to the man he held most
dear

---

Most of the drafting on this page is intermediate between the lines beginning "What place so fit . . ." on 50$^{v}$ and the further expansion of those lines on 48$^{v}$ (see note to 50$^{v}$); the "or" in the left-hand margin marks an alternate passage of drafting.

The last two lines at the foot of the page are revisions of the last two lines at the foot of 50$^{r}$, facing.

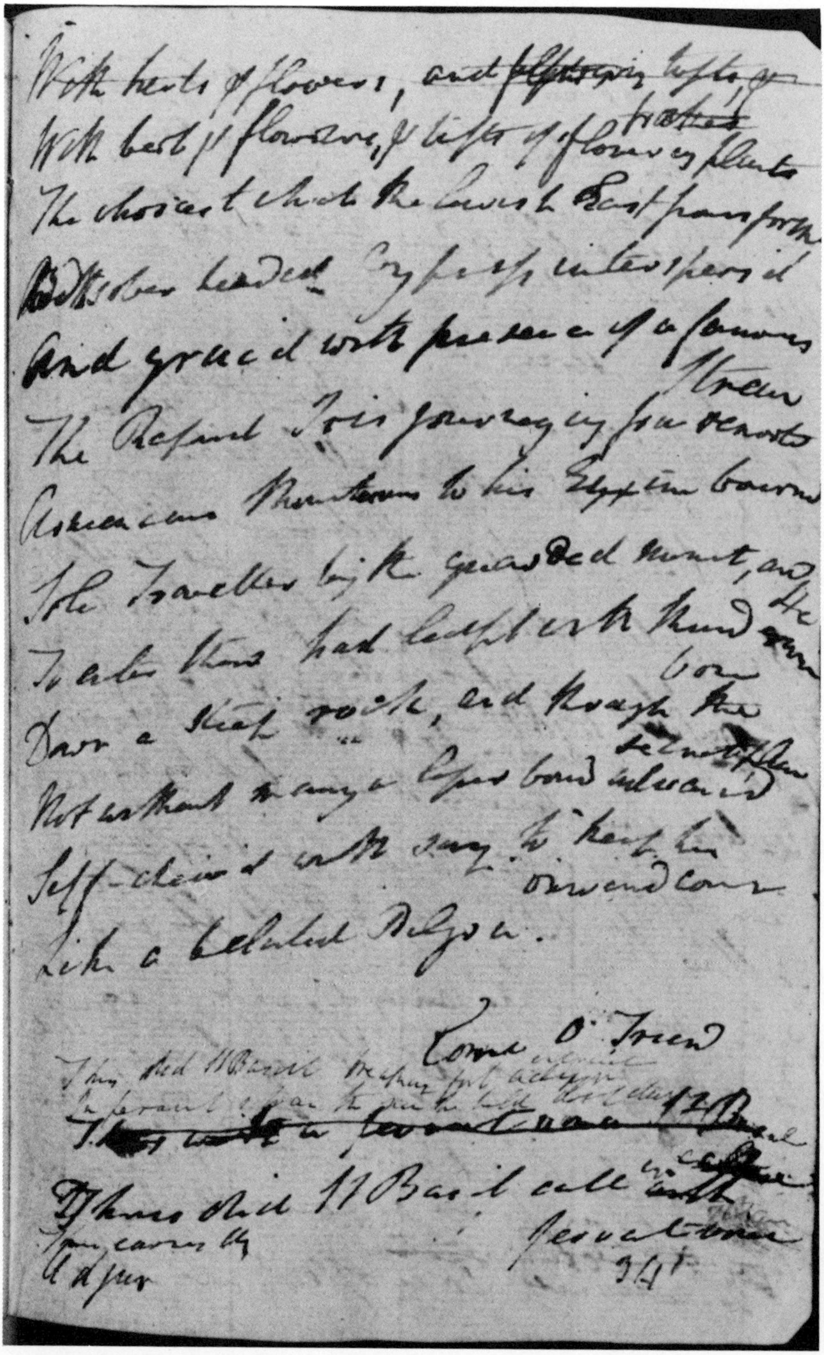

[DC MS. 65, 50$^{r}$] [*The Tuft of Primroses*]

{flowering
~~With herbs & flowers, and~~ {~~[?tufts] tufts, &~~
~~brakes~~
347 With herb & flowers, & tufts of flowering plants
348 The choicest which the lavish East pours forth
{And
349 {[?] sober headed Cypress interspers'd
350 And grac'd with presence of a famous
Stream
351 The Rapid Iris journeying from remote
352 Armenian Mountains to his Euxine bourne
353 Sole Traveller by the guarded mount, and
He
354 To enter there had leapt with thunderous
Voice
355 Down a steep rock, and through the
secret plain
356 Not without many a lesser bound advanc'd
357 Self-chear'd with song to keep his
onward course
358a Like a belated Pilgrim.

Come O Friend
entreat
Thus did St. Basil breaking fort adjur
In fervent strain the man he held most dear
~~Thus with a fervent voice St Basil~~
~~called~~

{T in
{Dhus did St Basil call ~~with~~
Thus earnestly strain
Adjur fervent ~~voice~~
340

---

The fair copy runs on from the foot of 49$^{r}$.

358 The address to Nazianzen that begins with the second half of this line continues on 51$^{r}$ and 52$^{r}$ and breaks off on 53$^{r}$; an expanded version of the address starts at the top of 54$^{r}$ and runs through 55$^{r}$ and 56$^{r}$ and ends on 57$^{r}$. The final version begins at the top of 58$^{r}$.

WW's count of 340 lines at the foot of the page follows from the "320" on 49$^{r}$.

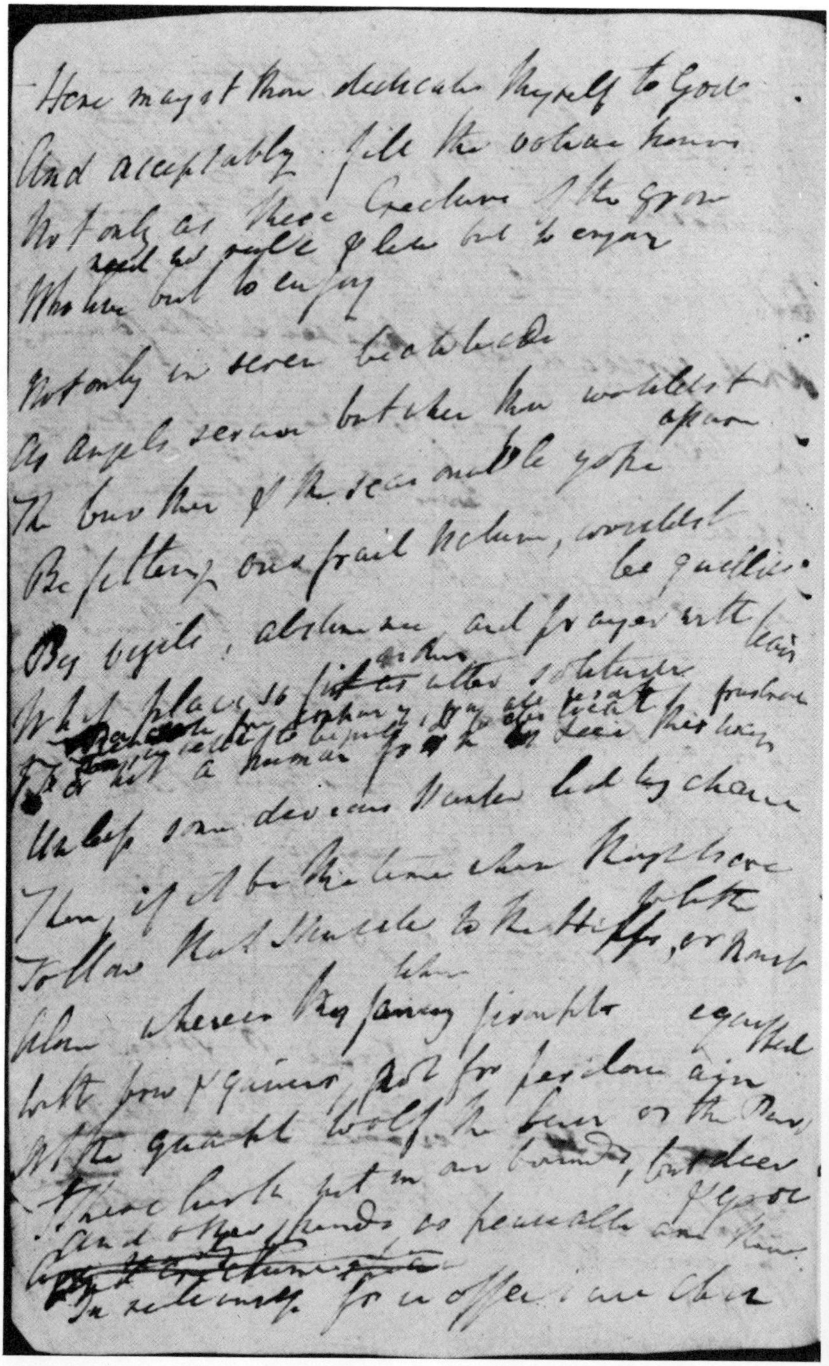

[DC MS. 65, 50$^{\text{v}}$] [*The Tuft of Primroses*]

Here mayst thou dedicate thyself to God
And acceptably fill the votive hours
Not only as these Creatures of the grove
need no rule & live but to enjoy
Who live but to enjoy
Not only in serene beatitude
As angels seruve but when thou wouldst
assume
The burthen & the seasonable yoke
Befitting our frail Nature, wouldst
be quelld
By vigils, abstinence, and prayer with tears
as this
What place so f~~it as~~ utter solitude
[?]
Remote from company, from all resort
frustrate
[ ? ] unsettle, to beguile or to distract
For not a human form is seen this way
Unless some devious Hunter led by chance
Then, if it be the time when thoughts are
blithe
{Hills
Follow that [?Hunter] to the {[?cliff], or mount
liking
Alone whereer thy fancy prompts equipped
{n
With bow & quiver, {fot for perilous aim
At the guant Wolf the Lion or the Pard
TThese lurk not in our bounds, but deer
& goat
And other kinds as peaceable are there
~~Are ready~~
~~And creatures [?peac]~~
In readiness for inoffensive chase

---

The drafting on this page develops work on 51$^{\text{v}}$ and continues the revision and expansion of the lines at the top of 52$^{\text{r}}$. The passage entered here, almost in fair copy, is meant to continue the poem from the last line on 51$^{\text{r}}$, facing. Further revision and expansion on 49$^{\text{v}}$ and then on 48$^{\text{v}}$ is incorporated in the fresh copy of the address to Nazianzen started at the top of 54$^{\text{r}}$.

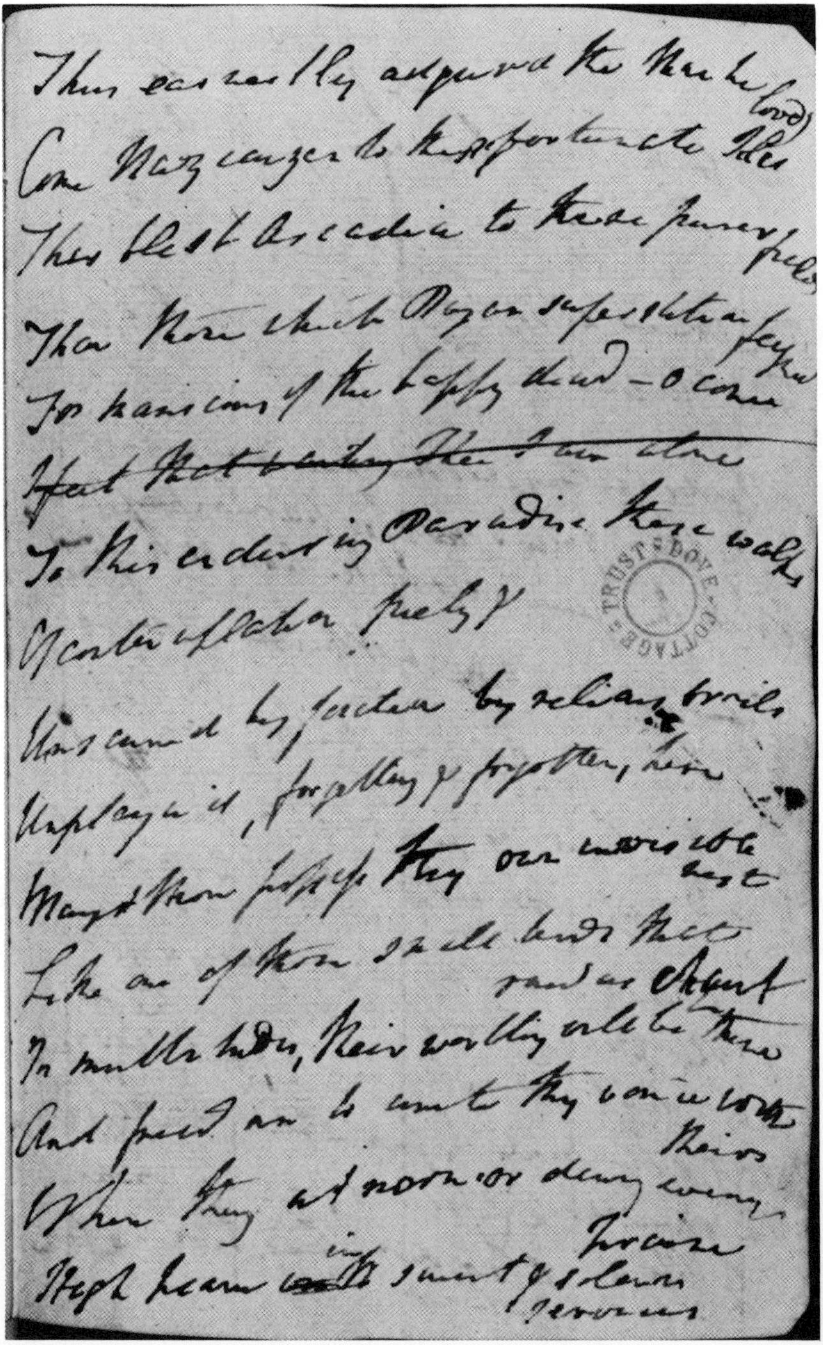

[DC MS. 65, 51r] [*The Tuft of Primroses*]

Thus earnestly adjurd the Man he lovd,
{se
Come Nazianzen to the{ fortunate Isles
This blest Arcadia to these purer fields
Than those which Pagan superstition feigned
For mansions of the happy dead—O come
~~I feel that wanting Thee I am alone~~
To this enduring Paradise these walks
Of contemplation piety &
Unscarred by faction by relious broils
Unplagu'd, forgetting & forgotten, here
Mayst thou possess thy own invisible
nest
Like one of those small birds that
{chant
round us {sing
In multitudes, their warbling will be thine
And freedom to unite thy voice with
theirs
When they at noon or dewy evening
in praise
High heaven ~~with~~ sweet & solemn
services

The fair copy on this page runs on from the foot of 50r.

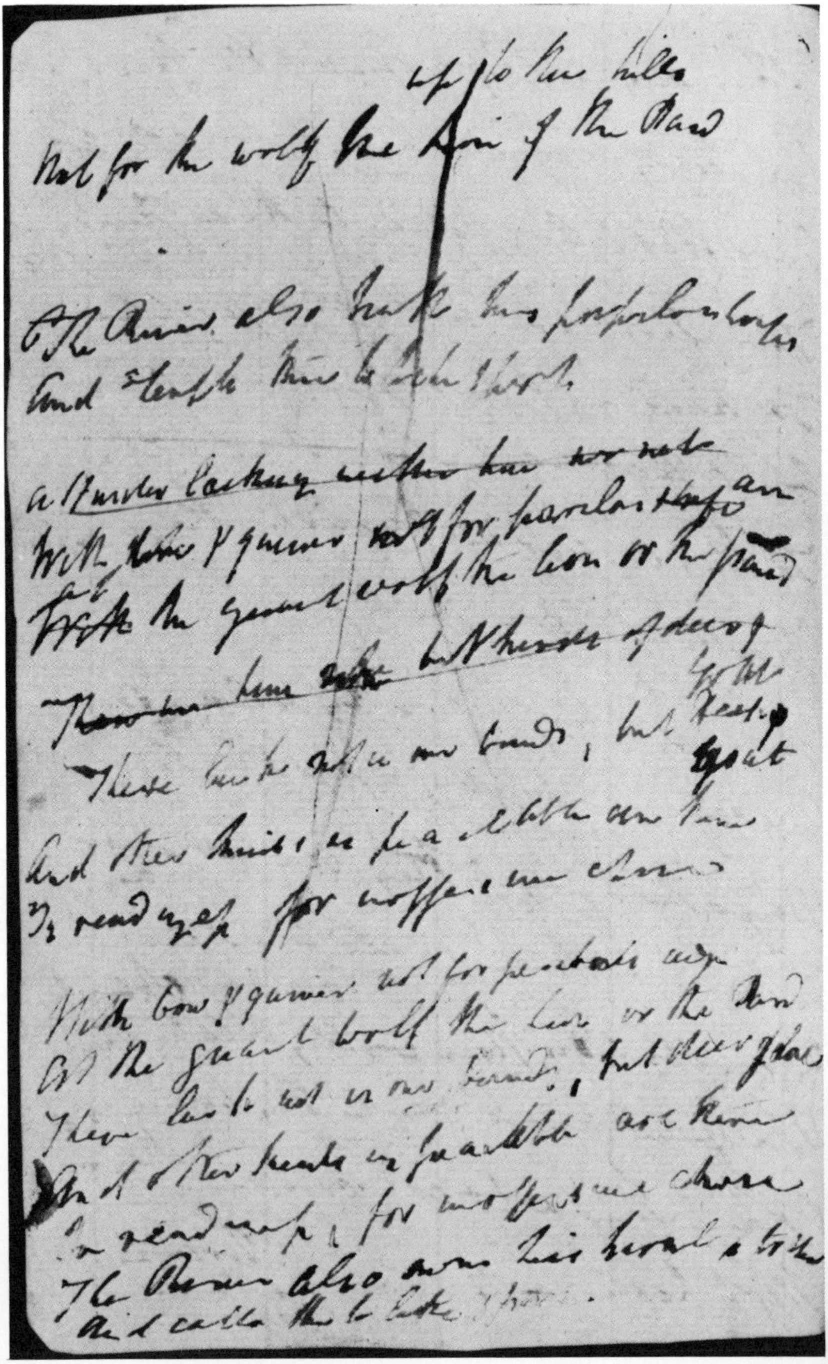

[DC MS. 65, 51v] [*The Tuft of Primroses*]

up to the hills
Not for the wolf the Lion of the Pard

~~R~~The River also hath his populous tribes
And tempts thee to like sport

~~A Hunter lacking neither bow nor net~~
With {bow / net} & quiver {not / [?]} for perilous aim ~~strife~~
at
~~With~~ the guant wolf the lion or the pard
~~These we have {none / [ ? ] but herds of deer &~~
Goat
These lurk not in our bounds, but Deer & {G / goat}
And other kinds as peaceable are here
In readiness for inoffensive chase

With bow & quiver not for perilous aim
At the guant Wolf the Lion or the Pard
These lurk not in our bounds, but deer & Goat
And other kinds as peaceable are there
In readiness, for inoffensive chase
The River also owns his harmless tribes
And calls thee to like sport

---

The drafting on this page is intermediate between the lines at the top of 52r and the further expansion and revision of those lines on 50v, 49v, and 48v.

[DC MS. 65, $52^r$] [*The Tuft of Primroses*]

And when is
~~Or if~~ thy mood be gay, up to the hills
With quiver shafts & bow the deer & Goat
And fiercer creatures [?we have none] are there
~~Are ready there~~
In readiness for inoffensive chase

owns
The River also {hath his harmless tribes
~~The River swarms with fish; labour itself~~
And calls thee to like sport
Is pastime here, for generous is the soil
~~And merciful the [?sun his]~~
~~Unless with large clouds that promise~~
~~lovely showers~~
And cool airs blowing from the mountain tops
Refresh the brow of him who in plain field
Or garden presses his industrious
Or if a different exercise thou chuse
And from boon Nature rather woulds
receive
Food for the day behold the fruits
that hang
In the primæval woods the wells & springs
Have each a living garland of ~~wild~~
~~flowers~~
green herbs

---

Fair copy on this page, degenerating into drafting, runs on from the foot of $51^r$. The lines at the top of the page were revised and expanded on $51^v$. Then a new version of the passage was entered on $50^v$; further expansion and revision on $49^v$ and then on $48^v$ are incorporated in the fresh copy of the address to Nazianzen, which starts at the top of $54^r$.

WW's count of 360 lines follows from the "340" at the bottom of $50^r$.

$52^v$ is blank.

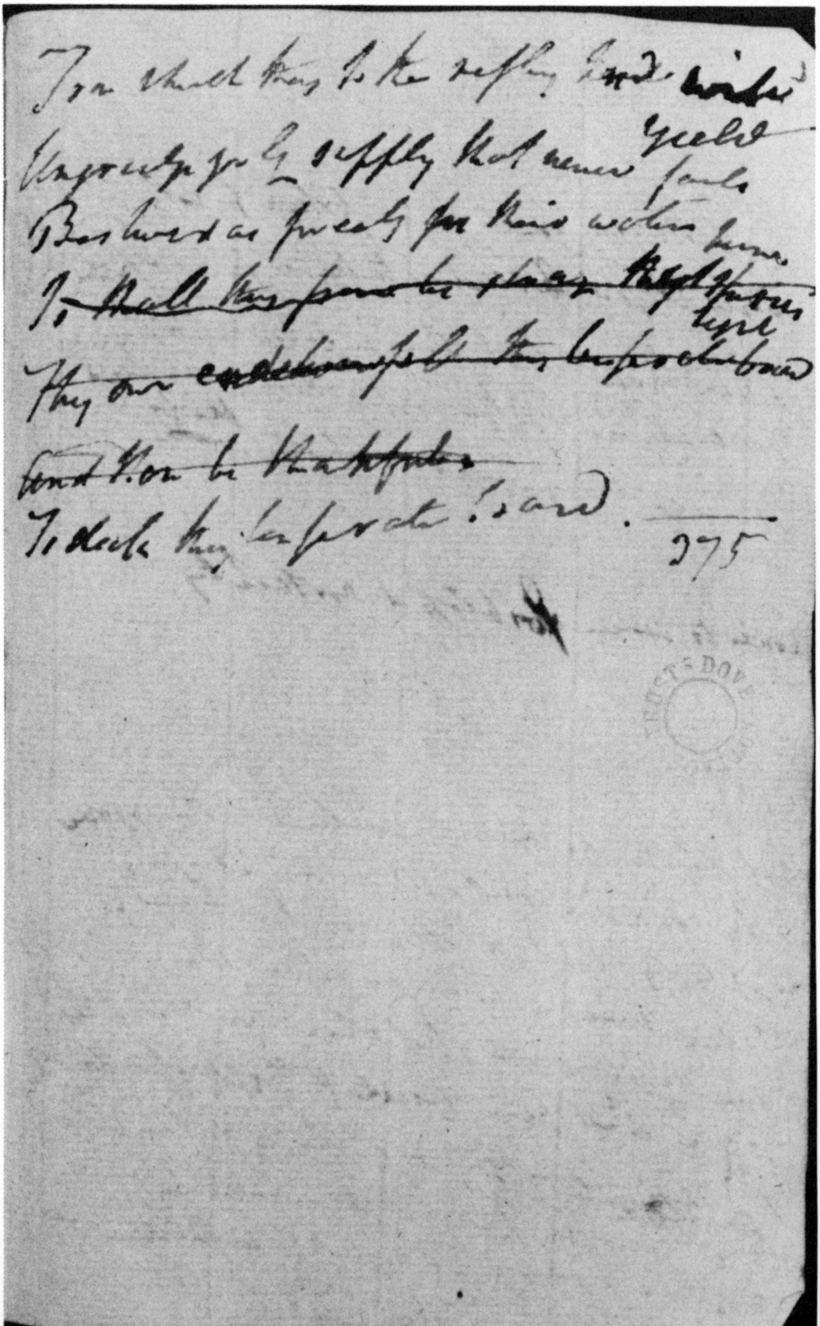

[DC MS. 65, 53r] [*The Tuft of Primroses*]

From which they to the rifling hand will
yield
Ungrudgingly supply that never fails
{as
Bestowd as freely {for their waters pure
{y
~~So shall thy frame be strong th{at spirits~~
{endeavour light
~~Thy own {[?exertion] fill thy temperate board~~
~~And thou be thankful.~~
To deck thy temperate board. __________

---

The fair copy runs on from the foot 52v. The rule followed by a count of 375 lines indicates a stopping place in transcription; the manuscript contains no further line numbers.

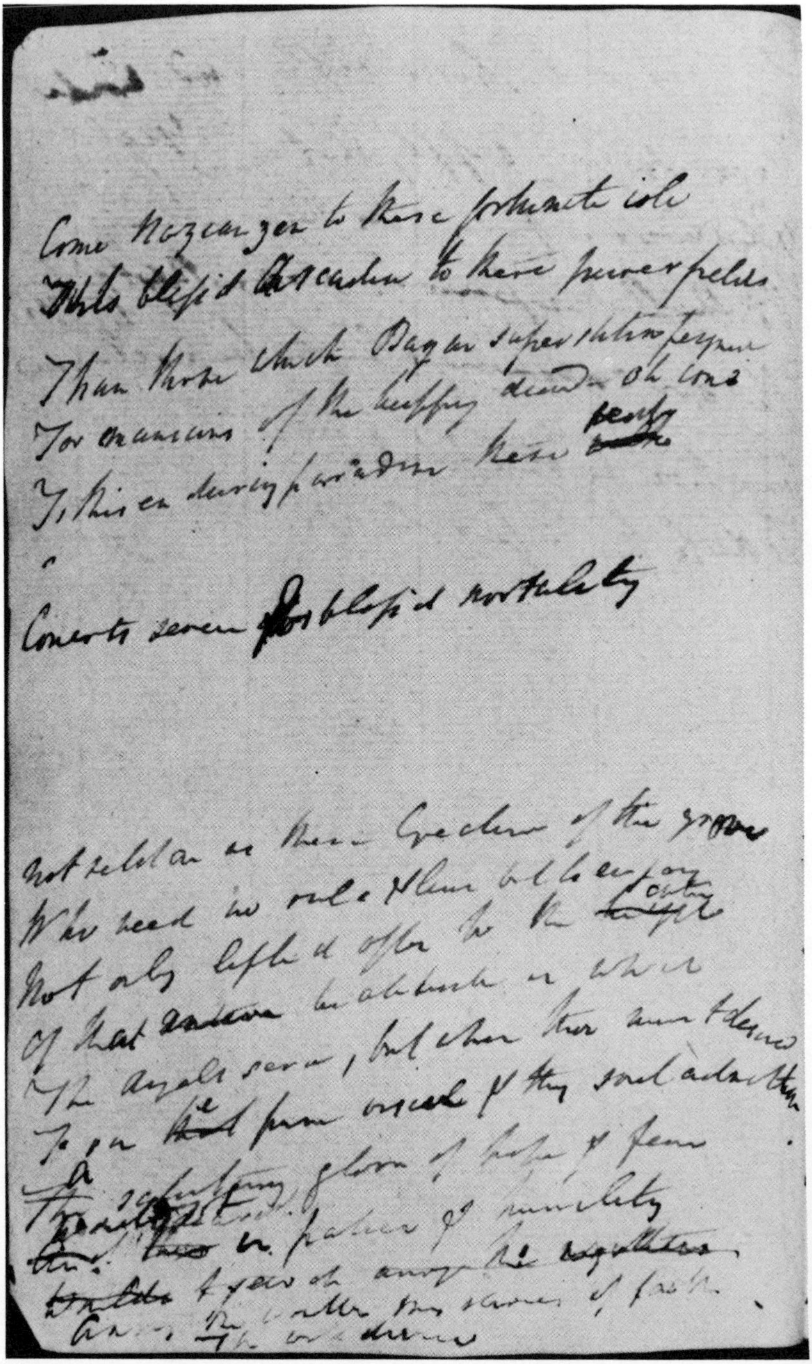

[DC MS. 65, 53v] [*The Tuft of Primroses*]

Come Nazianzen to these fortunate isle
{This {A
{To t bless'd {arcadia to these purer fields
Than those which Pagan superstition feigned
For mansions of the happy dead—oh come
seats
To this enduring paradise these ~~walks~~

{for
Coverts serene {of bless'd mortality

{ove
Not seldom as these Creatures of the gr{ave
Who need no rule & live but to enjoy
calm
Not only lifted often to the ~~height~~
at}{ entire
Of th[?e]}{[?serene] beatitude in which
The angels serve, but when thou must descend
e {ion {ting
From ~~that~~ pure vis{[?] & thy soul admit{s
A
~~The~~ salutary glow of hope & fear
Wouldst search
~~And thus~~ in patience & humility
{mysteries
~~Wouldst search among the {written~~
Among the written mysteries of faith
The will divine

---

Top: a draft version of the first lines of the address to Nazianzen, related to work on 54r, facing, and virtually identical to the lines as they appear at the top of 51r.

Middle: a draft of l. 364 meant to be inserted on 54r, facing, and incorporated in the fair-copy text on 58r.

Bottom: draft revision, developing the passage begun two lines from the bottom of 54r, facing, and yielding ll. 385–394 on 58v.

Come O Friend & Brother
(Thus didst thou Basil fervently break forth
Entreated thus the Man he held most dear)
Come Nazianzen to this blessed spot
To this enduring Paradise, there walk
Of contemplation piety and love
by no change disturbed
Unscared by faction, by seditious brawls
Unplagued, forgetting and forgotten, here
Mayst thou possess thy own invisible nest
Like one of those small Birds that round us throng
In multitudes, their warbling will be there
And freedom to unite thy voice with theirs
When they at morn or dewy evening praise
High Heaven in sweetly silent services.
Here mayst thou dedicate thy self to God
And acceptably fill the solemn hours
Not only as those Creatures of the grove
Who need no rule and have but to enjoy—

[DC MS. 65, 54[r]] [*The Tuft of Primroses*]

exclai
Come O Friend
did
(Thus St Basil fervently break forth
Entreated thus the Man he held most dear)
shelterd
Come Nazianzen to this blessed Spot
seats
To this enduring Paradise, these ~~walks~~
Of contemplation piety and love.
No loss lamenting by no change disturbed
Unscar'd by faction, by relious broils
Unplagu'd, forgetting and forgotten, here
Mayst Thou possess thy own invisible nest~~ed~~
Like one of those small Birds that round us
chant
sing
In multitudes; their warbling will be thine
And freedom to unite thy voice with theirs
When they at morn or dewy evening, praise
High Heaven in sweet & solemn services.
Here mayst thou dedicate thyself to God
And acceptably fill the votive hours
Not only as those Creatures of the groves
Who need no rule and live but to enjoy

---

On this page WW makes a fresh start at the address to Nazianzen that begins at the bottom of 50[r], continues on 51[r] and 52[r], and ends on 53[r].

The "ed" at the end of the line at mid-page was deleted by erasure.

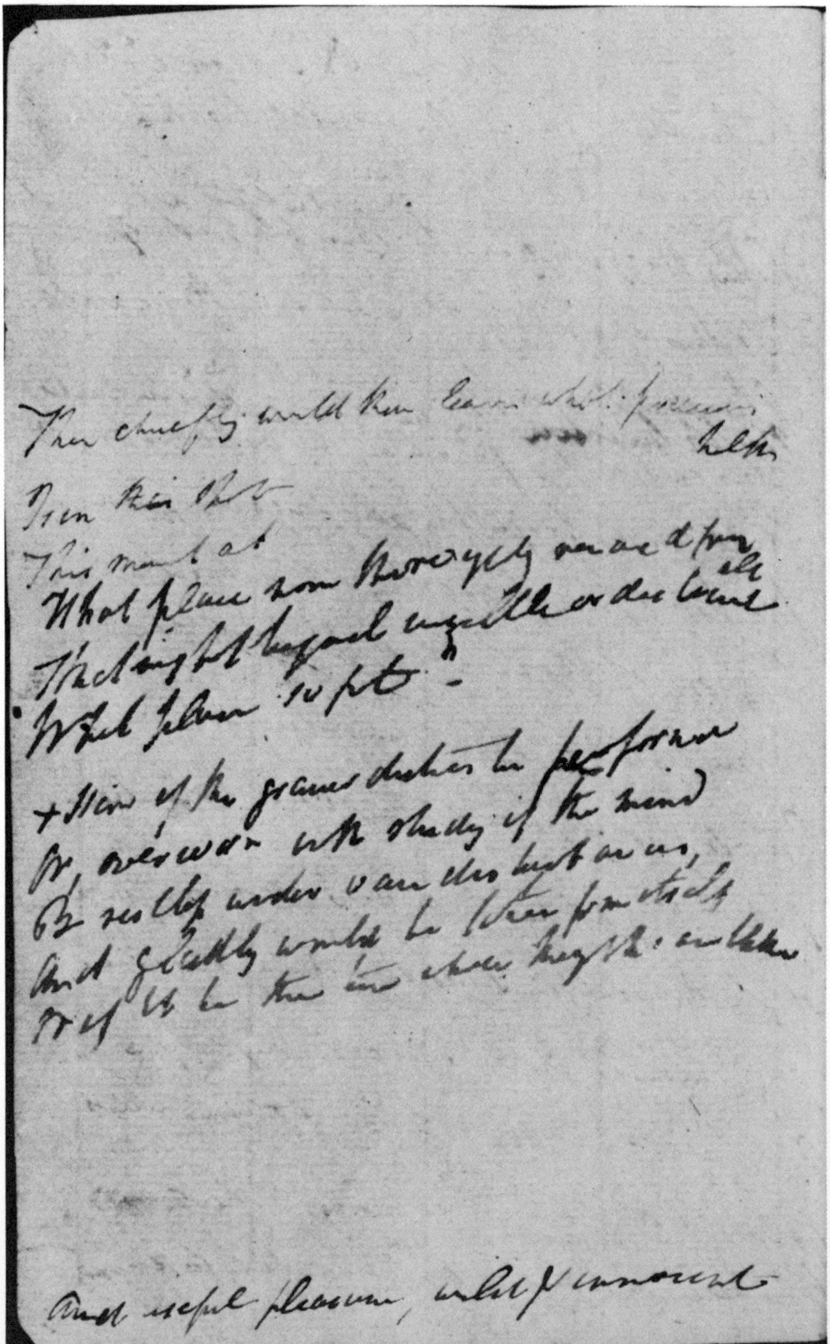

[DC MS. 65, 54v] [*The Tuft of Primroses*]

Then chiefly would thou learn what precious
help
Is in this spot
This must at

What place more thoroughly removd from
all
That might beguile unsettle or distract
?
What place so fit—

X Him if the graver duties be performd
Or, overworn with study if the mind
Be restless under vain disturbances,
And gladly would be taken from itself
Or if it be the time when thoughts are blithe

And useful pleasure, mild & innocent

---

The drafting at the top of this page is similar to draft lines on 50v, 49v, and 48v and may represent WW's intention to insert similar revisions on 55r, facing.

The five-line passage marked with an X (which becomes ll. 403–407 on 59r) is meant to be substituted for the two lines below the X on 55r, facing.

The line at the foot of the page is meant to follow the last line on 55r, facing.

That only in serene beatitude
As Angels serve, but when those worldlings spurn
The burthen and the seasonable yoke

by our frail Nature, would be

By vigils abstinence and prayers with tears
What place so fit? — a deeper solitude
The Cave, or the Pyrenean wilderness,
Continent [illegible], in its Forest barren round;
For not a human Form is seen there any
Unless some straggling Hunter led by chance
Him, if these sylvan duties be performed
And if it be the time when thoughts are blithe,
Him mayst thou follow to the hills, or mount
Alone, as fancy prompts, equipped with bow
And shafts and quiver, not for perilous aim
At the gaunt Wolf the Lion or the Bear
These bred not in our bounds, but Deer & Goat
And other kinds as peaceable as these
In readiness for inoffensive chase
[illegible]

[DC MS. 65, 55r] [*The Tuft of Primroses*]

Not only in serene beatitude
{A
As {angels serve, but when thou wouldst assume
The burthen and the seasonable yoke
by our frail Nature, woulds be
By vigils abstinence and prayer with tears
What place so fit?—a deeper solitude
Thebais, or the Syrian wilderness,
Contains not, in its dry & barren round;
For not a human Form is seen this way
Unless some Straggling Hunter led by chance
X graver
Him, if the ~~sterner~~ duties be perform'd
And if it be the time when thoughts are blithe,
Him mayst Thou follow to the hills, or mount
Alone, as fancy prompts, equipped with bow
And shafts and quiver, not for perilous aim
At th guant Wolf the Lion or the Pard
These lurk not in our bounds, but Deer
& Goat
And other kinds as peaceable are there
In readiness for inoffensive chase
and [?useful]

---

The fair copy runs on from the foot of 54r.
The X in the left-hand margin points to five lines of revision, similarly marked, on 54v, facing.

The River also owns his heartless tribes
And calls them to like sport: labour itself
Is pastime here;
And cool airs blowing from the mountain top
Refresh the brows of him who in plain field
Or garden prospers his under sultry shade.
Bring a different occasion those ...
And from ... Nature rather would ...
Food for the day, behold the Fruits that have
In the primaeval woods: the Wells & Springs
Have each a living garland of green herbs
From which they to the supply kind will yield
Ungrudgingly supply that never fails
Bestowed as freely as their waters ...
To deck thy temperate board.—
From them to them
Transported thus, and by a ... zeal
That slipp'd not him, the venerable Man
Holy & great, the institution framed

[DC MS. 65, 56r] [*The Tuft of Primroses*]

The River also owns his harmless tribes
And calls them to like sport: labour itself
Is pastime here,
And cool airs blowing from the mountain top
Refresh the brow of him who in plain field
Or garden presses his industrious spade.
Or if a different exercise Thou chuse
And from boon Nature rather wouldst recieve
Food for the day, behold the Fruits that hang
{W
In the primæval Woods: the {wells & Springs
Have each a living garland of green herbs
From which they to the rifling hand will
yield
Ungrudgingly supply that never fails
Bestow'd as freely as their waters pure
To deck thy temperate board.—
From theme to theme
Transported thus, and by a fervent zeal
That stopp'd not here, the venerable
Man
Holy & great, his invitation
framed

---

The fair copy runs on from the foot of 55r. At the foot of 55v, facing, WW drafted the following passage, intermediate between the second and third lines from the foot of 56r and the second and third lines at the top of 56v:

Thus}
[?en}r] ~~rapt~~ [?correspond]
Transported in this sort by fervent
zeal
That stoppd not here

From thence to thence
Transported in this sort by fervent zeal
That stopp'd not there the venerable Thane
Were in [illegible] fram'd: nor was it long
Ere Nazianzen broken loose from chains
Of the world's business at his call appear'd
And Amphilochius came; and numbers more
Men of all ages qualities estates
Came with one spirit, like a troop of fowl
That single, or in clusters, at a sign
Given by their Leader, settle on the breast
Of some broad pool, green field or lofty tree
In her wing [illegible]

[DC MS. 65, 56v] [*The Tuft of Primroses*]

From theme to theme
Transported in this sort by fervent zeal
That stopp'd not here the venerable Man
His invitation framd: nor was it long
Ere Nazianzen broken loose from {c / Chains}
Of the worlds business at his call appeard
And Amphilochius came; and numbers more
Men of all ages qualities estates
Came with one spirit, like a troop of fowl
That, single, or in numbers, at a sign
Given by their Leader, settle on the breast
Of some broad pool, green field or lofty tree
In harmony & undisturbed {repose / [?accord]}

---

These lines are a cleanly copied version of the passage that begins three and a half lines from the foot of 56r and ends on the top of 57r.

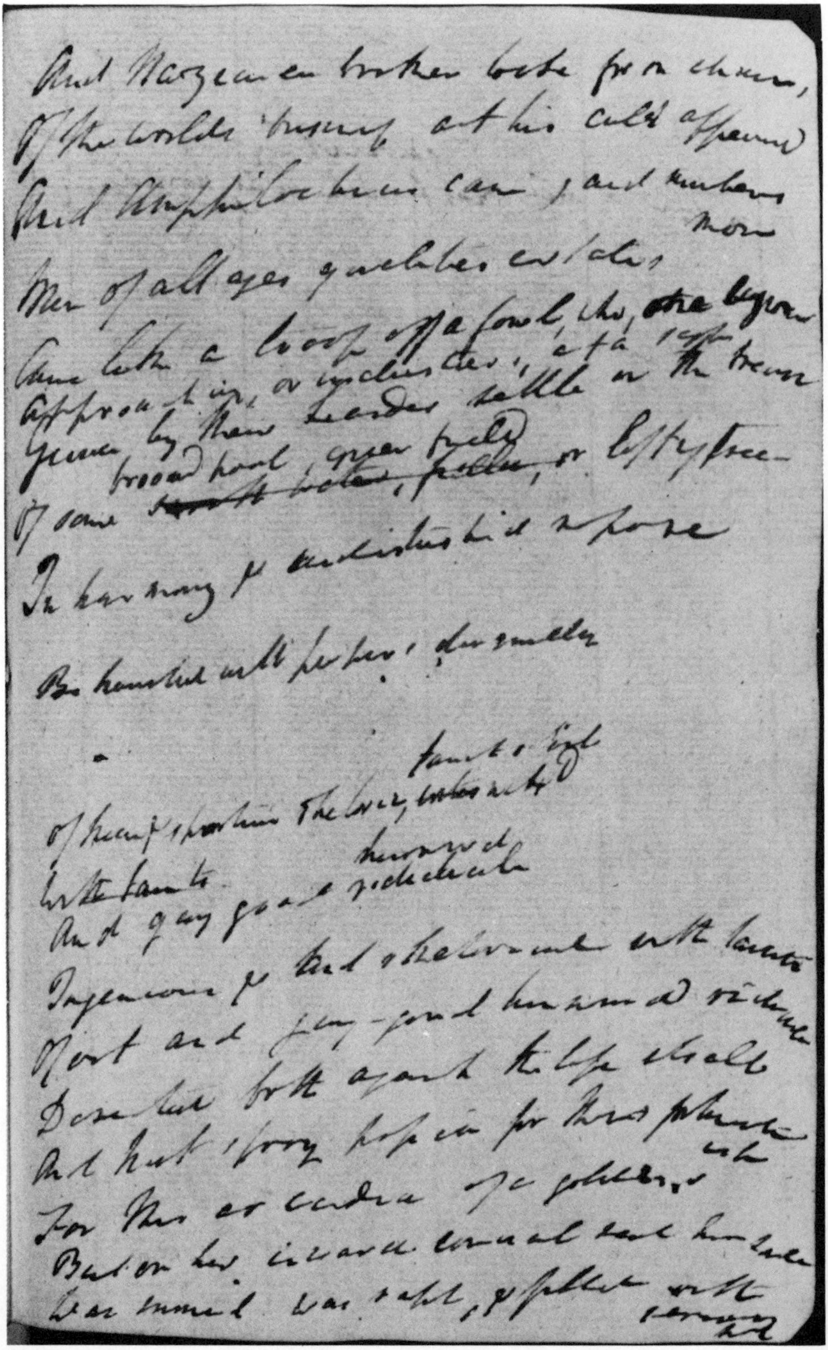

[DC MS. 65, 57r] [*The Tuft of Primroses*]

And Nazianen broken loose from chains
Of the worlds business at his call appeared
And Amphilochius came, and numbers
more
Men of all ages qualities estates
{one legion
Came like a troop off a fowl, who, {at a sign
Approaching, or in clusters, at a sign
Given by their Leader settle on the breast
broоad pool, green field
Of some ~~smooth water, fields~~ or lofty tree—
In harmony & undisturb'd repose

Be haunted with perfect tranquilly

taunts wit
Of keen & sportive rhetoric, ~~inter~~[ ? ]
~~With taunts~~
humourd
And gay good ridicule
{a
434 Ingenious & {tnd rhetorical with taunts
435 Of wit and gay-good humourd ridicule
436 Directed both against the life itself
437 And that strong passion for these fortunate
isle
438 For this arcadia of a golden [?d]
439 But on her inward council seat his soul
440 Was mov'd was rapt, & filld with
serious
ness

---

The fresh start begun at the top of 54r (and continued on 55r and 56r) breaks off here after eight lines.

The single line at the middle of the page appears to be related to the revision of l. 405 on 59r.

434–440 These lines incorporate revisions drafted at the foot of 59v and the top and bottom of 60r.

Come a Friend

Thus did St Basil fervently break forth
Entreating thus the man he held most dear
Come Nazianzen to these ~~sheltered spot~~ happier fields
To these enduring Paradise, these ~~seats~~ walks
Of contemplation piety & love,
Coverts serene of bless'd mortality.
What if the Roses and the flowers of kings
Princes and Emperors, and the crowns & palms
Of all the great are blasted, or decay,
What if the meanest of their subjects, each
Within the narrow region of ~~his~~ his cares
Tremble beneath a sad uncertainty;
There is a privilege to plead, there is,
Renounce, and thou shalt find that privilege here.
No loss lamenting, no privation felt,
Disturb'd by no vicissitudes, unscared
By civil faction by religious broils
Unplagued, forgetting, & forgotten here
Mayst thou possess thy own invisible rest

[DC MS. 65, 58r] [*The Tuft of Primroses*]

358b Come o Friend (
359 Thus did St Basil fervently break forth
360 Entreated thus the man he held most dear)
{e {e happy fields
361 Come Nazianzen to th{is { ~~shelterd spot~~
362 To this enduring Paradise, these ~~seats~~ walks
363 Of contemplation piety & love,
{ts
364 Cover{st serene of bless'd mortality.
365 What if the Roses and the flowers of Kings
366 Princes and Emperors, and the crowns & palms
{st}
367 Of all the great are bla{ts}ed, or decay,
{ bj
368 What if the meanest of their su{[?]ects, each
his
369 Within the narrow region of ~~their~~ cares
370 Tremble beneath as sad uncertainty
{ a
371 There is {[?] priviliege to plead, there is,
372 Renounce, and thou shall find that priviledge,
here.
373 No loss lamenting, no privation felt,
374 Disturb'd by no vicissitudes, unscared
375 By civil faction by religious broils
376 Unplag'd, forgetting, & forgotten here
377 Mayst thou possess thy own invisible
nest

---

At the top of this page WW doubles back to make a second fresh start at the lines originally begun at the bottom of 50r and again at the top of 54r.

359–360 On 57v, facing, is a draft revision by WW:

earnestly
Him who of all mankind he held most dear

Like one of those small birds that round us
chaunt
In multitudes, their warbling will be thine
That freedom to unite thy voice with theirs;
When they at morn or dewy evening praise
Of heaven in sweet and solemn services.
Here mayst thou dedicate thyself to God
And acceptably fill the votive hours
Not seldom as those Creatures of the grove
That need no rule, and have but to enjoy,
But only lifted often to the ~~[illegible]~~ calm
Of that entire beatitude in which
The Angels serve, but when thou must descend
From the pure vision, and thy soul admit
A salutary glow of hope and fear,
Searching in patience & humility
Among the written mysteries of faith
The will divine, or when thou wouldst repose
The burthen of the reasonable yoke
[illegible] by our frail Nature,
wouldst thou taste

[DC MS. 65, $58^{v}$] [*The Tuft of Primroses*]

378 Like one of those small birds that round us
chaunt
379 In multitudes, their warbling will be thine
380 And freedom to unite thy voice with theirs
381 When they at morn or dewy evening praise
382 High heaven in sweet and solemn services.
383 Here mayst thou dedicate thyself to God
384 And acceptably fill the votive hours
385 Not seldom as these Creatures of the grove
386 That need no rule, and live but to enjoy,
387 Not only lifted often to the ~~heigh~~ calm
388 Of that entire beatitude in which
389 The Angels serve, but when thou must descend
390 From the pure vision, and thy soul admit
391 A salutuary glow of hope and fear,
392 Searching in patience & humility
393 Among the written mysteries of faith
394 The will divine, or when thou wouldst assume
395 The burthen & the seasonable yoke
396 Required by our frail Nature,
wouldst be tamed

---

The fair copy runs on from the foot of $57^{r}$. WW's use of both rectos and versos for ll. 358–452 may indicate that the passage beginning with l. 453 had already been entered on $61^{r}$, making it necessary to fit ll. 358–452 into the available space, or, more probably, that WW considered the lines finished and did not anticipate any need for blank versos on which to draft further revisions (see note to $60^{r}$).

By vigils abstinence and prayer with tears
That place was fit:—and for solitudes
Thebais or the Syrian wilderness
Contains not in its dry and barren sand
For not a human form is seen there
Unless some wandering Hunter led by chance.
Here, if the grave duties be performed,
Or overthrown with stealthy of the mind
Be restless under vain distemperances
And gladly would be taken from itself,
Or if it be the time when thoughts are blithe
Then may it forth on to the hills, or wander
Alone as fancy prompts equipp'd with bow
And shafts and quiver not for peaceless aim
At the greatest wolf, the bear, or the Boar
These lurk not in our bounds, but Deer & Goat
And other kinds as peaceable are there
In readiness for wistful chase
The River also owns his harmless tribes
Which tempts thee to like sport; Release itself

[DC MS. 65, 59r] [*The Tuft of Primroses*]

By vigils abstinence and prayer with tears
What place so fit? —a ~~deeper~~ solitude
this
deep
Thebais or the Syrian Wilderness
Contains not in its dry and barren round
For not a human form is seen this way
Unless some straggling Hunter led by chance.
Him, if the graver duties be performed,
wrought
Or over~~wo~~rn with study if the mind
[ ? ]
haunted by a vain disquietude
Be restless under vain disturbances
And gladly would be taken from itself,
Or if it be the time when thoughts are blithe
Him mayst Thou follow to the hills, or mount
Alone as fancy prompts equipp'd with bow
And shafts and quiver not for perilous aim
{n
At the gua{tt wolf, the Lion, or the Pard
These lurk not in our bounds, but Deer & Goat
~~Are ready there f~~
And other kinds as peaceable are there
In readiness for inoffensive chase
The River also owns his harmless tribes
And tempts the to like sport; labour itself

---

The fair copy runs on from the foot of 58v.

To have been here forgotten as the sun
And cool air: blowing from the mountain top.
Respects the brow of him who tills our fields
Or yonder prospect his [illegible]
Or if a different [illegible] there choose
And from bare nature in their [illegible] [illegible]
Food for the day; behold the fruits that hang
In the primaeval woods. the Wells & Springs
Have each a living Garland of green herbs
From which they to the [illegible] hand will yield
Unreproachingly supply that never fails
Bestowed as freely as thy water-pure
To deck thy temperate board —
Far thence to those
Transported in this sort by fervent zeal
That stopped not here the invisible [illegible]
Holy and great, his [illegible] breathes
And Nazianzen fashioned a supply
Ingenious of the [illegible]
Of art of gay and [illegible] [illegible] —

[DC MS. 65, $59^{v}$] [*The Tuft of Primroses*]

417 Is pastime here for generous is the Sun
418 And cool airs blowing from the mountain top
419 Refresh the brow of him who in plain field
420 Or garden presses his industrious spade.
421 Or if a different exercise thou chuse
422 And from boon nature rather wouldst receive
423 Food for the day; behold the fruits that
hang
{w {s
424 In the primaval woods—the {Wells & {Springs
425 Have each a living garland of green herbs
426 From which they to the rifling hand will yield
427 Ungrudgingly supply that never fails
428 Bestowed as freely as their water—pure
429 To deck thy temperate board—
From theme to theme
430 Transported in this sort by fervent zeal
431 That stoppd not here the venerable Man
432 Holy and great, his invitation breathed
433 And Nazianzen fashiond a reply
Ingenious & rhetorical with taunts
{ridicule
Of wit & gay good humoured {[ ? ]

---

The fair copy runs on from the foot of $59^{r}$.

The two lines of revision at the foot of the page develop revision begun at the top of $60^{r}$, facing, and yield ll. 434–435, at the foot of $57^{r}$.

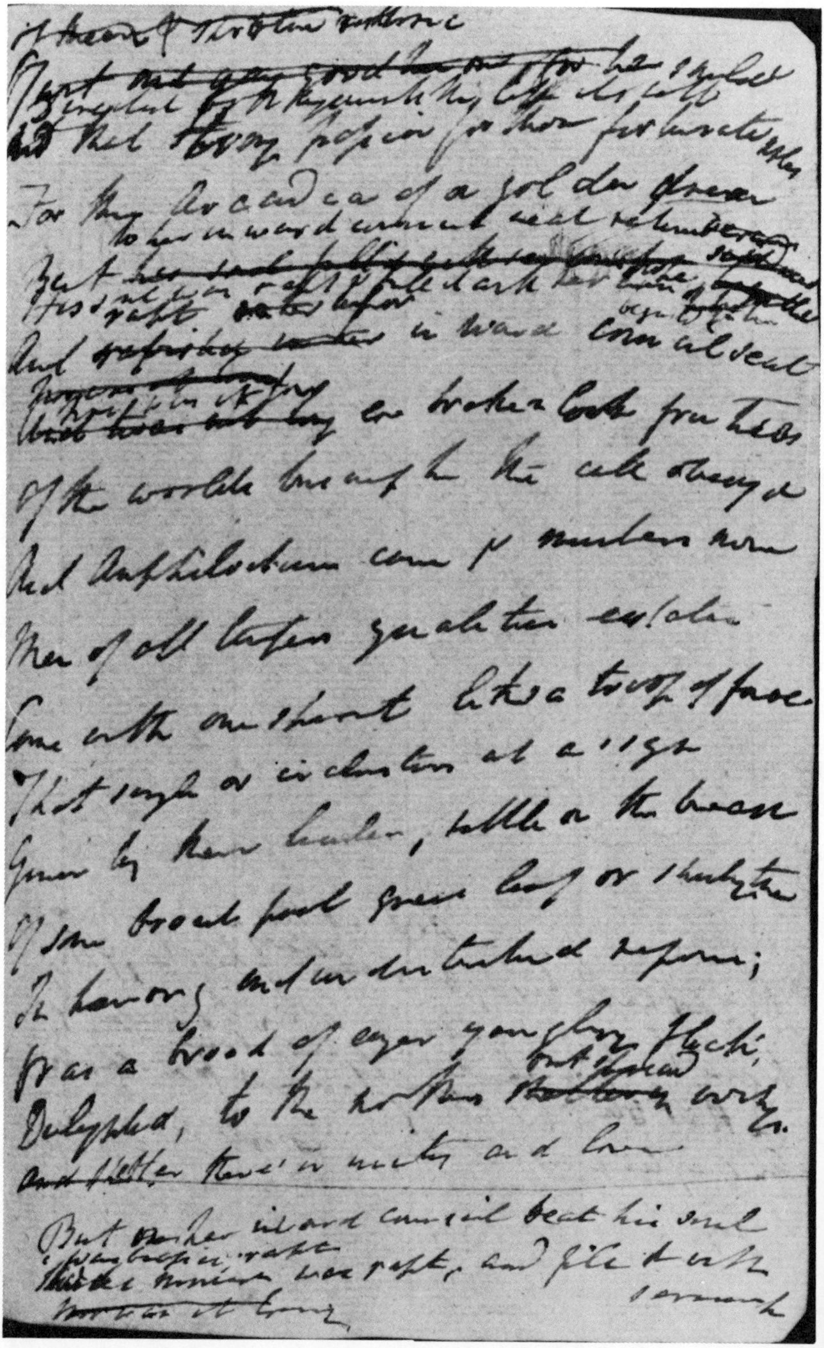

[DC MS. 65, 60ʳ] [*The Tuft of Primroses*]

~~Of keen & sportive~~ rhetoric
Of ~~wit and gay good humour, for~~ he smiled
Directed both against the life itself
{And str}
{At that thy long passion for those fortunate isles
{d
For the Arcadia of a golden {[?]ream
to her inward council seat return
~~serious~~
[~~?saddened~~]
But ~~his soul fill'd with serious hope beguild~~
His soul was rapt & filld with serious ~~of hope~~
rapt ~~on her~~ [?upon] beguild
And ~~refreshd in her~~ inward council seat
~~Nor was it long~~
Nor was it long {out
441 ~~And twas not long~~ ere broken {loose from ties
442 Of the worlds business he the call obeyd
443 And Amphilochius came & numbers more
444 Men of all tempers qualities estates
445 Came with one spirit like a troop of fowl
446 That single or in clusters at a sign
447 Given by their leader, settle on the breast
448 Of some broad pool green leaf or shady tree
449 In harmony and undisturbed repose;
450 Or as a brood of eager younglings flock,
outspread
451 Delighted, to the mothers ~~sheltering~~ wings.
452 And shelter there in unity and love

---

{on s}
But {in her inward council [?]}eat his soul
Was [ ? ], rapt
[ ? ] mov'd was rapt, and filld with
seriousness
~~Nor was it long~~

---

The fair copy runs on from the foot of 59ᵛ.

The revisions at the top of the page, developed in the two lines at the foot of 59ᵛ, facing, and in the two lines below the rule at the foot of the page, yield ll. 434–440 on 57ʳ.

The rule, and below it the extra space filled with revision, indicate either that composition paused with l. 452 before resuming at the top of 61ʳ or that 61ʳ had already been filled when WW arrived near the foot of 60ʳ.

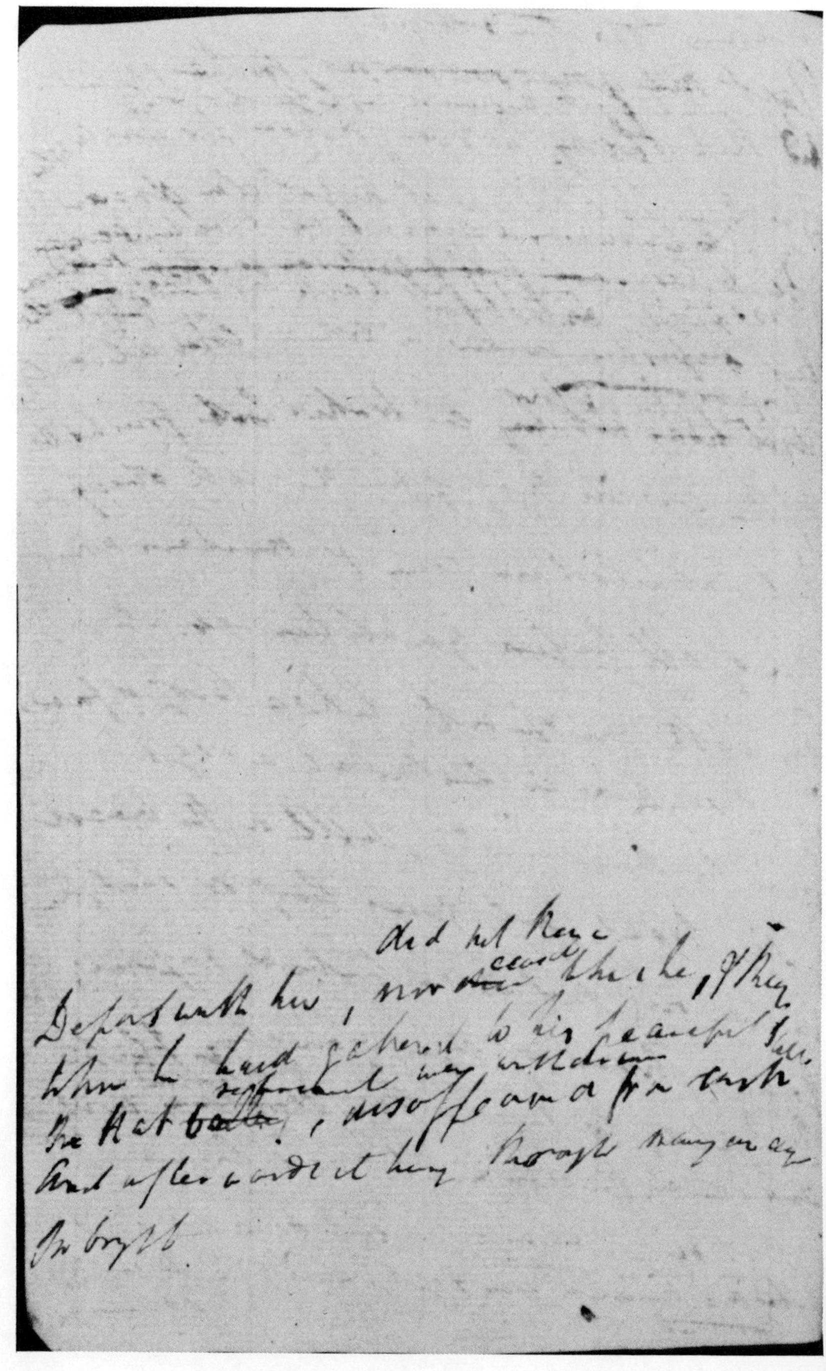

[DC MS. 65, 60v] [*The Tuft of Primroses*]

468b did not thence
ceasd
469 Depart with him, nor ~~died~~ when he, & they
470 Whom he haid gatherd to his peaceful Vale
retirement were withdrawn
471 In that ~~Valley,~~ disappeared from earth
472 And afterwards it hung through many an age
In bright

---

These lines are positioned opposite the passage they are meant to expand, ll. 468/473 on 61r, facing.

An intellectual Champion of the faith
Accomplish'd above all who then appeared
Or, haply, since victoriously have stood
In opposition to the desperate course
Of Pagan rites or specious heresy
St Basil, after lapse of years, went forth
To a station of authority and power
Upon an urgent summons, and resign'd
Ah not without regret, the heavenly Mount
The sheltering valley and his loved compeers
He parted from them, but their common life
Of neither first nor singular, at least
More beautiful than any of like frame
That hitherto had been conceived, a life
To which by written institutes and rules
He gave a solid being, did not fail
Nor die with him, and being through many an age
In bright remembrance, like a shining cloud
O'er the vast regions of the western Church
Whence those communities of holy men

[DC MS. 65, 61r] *[The Tuft of Primroses]*

of the
453 An intellectual Champion faith
454 Accomplish'd above all who then appeared
455 Or, haply, since victoriously have stood
456 In opposition to the desperate course
{eys
457 Of Pagan rites or [?] impious heres{ies
458 St Basil, after lapse of years, went forth
459 To a station of authority and power
460 Upon an urgent summons, and resignn'd
461 Ah not without regret, the heavenly Mount
{s
462 The {Sheltering Valley and his lov'd Compeers,
463 He parted from them, but their common life
464 If neither first nor singular, at least
465 More beautiful than any of like frame
466 That hitherto had been conceived, a life
467 To which by written institutes and rules
468a He gave a solid being, did not fail
Nor die with him, and hung through many an
age
473 In bright remembrance, like a shining cloud
{C {;
474 Oer the vast regions of the western {church{
Whe }
475 He}nce those communities of holy men

---

The fair copy here runs on from the foot of 60r, but in a new ink or with a newly sharpened pen.

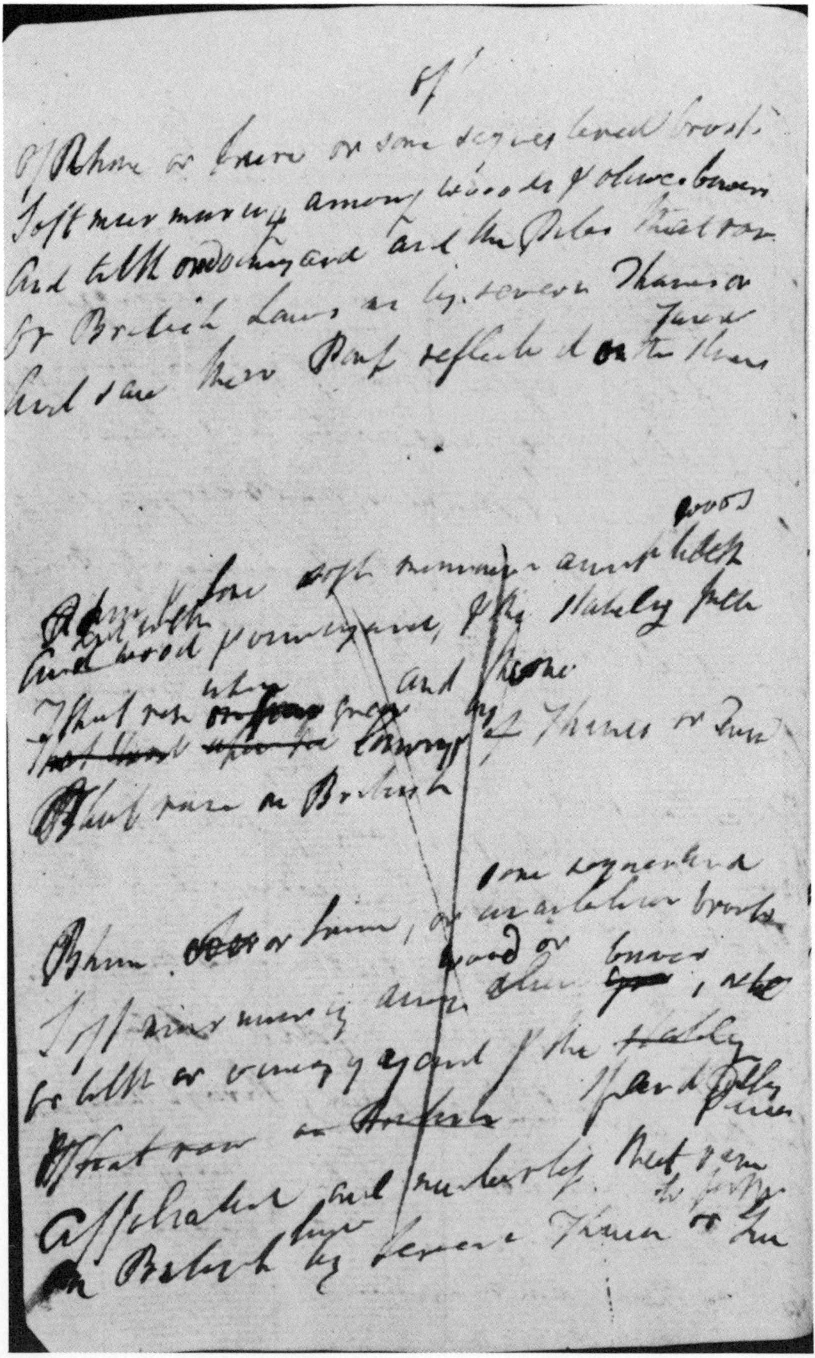

[DC MS. 65, 61v] [*The Tuft of Primroses*]

of
Of Rhone or Loire or some sequestered brook
Soft murmuring among wooods & olive bowers
{nd
And tilth o{r vineyard and the Piles that rose
On British Lawns as by severn Thames or
Tweed
{on
And saw their Pomp reflected {in the stream

wood
[?Rhone] & [?Loire] soft murmurs among tilth
and tilth
~~And wood~~ & vineyard, & the stately pile
where and [?Rhone]
Tthat rose ~~on [ ? ]~~ green
by
~~That stood~~ ~~upon the~~ [?lawns] ~~of~~ Thames or Tweed
{T
{[?]hat rose on British

{[?or] some sequestered
Rhone {~~L~~ ~~[?or]~~ or Loire, or inarticlate brook
wood or bower
Soft murmuring among olive ~~gro~~, or bo
Or tilth or viney y yard & the ~~stately~~
[?splendidly]
[ ? ]
{That
{~~[?Of] rose on British~~
Affiliated and nurturless that rose
lawn [?to] [?forth]
On British by Severn Thames or Twee

---

The block of drafting at the middle of the page was entered first, opposite the related fair-copy lines on 62r, facing; it was followed by the lines at the bottom of the page and then by those at the top. This series of revisions is intermediate between the passage at mid-page on 62r and ll. 484–488 on 62v and 63r.

That spread so far, to shroud a gracelessness
Devoted, and of seemingly virgin power.

Fallen, in a thousand vales, the stately towers
And branching windows gorgeous to the view
And aisles & roofs magnificent that thrilled
With hallelujahs; and the thronged abbot vault
Are crushed, and buried under weeds & earth
The cloistral avenues; they that heard the voice
Of Rhine or Seine, of British Thames or Tweed,
And saw their pomp reflected in the stream
As Tarleton saw, and to this day beholds
Her faded image in the depths of Wye.
Gone are they, levelled with ground, or left
To encounter friendless the beating storm
~~And perish under heaven~~ of storm or care
And stand or fall
~~Abandoned~~ as an ever ready prey
Torn hour by hour
To hands
time to feed upon a thievish hope
but not the fables, not the care

[DC MS. 65, 62r] [*The Tuft of Primroses*]

476 That spread so far, to shrouded quietness
477 Devoted, and of saintly Virgins pure.

Fallen, in a thousand vales, the stately toTower
And branching windows gorgeously
And aisles & roofs magnificent that thrilled
With halleluiahs, and the strong-ribbed
vault
Are crushed, and buried under weeds & earth
The cloistral avenues; they that heard the
{R {or voice
Of {Shone {and Loire, of British Thames or Tweed,

{pomp
And saw their {[ ? ] reflected in the
stream
As Tintern saw, and to this day beholds
Her faded image in the depths of Wye
dust
Gone are they, levelld with ground, or left
To encounter friendlessly the beating storm
~~And perish under heaven of human care~~
And stand or fall
~~As ordaind, as~~ an ever ready prey
For hungry time to feed upon their hope
Is hers but not the feeling not the
sense

---

The fair copy runs on from the foot of 61r; the canceled passage is recopied on 63r.

Fallen in a thousand vales, the stately Towers
And branching windows gorgeously array'd,
And aisles and roofs magnificent that thrill'd
With hallelujahs and the strong-ribb'd vaults
Are crush'd, and buried under weeds & earth
The cloistral avenues—they that heard the voice
Of Rhone or Loire, or some sequestered brook
Soft murmuring among woods and olive bowers
And tilth and vineyards, and the Piles that rose
On British lawns by Severn Thames or Tweed
And saw their pomp reflected in the stream
As Tintern saw; and, to this day, beholds
Her faded image in the depths of Wye
Of solemn port smitten but unsubdued
She stands, nor [illegible] of her [illegible]
[illegible] Fountains Abbey glorious in decay
[illegible] yet uplifts a venerable brow
Before the [illegible] Traveller's lifted eye
And Fountains Abbey glorious in decay
Threatening to outlive the ravages of Time
And bear the cross till Christ shall come again.

[DC MS. 65, 63r] [*The Tuft of Primroses*]

478 Fallen, in a thousand vales, the stately Towers
479 And branching windows gorgeously array'd,
480 And aisles and roofs magnificent that thrill'd
481 With halleluiahs and the strong-ribb'd vaults
482 Are crush'd, and buried under weeds & earth
483 The cloistral avenues—they that heard the
voice
Of Rhone or Loire, or some sequesterd brook
485 Soft murmuring among woods and olive bowers
486 And tilth and vineyards, and the Piles that
rose
487 On British lawns by Severn Thames or Tweed
488 And saw their pomp reflected in the stream
489 As Tintern saw; and, to this day, beholds
490 Her faded image in the depths of Wye.—
491 Of solemn port smitten but unsubdued
492 She stands, nor less tenacious of her rights
{A
493 F f Fountain {abbey glorious in decay
Stands
~~Doth yet uplift a reverend brow~~
494 Before the pious Travellers lifted eyes
~~And Fountains Abbey glorious in decay~~
{ing
495 Threaten{s to outlive the ravages of Time
496 And bear the cross till Christ shall
come again.

---

WW here makes a fresh start at the passage canceled on 62r.
On 62v, facing, WW entered a line of revision which becomes l. 484:

Of some sequesterd brook in Gallias Vales

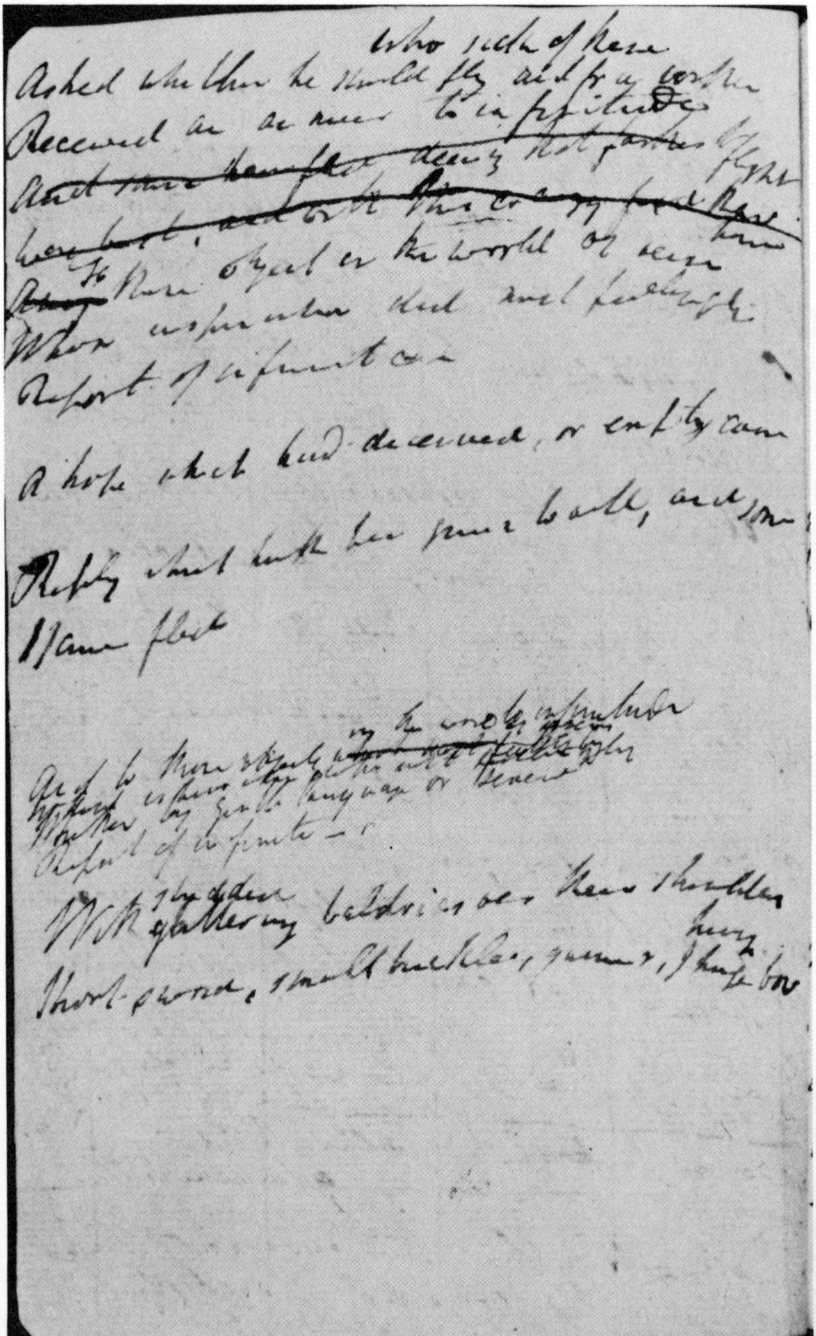

[DC MS. 65, $63^{v}$] [*The Tuft of Primroses*]

who sick of these
Asked whither he should fly and from within
Received an answer to infinitude
~~And some have fled deeming that farthest~~ flight
~~Was best, and with this [?craving] fixd [?their]~~
To [?home]
~~Among~~ those object in the world of sense
Where inspiration did most feelingly
Report of infinite—

503 A hope which had deceived, or empty came

Reply which hath ben given to all, and some
Have fled

to infinitude
in the world of sense
And to those objects ~~which most feelingly~~
Where inspiration doth most lastingly
Whether by gentle language or severe
Report of infinite—.

studded
With glittering baldrics oer their shoulders
hung
Short-sword, small buckler, quiver, & huge bow

---

The lines on this page (not including l. 503 and the two lines at the foot of the page) were probably drafted to replace the passage deleted with a large X at the bottom of $64^{r}$, starting with the second half of l. 507. It is possible that the half line "Report of infinite—." was meant to lead to the second half of l. 507, on $65^{r}$, but it seems more likely that the lines drafted here were superseded by the Chartreuse passage, ll. 507b–567.

503 This line was probably meant to follow l. 502, which it faces on $64^{r}$.

The two lines at the bottom of the page were meant to follow the fourth line from the bottom of $64^{r}$, facing.

To cleave they to the earth, in monuments
Of Revelation, nor in memory less
Of natures pure religion as in line
Uninterrupted it hath travelled down
From the first man who heard a lonely storm
Or ever felt a troubled thought, or vain desire,
or in the very sunshine of his joy
Was saddened at a perishable bliss,
Or languished idly under sad respects
That world must be subdued. —— He thinks I hear,
Not from these woods, but from some mossy grove
That lies I know not where, the sprightly blast
Of the clear bugle, and from thicket green
Of hollies sparkling in an April sun
Forth, in a moment, issue to the glade
A Troop of green clad Foresters in arms
Blithe Outlaws and with their Chieftain? — would
The Stag, dear lady — the Hart, or will they range
Their oaths in presence of Maid Marian sworn

[DC MS. 65, 64r] [*The Tuft of Primroses*]

497 So cleave they to the earth, in monument
498 Of Revelation, nor in memory less
499 Of natures pure religion as in line
500 Uninterrupted it hath travelled down
{From
501 {To the first man who heard a howling
ever storm
502 Or felt a troubled thought, or vain desire,
504 Or, in the very sunshine of his joy
{And
505 {Or saddened at a perishable bliss,
506 Or languishd idly under fond regrets
might
507a That would not be subdued.——Me thinks
I hear,
Not from these woods, but from some merry grove
That lies I know not where, the spritely blast
Of the clear bugle, and from thicket green
Of hollies sparkling in an April sun
Forth, in a moment, issues to the glade
A Troop of green clad Foresters in arms
{O and :}
Blithe {outlaws ~~with~~ their Chieftain?}—would
the rouze
The Stag, dislodge the Hart; or will they keep
Their oath in presence of Maid Marian
sworn

The fair copy runs on from the foot of 63r. The canceled passage was replaced first with lines drafted on 63v, facing, and then with the passage beginning at l. 507b, on 65r.
64v is blank.

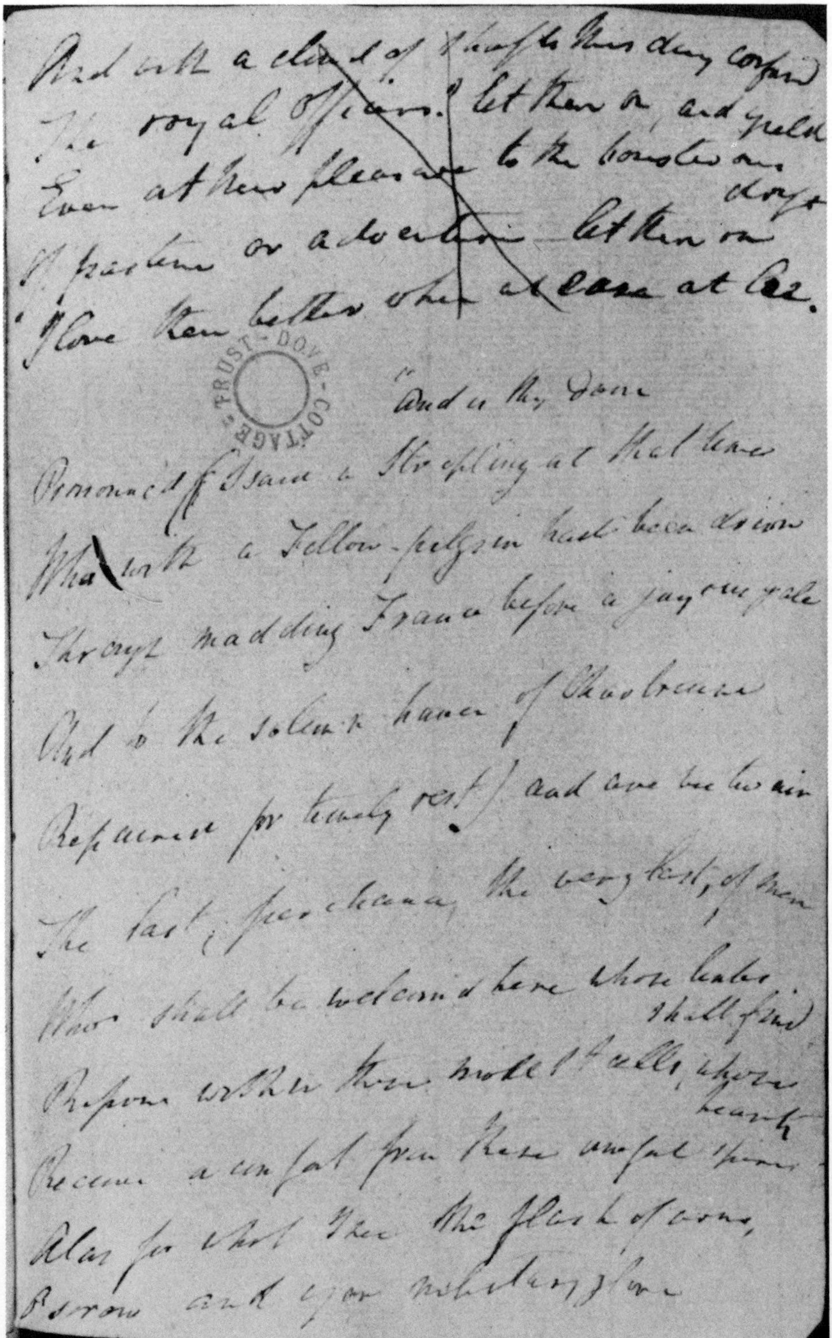

~~And with a cloud of thoughts thus deeply confin'd~~
~~The royal Officers. Let them on, and yield~~
~~Even at their pleasure to the boisterous drops~~
~~Of fortune or adventure—let them on~~
~~I love them better when at anchor at ease.~~



And as thy Dame [illegible]
Pronounc'd of Isaac's Stripling at that time
Who with a Fellow-pilgrim had been driven
Through madding France before a joyous gale
And to the solemn haven of Chartreuse
Repaired for timely rest) and are but twain
The last, perchance, the very last, of men
Who shall be welcom'd here whose limbs shall find
Repose within these holy cells, whose hearts
Receive a comfort from these awful Spires
Alas for what I see the flash of arms,
O sorrow and upon [illegible]

[DC MS. 65, 65$^r$] [*The Tuft of Primroses*]

And with a cloud of shafts this day confound
The royal Officers? let them on, and yield
Even at their pleasure to the boisterous drift
Of pastime or adventure—let them on
I love them better when at ease at lie.

507b "And is thy doom

( )(
508 Pronounc'd;} I said a Stripling at that time
509 Who with a Fellow-pilgrim had been driv'n
510 Through madding France before a joyous gale
511 And to the solemn haven of Chartreuse
512 Repaired for timely rest) and are we twain
513 The last, perchance, the very last, of men
514 Who shall be welcom'd here whose limbs
shall find
515 Repose within these modest cells, whose
hearts
516 Receive a comfort from these awful spires
517 Alas for what I see the flash of arms,
518 O sorow and yon military glare

---

The fair copy runs on from the foot of 64$^r$. The passage below the five lines deleted with an X was entered in a different ink or with a newly sharpened pen.
65$^v$ is blank.

That burst from voices! Let us hide our glow
Protected of St Bruno's wood, here high
Those whispers that surround, or meet, or where
are they but a common
From the two kindred streams of life proceed
Or are they by the parting Genius sent
Unheard till now, and to be heard no more.
Yes I was moved and to this hour am moved.
What man would bring to nothing if he might
A natural power or element? and who
If he had ability were he would dare
To kill a species of insensate life
Or to the bird of meanest wing would say
Thou, and thy kind, must perish. Even
So consecrated, almost, might he deem
That power that organ, that
transcendent frame

[DC MS. 65, $66^{r}$] [*The Tuft of Primroses*]

And hark those voices! let us hide in gloom
Profoundest of St Bruno's wood, these sighs
These whispers that pursue, or meet, me, whence
are they but a common
{D
From the two Sister Streams of Life & {death
Or are they by the parting Genius sent
Unheard till now, and to be heard no more.
Yes I was moved and to this hour am moved.
What Man would bring to nothing, if he might,
A natural power or element? and who
If the ability were his would dare
To kill a species of insensate life
Or to the bird of meanest wing would say,
Thou, and thy kind, must perish.—Even
so
So consecrated, almost, might he deem
That power that organ, that
transcendent frame

---

The fair copy runs on from the foot of $65^{r}$.

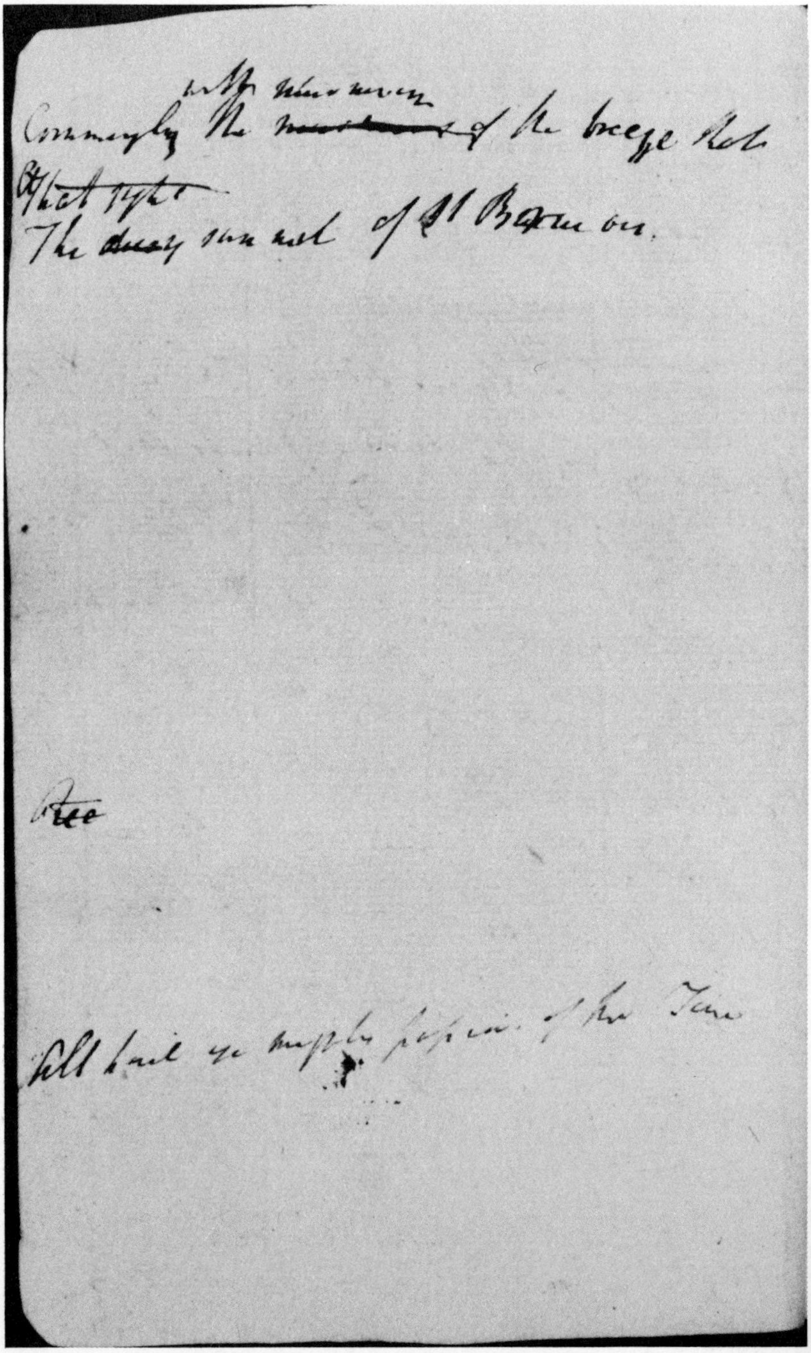

[DC MS. 65, $66^{v}$] [*The Tuft of Primroses*]

with murmuring
Commingling the ~~murmurs~~ of the breeze that
A
~~That sighs~~
{ru}
The [?dewy] summit of St B{ as }nos

~~Rec~~

547 All hail ye mighty passions of the Time

---

The drafting at the top of the page—in a dark ink matching "Rec" at mid-page and the revisions on $67^{r}$, facing—is part of WW's adaptation of ll. 507–567 to *The Prelude* ([1850], VI, 415–488) and appears to be an expansion of ll. 544–545 on $67^{r}$ (see *Prelude* MS. $A^{2}$, ll. 42–46, in *Prel.*, pp. 198–200).

The line at the bottom of the page faces the line it replaces at ll. 546/548 on $67^{r}$.

Of social being.— "Stay your impious hand,"
Such was the vain injunction of that hour,
By Nature uttered from her Alpine throne
transcendent from
O leave in quiet this embodied dream,
Of social being
This substance by which mortal men have clothed
Humanly clothed the ghostliness of things
In silence visible and perpetual calm
Let this one temple last—be this one spot
Of earth devoted to Eternity."—
I heard, or seemed to hear, and thus the voice
Proceeded—"honour to the Patriot's zeal
Glory and life to new-born Liberty—
Hail to the mighty projects of the State
The vengeance and the transports of the hope,
But spare, if past ~~[illegible]~~ future be the wings:
On whose support harmoniously conjoined
Moves the great Spirit of human
[illegible] spare

[DC MS. 65, 67r] [*The Tuft of Primroses*]

Of social being.—"Stay your impious hand,
Such was the vain injunction of that hour,
By Nature uttered from her Alpine throne
                    transcendant frame
O leave in quiet this embodied dream,
    Of social being {b
This substance {wy which mortal men
                        {c
                    have {[?]lothed
Humanly clothd the ghostliness of things
In silence visible and perpetual calm
Let this one Temple last—be this one spot
Of earth devoted to Eternity."—
I heard, or seemd to hear, and thus the Voice
Proceeded—honour to the Patriots zeal
Glory and life to new-born liberty—
Hail to the mighty Passions of the
The vengeance, and the transport & the hope,
                    future
But spare, if past & ~~present~~ be the wings
On whose support harmoniously conjoined
Moves the great Spirit of human
                    knowledge, spare

---

The fair copy runs on from the foot of 66r.

The interlinear revisions on this page, in a dark ink matching the drafting at the top and middle of 66v, facing, are related to WW's adaptation of ll. 507–567 to *The Prelude* ([1850], VI, 415-488).

67v is blank.

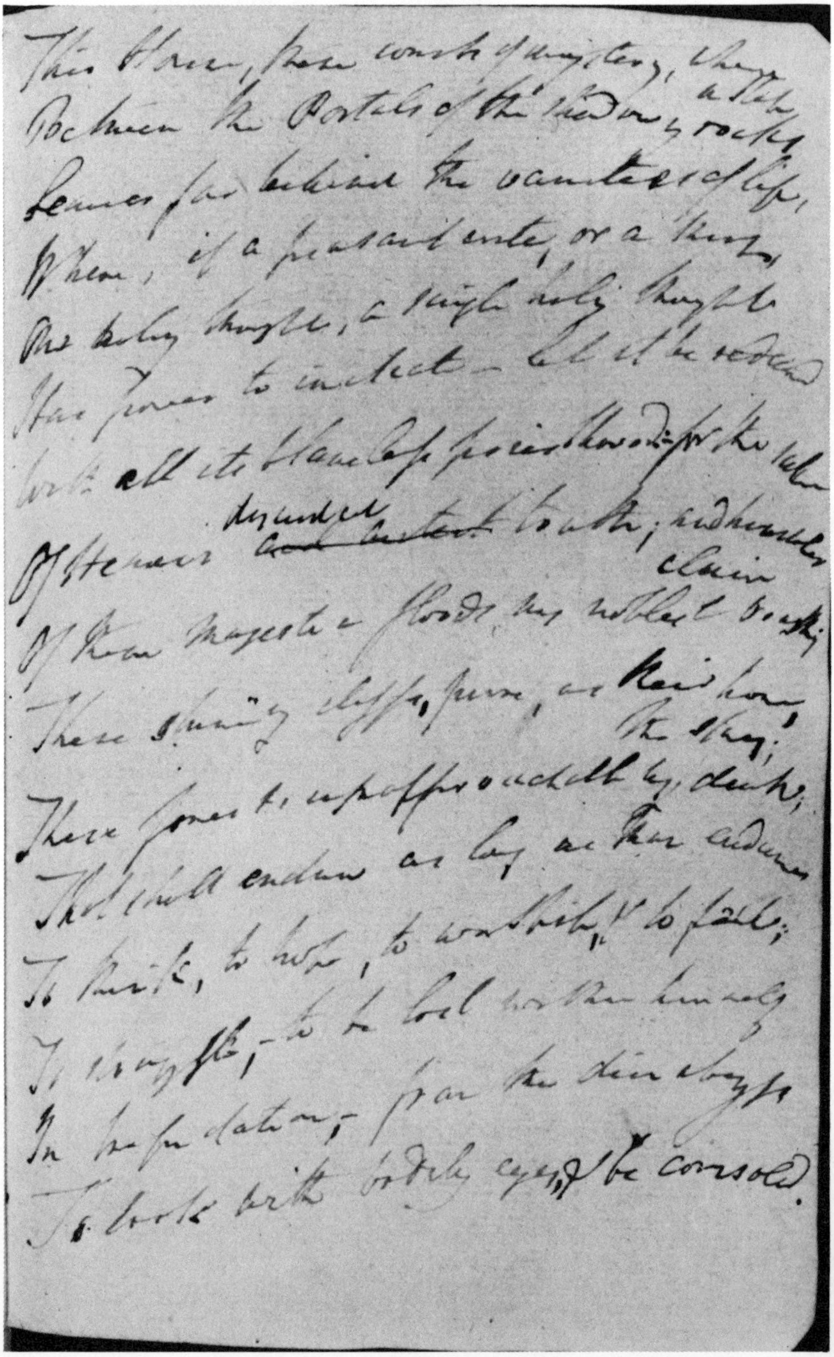

[DC MS. 65, 68r] [*The Tuft of Primroses*]

552 This House, these courts of mystery, where
a step
553 Between the Portals of the shadowy rocks
554 Leaves far behind the vanities of life,
555 Where, if a peasant enter, or a king,
556 One holy thought, a single holy thought
557 Has power to initiate—let it be redeemed
{:—
558 With all its blameless priesthood{ for the sake
descended
559 Of Heaven ~~and [?constant]~~ truth; and humbler
claim
560 Of these majestic floods, my noblest boast;
561 These shining cliffs, pure, as their home,
the sky;
562 These forests unapproachable by death,
563 That shall endure as long as Man endures
564 To think, to hope, to worship, & to feel;
565 To struggle,—to be lost within himself
566 In trepidation,—from the dim abyss
567 To look with bodily eyes, & be consoled.

---

The fair copy runs on from the foot of 67r.

558–559 Revision of these lines, in a dark ink matching other revisions on 67r and 66v, is related to WW's adaptation of ll. 507–567 to *The Prelude* ([1850], VI, 415–488).

68v is blank.

Such repetition of that

My thoughts demanded now an humbler task

Desarts are for the unwearied Song I will leave

Yet & lonely Isle the [illegible] abode

Of female Votaries. No                    plain

Placid as the Arabian water[?] wells descends

This chosen spot nor is it

By rocks like those of Camaldoli or Alps

~~Shapes untransmuted of successive worlds~~

Sole untransmuted shapes of many worlds

Nor can it boast a mossy structure huge

Founded & built by hands with arch & towers

Pillar and pinnacle and gables in shine

Sublime as if in Emulation reared

Of the eternal Architects— these types

These tokens— admonitions to recall

Minds to reverence [illegible] or stages to lean upon

Such forms to nourish or appease the soul

The gentle Being who found harbour here

[DC MS. 65, 69r] [*The Tuft of Primroses*]

Such repetition of that
My thoughts demanded now an humbler task
Awaits us for the unwearied Song will lead
{a
Into {l lonely Vale the mild abode
Of female Votaries. No plain
{a
Blaink as the Arabi{[?e]n wilderness defends
This chosen Spot nor is it
By rocks like those of Caucasus, or Alps
Shapes untransmuted of successive worlds
The untransmuted Shapes of many worlds,
Nor can it boast a massy Structure huge
Founded & built by hands with arch & towers
Pillar and pinacle and glittering spire
Sublime as if in Emulation reared
{A
Of the eternal {architect—these signs
These tokens—admonitions to recall
Curbs to restrain or stays to lean upon
Such food to nourish or appease the Soul
The gentle Beings who found harbour here

---

The fair copy runs on from the foot of 68r.
576 The revision above this line, in pencil, may be part of WW's adapation of ll. 507–567 to *The Prelude* ([1850], VI, 415–488).
69v is blank.

[DC MS. 65, 70r] [*The Tuft of Primroses*]

Required not. Them a lowly Edifice
{[?lowly]
Embracd by {[ ? ] grounds that did not aim
To overshadow but to screen & hide,
Contented,—and an unassuming brook
between these hills
Working its aimless way ~~between these~~
Through meadow, chestnut wood, and
olive bowers
And tilth and vineyard.———

---

The fair copy runs on from the foot of 69r and breaks off on this page; 70v–113r are blank.

I raised

My heavy eyes which passing thus I saw

Saw at a glance

[DC MS. 65, 118v] [*St. Paul's*]

I raised
My heavy eyes while pacing thus & saw
Saw at a glance

---

The revision for *St. Paul's* conflates the two lines at ll. 11b–14a, on 119r, facing.

Press'd with conflicting thoughts of love and fear
I parted from thee, Friend! and took my way
Through the great City, pacing with an eye
Downcast, ~~feet~~ ear sleeping, & feet masterless
That were sufficient guide unto themselves,
And step by step went pensively. Now, mark!
Not how my trouble was entirely hush'd,
(That might not be) but how by sudden gift
Gift of Imagination's holy power
My Soul in her uneasiness received
An anchor of stability. It chanced
That while I thus was pacing I raised up
My heavy eyes and instantly beheld
Saw at a glance in that familiar spot
A visionary scene a length of street
Laid open in its morning quietness
Deep hollow unobstructed vacant smooth
And white with winter's purest white, as fair
As fresh and spotless as he ever sheds
On field or mountain. Moving Form was none
Save here & there a shadowy Passenger
Slow shadowy, silent, dusky, and beyond
And high above this winding length of street
This moveless and unpeopled avenue
Pure silent solemn beautiful was seen

[DC MS. 65, $119^{r}$] [*St. Paul's*]

Press'd with conflicting thoughts of love and fear
I parted from thee, Friend! and took my way
Through the great City pacing with an eye
Down cast, ~~feet~~ ear sleeping, & feet masterless
That were sufficient guide unto themselves
And step by step went pensively. Now, mark!
Not how my trouble was entirely hush'd,
That might not be) but how by sudden gift
    Gift of imagination holy power
My Soul in her uneasiness received
An anchor of stability. It chanced
That while I thus was pacing I raised up
My heavy eyes and instantly beheld
Saw at a glance in that familiar spot
A visionary scene a length of street
Laid open in its morning quietness
Deep hollow unobstructed vacant smooth
And white with winters purest white, as fair
As fresh and spotless as he ever sheeds
On field or mountain. Moving Form was none
Save here & there a shadowy Passenger
Slow shadowy, silent, dusky, and beyond
And high above this winding length of street
This noiseless and unpeopled avenue
Pure silen        solemn beautiful was seen

---

9 This line is present in DC MS. 18, $1^{v}$; its omission from the base text here was probably inadvertent.

17 This line is an interlinear insertion in DC MS. 18, $1^{v}$.

25 The gap left in this line may be related to WW's attention to the words "silent," "soundless," and "noiseless" in ll. 22–25 (see revisions to these lines on DC MS. 18, $1^{v}$).

The huge majestic Temple of St Paul
In awful sequestration through a veil
Through its own sacred veil of falling snow

[DC MS. 65, 120$^{r}$] [*St. Paul's*]

The huge majestic Temple of St Paul
In awful sequestration through a veil
Through its own sacred veil of falling snow

---

120$^{v}$–128$^{r}$ are blank.

# DC MS. 143: *To the Clouds*

DC MS. 143 (formerly MS. Verse 92) is a calf-bound notebook in use at Rydal Mount in the 1830s and 1840s. The notebook is fully described in *Poems, in Two Volumes, by William Wordsworth,* edited by Jared Curtis (Ithaca, 1983), page xxvi.

Toward the end of the notebook Mary Wordsworth entered an untitled fair copy of *To the Clouds,* probably in preparation for *Poems, Chiefly of Early and Late Years,* published in 1842. The fair copy follows generally from the version of the poem on $8^r$–$10^v$ in DC MS. 65, incorporating most revisions made there. Wordsworth's drafting of the concluding lines of the poem on $11^v$–$12^r$ in DC MS. 65 appears to be contemporary with his entry and further revision of those lines in DC MS. 143. Revisions made by Wordsworth himself throughout the text of *To the Clouds* in DC MS. 143 are incorporated in the penultimate fair copy of the poem in DC MS. 151/3.

Editorial numbers in the left-hand margins of the transcriptions correspond to lines in the 1842 reading text.

# [DC MS. 143: *To the Clouds*]

[107v]

12 Beheld in your impetuous march the likeness
13 Of a wide army pressing on to meet
{m
14 Or overtake some unknown ene{yy.
smooth as swift and keen
{C
But smooth your motion ~~is~~, Ye {clouds, [?as swift]
once more bold Fancy better pleased
And you ~~doth Fancy, better pleased, compare~~
Compares with
~~Once more~~ ~~to~~ things in character and aim
Peaceful,—a never ending flight of Birds

---

[108r]

1 *Army of clouds equestrian host on wings*
2 *Ascending from behind the motionless brow*
3 *Of that tall rock as from a hidden world*
4 *O whither with such eagerness of speed*
5 *What seek ye or what shun ye of the gale*
6 *Companions, fear ye to be left behind*
7 *Or racing oer your blue etherial field*
8 *Contend ye with each other? Of the sea*
9 *Children thus post ye over Vale & height*
10 *To sink upon your Mother's lap & rest* 10
11 *Or were ye rightlier hailed when first mine*
*eyes*
*Be*} in your impetuous march the likeness
*~~For~~*} *held you, for ye still are sweeping on*
Of pressing on to meet
*~~Like~~ a wide Army ~~in impetuous march~~*
~~Or would it please you less to be comp~~
Or overtake
*~~Eager to meet~~ some unknown Enemy*
Or may ye not as fitly aptly
~~it please you less to be compared~~
*~~Or would ye rather once again be likened~~*
Once more to things in character and aim
*~~To things of peaceful character & aim~~*

---

Work on 107v follows from revision of the last five fair-copy lines on 108r and the first line on 109r.

---

10 The "10" in the right-hand margin of 108r is the first of WW's line counts.
11/ "For" was deleted by erasure.
108v is blank.

---

[109r]

Peaceful,
~~*Say to*~~ *a never-ending flight of birds* ~~*aerial*~~
18 Aerial *upon due migration bound* 20
ye {e
19 *To milder climes or rather do* ~~*you*~~ *urge*
~~*To pause at last*~~
20 *In caravan your hasty pilgrimage*
21 *To pause at last on more aspiring heights*
22 *Than these, & utter your devotion there*
23 *With thunderous voice? or are ye jubilent*
24 *And would ye, tracking your proud Lord the*
*sun*
25 *Be present at his setting, or the pomp*
Persian
26 *Of* ~~*Indian*~~ *mornings would ye fill & stand*
27 *Poizing your splendours high above the heads*
28 *Of worshipers kneeling to their up-risen God?*
29 *Whence, whence ye Clouds this eagerness of speed*
30 *Speak silent creatures—they are gone are fled*
31 *Buried together in yon gloomy mass*
32 *That loads the middle heaven & clear & bright*

---

[110r]

33 *And vacant doth the region which they thronged*
34 *Appear—a calm descent of sky conducting*
35 *Down to the unapproachable abyss*
36 *Down to that hidden gulf from which they*
*rose*
37 *To vanish fleet as days & months & years*
*d*}
38 *Fleet as the generations of manking* 40
39 *Power glory empire as the world itself*
40 *The lingering world, when time hath ceased to*
*be.*
41 *But the winds roar shaking the rooted trees*
42 *And see a bright precursor to a train*
43 *Perchance as numerous overpeers the rock*
44 *That sullenly refuses to partake*
45 *Of the wild impulse, from a fount of life*
46 *Invisible the long procession moves*
*A multitude as rapid of like shapes*
47 *Radient or gloomy welcome to the Vale*
48 *Which they are entering welcome to mine eye*
49 *That sees them to my soul that* ~~*owns*~~ *in them*
owns

---

In the first line on 109r "aerial" was deleted by erasure.
18 WW's line count, which includes his revisions on 107v, is one line too high; perhaps he counted the line beginning "Peaceful" both at the foot of 107v and at the top of 109r.
20/21 MW inadvertently began to copy l. 21 here.
109v is blank.

---

38 WW's line count follows from the "20" at the top of 109r.
110v is blank.

---

[111r]

                fir}   m}
*And in the bosom of the per}man}ent*
Oer which they wherein
*~~Wherein~~ they move ~~in which~~ they are contained*
*A type of her capacious self & all*
*Her restless progeny.*
*A humble walk*
*Here is the body doomed to tread, this path*
*A little hoary line & faintly traced*
*Work shall we call it of the Shepherd's foot*
*Or of his Flock, joint vestige of them both*
60
*I pace it unrepining for my thoughts*
*Admit no bondage & my words have wings.*
*Where is the Orphean Lyre or Druid Harp*
?}
*To accompany the verse } the mountan blast*
*Shall be our* <u>*hand*</u> *of music he shall sweep*
*The rocks & quivering trees & billowy Lake*
*And search the fibres of the Caves & they*
*Shall answer for our Song is of the Clouds*
*And the Wind loves them & the gentle*
*glales*

---

[112r]

*Which by their aid reclothe~~d~~ the naked lawn*
*With anual verdure & revive~~d~~ the woods*
*And moistene~~d~~ the parched lips of thirsty flowers*
*Love them, & every idle breeze of air*
*Bends to the favourite burthen. Moon & stars*
*Keep their most solem vigil when the clouds*
s}   {ftin }
*Watch also c}ha{ngin}g peaceably their place*
lie
*Like bands of ministering Spirits or when they*
*~~lie~~*
As if some Protean act the change ha wrought
~~etherial~~
*~~Blank forms & listless thro' the azure~~ deep*
In listless quiet oer the etherial deep
*~~Dispersed in island quiet~~*
Scatterd a of various shapes
80 [?*Sctterd*] *like*^*Cyclades from hour to hour in*
And all degrees of beauty
*~~Islands in perfect quiet.~~ O ye lightenings!*

---

57 WW's line count follows from the "40" toward the top of 117r.
111v is blank.

---

73 WW seems to have meant to convert "changing" into "shifting."
77/78 WW's line count follows from the "60" at mid-page on 111r.

79 *Ye are their perilous offspring & the Sun*
80 *Source inexhaustible of life & joy*
thence
H}
81 *And type of Man's far-darting reason*∧~~*th*~~}~~*ence*~~
82 In old time worshipped as the God of verse
~~*Therefore by man esteemed in ancient times*~~
~~*The God of verse as in their sight he moved*~~
83 *A blazing intellectual deity*

---

[113r]

84 Loves his own glory in their looks, and showers
~~*Loves in the Clouds his own reflected glory*~~
~~*He from his throne to sight impervious,*~~ shower
{And
~~*Showers,*~~ {~~*& not without regard to human kind*~~
*U*} Upon
85 ~~*Showers*~~ *u*}~~*pon*~~ *that unsubstantial brotherhood*
with all but beatific light
86 *Visions* ~~*as of beatitutde, revealed.*~~ alas!
87 Enriched—too transient were they not renewed
~~Too transient were they not from age to age~~
age age
88 From ~~year~~ to ~~year~~, and did not while we gaze
~~Renewed, and did not Memory give bond~~
89 In silent rapture, credulous desire
~~Fallacious as at best it needs must~~
be
not power
{not
90 Nourish ~~the hope~~ that Memory lacks {[ ? ] power
the hope
~~To keep the silent treasure unimpaired~~
~~hold~~ ~~fast, illusive~~ hope
To ~~keep the treasure, for her grasp un[ ? ]~~!
91 To keep the treasure unimpaird—vain thought
92 Yet while repine created as we are
to
93 For joy and rest, albeit ~~we~~ find them only
94 Lodged in the bosom of enduring things?
107

---

112v is blank.

---

94 WW's line count, following from the "80" at mid-page on 112r, should be 97; "107", a mistake, was copied by MW in the penultimate fair copy of the poem, DC MS. 151/3.

# DC MS. 105: Manuscripts Contributing to *Composed when a probability existed . . .*

## MS. A

DC MS. 105 consists of five parts. The first is an early fair copy of *Composed when a probability existed . . .* in 101 lines, much revised, here labeled MS. A. The second is a bifolium taken out of another notebook, *Peter Bell,* MS. 7—here labeled MS. A(1)—adding some fifty lines on Joan of Arc. The third part is an expanded fair copy, in 182 lines (one leaf is missing and twenty of these lines must be supplied conjecturally), here labeled MS. B. The fourth part consists of two scraps of manuscript—MS. B(1) and MS. B(2)—intermediate between revisions in MS. B and the penultimate fair copy of the poem in DC MS. 89. The fifth part, MS. C, consists of two brief drafts written in pencil on the back of a piece of calligraphy.

MS. A is formed of two sheets of wove paper watermarked STAINS & C° above the date 1824; the sheets are folded once to make a manuscript of four leaves, each measuring approximately 18.5 by 22.5 centimeters. Beginning on $1^r$ Mary Wordsworth entered a fair copy of *Composed when a probability existed . . .*, incorporating two sections of fair copy cut out of an earlier manuscript in Dora Wordsworth's hand (the rest of which is now lost), which were pasted on to $1^v$ (ll. 28–44) and $3^r$ (ll. 94–101). The versos of these paste-overs, affixed with sealing wax and lifted away during recent restoration, contain further fragments of Dora's fair-copy version. Mary Wordsworth's patched-together fair copy is the earliest complete form of the poem that can now be recovered. Editorial line numbers in the left-hand margins of the transcriptions indicate lines that make up the early reading text.

After MS. A had been prepared, further revision was extensive: two additional scraps of paper containing new work (again with early work on their versos) were pasted onto $1^v$, and new passages of fair copy were entered on $1^v$, $4^r$, and $4^v$. An entirely new section of the poem—the lines on Joan of Arc in MS. A(1)—was added, on leaves taken from another notebook (*Peter Bell,* MS. 7). Thus cobbled together the extended poem had assumed a complicated shape, so that a new fair copy, MS. B, must have seemed necessary.

Pellucid Spring! unknown beyond the verge
Of a small Hamlet, there, from ancient time
Not undistinguished; (for of wells that ooze
Or Founts that gurgle from thy ~~[illegible]~~
~~And craggy forehead of the~~ cloud-capp'd hill,
Their common Sire, thou only bear'st his Name)
One of my last fond looks is fix'd on Thee;
Who with the comforts of my ~~daily meal~~ simple board
Hast blended, thro' the space of twice seven years,
Beverage as choice as ever Hermit prized,
That Persian Kings might envy; & whose pure
And gentle aspect oft has minister'd
To finer uses. They for me must cease;
the years of years we gain
Days shall pass on; ~~& months revolve~~, & years
Fade, & the moralizing mind derive
No lesson from thy presence, Gracious Power
By the inconstant nature we inherit
Unmatch'd in delicate beneficence;
For neither unremitting rains avail

[DC MS. 105, MS. A, 1r] [*Composed when . . .*]

*Pellucid Spring! unknown beyond the verge*
*Of a small Hamlet, there, from ancient time,*
*Not undistinguished; (for of Wells that ooze*
*Or Founts that gurgle from this ~~moss-grown side~~*
*~~And craggy forehead of this~~ cloud-capp'd hill,*
*Their common Sire, thou only bear'st his Name)*
*One of my last fond looks is fix'd on Thee;*
*simple board*
*Who with the comforts of my ~~daily meal~~*
*Hast blended, thro' the space of twice seven years,*
*{ce*
*Beverage as choi{se as ever Hermit prized,*
*That Persian Kings might envy; & whose pure*
*And gentle aspect oft has minister'd*
*To finer uses. They for me must cease;*
*the year, if years be given,*
*Days shall pass on, ~~& months revolve, & years~~*
*Fade, & the moralizing mind derive*
*No lesson from thy presence, Gracious Power*
*By the inconstant nature <u>we</u> inherit*
*Unmatch'd in delicate beneficence;*
*For neither unremitting rains avail*

---

All work on this page is in the hand of MW, except for revision to l. 14, which is in Dora Wordsworth's hand.

To swell thee into voice, nor hottest drought
Can shrink thy bounty, nor thy beauty mar.
Henceforth what summer loiterer, with regard
What loiterer now with aid of slope of ground
Inquisitive, thee examines
From summer's kisses that countenance will peruse
Pleas'd to detect the dimpling stir of life
The breathing faculty with which thou yield'st
Tho' a mere goblet to the careless eye
Boons inexhaustible. Who hurrying on

Let light propitious? and dead air consent?—
Then would the limitary floor elude the searching eye
The searching eye, that and distinctly vanished, nothing checks
An exquisite communion, flowrets, plants, herbs
And the whole body of grey vault they deck,
Imaged in downward show; the flowers, the herbs flowers
There not of earthly texture, and the vault
Not there diminutive; but thro' a scale
Of [illegible] less and less distinct [illegible]

[DC MS. 105, MS. A, 1$^{v}$] [*Composed when . . .*]

e
20 *To swell the{ into voice, nor hottest drought*
21 *Can stint thy bounty nor thy beauty mar.*
Henceforth what summer Loiterer, with regard
22 *What Loiterer now, with aid of sloping beams*
Inquisitive, ~~that counten~~
23 *~~From summer suns~~ that countenance will peruse*
24 *Pleas'd to detect the dimpling stir of life*
w
25 *The breathing faculty th}ith which thou yield'st*
26 *Tho' a mere goblet to the careless eye*
27 *Boons inexhaustible. Who hurrying on*

Was id
~~Is~~ *light propitious? and d{oes air consent?—*
would
*Then ~~may~~ the limitary floor elude ~~the searching ey~~*
and instantly behold
*The searching eye, <u>that</u> vanished, nothing checks*
*An exquisite communion, flowrets, ~~plants,~~* herbs
*And the whole body of grey vault they deck,*
thee
*Imaged in downward show; the ~~flowers,~~ the ~~plants, the~~ flowers*
herbs
*There not of earthly texture, and the vault*
[?]
*Not there diminutive; but, thro' a scale—*
Of vision less and less distinct descending
*Of vis*

---

27 MW's fair copy breaks off after l. 27, indicating that MS. A was prepared in order to lead into ll. 28–44 on the middle paste-over, cut from a leaf containing these and probably more lines in Dora Wordsworth's hand.

The eight fair-copy lines on the lower part of the page, in Dora's hand, were entered over WW's pencil drafting, now illegible, in the blank space covered by the middle paste-over.

Dora's lines incorporate revisions of ll. 54–61, deleted on the lower half of 2$^{r}$, facing, and contribute to lines on the lower half of 4$^{v}$. Sealing wax over the revision "Was" in the first of the lines shows that the middle paste-over was affixed to the page after the lines beneath it had been entered; the paste-over was then affixed only along its upper edge, allowing it to be lifted to reveal the lines beneath.

Dora Wordsworth's drawing of a hand, at the foot of the page, points to a wavy line linking the phrase "Of vision" to l. 62 on 2$^{r}$.

The phrase "the searching ey" in Dora's second line is erased.

The single line entered by WW at the foot of the page links eight lines of fair copy on the bottom half of the page to the lines in WW's hand on the bottom paste-over.

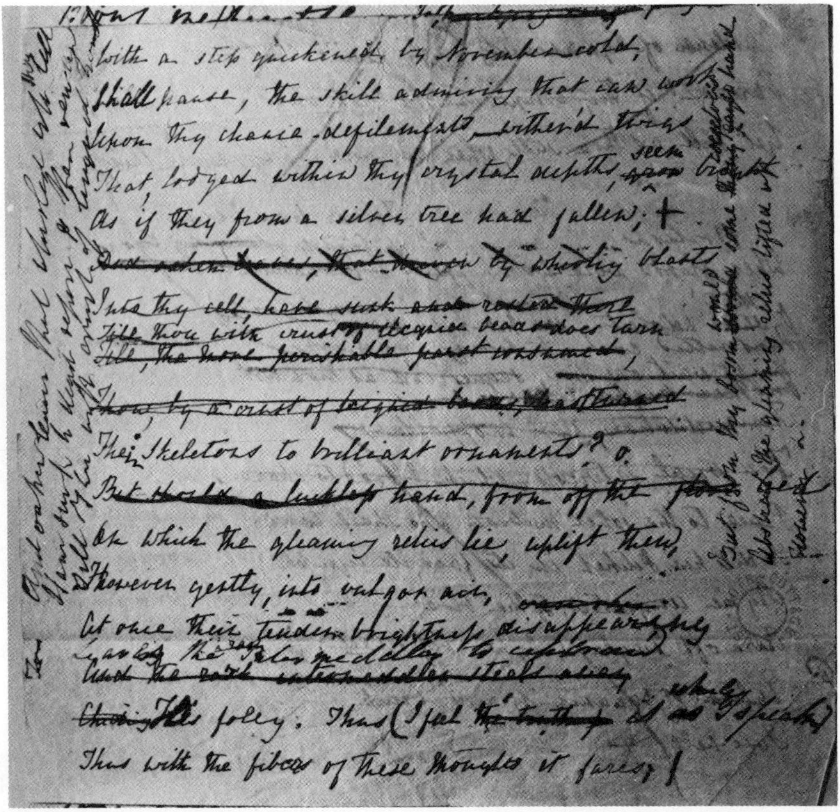

[DC MS. 105, MS. A, 1v] [*Composed when . . .*]

[Middle paste-over, recto]

, ~~*hurrying on*~~
28 *With a step quickened by November-cold,*
{*Shall*
29 {*Will pause, the skill admiring that can work*
{*s—*
30 *Upon thy chance-defilement*{, *wither'd twigs*
*seem*
31 *That, lodg'd within thy crystal depths,* ~~*grow*~~ *bright*
∧
32 *As if they from a silver tree had fallen;* +
33 ~~*And oaken leaves, that—driven by whirling blasts*~~
34 ~~*Into thy cell, have sunk and rested there*~~
~~*Till thou with crust*~~ *of licquid beads does turn*
35 ~~*Till, the more perishable parst consumed,*~~
{*t*
36 ~~*Thou, by a crust of lciquid beads, has*{ *turned*~~
{*ir*
37 *The*{ *Skeletons to brilliant ornaments?* O
38 ~~*But should a luckless hand, from off the floor*~~ bed
39 *On which the gleaming relics lie, uplift them,*
40 *However gently, into vulgar air,*
~~vanishes~~ {*ing*
41 *At once their tender brightness disappear*{*s,*
{es rash
Leav{ing the Intermeddler to upbraid
42 ~~*And the rash intermeddler steals away*~~
{Hi while
43 ~~*Chiding*~~ {*his folly. Thus (I feel* ~~*the truth)*~~ it ~~as~~ I speak)
{*er*
44 *Thus with the fib*{*res of these thoughts it fares;* 1

[Left margin, written vertically:]
Have sunk to dead repose & there reman
Till Thou with crust of liciquid [?hast] turnd

[Right margin, written vertically:]
*would* {*ve*
*But from thy bosom* ~~*should*~~ *some* *co*{[?]}*tous* ~~*strong*~~∧~~*eager*~~ *hand*
*Abstract the gleaming relics lifted up*
*However &c.*

---

MS. A was prepared with the intention of including ll. 28–44 on this scrap of paper, in Dora Wordsworth's hand.

32 The + points to the two lines similarly marked below the rule on 4r.

37 The O at the end of the line points to the three lines similarly marked at the foot of 4r.

44 The vertical mark, perhaps a "1," at the end of the line is meant as a link to the "2" that marks the beginning of l. 45 at the top of 2r.

Revisions by WW, in the left margin, and by Dora Wordsworth, in the right margin, contribute to the fair-copy revisions entered by Dora on the bottom half of 4r and marked for insertion at l. 32 and l. 37; the last word in the left margin, "turnd," is written partly on 1v, showing that the lines in the left margin were entered after the paste-over had been affixed to the page.

Can swell thee into voice; nor hottest drought
Can stint thy bounty, nor thy beauty mar.
—Such calm attraction have I found in thee
My private treasure, while the neighbouring stream
Famed through the Land for turbulent cascades,
Not seldom forfeits his dependent praise,
Until disappoints the ~~Traveller~~ Stranger, lured from far.
Henceforth, what [illegible] [illegible] [illegible] with regard
[illegible] thy [illegible] will peruse
Pleased [illegible]

[DC MS. 105, MS. A, 1v] [*Composed when . . .*]

[Top paste-over, recto]

To
~~Can~~ swell thee into voice, nor hottest drought
Can stint thy bounty, nor thy beauty mar.
—Such calm attraction have I found in thee
My private treasure, while the neighbouring
Stream
Fam'd through the Land for turbulent cascades,
{ praise
Not seldom forfeits his dependent { [ ? ]
Stranger
And disappoints the ~~Traveller~~, lured from far.
~~standing~~
w vacant
Henceforth, what summer Loiterer with regard
Inquisitive thy countenance will peruse
Pleas'd,

---

The lines on this scrap of paper, pasted on during revision of MS. A, replace and expand ll. 20–24 at the top of 1v and become ll. 19–27 in MS. B.

To gloom unfathomable. So ~~in moods~~ of thought
From help from something guiding thee by will
~~Of contemplation, without taste or will~~
By the scarce bases of habitual sense
Supplanted, not for treacherous vacancy
blank dissociation
And ~~utter separation~~ from the world
We love, but that the Residence of Flesh
Mirrored, yet not too strictly, may repair
To Spirit; — for the Idealizing Soul
Time wears the colours of eternity
And Nature deeper into Nature's God!

[DC MS. 105, MS. A, $1^{v}$] [*Composed when* . . .]

[Bottom paste-over, recto]

if thought
To gloom inpenetrable. So ~~in moods~~
Win help from something greater than himsel
~~Of Contemplation, without wish or will~~
Is the coarse basis of habitual sense
Supplanted; not for treacherous vacancy
blank dissociation
And ~~utter separation~~ from the world
S
We love, but that the Residues of ~~Flesh~~
Mirrord, yet not too strictly, may refine
{for
To Spirit;—{to the Idealizing Soul
Time wear the colours of eternity
And Nature deepen into Natures God!

---

These lines are a revision and expansion of ll. 63–70 on $2^{r}$–$2^{v}$ and become ll. 90–99 in MS. B.

Might wait on Thee— a bashful little one
Yet, to the measure of thy promises,
[illegible] as the [illegible] on thee, sequestered
For meditation—nor inopportune
For social interests, such as I have shared.
Peace to the Matron who shall bend to dip
Her pitcher in its fragrant lymph, by me
No longer greeted— to the blushing Girl
Oft tempted here to linger when waylaid
By her Betrothed, peace & happiness.
The cloud of rooks descending from mid air
Softens its evening uproar towards a close

[DC MS. 105, MS. A, 1v] [*Composed when . . .*]

[Top paste-over, verso]

Might wait on Thee— bashful
~~On thee might wait, on thee~~ *a^little one*
{,
~~Tho'~~ *Yet, to the measure of thy promises*{
{— {,
~~T~~ *Strict as the mightiest*{; *on thee*{ *sequestered*
{—
True *For meditation*{ *nor inopportune*
{.
*For social interests, such as I have shared*{,
*Peace to the* ~~sober~~ *Matron who shall bend to dip*
{*H* *favourite*
~~To dip~~ {*her pitcher in its^lymph, by me*
ushing {*G*
*No longer greeted—to the bl*~~ooming~~ {*girl*
~~Her~~ *Oft tempted here to linger when waylaid*
{*B*
*By her* {*betrothed, joy & happiness!*
{*T*
{[?]*he cloud of rooks descending from mid air*
{,
*Softens its evening uproar tow*{~~a~~*rds a close*

---

Work on this scrap of paper, earlier than MS. A, contributes directly to ll. 78–89 on 2v–3r; the hand is MW's, and the fragment of fair copy continues on the verso of the bottom paste-over, part of the leaf from which this paste-over was cut.

Emblem of equanimity and peace
Farewell! if thy composure be not ours
Yet still as thou still, when we are gone wilt keep

Time has been
British & faint [illegible] trace
When floods were worshipped [illegible]
Of that idolatry through monkish rites
Transmitted even to living memory.
[illegible], sequestered as thou art
[illegible]
For meditation [illegible]
For social interests, which I [illegible] to share.
Peace to the sober matron who shall bend
To dip her Pitcher in its favorite lymph
By me ungreeted; to the blooming girl
Here oft waylaid by her betrothed, joy.—
Emblem of equanimity and truth
Fare-well

Near & more near for this protracted strain
A warning not unwelcome. Fare thee well
Emblem of equanimity & truth

[DC MS. 105, MS. A, $1^v$] [*Composed when . . .*]

[Middle paste-over, verso]

*Emblem of equanimity and peace*
*Farewell! if thy composure be not ours*
*Yet ~~still~~ as thou still, when we are ~~gone wilt keep~~*

*Time has been*
*& faint ~~gleams~~ trace*
*British* ' R
*When*^*floods were worship ~~ped~~ ~~& transmitt'd rights~~*
*that through ~~clouds~~ rites*
*Of ~~such~~ idolatry ~~in~~ monkish ~~days~~*
*Transmitted even to living memory*
*~~Might wait on thee, sequester'd as thou art~~*
*~~On thee might fall^[ ? ] to art~~*
*~~For meditation, nor inopportune~~*
*F '*
*~~for social interests, which I lov ed to share.~~*
*Peace to the sober matron who shall bend*
*To dip her Pitcher in its favorite lymph*
*By me ungreeted; to the blooming girl*
*P Here oft waylaid by her betrothed, joy.*
*~~Emblem of equanimity and truth~~*
*Fare-well**

---

The three lines deleted at the top of this scrap of paper are related to ll. 92–94 on $3^r$. The rest of the work here contributes to ll. 73–93 on $2^v$–$3^r$. The hand is Dora's; revisions appear to be MW's.

The "P" in the left-hand margin is probably meant to signal the insertion of something like ll. 88–91 on $3^r$. The short rule below the "ed" in "betrothed" may signal that the word was meant to have three syllables.

The asterisk after "Fare-well" is probably a link to another section of manuscript, now lost.

[$1^v$, bottom paste-over, verso]

*Near & more near, for this protracted strain*
*A warning not unwelcome. Fare thee well*
*a*
*Emblem of equ inimity & truth*

---

These lines, related to ll. 90–92 on $3^r$, are in MW's hand; they follow from the lines on the verso of the top paste-over, part of the leaf from which this scrap of paper was cut.

2 And O how much of all that Love creates
Or beautifies like changes undergoes
Suffers like loss when drawn out of the soul
Its silent laboratory Words should say
Could they ~~but paint~~ depict the wonders of thy All.
How often I have mark'd a plumy fern
Bending ~~its~~ apex towards ~~its~~ the paler self
Reflected all in perfect lineaments
Shadow & substance keeping point to point. †
A subtler operation may withdraw
From sight the solid floor that limited
The nice communion ~~but that barrier gone~~ that gone nothing checks
~~Nought checks nor intercepts the downward thr~~
~~Created for the moment~~ Nothing precludes the downward thre of Flowerets, slants
And the whole body of grey wall they deck
Reflected but not there dimensions
There not of ~~ethereal~~ earthly texture, ~~& thro' a vale~~
~~Of~~ vision less & less distinct descending
To gloom impenetrable. So in moods
Of ~~thoughts~~ pervaded by supernal grace
~~Is the firm base of ordinary sense~~
Is the coarse basis of habitual sense

[DC MS. 105, MS. A, 2r] [*Composed when . . .*]

2 *And O how much of all that Love creates*
*Or beautifies like changes undergoes*
*when*
*Suffers like loss & drawn out of the Soul*
*Its silent laboratory Words should say*
*depict* {*C*
*Could they ~~but paint~~ the wonders of thy* {*cell*
*How often I have mark'd a plumy fern*
{*its a*
*Bending* {*an apex towards ~~its~~ paler self*
*Reflected all in perfect lineaments*
*Shadow & substance kissing, point to point.*
Erelong the limitary floor eludes
*A subtler operation may withdraw*
Thy searching eye that vanishd nothing checks
*From sight the solid floor that limited*
*that gone nothing checks*
*The nice communion ~~but that barrier gone~~*
An exquisite communion flower
*~~Nought checks nor intercepts the downward shew~~*
*Nothing precludes the downward shew*
*~~Created for the moment~~^~~flowrets,~~ plants* flowers
vault
*And the whole body of grey ~~wall~~ they deck*
United
*Reflected but not there diminutive*
not earthly
*There^of ~~etherial~~ texture, ~~&, thro' scale~~*
*Of vision less & less distinct descending*
*To gloom impenetrable. So in moods*
{*t*
*Of though*{*~~ts~~ pervaded by supernal grace*
*~~Is the firm base of ordinary sense~~*
Is the coarse basis of habitual sense

---

The hand is MW's.

45 The "2" in the left margin shows that this line is meant to follow l. 44, marked with a slash (perhaps a "1") at the foot of the recto of the middle paste-over on 1v.

53 The mark at the end of the line shows the location of the passage identified by a similar mark at the top of 4r.

53/54, 54/55, 56/57 WW's revisions are in pencil, partially erased.

58 The word "flowers" is in pencil; "flowrets" is canceled in pencil.

59–60 Revisions and deletion in pencil.

62 The end of the link drawn across the foot of 1v is visible at the beginning of the line.

Supplanted & the residues of flesh
Are linked with spirit; shallow life is lost
In being; to the idealizing soul
Time wears the colors of Eternity
And Nature deepens into Nature's God.—
Millions of kneeling Hindoos at this day
Bow to the watery element adored
In their vast stream; & if an age hath been
As books & haply votive Altars vouch
When British floods were worshipped some faint trace
Of that idolatry thro' monkish rites
Transmitted even to living memory
Might wait on thee a bashful little one
Yet to the measure of thy promises
Strict as the mightiest; upon thee sequestered
For meditation, nor inopportune
For social interests such as I have shared
—Peace to the sober Matron who shall bend to dip
Her pitcher in the favourite Lymph
No longer greeted; to the blushing girl

[DC MS. 105, MS. A, 2v] [*Composed when . . .*]

66 *Supplanted & the residues of flesh*
*formal* *merg'd*
67 *Are linked with spirit; ~~shallow~~ life is lost*
{;
68 *In being{ to the idealizing soul*
69 *Time wears the colors of Eternity*
70 *And Nature deepens into Nature's God.—*
71 *Millions of kneeling Hindos at this day*
72 *Bow to the watery element adored*
73 *In their vast stream; & if an age hath been*
74 *As books & haply votive Altars vouch*
{W
75 {~~B~~*hen British floods were worshipped some faint*
*trace*
76 *Of that idolatry thro' Monkish rites*
far as
77 *Transmitted even to living memory*
78 *Might wait on Thee a bashful little one*
79 *Yet to the measure of thy promises*
*up*}
80 *Strict as the mightiest;* }*on thee sequestered*
81 *For meditation, nor inopportune*
82 *For social interests such as I have shared*
{*sober*
{[ ? ] ~~*to dip*~~
83 *—Peace to the*^*Matron who shall bend* ~~*to dip*~~
~~To dip~~ {*H*
84 ~~*To dip*~~ {*her pitcher in the favourite lymph* ~~*by me*~~
By me un
85 *No longer*^*greeted; to the blushing Girl*

---

The copyist was MW.

67 The word "shallow" is canceled in pencil; "formal" is in pencil.

68 Revision in pencil.

75 Deletion by erasure.

83 The revision "sober" is written over an illegible word in pencil; "to dip" is canceled in pencil.

83/84, 84/85 Interlinear revisions are in pencil, reinforced in ink.

Oft tempted here to linger when waylaid
By her Betrothed, joy & happiness ——
The cloud of rooks descending from mid air
Softens its evening uproar towards a close
Near & more near, for this protracted strain
A warning not unwelcome — Fare thee while
Emblem of equanimity & ~~truth~~ peace truth
Farewell if thy composure be not ours

Yet ~~of~~ as thou still, when we are gone, will keep
Thy living chaplet of moist fern and flowers
Cherished in shade tho' peeped at by the Sun
So shall our bosoms feed a covert growth
Of grateful recollection, tribute due,
(Not less than to wide lake and foaming rill)
To thy obscure and modest attributes
To thee, clear Spring! ~~and~~ all-sustaining Heaven.
the aid

[DC MS. 105, MS. A, 3r] [*Composed when . . .*]

86 *Oft tempted here to linger when waylaid*
87 *By her Betrothed, joy & happiness* ———
88 *The cloud of rooks descending from mid air*
 '
89 *Softens its evening uproar towa*|*rds a close*
90 *Near & more near, for this protracted strain*
91 *A warning not unwelcome—Fare thee well*
 truth
92 *Emblem of equanimity & ~~truth~~ peace*
93 *Farewell if thy composure be not ours*

[Paste-over, recto]

 *as*
94 *Yet ~~if~~ thou still, when we are gone, will keep*
 *2 1*
95 *Thy living chaplet of moist fern and flowers*
96 *Cherished in shade tho' peeped at by the Sun*
 *sha*
97 *So wi*|*ll our bosoms feed a covert growth*
98 *Of grateful recollections, tribute due,*
99 *(Not less than to wide lake and foaming rill)*
100 *To thy obscure and modest attributes*
101 *To thee, clear Spring! and all-sustaining Heaven.*

———

———

*aid*

---

The copyist was MW.

92 The word "truth" is in pencil.

93/ Fair copy breaks off with l. 93, showing MW's intention to add the paste-over containing ll. 94–101.

The hand of the paste-over is Dora Wordsworth's.

95 The numbers above the line show that "fern" and "flowers" are to be transposed.

3v is blank.

y forehead of this cloud capped hill,
As books
[kn]own Sire, thou only bearst his name]
When my last fond looks is ~~turned to thee~~; fixed on thee;
the comforts of my simple board
Of that
ndeed, thro' the space of twice seven years,
Trans g.
as choice as ever Hermit prized,
Might raw things might envy; & whose pure
Yet ttle aspect oft has ministered
Strict uses. Shall they ~~cease & henceforth~~ for me must cease;
shall on the months and years complete
For [illegible]

[DC MS. 105, MS. A, 3r] [*Composed when . . .*]

[Paste-over, verso]

]y *forehead of this cloud cappd hill,*
]}
]*mmon Sire, thou only bearst his name,*}
*my last fond looks is* ~~*turned*~~ *to thee; fixed on thee;*
~~*fixed*~~
*the comforts of my simple board*
]*nded, thro' the space of twice seven years,*
*as choice as ever Hermit prized,*
]*sian Kings might envy; & whose pure*
{,
]*tle aspect oft has minister*{*ed*
{for {me must cease,
{*T* {*must*}
*uses. Shall* {*they cease? henceforth*
*shall on the months and years complete*
[ ? ]

---

The line endings visible here are the earliest extant version of ll. 5–14; the hand is Dora's.

* Such delicate caress as in the shape
Of this green plant had aptly recompensed
For baffled lips & disappointed arms
And hopeless pangs the spirit of that youth
The fair Narcissus whom some pitying God
Changed to a crimson flower when he for whose pride
Probably a retribution too severe
Had pined, upon a watery duplicate
Wasting that love the Nymphs implored in vain

+ And oaken leaves that driven by whirling blasts
Have sunk & lain immersed in dead repose

But from thy bosom would some covetous hand
Abstract the gleaming relics & uplift them
However gently towards the vulgar air

[DC MS. 105, MS. A, 4r] [*Composed when . . .*]

*Such delicate caress as in the shape*
*Of this green plant had aptly recompensed*
*For baffled lips & disappointed arms*
*And hopeless pangs the spirit of that youth*
*Then fair Narcissus whom some pitying God*
*whose*
*Changed to a Crimson flower when he ~~for~~ pride*
*{'d {a ^*
*Provok{ig { retribution too severe*
*Had pined, upon a watery duplicate*
*Wasting that love the Nymphs implored in vain*

---

\+ *And Oaken leaves that driven by whirling blasts*
*Have sunk & been imersed in dead repose*

*{B*
*o {but from thy bosom would some covetous hand*
*Abstract the gleaming relics & uplift them*
*However gently towards the vulgar air*

---

Work on this page, in Dora Wordsworth's hand, is part of the revision of MS. A.

The mark to the left of the first line on the page shows the point at which the passage at the top of the page is to be inserted, following a similar mark at l. 53 on 2r.

The passages below the rule are marked for insertion on the middle paste-over on 1v, at l. 32 and l. 37.

loveliest will meet

A parting moment with her ~~fairest~~ look
And seemingly her happiest look so fair
It frustrates its own purpose & recals
The grieved one whom it went to send away
Dost tempt me by disclosures exquisite
To linger hanging over thee—
Eager as one who on some pleasant day
Peers from a head-land searching the sea-clouds
For coming sails or as a simple child
Who deaf to plaudits that proclaim the joy,
Of all around him sits by some new charm
Of scenic transmutation wonder bound.
Where is thy earthy floor from keenest sight
That obstacle is vanished & slant beams
The silent inquest of a western sun
Aspiring, air propitious, thou revealest
Communion without check of herbs & flowers
And the vaults hoary sides to which they cling
Imaged in downward show the flowrets herbs
Not there not of earthly texture & the vault
Not there diminutive —

[DC MS. 105, MS. A, 4v] [*Composed when . . .*]

*will meet*

*loveliest*

*A parting moment with her ~~fairest~~ look*
*And seemingly her happiest look so fair*
*It frustrates its own purpose & recalls*
*The grieved one whom it meant to send away*
*Dost temp't me by disclosures exquisite*
*To linger hanging over thee—*
*Eager as one who on some pleasant day*
*Peers from a head-land searching the sea-clouds*
*For comig sails or as a simple child*
*Who deaf to plaudits that proclaim the joy,*
*Of all around him sits by some new charm*
*{c*
*Of scenis transmutation wonder bound*
*Where is thy earthy floor from keenest sight*
*That obstacle is vanished & slant beams*
*The silent inquest of a western sun ~~ass~~*
*Assisting, air propitious, thou reveale'st*
*Communion without check of herbs & flowers*
*And the vaults hoary sides to which they clig*
*Imaged in downward show the flowrets herbs*
*T}*
*~~Not~~ there not of earthly texture & the vault*
*Not there diminutive—*
*n*

---

The passage on this page, part of the revision of MS. A, becomes ll. 67–88 of MS. B; the copyist is Dora Wordsworth. The letters "ass" at the end of the seventh line from the foot of the page were deleted by erasure.

# DC MS. 105, MS. A(1)

Work on these pages, taken from a notebook containing a late fair copy of *Peter Bell,* contributes directly to the fair copy in DC MS. 105, MS. B, lines 120–168. The leaves measure 18.2 by 22.5 centimeters, and the wove paper is watermarked with the date 1816; the notebook from which they were taken is fully described in *Peter Bell,* edited by John Jordan (Ithaca, 1985), page 16. Editorial numbers in brackets at the upper right-hand corners of the transcriptions correspond to the numbers assigned to fair-copy lines in the transcriptions of DC MS. 105, MS. B. The hand is Dora Wordsworth's.

But
And should these hills be ransacked by one whose soul
Scorning love whispers shrinks from love itself
As fancy's snare for female vanity
Here may the aspirant find a trusting place
For loftier intercourse the muses crowned
For mountain airs made vocal through their lips
In notes what mountain echoes, taken up
Boldly, & bear away for softer life
Hence Deified as Sisters, bound
Together in a never dying choir
Who with their Hippocrene & grotted fount
Of Castaly attest that womans heart
Was in the limpid age of this staind world
The most reverd seat of fine ecstasy
And new born waters deemd the happiest source
Of inspiration for the conscious Lyre
Sought not in harsher times the Maid of lore
Her fountain of the fairies whose still notes
Pondering in quiet only the attuned her soul
For the reception of a deeper voice
There the Enthusiast sate gazing intensely
Till the innocent current turned into

[DC MS. 105, MS. A(1), 1r] [*Composed when . . .*, ll. 120–136]

But be ranged by one
*And should these hills ~~give birth to one, whose soul~~*
*Scorning love whispers shrinks from love itself*
*As fancy's snare for female vanity*
*Here may the aspirant find a trysting place*
muses cround
*For loftier intercourse the ~~sacred nine~~ muses crowned*
With wreathes *that have not faded to this hour*
*~~Certes were self taught Grecian damsels, famed~~*
*What were they certes grecian Damsels famed*
*For mountain air made vocal through their lips*
*wh that* *wd*
*In notes ~~by~~ mountain echos∧taken up*
*{& bear*
*Boldly, {or ~~borne~~ away for softer life*
*as* they were
*Hence ~~were they~~ Deified ~~for~~ Sisters, bound*
*Together in a never dying choir*
*{ip}*
*Who with their h{on}ocrene & grotto'd fount*
*Of Castaly attest that womans heart*
*Was in the limpid age of this staind world*
*{' ecs}*
*The most rever{ed seat of fine ec}tasy*
*{e*
*And new born waterns deem'd the happi{sst source*
*Of inspiration for the conscious Lyre*
*Sought not in harsher times the Maid of Arc*
*Her fountain of the fairies whose still notes*
d ness *she*
*Ponder~~ing~~ in quiet ~~the Enthusiast she~~∧attuned her Soul*
*For the reception of a deeper voice ~~& holier listenings~~*
*~~And holier listenings~~ ~~There the Enthusiast~~ sate gazing intensely*
*innocent*
*Till the∧current turned into*

[left margin, vertical:]
The Muses crownd
With wreathes that havent faded to this hour
What were they? certes Grecian Damsels fair

[right margin, vertical:]
*se}*
*Certes were [?]{lf taught damsels scatter'd births*
*Of may a Grecian vale who sought not praise*
*&*
*~~Were~~ heedless even of listeners—warbl{'ed ing out*
*[?] Their own emotions given to mountain air*

---

The first three lines at the top of this page probably became the last three at the foot of the missing leaf 6 (recto) in MS. B.

The four lines in the right margin are meant to replace the three lines canceled at mid-page. The last six lines at the foot of the page are revised on 2v.

WW's drafting in the left margin is intermediate between the interlinear revisions at mid-page and the four lines in the right margin.

1v contains *Peter Bell* material, inverted.

And holier listenings There ~~would~~ the Enthusiast sate
There would she gaze intensely till the current
Turned into blood before her heart sick eye
Then tinkled audibly the fairy fount
Till haply that mysterious voice again
Roused her & from the agonies of France
Sucking resentment the moist eye ~~caught~~ took fire
Her out stretch'd arms as oft in midnight dreams
Petitioned the blank air for space & shelter
And her breast heaved Labouring beneath a soul
Wild ~~with impatience~~ as the wind & when the fit was past ~~as the blasts of air~~
~~Yet not to be diverted from its course~~
Not less determin'd than a torrent stream
That having smooth'd its brow ~~from~~ on some dread brink
Drops headlong resolute to find or make
A Gulph of rest deep as the height it falls from
Bestowing her Lowly tasks & natural hopes &
~~So the due season from the servile tasks~~
Religious but treasuring every law
~~Of Faith & Vineyard & the pastoral mead~~
And grace of feminine humanity
The chosen rustic urged ~~the~~ a warlike steed
~~Urged the chosen rustic in the might of Prophecy~~
Towards the beleaguer'd city in the might
of Prophecy Decreed to fulfil ~~at the swords point~~
At the swords point Visions conceived in tears — ~~a cloud of [illegible]~~

Turn

[DC MS. 105, MS. A(1), 2r] [*Composed when . . .*, ll. 150–168]

*the*
*And holier listenings there ~~would~~ Enthusiast sate*
*Th*
*An ere would she gaze intensely till the current*
*Turned into blood before her heart sick eye*
X*Then tinckled audibly the fairy fount*
*Till haply that mysterious voice again*
*Roused her & from the agonies of France*
took
*Sucking resentment the moist eye ~~caught~~ fire*
*Her out stretch'd arms as oft in midnight dreams*
*Petioned the blank air for spear & shiel*
*And her breast heaved laboring beneath a soul*
*as the wind & when the fit was past*
*Wild ~~with impatience as the blasts of air~~*
*~~Yet not to be diverted from its course~~*
*t*
*No r less determin'd than a torrent stream*
*on*
*That having smooth'd its brow ~~from~~ some dread brink*
*Drops headlong resolute to find or make*
*ph*
*A Gul f of rest deep as the height it falls from*
*Erelong her lowly tasks & natural haunts r*
*~~So in due season from the servile tasks~~*
*ig*
*t Relinquishing but treasur es every law*
*~~Of T ilth & vineyard & the pastoral mead~~*
*And grace of feminine humanity*
*a*
*The chosen rustic urged ~~the~~ warlike Steed*
*~~Issued the chosen rustic in the might of Prophecy~~*
*OfProphecy Towards the beleaguer'd city in the might*
*Accoutred to fulfil ~~at the swords point~~*
*a*
*Visions conceived in tears ~~a cloud of rooks &c &~~ — —*
*At the swords point* [ ? ]

---

The first three lines at the top of the page, deleted here, are revised on 2v. The X to the left of the fourth line on the page marks the point at which the passage of revision on 2v ends.

The two phrases entered in the lower left-hand margin extend onto 1v.

In harsher times the Maid of Lire w[oul]d steal
From human converse to frequent alone
The fountain of the fairies what to her
Were the repeated doings what their joys of the Elves
Their merriment & revelry to her
Whose country groaned beneath a foreign scourge
It was a sacred fountain by whose side
She pondered murmurs that attuned her ear
For the reception of a deeper voice holier listenings
It was a sacred fountain by whose side
And holier listenings the translucent lapse
Darkened beneath the shadows of her thoughts
As if swift clouds pass over it or caught
War's tincture mid the [illegible] green & still
Turning to blood before her heart sick eye
Then &

[DC MS. 105, MS. A(1), 2v] [*Composed when . . . ,* ll. 137–150]

*In harsher times the Maid of Arc wd steal*
*F}*
*In} rom human converse to frequent alone*
*The fountain of the fairies what to her*
*of the Elves*
*Were the reputed doings ~~what their jo~~ys*
*Their merryment & revelry to her*
*{[?under]*
*Whose country groaned {~~beneath~~ a foreign scourge*
*~~It was a sacred fountain by whose side~~*
*She pondered murmurs that attuned her ear*
*For the reception of a deeper voice ~~& holier listenings~~*
*~~It was a sacred fountain by whose side~~*
*And holier listenings the translucent lapse*
*{t*
*Darkened beneath the shadows of her {Thoughts*
*As if swift clouds past over it or caught*
*War's tincture mid the forest green & still*
*Turning to blood before her heart sick eye*
*Then &—*

---

The lines on this page are a revised version of the passage beginning six lines from the foot of 1r and ending three lines from the top of 2r.

The bottom of the page contains three stanzas of *Peter Bell,* inverted, and not transcribed.

# DC MS. 105, MSS. B and B(1)

The base text of MS. B, in the hand of Dora Wordsworth, incorporates the latest work in MS. A and MS. A(1). Complete except for leaves 6 and 12, MS. B is formed of sheets of laid paper watermarked with a shield containing images of harp, bear, lion, and horse, and countermarked GILLING / & / ALLFORD above the date 1821. Each sheet is folded once to form leaves measuring about 15.5 by 19.2 centimeters; chain lines are at intervals of 2.4 centimeters. Editorial line numbers in the left-hand margins of the transcriptions indicate fair-copy lines, but no reading text has been constructed for MS. B. Lines 100–119, which would have been on the missing leaf 6, can be supplied from $2^v$ of MS. A and $1^r$ of MS. A(1); leaf 12 was apparently torn away before Dora began her transcription.

MSS. B(1) and B(2), both in Wordsworth's hand, contain fair copy intermediate between revisions in MS. B and the penultimate fair copy of the poem in DC MS. 89. MS. B(1) is formed from a single sheet of laid paper folded and torn to form four leaves, each measuring approximately 15 by 19 centimeters. The paper is watermarked with a shield containing images of lion, bear, harp, and horse and countermarked with the letters WP over the date 1815; chain lines are at intervals of 2.5 centimeters. In the transcription of MS. B(1) bracketed editorial line numbers indicate passages in the late reading text to which the work on each leaf is related.

MS. B(2) is fully described in the headnote to the reading texts of *Composed when a probability existed . . .*, above.

# [DC MS. 105, MS. B:
*Composed when a probability existed . . .*]

[1r]

[?Suffice to give]
*Pellucid Spring! unknown beyond the verge*
*Of a small Hamlet, there, from ancient time*
*Not undistinguished; (for, of wells that ooze,*
{is
*Or founts that gurgle, from th{e cloud-capp'd hill,*
*Their common Sire, thou only bears't his name)*
{t
*One of my last fond looks is fix'd on {Thee;*
*Who with the comforts of my simple board*
*Hast blended, thro' the space of twice seven years,*
*Beverage as choice as ever Hermit prized,*
*That Persian Kings might envy; & whose pure*
*And gentle aspect oft has minister'd*
*To finer uses. They for me must cease;*
{,
*Days shall pass on{ the year, if years be given,*
{,— {i
*Fade{ & the moral{ zing mind derive*
*No lesson from thy presence, Gracious Power!*
*By the inconstant nature we inherit*
*Unmatch'd in delicate beneficence;*
*For neither unremitting rains avail*
*To swell thee into voice, nor hottest drought*

---

[1v]

Thy bounty stints: nor can thy beauty mar.
Such calm attractions have I found in thee
My private treasure, in all change a Friend
True as unboastful—while

~~Perchance, the Norman curfew had not toll'd~~

Not yet, perchance, translucent Spring
had toll'd

---

WW's phrase at the top of 1r, possibly "Suffice to give," is in pencil.
3,4 The deleted commas are erased.

---

The block of lines at the top of 1v represents revision of ll. 20–22 at the top of 2r. Drafting on the rest of 1v is WW's earliest work toward ll. 30–36 in the Morgan MS.

The Norman curfew-bell, when human hands
First have their help that the deficent rock
Might over arch thee from the heat of noon
Sheltered, ~~and unapparent to the [ ? ]~~
~~Of any star that looks not from the west~~

age
rude ~~time~~ were herds
{at
Nor haply cam in th{ose unsteadfast times
Or wild deer
~~[?Were] Cattle~~ pasturing the green hill allowd
To trouble thee appropriate to mans need
~~like selfish~~ cares
These Grosser ties will last, ~~such c~~are ~~bright~~
Sprin
Shall not be wanting, but when we are gone
~~Will not~~
pensive
What va~~cant~~ summer Loiterer

---

[2r]

~~Yet a little world~~
~~Which change of season [?injures] not a world~~
*~~Can stint~~ thy bounty, nor thy beauty mar.*
Of
*~~Such~~ calm attraction have I found in thee*
Our {S
*~~My~~ private treasure, while the neighbouring* {*stream,*
*Fam'd through the land for turbulent cascades,*
{time
Will oft{en {a
*Not seldom forfeits his depend{ent praise*
*And disappoints the Stranger, lured from far.*
vacant
*—Henceforth what summer Loiterer, with regard*
*Inquisitive, thy countenance will peruse,*
*Pleased to detect the dimpling stir of life,*
*The breathing faculty with which thou yield'st,*
*Tho' a mere goblet to the careless eye,*
{*i*
*Boons inexhaust{able?—who, hurring ~~on~~* past
*With a step quickened by November cold,*
*Shall pause, the skill admiring that can work*
*Upon thy chance defilements,—wither'd twigs*
*That lodged within thy crystal depths seem bright*
{;
*As if they from a silver tree had fallen{!*
O}
*And o}aken leaves, that driven by whirling blasts,*
*Have sunk, and lain imersed in dead repose,*
hast {d
*Till thou, with crust of licquid beads, ~~does~~ turn{*
*Their skeletons to brilliant ornaments?*

---

22 "Stream" is capitalized in pencil.
26 The alternate "vacant" is in pencil.

[$2^{\text{v}}$]

{S
Not yet, perchance, translucent {spring, had
toll'd
The Norman Curfew-bell when human hands
First gave their help that the deficient Rock
cool as thou art clear
Might over arch thee from pernicious heat
defended and appropriate to Man's need
Shelterd, and haply even in that rude age
Nor beast that dwelt in woods nor household
Kine
~~Might trouble thee, appropriate to man's need.~~
These grosser ties will last,—these antient cares
Shall not be wanting; but, when we are gone,
What pensive summer loiterer with regard
Inquisitive [?&c]
Then haply, too, nor beast that dwells
in wood
{[?at]
And haply see this beast of ~~foul~~ {prey or chase
Nor household kine—wherever else they
~~bathed~~ slake
At will the thirsty lip or plunge the hoof
Might trouble thee

Might over arch thee from pernicious heat
Defended, and appropriate to Mans need.
These grosser ties will last—these antient cares
~~Will~~ t
Shall not be wanting, but when we are gone
What pensive Summer Loiterers

[$3^{\text{r}}$]

*But, from thy bosom, would some covet~~o~~sus hand*
lifted
*Abstract the gleaming relics, and uplift them,*
into
*However gently,* ~~*into*~~ ~~*vul*~~ *towards the vulgar air*
*At once their tender brightness disappears,*
*Leaving the Intermeddler to upbraid*
*His folly. Thus (I feel it while I speak)*
*Thus with the fibres of these thoughts it fares;*
*And O! how much of all that Love creates,*
*Or beautifies, like changes undergoes,*
*Suffers like loss, when drawn out of the Soul*

Drafting on $2^{\text{v}}$—the second stage of work toward ll. 30–36 of the Morgan MS—follows from work on the bottom two-thirds of $1^{\text{v}}$ and leads to another version of the passage on MS. B(1), $2^{\text{r}}$.

A diagonal deletion line cancels everything between "Rock" at the end of l. 3 and "Might over arch" five lines up from the bottom.

41/42, 42/43 Interlinear revisions are in pencil.

The passage in the right margin of $3^{\text{r}}$, meant to be inserted at ll. 56/57, becomes ll. 69–73 in the Morgan MS.

*Its silent laboratory.—Words should say,*
features
*Could they depict the wonders of thy cell*
~~From the live rock with grace inimitable~~
*How often I have mark'd a plumy fern*
From the live rock with grace inimitable
*Bending its apex towards a paler self*
*Reflected all in perfect lineaments,*
*Shadow & substance kissing, point to point,*
*Such delicate caress, as, in the shape*
*Of this green plant, had aptly recompensed*
,still baffled
*For ~~baffled~~ lips & disappointed arms,*
*And hopeless pangs, the spirit of that youth*

In mutual stillness, or if some bold breeze
s
Enter{ing the cell gave restlessness to One
The other glassd in thy unruffld breast
Partook of every motion met retired
And met again, such playful sympathy
Such delicate caress

---

[3v]

And seemingly her happiest tempt'st me yet
And yet to linger bending over thee:
For now thy earthy bed (a moment past
[?] grounds
Palpable unto sight as the dry ground)
[ ? ] [ ? ? ]
Eludes perception by some sleight or charm
Of wonder working Nature; and slant beams

When I would turn aside, to linger—yet
And yet a little—hanging over thee
Earnest as One—

~~*To turn & linger hanging over thee,*~~

*en* *a*
*Wh{ile deaf to plaudits that proclaim ~~the~~ joy*
*Tumultuous* *sits still*
*~~Of all~~^ ~~around him~~ he^by some new charm*
*transmutation*
*Of scenic ~~witchery, sits~~ wonder bound.*

---

The entries by WW on the top half of 3v lead from ll. 69–81 on 4r–5r to work in MS. B(1), 1r–1v and finally to the Morgan MS, ll. 88–97.

The words below the third and fourth lines from the top of 3v are in pencil, and traces of pencil are visible beneath the fifth line from the top of the page.

The canceled line at mid-page is in MW's hand.

The three lines at the foot of 3v, in Dora Wordsworth's hand, are a revision of ll. 77–79 on 4r, facing.

---

[4r]

by
61 *The fair Narcissus, ~~whom~~ some pitying god*
62 *Changed to a crimson flower when he, whose pride*
63 *Provok'd a retribution too severe,*
64 *Had pined, upon a watery duplicate,*
65 *Wasting that love the Nymphs implored in vain.*
*bright*
66 *—This fancy is forgiven & thou ~~clear~~ spring*
*~~Moved~~ like ∧*
*~~Like (shall I say) to a dear friend who meets~~ ~~shall I~~*
67 *~~As oft the face of a~~ ~~Like a dear friend whose face will often meet~~*
*(Moved (shall I say) like a dear friend who meets*
*~~its~~*
68 *A parting moment with ~~her~~ loveliest look,*
*~~its~~ her*
*her*
69 *And seemingly ~~his~~ happiest,—look so fair*
70 *It frustrates its own purpose, & recalls*
*' a*
71 *The griev{ed one whom it ment to send away)*
*∧*
72 *Dost temp't me by disclosures exquisite* X
in *~~To lin when I would turn aside to linger—yet~~*
in *~~And yet a little~~*
73 *~~To linger ∧ hanging over thee—~~*
Earnest
*~~Earnest~~ ~~Intent~~ at ~~who the break of day~~*
74 *~~Eager~~ ∧ as he, who ~~on some pleasant day~~*
[ ? ] *on some pleasant day*
75 *Peers from a head-land, searching the sea clouds*
*~~earnest~~*
76 *For coming sails; as as a~~n~~ ~~simple~~ child*
*ile*
77 *Wh{o deaf to plaudits that proclaim the joy*
*n*
78 *Of all around him sits by some new charm*
79 *Of scenic transmutation wonder bound*
bright Spring a moment
bed *F*}
80 *~~Where is thy~~ earthy floor? ~~from keenest sight~~*
clear
Thy earthy floor, ~~bright~~ Spring, a moment past

---

66/67 The word "to" is canceled twice; "shall I" is deleted by erasure.
67/68 The inserted line is MW's, as are the words "Moved" and "like" beneath l. 66.
72/73 The word "in" entered twice in the left margin indicates WW's intention to keep MW's revision lines canceled here; the X after l. 72 probably points to his copy of these canceled lines at mid-page on 3v, facing.
74/75 The illegible word is in pencil.
75/76 The word "earnest" is canceled in pencil.
79/80 The word "bed" is in pencil.
77 "When" may at one stage have been intended.
At the top of 4v, in pencil, WW drafted "From the live Rock with grace inimitable"—the line entered in ink at ll. 53/54 on 3r.

[5r]

~~Was palpable to sight as the dry ground~~
~~On which are [ ? ? ] vanishd, &~~
81 *That ~~obstacle is vanished; & slant beams,~~*
{~~setting~~
{[ ? ]
82 *The silent inquest of a ~~west~~ern sun,*
~~lucid well-spring~~ {o {'
83 *Assisting, ~~air propitious~~, th{eu reveal{st*
84 *Communion, without check, of herbs & flowers,*
{l
85 *And the vau{ts hoary sides to which they cling,*
86 *Imaged in downward show; the flowrets, herbs,*
87 *There not of earthly texture, & the vault*
88 *Not there diminutive; but, thro' a scale*
89 *Of vision less & less distinit, descending*
90 *To gloom impenetrable!—So, if thought*
91 *Win help from something greater than herself,*
92 *Is the coarse basis of habitual sense*
93 *Supplanted; not for treacherous vacancy,*
94 *And blank dissociation from the world*
95 *We love, but that the Residues of Flesh,*
96 *Mirror'd—yet not too strictly, may refine*
97 *To Spirit;—for the Idealizing Soul,*
98 *Time wear the colors of eternity,*
99 *And Nature deepen into Nature's God!*

[5v]

To the tottering Sire
For
[ ? ] whom like
Who with like service, now & then his
To the tottering Sire

like service
[ ? ? ] now & then his choice
Relieves the tedious holiday of age
Thoughts raisd above the earth while here he rests
Feeding on sunshine

No longer greeted;—to the tottering Sire
For whom like service, now and then his choice,
Relieves the tedious holiday of age
Thoughts raised above this earth while
here he rests
Feeding on sunshine;—to the blushing Girl

*that*
*~~Peace to the Matron who with cautious hand~~*
∧

*~~Shall dip her pitcher in its favorite lymph~~*
*~~By me ungreeted~~, to the blushing Girl*
speed their flight
*Who, as the minutes ~~steal away,~~ forgets*
*Her errand, nothing loath to be way-laid*
while years roll on
*By her Betrothed—peace thro' all her days*
*And pleasure sober'd down to happiness*

---

[$7^r$]

*Here may the aspirant find a trysting place*
*For loftier intercourse!—the muses, crowned*
*With wreaths that have not faded to this hour,*
*Certes were self taught damsels, scatter'd births,*
*Of many a Grecian vale, who sought not praise,*
*And, heedless even of listeners, warbled out*
*Their own emotions given to mountain air*
*In notes that mountain echos would take up*
*Boldly, or bear away for softer life;*
*they*
*Hence Deified as Sisters ~~they~~ were∧bound*
*Together in a never dying choir;*
*Who, with their hipocrene & grott'd fount*
*Of Castaly, attest that woman's heart*
*Was, in the limpid age of this stain'd world,*
*fine*
*The most rever'd seat of∧ecstacy,*
*And new born waters deem'd the happiest source*
*Of inspiration for the conscious Lyre.*
*withdrew*
*In harsher times the Maid of Arc ~~would steal~~*
*From human converse, to frequent alone*
*The fountain of the Fairies* .} {*W* / *what to her*}

---

The work toward the top of $5^v$, leading to ll. 133–137 in the Morgan MS, was drafted twice in pencil and then recopied in ink; in the transcription, the ink lines are indented and placed below those in pencil.

The fair-copy passage in Dora's hand at the foot of $5^v$ is from MS. A, $2^v$–$3^r$, ll. 83–87, and leads to ll. 131–140 of the Morgan MS. The lines were probably entered opposite a fair-copy passage on leaf 6, now missing. WW's revision between the second and third lines from page foot is in pencil, reinforced by ink.

---

The fair copy begins again on $7^r$ after a gap of 20 lines that would have been on the recto of the missing leaf 6. See headnote to DC MS. 105, MSS. B and B(1).

120–123 Canceled with a vertical ink line.

[$7^v$]

Wars tincture mid the forest green & still
Turnd
Turnd into blood before her heart-sick eye
her natural
those
Erelong forsaking all her cherished haunts
All her acustomd offices & cares

for this [?] shunned the marge
Yet not the less the Enthusiast loved to sit
[?]
~~By~~ the green fount that tinkling audibly
Resum'd a soothing influence till the voice
The [?monitory] voce from heaven again
and
Rouzd her, ~~made~~ restless to deliver Fran

heaved th Virgin's chest
Then with resentment throbbd her breast—
Her arms as if her arms
Outstreth'd as many a time in midnight
dreams
Petitioned the blank air for spear & shield
wood
was the forest leafless ere
Nor ~~haply waned the moon before~~ her Sire
Trembles to see them in her solid [?] grasp
Wield at will for martial exercise
And now forsaking all those natural haunts

S
Nor was the forest leafless e're her sire
Trembles to see them in her solid grasp
Wielded at will for martial exercise
Ere long
Forsaking forsaking a

[$8^r$]

140 *Were the reputed doings of the Elves,*
*pageants their*
141 *Their ~~merryment~~, and∧revelries; to her*
142 *Whose crountry groaned under a foreign scourge?*
143 *She pondered murmurs that attuned her ear*
144 *For the reception of a deeper voice*
145 *And holier listenings; the translucent lapse*
146 *Darkened beneath the shadows of her thoughts,*

---

The four lines at the top of $7^v$ represent a drastic condensation of ll. 148–163 on $8^r$–$9^r$. The block of lines at mid-page is canceled by two vertical ink strokes; it represents an expansion and revision of ll. 150–152 on $8^r$. The blocks of drafting on the bottom half of $7^v$ represent revision of ll. 153–162 on $8^r$–$9^r$.

*As if swift clouds past over it; or caught*
*War's tincture, mid the forest green & still,*
*Turning to blood before her heart sick eye.*
*Then tinckled audibly the fairy fount*
*Till haply, that mysterious voice again*
*Roused her, &, from the injuries of France,*
*Sucking resentment, the moist eye took fire.*
*Her out stretch'd arms, as oft in midnight dreams,*
*Petition'd the blank air for spear & shield;*
*And her breast heaved laboring—beneath a soul*
but
*Wild as the wind; & when the fit was past*
*Not less determin'd than a torrent stream*
*That, having smooth'd its brow on some dread brink,*

---

[9r]

*Drops headlong, resolute to find or make*
*A Gulph of rest, deep as the height it falls from!*
forsaking all her natural cherished
*Ere long, her lowly tasks & natural haunts*
All her accustom'd offices and cares
*Relinquishing, but treasuring every law*
*And grace of feminine humanity,*
*The chosen rustic urged a warlike steed*
*Tow'~~a~~rds the beleaguer'd city, in the might*
*Of prophecy~~,~~ accoutred to fulfil,*
*At the sword's point, visions conceived in tears.*

*The cloud of rooks, descending from mid air,*
*Softens its evening uproar towards a close,*
*Near & more near, for this protracted strain*
*A warning not unwelcome.—Fare thee well*
*Emblem of equanimity & ~~peace~~ truth*
*Farewell! if thy composure be not ours,*
*Yet as thou still, when we are gone will keep*
*fresh*
*Thy living chaplet of ~~moist~~ flowers & fern*

---

Ll. 150–161, marked for deletion here on 8r and on 9r, are omitted in MS. B(1), 4v, and in DC MS. 89, 3r, at ll. 183/184.
8v is blank.

---

160–161 Marked for deletion, as are ll. 150–159 on 8r; ll. 160–162 are also crossed out by a vertical ink stroke, probably to be replaced by lines at the top of 7v.
167 The comma is erased.
9v is blank.

---

[10r]

*Cherished in shade tho' peeped at by the sun,*
*So shall our bosoms feed a covert growth*
*Of grateful recollections, tribute due*
*((Not less than to wide lake & foaming rill)*
*To thy obscure & modest attributes,*
*To thee clear Spring! and all-sustaining Heaven.*

---

[11v]

~~To the tot~~
No loger greeted to the tottering sire
For whom like service now & then his choice
Relieves the tedious holiday of age,
Thoughts raised above this earth while here he
rests
Feeding on sunshine to the blushing Girl
{e
~~Who as the minut{ts speed their flight forgets~~
Her errand, nothing loth to be way-laid
By her Betrothd peace while years roll on
And pleasure soberd down to happiness
{th
Who here forgets her errand, nothing lo{s
{tr
To be way laid by her Be{thothed, peace
While years roll on the sanctity of heaven
And pleasure soberd down to happiness

But should these Hills be ranged by one whose Soul
Scorning loves whispers shrinks from love itself
As fancys snare for female vanity
Here may the Aspirant find a trysting place
For loftier intercourse—The Muses crowned
With wreathes that have not faded to this hour
Sprang from high Jove of sage Mnemosyne

---

10v is blank; 11r contains only the closing line and a half of the passage started on 11v.

---

The lines on 11v follow from the drafting toward the top of 5v and lead to ll. 133–147 of the Morgan MS. The passage is continued with a line and a half at the top of 11r:

Enamoured, so the fable runs, but they
Certes were self

The three lines below the line crossed out at mid-page are also canceled with vertical ink strokes.

## [DC MS. 105, MS. B(1): *Composed when a probability existed . . .*]

[1r] [Ll. 2–12]

Sky-piercing mountains son must we depart
Willing or not, must bid farewell to you
Depart we must, willing or not—the time
Approaches when my voice must bid farewell
{!
Sky piercing Mountains{—bid farewell to you
And all which ye look down upon with pride,
paths
With tenderness embosom to your ~~groves~~
And ~~Dwellings and~~
~~Fields, pleasant habitations with the paths~~
And pleasant Dwellings
~~That wind among them,~~ to familiar ~~flowers~~ trees
And wild flowers known as well as if our hands
Had tended them. And Thou pellucid Spring
Unheard of save in this small hamlet, here
(}
Not undistinguish'd,} for of Wells that ooze
Or fonts that gurgle from a craggy Steep
Their common Sire Thou only bear'st his name
What wonder if the foretaste of such Parting
me at thy
{at
Hath ruled my steps & seals me {at thy side?
me near thee mindful
For with the comforts of my daily meal
That
~~Thou~~ through the space of twice seven years
has blended

---

[1v] [Ll. 13–25]

Beverage as pure as ever fix'd the choice
Of Hermit doubting where to scoop his
cell
thy
Which Persian Kings might envy and ~~whose~~
pure
And gentle aspect oft has minister'd

---

Three lines at the top of 1r ("Depart we must . . . farewell to you") and four lines toward the bottom ("Unheard of . . . bear'st his name") are boxed in ink as a signal for deletion or revision. The latter passage is similar to ll. 2–6 of the early reading text of *Composed when a probability existed . . .*

To finer uses. They for me must cease
Days will pass on—the year, should years be given,
Fade, and the moralizing mind derive
No lesson from the presence of a power
By the inconstant nature we inherit
Unmatchd in delicate beneficence
For neither unremitting rains avail
s{ thee {r
To v{well into voice no{t hottest drought
Thy bounty stints nor can thy beauty mar.
Such calm attraction have I found in thee
My private treasure while the neighbouring Stream
Famed through the Land for turbulent cascades
Not seldom forfeits his dependant praise,
And disappoints the traveller lured from
far

---

[2r] [Ll. 28–35]

Not yet perchance translucent Spring had
{N toll'd
The {norman curfew bell when human hands
First offerd help that the deficient rock
Might over arch thee, sacred to mans use
Such ties will not be wanting
~~These grosser ties will last~~ but when we
Are gone, what summer loiterer with regard
Inquisitive

---

[2v] [Ll. 51–53]

But from thy bosom would some covetous hand
Abstract the gleaming Relics and uplift them
However gently towards the vulgar air

---

[3r] [Ll. 68–85]

In mutual stillness or if some bold breeze
Entering the Cell gave restlessness to one
The Other glassd in thy unruffled breast
Partook of every motion met returned
{p
And met again such {flayful sympathy
Such delicate caress as in the Shape

---

The last five lines on 1v are boxed and deleted by a large X; they are essentially the same as the unrevised fair copy in ll. 21–25 on 2r of DC MS. 105, MS. B.

Of this green plant had aptly recompensed
For baffled lips and disappointed arms
And hopeless pangs the spirit of that Youth
The fair Narcissus, by some pitying God
Changed to a crimson Flower, when He whose
pride
Provoked a retribution too severe
Had pined, upon a watry Duplicate
{N
Wasting that Love the {nymphs implored
in vain
Thus while my Fancy wanders, Thou clear
Spring
Movesd shall I say like a dear Friend who meets
A parting moment with her loveliest look
And seemingly her happiest, looks so fair

---

[3v] [Ll. 86–98a]

It frustrates its own purpose and recalls
The griev'd one whom it meant to send away)
Dost tempt me by disclosures exquisite
To linger bending over thee
Earnest as one who on a summer day
Peers from a headland searching the sea clouds
[?~~bres~~]
For coming sails, or as a ~~simple~~ child
o
Wh~~ile~~ deaf to plaudits that proclaim the joy
feat
Of all around her, sits by some new ~~charm~~
sits, spell
Of scenic transformation, ~~wonder~~-bound.
{ bed
For now thy earthy {[ ? ], a moment past
Palpable unto sight as the dry ground,
Eludes perception, by some slight or chance
Of wonder working nature, and slant beams
The silent inquest,

---

[4r] [Ll. 166–180]

The fountain of the fairies. What to her
o}
Smooth summer dream of}ld favors of the place

---

Ll. 5–10 on 3v are bracketed for deletion; they are essentially the same as ll. 74–79 on 4r of DC MS. 105, MS. B.

Pageants
Pageants & revels of the Elves to her
Whose Country groaned under a foreign scourge.
She ponderd murmurs that attuned her ear
holier voce
For the reception of a ~~deeper~~
{ir
Than the{ir music—mandates, truthes
More awful than the chambers of dark earth
l}
Have Virtue to send forth. She knen}t & prayd
For ravaged France implore the King of Kings
To liberate the Realm by [?saintly] meek
[~~—?—~~]
Expelling
Subduing worldly strong if such his will
l}
And sometimes why}e beside the font she sate
Gazing intensely the translucent lymph
Darkend beneath the shadows of her thoughts
As if swift clouds passed over it, or caught
Wars tincture, mid the forest green & still

---

[4v] [Ll. 181–184]

Turned into blood ~~into~~ before her heart sick eye.
——Erelong forsaking all her natural haunts
All her accustomed offices & cares
Relinquishing

---

Ll. 7–13 on 4r are deleted with a large X; they do not appear in other manuscripts.

# DC MS. 105, MS. C

DC MS. 105, MS. C is a sheet of wove paper, 20.4 centimeters wide by 25.2 centimeters high, watermarked with a fleur-de-lis over a cursive HB, over the date 1824. One side of the sheet contains calligraphy in an unknown hand, preserving an old-spelling record of the circumstances surrounding the deaths of William Hountire and Robert Smith in 1684. The other side contains pencil draft work and fair copy for *Composed when a probability existed* . . . The fair-copy passage corresponding roughly to lines 30–36 of the late reading text is in the hand of an unidentified copyist, probably John Carter; the drafting corresponding to lines 91–97 of the late reading text is in Wordsworth's hand.

# [DC MS. 105, MS. C:
# *Composed when a probability existed . . .*]

[Top] [Ll. 91–97]

pebbly
Where is thy earthy floor—a moment past
Twas palpable to sight as the dry grou
[ ? ]
On which we tread now thou art fathomless
B
Thy ~~pebbly bed~~ is vanishd—
[ ? ? ? ]

---

[Bottom, reversed] [Ll. 30–36]

*lose*
*We go, And losing us thou willt not lack*
*Such case as aided the deficient rock*
*To overarch thee, shelterd from the beems*
*ken*
*Of Noon, and unapparent to the eye*
*Of every stag that looks not from the well*
*Nor shall the thirsty heifer be allowed*
*To trouble thee, appropriate to Man's need.*
*Yet then what pensive loiterer with regard*
*Inquisitive thy countenance will peruse*
*Pleased to detect &c*